LAS VEGAS

& DAY TRIPS

ARIZONA, UTAH & CALIFORNIA

2008/9

LAS VEGAS

& DAY TRIPS
ARIZONA, UTAH & CALIFORNIA

2008/9

Karen Marchbank
with Richard Evans

foulsham
LONDON • NEW YORK • TORONTO • SYDNEY

foulsham
The Publishing House, Bennetts Close, Cippenham, Slough, Berkshire, SL1 5AP, England

Foulsham books can be found in all good bookshops and direct from www.foulsham.com

ISBN: 978-0-572-03403-0

A CIP record for this book is available from the British Library

Look out for the latest editions of Foulsham's other travel guides:
Brit Guide to Orlando and Walt Disney World by Simon and Susan Veness
Brit Guide to Disneyland Resort Paris by Simon and Susan Veness
Brit Guide to New York by Amanda Statham
Top 50 Ski and Snowboard Resorts in Europe by Pat Sharples and Vanessa Webb

Printed in Dubai

CONTENTS

A note on the Brit Guides

This *Brit Guide* is one of an innovative series of travel guides that aim to offer practical, user-friendly guidance for the British traveller abroad. Focusing on clear, honest information, it is one British traveller's advice to another – without the jargon or sales pitch of the brochures.

The Strip, one of the world's most recognised thoroughfares

INTRODUCTION

Sin City continues to grow and remake itself in astonishing ways, and yet it is the same old Las Vegas. Where else can mum relax in the embrace of a world-class spa treatment while dad fires golf balls about a quality nine holes? Then you meet later for a few hours of blackjack, poker or some time pulling on the 'one-armed bandits', before strolling through the fabulous plazas of Caesar's shops. Next, you stop and enjoy a romantic dinner at Delmonico's before claiming marvellous seats for Elton John's Red Piano extravaganza. Then it's drinks and dancing into the small hours and before you know it, the sun is peeking over the horizon and you stagger off for a few moments of sleep before rising to do it all over again.

Legions of visitors descend on this isolated city in the desert to spend long, sleepless nights losing their inhibitions in an orgy of memorable good times, best confided with great prudence to family back home! In fact, it is often hard to keep track of everything, from how many glittering resorts are rising on the Strip skyline to which day it is!

Las Vegas is continuing to grow at an astonishing rate, but also in depth and complexity, and with it – in America at least – there's a change of Las Vegas's image. For recent decades a city associated with tacky brashness has seen the city transformed. The monstrous, themed resorts like the Venetian, Caesars Palace, Excalibur, Mandalay Bay and Bellagio are being challenged by new, even more titanic, wantonly decadent creations like Wynn Las Vegas, City Center, Trump International and The Cosmopolitan.

Two sides to every adult

After a brief, unsuccessful flirtation with selling itself as a family destination in the 1980s, Las Vegas realised it could never compete with the massive theme parks of Orlando, Florida. Adults were the natural market for Vegas. So, with Circus Circus and Excalibur standing as notable exceptions, Las Vegas has melded itself into an adult playground of such awesome scale and complexity as to be unrivalled by anything on Earth.

Entertainment has topped the list, and Vegas has invested billions of dollars in bringing the finest to Las Vegas venues. The visually stunning production shows of the Canadian troupe Cirque du Soleil® reigns supreme as people literally fight to acquire a ticket to the habitually sold-out shows. But there are also stunning shows by Elton John, Toni Braxton, Blue Man Group, Penn & Teller and a legion of others to beguile you. Then there are a constant stream of special concerts, championship boxing matches, Miss Universe pageants and more to draw in the crowds.

Steve Wynn started the Vegas tradition of bringing in greater cultural aspects to Vegas and his Wynn Las Vegas joins Bellagio, Caesars Palace, Venetian and

The iconic Las Vegas sign

Tropicana with impressive displays of art and museum displays. During a visit to Las Vegas in June 2007, I was able to see gorgeous collections of Matisse at the Venetian, Picasso at Wynn Las Vegas, two impressive museum collections of 'Titanic Artefacts' and 'The Human Body' at the Tropicana and a lovely collection of French Impressionists at Bellagio.

The active crowd also has the attention of the resort moguls. A score of world-class golf courses has turned Las Vegas into a top golfing destination. Meanwhile a host of tour operators has opened up rock climbing, horse riding, desert walking, parasailing, boating, rollercoastering and nearly any other activity one could imagine, done with style and flair.

But the refined end of Las Vegas aside, Sin City has a reputation, well deserved, of sex and titillation. Has Vegas helped engineer the world's embrace of things once considered naughty, or has Sin City simply welcomed the shift in morality? In any case the number of 'skin' bars has tripled in recent years.

The arrival of the new millennium has ushered in a new age of ever-more-raunchy nightclubs where beds not settees, sofas not chairs give rise to a greater degree of intimacy. A venue's success in the last few years has gone hand in hand with its ability to offer both exclusive facilities for VIPs and saucy settings for a live-hard, work-hard and play-hard clientèle.

The hottest Las Vegas *tour de force* is resorts with 'European-style sunbathing' – Las Vegas code for adult-only poolsides where topless lounging is decadently embraced. Many of these areas are tied to some of Las Vegas' hottest nightspots, such as Venetian's Tao Beach and Hard Rock Café's Sunday Pool Party. Here beautiful people dance and swill unbridled either by children or bikini tops.

Where the shopping is easy

Another Las Vegas trend has been the move towards high-class shopping outlets. Forum Shops at Caesars Palace led the way and now offers a new, three-storey complex of shops and restaurants. The Fashion Show Mall offers seven fashion department stores in a one-stop destination and the Bellagio, Wynn Las Vegas and the Venetian have whole promenades of designer shopping. Meanwhile, Chelsea Premium Outlets, which specialises in Bicester Village-style designer outlet stores, is now firmly established with two large locations in the city. Finally, Miracle Mile Shops (formerly Desert Passage) has over 170 mid-to-high-priced shops.

Shops at the Mandalay Bay

Big is beautiful

None of this has happened by accident. The city has one of the most well co-ordinated and determined marketing strategies of any city in America (if not the world). Galvanised into action in the 1980s and '90s by the growth of Atlantic City, the Las Vegas Convention and Visitors Authority (LVCVA) – which has overseen marketing strategies that have helped the city reach a figure of 39 million visitors per annum – has no intention of sitting on its laurels. Its current five-year plan is to attract a phenomenal 43 million visitors per annum by 2009.

Developers plan to add 20,000 hotel rooms by that year (at an estimated cost of $18 billion) – bringing the total number to a whopping 150,000 rooms – so the city's management aims to ensure those rooms are filled. And the developers only plan new resorts because the LVCVA works tirelessly both to maintain existing visitor levels and to attract both new ones and increase repeat customers.

One of the most important sources of visitors is the ever-expanding convention industry that ensures those all-important bums are plopped on hotel beds during the week. As the party capital of America, the city has no problem reaching near 100% occupancy at the weekend, but to be truly successful (and provide the expected levels of return on the billion-dollar investments made in resort hotels) the hotels need to reach 80% occupancy all week long, all year round. And they are dazzlingly successful, as in 2006 Las Vegas hotels averaged a 92.7% occupation rate, well over the 65% rate typical of hotels throughout the States.

So, Las Vegas will just continue to grow and grow – at least through 2010. A forest of construction cranes reach into the Strip's skyline as the newest creations take shape to shock, inspire and lure us back again and again.

1 ENTERTAINMENT CITY

What the city is all about, when to go and other useful information

Las Vegas is a mere 100 years young, built in the middle of the desert, and lives like some old American West frontier town. In many ways it is the modern equivalent of an 1880s gold rush town, where thousands of hopeful miners elbowed space on to gaming tables next to Chinese coolies and ranching cowboys. Piano players played loudly, dance hall girls swished their dresses provocatively and the drunken crowds whooped and fired their guns in the air.

Today's Las Vegas is just a bit more modernised, with her casinos, shows, nightclubs and showgirls. Sin City has it all, yet it's not until you see the staggering line-up of monster-sized hotels for yourself that the enormity of it sinks in. In fact, the city never fails to impress. From the revolving restaurants and bars, to the chichi lounges, spectacular thrill rides and state-of-the-art nightclubs, it is such an incredible experience from beginning to end that you'll need to remind yourself to close your mouth on a regular basis!

In this chapter

As you drive up Las Vegas Boulevard South – the Strip, as it is known – from the airport, you'll encounter the triple-pronged Mandalay Bay resort, then the amazing pyramid of the Luxor on your left and the gigantic golden lion of the MGM Grand to your right. Other wondrous sights appear, including the beautiful drawbridge castle of the Excalibur and a complete replica of New York's skyline at the New York-New York resort. And that is before you even reach what used to be the most famous part of the Strip – the old Four Corners that include the Greco-Roman empire of

A great experience at Fremont Street

Caesars Palace and the Flamingo Hilton. Then it all comes in a rush, with the massive resorts of City Center, Planet Hollywood (the old-new Aladdin), Paris, Mirage, Treasure Island, Venetian, the Wynn and many more.

Towering over it all is the Stratosphere, the world's tallest free-standing observation tower at the top end of the Strip on the way to Downtown Las Vegas. Head farther down Las Vegas Boulevard and you'll run across the Old Las Vegas. Here you'll find the last vestiges of Las Vegas's former neon culture known as Glitter Gulch in the Fremont Street Experience that totally encloses Fremont Street. Then on your right is the new East Fremont Entertainment District, a three-block cluster of cool nightclubs, jazz venues and chic eateries, all within walking distance of each other.

What it's all about

Las Vegas is a great place to work. Up to 6,000 people move into the area every month from southern California, Utah and beyond. The predictions are that the current population of 1.6 million in Clark County, which encompasses Las Vegas, will have increased by over 50% to 2.7 million by the year 2018, after expanding from just 350,000 in 1992. They come because the jobs are here. The Las Vegas area created 47,000 new jobs in 2006, with employment up 5.7% to 875,000. The unemployment rate held steady at a mere 4%.

But not all the jobs are in the gambling industry. Many other businesses, especially those in the high-tech industry, are attracted by the low property tax and the lack of income or corporate income taxes. Aggressive advertising campaigns in trade publications such as the *Hollywood Reporter* have played a key part in the expansion of Nevada's film industry, leading to an income state wide of $100m from this source alone.

There are plenty of opportunities to relax

An awesome view down the Strip

The golfing industry, too, has had a massive impact, creating 4,500 jobs and bringing $891m to the southern Nevada area, with Las Vegas at its epicentre. All these growth areas have been supported by a $91m expansion of the city's airport, McCarran International, and the opening in the summer of 2005 of the $650m Las Vegas Monorail.

Developers have been quick to spot the influx of smart, young professionals – lured by wages that vastly outstrip other American cities and have rushed to provide a wealth of sparkling condos in the heart of the city's most exciting corridor: the Strip. It is these professionals – along with cooler, smarter types of visitor – who have contributed to the explosion of trendy bars, ultra-lounges (see page 143), sophisticated nightclubs and an array of celebrity-chef restaurants.

They also played a part in the growth of thrill rides, such as the heartline-twister Manhattan Express™ around New York-New York and Speed at the Sahara Hotel. It is even possible to have a family holiday here and see the fabulous natural sights of the Red Rock Canyon, Valley of Fire, Grand Canyon (by helicopter or plane in a day) and Mount Charleston, not so far away.

You can find a venue for nearly every activity you fancy and there are plenty of opportunities to experience the real West. You can go horse riding at any of the national parks, go on a cowboy trail, meet the Native American tribes north and south of the city, go swimming, water-skiing and fishing at Lake Mead and even go skiing in Lee Canyon in winter. If that's not enough action for you, then try skydiving from Boulder City airport near the Hoover Dam.

The power of plastic comes into its own in the myriad shopping centres that have sprung up since Caesars Palace's Forum Shops gave a whole new meaning to the word 'mall'. Now locals and tourists spend even more money flexing their credit-card muscle shopping than they do on gambling, making Las Vegas the most successful place for the retail industry in all of America.

History in brief

It's a long way from the days of mobster Bugsy Siegel and, before him, the railroad settlers and Mormons. In fact, the history of southern Nevada reaches back into prehistoric times when it was a marsh full of water and lush vegetation that was home to dinosaurs.

Eventually, as millions of years went by, the marsh receded, rivers disappeared beneath the surface and the wetlands evolved into a parched, arid landscape that can now only support the hardiest of plants and animals. Water trapped underground in the geological formations of the Las Vegas Valley sporadically surfaced to nourish plants and create an oasis in the desert, while life-giving water flowed to the Colorado River.

Hidden for centuries from all but Native Americans, the Las Vegas Valley oasis was protected from discovery by the surrounding harsh and unforgiving Mojave Desert until around 1829 when Mexican trader Antonio Armigo, leading a 60-man party along the Spanish Trail to Los Angeles, veered away from the route and discovered Las Vegas Springs.

On the gold rush trail

The discovery of this oasis shortened the Spanish Trail to Los Angeles and hastened the rush west for the California gold. Between 1830 and 1848, the name Vegas was changed to Las Vegas, which means 'the meadows' in Spanish. In 1844, John C Fremont camped at the springs while leading an overland expedition west, and his name is immortalised in the downtown Fremont Hotel and Fremont Street.

In 1855, Mormon settlers from Salt Lake City started to build a fort of sun-dried adobe bricks in Las Vegas to protect pioneers travelling between Utah and Los Angeles. They planted fruit trees and vegetables and made bullets from lead mined at Potosi Mountain, 30mls/48km from the fort. Here, with Mormon influence, Las Vegas could have become a conservative, religious oasis in the desert.

Lake Mead is only 25mls/40km from Las Vegas

But it wasn't to be. The Mormons abandoned the settlement in 1858, largely because of Indian raids. It remains as the oldest non-Indian structure in Las Vegas and has been designated a historic monument. Las Vegas had a different future ahead of her.

Working on the railroad

By 1890, railroad developers had chosen the water-rich valley as a prime location for a stop facility and town. When work on the first railroad into Las Vegas began in 1904, a tent-town sprouted, with saloons, stores and boarding houses, and the San Pedro, Los Angeles and Salt Lake Railroad (later absorbed by Union Pacific) made its first run east from California. The advent of the railroad led to the founding of Las Vegas on 15 May 1905. The Union Pacific auctioned off 1,200 lots in a single day in an area that is now known as the Fremont Street Experience.

Gambling got off to a shaky start in the state, which introduced anti-gambling laws in 1910. They were so strict that even the western custom of flipping a coin for a drink was banned. But the locals set up underground gambling dens for their roulette wheels, dice and card games. They stayed illegal but were largely accepted, and flourished until 1931 when the Nevada Legislature, cash starved by the horrific economic depression sweeping America, approved a legalised gambling bill that was designed to generate tax revenue to support local schools. Now more than 41% of Nevada's income comes from gambling tax revenue and more than 31% of its fund is used to provide state education.

In the same year, construction work began on the Hoover Dam project, which at its peak employed more than 5,000 people. During these economically disastrous years, employment was scarce and money was hard to come by. Yet here were legions of men from the project seeking a break from their 12-hour-a-day, six-days-a-week work regimen. They descended on the town with ample coin in their pocket and normally only 12 to 24 hours to enjoy their riches. After a tour of gambling, drink and women, the men would tumble into the bed of a truck and blearily head back to work. Las Vegas traditions of 24-hour fast times and midnight breakfast specials became iconic fixtures. The young town of Las Vegas thrived even during the harsh realities of America's Great Depression.

The Second World War delayed major resort growth, but the seeds for development were sown when Tommy Hull opened the El Rancho Vegas Casino in 1941 on land opposite what is now the Sahara Hotel. During the Second World War, the nearby Nellis Air Force Base was a key military installation and later became a training ground for American fighter pilots and provided more gamblers to swell the city's halls.

Mob rules

The success of El Rancho Vegas triggered a small building boom in the late 1940s. Capitalising on the expanding traffic from Los Angeles, several hotel-casinos were

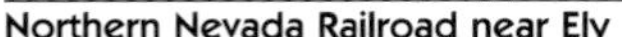

Northern Nevada Railroad near Ely

The plume of lights at the Flamingo

launched on the two-lane highway leading into Las Vegas from Los Angeles and these evolved into today's Strip. Early hotels included the Last Frontier, Thunderbird and Club Bingo.

By far the most famous was the Flamingo Hotel, built by mobster Benjamin 'Bugsy' Siegel, a member of the Meyer Lanksy crime family. Complete with a giant pink neon sign, replicas of pink flamingos on the lawn and a bullet-proof, high-security apartment for Bugsy, the hotel opened on New Year's Eve in 1946. Nevertheless, Bugsy was gunned down six months later as he sat in the living room of his girlfriend's home in Beverly Hills. After numerous owners, the Flamingo now belongs to the Hilton Hotel Group. Today, only the name remains as the last of the original motel-like buildings were replaced by a $104m tower in 1995.

The early building boom continued and Wilbur Clark, a former hotel bellman, opened the Desert Inn in 1950. Two years later, Milton Prell opened the Sahara Hotel on the site of the old Club Bingo. Despite many changes of ownership, the Sahara has survived. So, too, has the Desert Inn, which underwent a $200m remodelling and construction programme in 1997 and remains a part of Steve Wynn's new Wynn Las Vegas resort, which opened in March 2005.

The Sands Hotel, a showroom and once the playground for the 'Rat Pack' of Frank Sinatra and his buddies, high-rollers and Hollywood stars, opened in 1952, but was demolished in 1996 to make way for the fabulous Venetian.

In 1976, Atlantic City in New Jersey legalised gambling and so began a new era in Las Vegas's history, as gamblers from the American East Coast were kept away by Atlantic City's proximity. Las Vegas hotel-casinos saw they would need to create a true resort destination to compete. Caesars Palace had been the first hotel on the Strip to create a specific theme for its resort hotel when it opened in 1966, and two years later Circus Circus opened its tent-shaped casino with carnival games and rides. But it was not until the late 1980s and early 1990s that the boom in resort hotels began in earnest.

A new day dawns

In 1989, the $630m upmarket Mirage Hotel opened with a white tiger habitat, dolphin pool, elaborate swimming pool and waterfall and a man-made volcano that belched fire and water. Mirage's owner at the time, Steve Wynn, then built the $430m Treasure Island resort next door, which is now home to the *Sirens of TI* show. Wynn also went into a joint venture with Circus Circus Enterprises to develop another luxury resort hotel – the Monte Carlo, which opened in 1996 – and his next venture – the luxurious Bellagio, styled as an Italian lakeside village – opened in 1998 on the site of the former Dunes Hotel. Wynn sold all his holdings in these hotels in June 2000 and snapped up the Desert Inn ten days later.

The Excalibur medieval castle opened in 1990 with court jesters and King Arthur's jousting knights entertaining visitors to the massive $290m complex. Circus Circus Enterprises then developed the amazing $375m Luxor next door, opening in 1993.

The quiet beauty of Deer Springs

In the same year, Grand Slam Canyon Adventuredome opened at the Circus Circus hotel, as did Treasure Island and the MGM Grand Hotel and Theme Park. Now one of the world's largest resorts, the MGM Grand has three of the largest concert and sports venues in Las Vegas, some of the top restaurants and myriad swimming pools and tennis courts.

In 1997, the £460m resort hotel New York-New York that re-creates the Big Apple's skyline, added 2,000 rooms. Then came a whole raft of luxury resorts aimed specifically at the sophisticated traveller, including the Mandalay Bay, Paris and Venetian in 1999 – themed as a South Seas island, the French capital and Venice respectively. The Aladdin opened in 2000, almost immediately faced a host of economic problems and descended into bankruptcy. Then the Palms opened in 2001. It all went quiet for a few years until the unveiling of Wynn Las Vegas in 2005, which coincided with a new round of building projects. The Aladdin became Planet Hollywood, and in 2008 the massive constructs of the Cosmopolitan, Trump International and the greatest of them all, City Center, are due to open their doors. The City Center Project, built by MGM/Mirage, is the most massive privately financed building project. These new hotels break from the Las Vegas of decadent, themed resorts. Instead all of them, starting with the Wynn Las Vegas, are not just the last word in luxury, or just magnificent creations of a theme, but they have also swelled the cultural and dining coffers of the city.

It seems that after going through all its different marketing ploys – the city that never sleeps, a family town, adults only – Las Vegas has finally become the sophisticated mecca of fun Bugsy Siegel envisaged so many decades ago, and to go with it, the city's marketing theme: 'What happens in Las Vegas stays in Las Vegas' – unless you've put it on the credit card, of course!

BRITTIP

Don't hire a car from the airport or you'll be charged exorbitant airport 'surcharges'. Take a cheap shuttle to your hotel and sort it out from there.

Getting around

Las Vegas has been growing at such a phenomenal rate in the last 20 years that her roads, especially around the Strip, are hopelessly clogged, especially in the afternoons. In the evenings, it is much faster to walk than to drive along Las Vegas Boulevard, especially if there is a special event happening.

If you arrive by plane, a taxi ride to a Strip hotel (where most of the major theme resorts are located) will cost $10–20, and to a downtown hotel $20–30, depending on the route taken and the time of day. Airport shuttle fares cost $8 to Strip hotels. They're excellent value for money and can be found immediately on your right as you exit the baggage reclaim area. The ticket office is on your left. In addition, most major hotels run shuttles to and from the airport.

Sam's Town Hotel and Casino

BRITTIP

Many upmarket resorts like the Venetian and Bellagio have counters at the airport where you can check in to your room at the airport. You'll save lots of time doing it there!

Walking

Let's face it; walking is the way most people want to explore the Strip, yet it can be a highly dodgy activity. For one, in the summer months the heat is suffocating, and while you might see your destination, trust me, it is still a very long way off. Resorts seem so near because they are so massive!

Also, the city – like most of those in America – is mostly geared to cars and is not just pedestrian-unfriendly, but here it is downright dangerous. The seemingly never-ending construction and the heavy traffic make drivers frustrated and hasty: dangerous conditions for pedestrians. In some parts of the Strip, where many of the never-ending construction sites are located, there are no pavements at all. In other parts, where there are pavements and even pedestrian crossings, there is not enough time to get across the road before the lights change. What's worse is that most of the road-users seem to see pedestrians as targets. When the light changes they have the right of way and you'd better dash across!

However, the hotels and city councillors have been taking action – footbridges have been built at many of the junctions and I strongly advise you to use them!

The monorail

Web: lvmonorail.com
Prices: Single ride ticket $5; 10-ride ticket $35 (one ride equals one trip of any distance); 1-day ticket $15, valid for unlimited travel for any 24-hour period; 3-day ticket $40, valid for 72 hours from first use. Automated ticket machines can be found at all the stops and some of the resorts.
Hours: 7am–2am daily.

BRITTIP

Websites are all preceded by 'www.' unless they are indicated as 'http://'.

The $650m monorail opened in 2004 and is a happy, if somewhat flawed, way to get around. In fact, most times it is by far the fastest way to travel from one part of the Strip to another. The monorail grew from an original transit venture between the MGM Grand and Bally's Hotel in 1993. The Las Vegas Monorail Company, which owns the new transit service, was created in 2000 as a non-profit corporation and now owns the original monorail system.

Monorails come every six minutes and whisk you along to your destination, avoiding the horrid traffic of the Strip. There are two niggles about the monorail service. First, when it opened in 2004 a single fare was only $3, but this was raised in 2007 to $5, which makes it far less of a bargain than originally. Second, all the stops are poorly marked, often difficult to find, and they are also in the very back of each property. This means you must do a lot of walking through these massive resorts to get there, then another long walk to get to where you want. It can be much faster to simply walk to your destination, if it is only one or two stops down the line.

It runs on the east side of the Strip, and these are the various stops, starting with the southernmost stop:

- MGM Grand main hotel entrance services the Tropicana, Mandalay Bay, Luxor, Excalibur, New York-New York and Monte Carlo
- Bally's and Paris Las Vegas services the Paris, Planet Hollywood, Bellagio, City Center and Bally

The monorail is a great way to get around

Napoleon's lounge at Paris Las Vegas

- Flamingo/Caesars Palace
- Harrah's/Imperial Palace services the Mirage, Treasure Island and Venetian
- Las Vegas Convention Center and Las Vegas Hilton
- Sahara services Circus Circus and Stratosphere

Three other monorails run on the western side of the Strip between Treasure Island and the Mirage; the Bellagio and the Monte Carlo; and the Excalibur, Luxor and Mandalay Bay resorts. These monorails are free. In the meantime, an extension has already been approved to connect the Sahara to Fremont Street in the downtown area, but it has run into a series of delays and there is no current completion date.

Buses and taxis

If you're sticking to the main drag, the monorail will be the fastest bet. However, the bus service – Citizens Area Transit (CAT) – has a 24-hour service on the Strip and downtown, plus 40 other routes that operate 5.30am–1.30am daily.
'The Deuce' is the route for Las Vegas Boulevard, sporting double-decker buses that come approximately every 5–10 minutes. Exact change is required, but you can get all-day passes that are reasonably priced at $5.00. In the afternoons and evenings they can be terribly crowded, with long queues at the (fortunately) shaded bus stops. For information about routes and schedules, call 702 228-7433.

BRITTIP

Not only is taking a taxi pricey, but also it is almost impossible to flag one down on the street. You must either pick one up from a hotel (where there's often a queue) or from designated stops.

More than 1,100 taxis service the city but costs will mount if you use them all the time. My caveat would be to avoid using taxis where possible and try to use the monorail.
Services include: ABC Union: 702 736 8444; Ace Cab Co.: 702 736 8383; Checker Yellow Star: 702 873 2227; Desert Cab: 702 386 9102; A North Las Vegas Cab Co.: 702 643 1041; A Vegas Western Cab Co.: 702 736 6121; Western Cab Co.: 702 736 8000; Whittlesea Blue Cab 702 384 6111.

The trolley

The Las Vegas Trolley runs 9.30am–2am every day at roughly 20-minute intervals. Northbound from the Mandalay Bay to the Stratosphere, it stops at the Tropicana, MGM, Bally's, Imperial Palace, Harrah's,

BRITTIP

Some trolley stops are harder to find than others – especially at Caesars Palace where there are no signs at all and the bellboys are the rudest on the Strip if you don't brandish a tip. The first stop is on the right-hand side of the road just by the entrance to the Forum Shops. The second stop is at the end of the entrance to Caesars hotel, just by the bus stop.

Riviera, Hilton and Sahara. Southbound from the Stratosphere, it stops at Circus Circus, Slots of Fun, Stardust, Fashion Show Mall, Caesars, Jockey Club, New York-New York, Excalibur and Mandalay Bay. It costs $1.75 for all journeys and exact change is required. This is a very cheap way of seeing the Strip, but also the slowest – it takes about 50 minutes to travel the entire length in one direction.

BRITTIP

The one bonus to riding the trolley is the close-up views you'll get of the Strip and the major resorts – without pounding the streets or getting run over!

Car rental

For travelling about the Strip or downtown, you are best off without a car. However, if you want to explore the outlying areas like the Grand Canyon, Hoover Dam and elsewhere a car is a necessity.

Before hiring a car, read Chapter 14 (see page 255) first so you know exactly what you'll have to pay for. Most cars can be hired locally to travel throughout California, Nevada and Arizona. However, if you are travelling outside that area, check with the car hire firm for limitations.

If you do plan to arrange car rental on arrival in Las Vegas, look out for special deals advertised in the local press. You might find excellent prices and extras such as free long-distance phone cards. You should also look at the offers with our *Brit's Guide* partner, Alamo.

Car rental companies in Las Vegas include: Airport Rent-A-Car: 702 795 0800; Alamo: 702 263 8411; All State: 702 736 6147; Avis: 702 261 5995; Budget: 702 736 1212; Dollar: 702 739 8408; Enterprise: 702 795 8842; Hertz: 702 736 4900; National: 702 261 5391; Practical: 702 798 5253; Rent A Vette Sports Cars/Exotics/Motorcycle Rentals: 702 736 2592; Thrifty: 702 896 7600.

BRITTIP

Be careful of what the total cost of a car hire will be. Many car hire firms advertise an extremely low rate from the airport, but then you are charged exorbitant airport 'surcharges' that often make the total cost much higher than if you'd rented at your hotel. On the other hand, at relatively quiet times in Vegas, the specials offered at the airport are much cheaper than those in town. Make a few phone calls, asking for the total price 'including all taxes and fees'.

Some companies have rental sites at many of the major resort hotels. If booking on site in Las Vegas at a quiet time, you may be offered very cheap upgrades, but beware of hard-sell tactics and if you're certain you don't want or need a bigger car, don't be persuaded.

Limos

It won't cost you an arm and a leg to travel in style in Las Vegas; you can rent a limo for the ride into town from the airport for as little as $7 a person if there are several of you. Check out the deals available on

Hire a limo for that special night out

arrival. If you're having a big night out on the town and want to have a drink, hiring a limo for the night often works out at about the same price as a taxi.
Limo companies include: Ambassador Limousines: 702 362 6200; Bell Trans/Limousines and Buses: 702 739 7990 or toll-free 1 800 274 7433; Las Vegas Limousines: 702 736 7990 or toll-free 1 800 274 7433; On Demand Sedan-Black Car Service: 702 876 2222; Presidential Limousines: 702 731 5577 or toll-free 1 800 423 1429.

BRITTIP
Some of the smaller rental companies may be cheaper, but always ensure that your rental agreement will allow you to drive outside the state of Nevada.

The best times to go

Las Vegas in 2007 had a staggering 130,000 rooms, but at many times of the year it still gets absolutely packed. The average room price skyrocketed from 'only' $104 in 2005 to a hefty $120 in 2006 and is still rising in 2007. The new resorts expected to open in 2008 should swell the number of rooms to over 150,000, to provide some relief, but at times, hotel rooms will be hard to find.

The busiest times are Christmas, June, July, August, Easter and the American bank holidays: President's Day (George Washington's birthday) – the third Monday in February; Memorial Day – the last Monday in May and the official start of the summer season; Independence Day – 4 July (slap bang in the middle of the high season anyway); Labor Day – the first Monday in September and last holiday of summer; and Thanksgiving – always the fourth Thursday in November.

The best times to visit – providing there are no major conferences or boxing matches going on – are from January to the end of April (excluding the bank holidays) and Easter, and October to November. August and September are busier, but are still good times to go.

The weather

One thing you can be sure of – you're not going to freeze! Having said that, in December 2006, temperatures only got as high as 6°C/42°F, which is 7°C/45°F below the daytime norm, and there was the briefest flurry of snow. You'll be pleased to know that those poor Las Vegas dwellers did recover from their small taste of our normal springtime!

Generally, Las Vegas has about 300 days of sunshine a year, with an average rainfall of 4.2in/10.2cm throughout the year, making it an arid climate. June to

The Conservatory at the Bellagio

Month	Temperature °C/°F min	max	Humidity % am/pm	Rainfall in/mm	Sunshine %
January	1/34	13/55	41/30	.5/13	77
February	3/37	19/66	36/26	.46/12	80
March	5/41	20/68	30/22	.41/10	83
April	9/48	25/77	22/15	.22/6	87
May	15/59	30/86	19/13	.22/6	88
June	20/68	36/97	15/10	.09/2	92
July	24/75	40/104	19/15	.45/11	87
August	22/72	38/100	14/18	.54/14	88
September	18/64	34/93	23/17	.32/8	91
October	11/52	27/81	25/19	.25/6	87
November	5/41	19/66	33/27	.43/11	80
December	1/34	14/57	41/33	.32/8	77

September tends to be the hottest period, with daytime temperatures above 38°C/100°F in July and August. So if you're going out for the day, always make sure you put a good sunblock on before you leave your hotel, cover up when necessary and carry water with you.

What to wear

Fortunately, given the climate, the dress code is pretty relaxed in Las Vegas with casual clothes permitted around the clock. But wearing swimming costumes inside a casino or restaurant is not acceptable and it is normal to dress up for a big evening out. If you're visiting in early spring or late autumn, take a sweater or light jacket for the evening and something a bit warmer for winter.

Tips on tipping

Tipping is not just a way of life in America but a genuine source of income for most employees in the hotel and casino industries and they are even taxed on an expectation of tips received. Sadly, tipping is something that we Brits tend to overlook.

BRITTIP

When buying US dollars before your trip, always ask for plenty of $1 bills – known as singles – so you can tip porters and taxi drivers on arrival. Also, at many American airports it will cost you $1 to use a baggage trolley.

There are some fairly loose customs in Las Vegas, but here is a guide to how much we should tip.

- Bartenders and cocktail waitresses: $1 a round of drinks for parties of one to four people, more for larger groups.
- Bellboys: $1–2 per piece of luggage.
- Concierge service: $5.
- Food servers and room service: 15–20%.
- Hotel maids: $2 a day at the end of a visit.
- Keno runners (see Chapter 7, page 169), slot machine change girls/men and casino dealers: $1–2 for the service and at least a small percentage of any win. Some gamblers who play for long periods tip even if they've lost!

Don't forget to tip friendly staff

Chinese New Year is an extravagant celebration

- Maître d': Many showrooms sell assigned seating tickets, which may include the tip. In resort showrooms that have restaurant-style reservations and seating, you can tip the maître d' (Americans don't have head waiters, they have maître d's like the French!) $5–20 to improve your seats.
- Pool attendants: 50 cents–$1 for towels, pads, loungers, etc.
- Showroom servers: $5–10 for a party of two to four people at a cocktails-only show, or $10–20 for a dinner show depending on the service and food quality.

BRITTIP

Be generous with taxi drivers. Unlike most other cities, it is rare for drivers in Las Vegas to be their own bosses and wages are low, so a decent tip would be appreciated!

- Taxi drivers: $1–2 per person at the end of the trip, or follow the 15–20% rule, whichever is greater.
- Valet parkers: $2, depending on how quick the service has been.

You can often get great room upgrades for a $20 tip to the desk clerk when you book in. Take a look at the Brit tip on page 27.

BRITTIP

Most casinos provide free drinks for gamblers, but at busy times the service can become quite slow. One way to receive fast attention is ask everybody in your party or at your gambling table to offer an additional dollar tip when you first sit down. Give it to the server when you make your first order. Guaranteed, she'll always check your table first and most often!

Medical emergencies

The number for the emergency services is 911.

Medical help: If you need medical help in Las Vegas that does not require an ambulance, there are three main options, all of which are open 24 hours a day seven days a week: Harmon Medical Center, 150 East Harmon Avenue (702 796 116); Fremont Medical Center, 4880 South Wynn Road (on the corner of Tropicana and Wynn, 702 871 5005); and UMC Hospital, 1800 W Charleston Boulevard (702 383 2000).

Many prescription and over-the-counter drugs are produced under different generic names in America. If you take any kind of regular medication, e.g. for a heart

'Vegas Vickie' at Glitter Gulch

condition or epilepsy, it's a good idea to ask your doctor or pharmacy to find out the American name for your particular prescription drug. Keep this written down with your prescription or put both English and American drug names inside a clear plastic case that is easily accessible for medical crews, in case you are involved in an accident. The American term for paracetamol is acetaminophen.

Useful websites

visitlasvegas.com: Run by the city's Convention and Visitors Authority, this website not only supplies information but also carries a preview of good deals.

BRITTIP

The city's Information Center can be found at 3150 Paradise Road, 1 877 VISITLV (847 4858).

ilovevegas.com: Provides current information, supplied by the magazine *What's On, The Las Vegas Guide*, about hotels, casinos, dining, entertainment and recreation.
lasvegasadvisor.com: Run by Huntington Press and Anthony Curtis, a Las Vegas icon for good deals and bargain hunting. Here are rankings of the best deals for gambling, meals, drinks and shows. It also has one of the best web portals for finding cheap Las Vegas hotel rooms.
lasvegas.com: Excellent source of information, discounts and pre-booking for restaurants and clubs.
lasvegasgolf.com: First-rate guide for golfers with great deals on packages.
reviewjournal.com: One of the most useful websites with links to entertainment, local news and maps, run by *The Las Vegas Review Journal*.

BRITTIP

If you run out of cash, you'll find many ATMs (cash machines) in virtually every hotel.

Useful numbers

Airport information:	702 261 5743
Airport parking:	702 261 5121
Citizens Area Transit:	702 228 7433
Convention information:	702 892 0711
Directory assistance:	702 555 1212
Emergency Service Dispatch:	911
Highway Patrol:	702 385 0311
Las Vegas Fire Department:	702 383 2888
Las Vegas Transit System:	702 228 7433
Marriage License Bureau:	702 455 4415
Metro Police:	702 795 3111
Poison Information Center:	702 732 4989
Road conditions:	702 486 3116
Show Hot Line:	702 225 5554
Tourist information:	702 892 7575
Weather:	702 736 3854

Fireworks light up the Stratosphere

Language in Las Vegas

It has often been said that Brits and Americans are divided by a common language and when you make an unexpected *faux pas* you'll certainly learn how true this is. For instance, never ask for a packet of fags as this is the American slang word for gays and a sense of humour is not their strong point! There are plenty of other differences, too, so this list should help to avoid confusion. Remember, too, that spellings sometimes vary.

Travelling around

English	*American*
Aerial	Antenna
Articulated truck	Semi
Bonnet	Hood
Boot	Trunk
Caravan	House trailer
Car park	Parking lot
Car silencer	Muffler
Crossroads/junction	Intersection
Demister	Defogger
Dipswitch	Dimmer
Dual carriageway	Four-lane or divided highway
Flyover	Overpass
Give way	Yield
Jump leads	Jumper cables
Lay-by	Turn-out
Lorry	Truck
Manual transmission	Stick shift
Motorway	Superhighway, freeway, expressway
No parking or stopping	No standing
Pavement	Sidewalk
Petrol station	Gas station
Request stop	Flag stop
Ring road	Beltway
Slip road	Ramp
Subway	Pedestrian underpass
Transport	Transportation
Turning	Turnoff
Tyre	Tire
Underground	Subway
Walk	Hike
Wheel clamp	Car boot
Windscreen	Windshield
Wing	Fender

BRITTIP

If you arrive at a hotel by car or taxi, one bellhop will take your luggage out of the boot (trunk) – for which you have to tip him – then another takes it up to your room – and, yes, he needs a tip, too.

Food and drink

There are plenty of differences in US and UK food terms. The Americans don't flick fat over the top of the egg when frying it, but turn it over to cook on both sides, so for eggs the way I like them, cooked on both sides but soft, I don't order 'sunny-side up' but 'over easy' and if you like yours well done, then ask for eggs 'over hard'. Many standard American dishes come with a biscuit – which is a corn scone to us! They also have something called grits, which is a porridge-like breakfast dish made out of ground, boiled corn, plus hash browns – grated, fried potatoes.

English	*American*
Aubergine	Eggplant
Bill	Check or tab
Biscuit (sweet)	Cookie
Biscuit (savoury)	Cracker
Chickpea	Garbanzo bean
Chips	French fries or fried potatoes
Choux bun	Cream puff
Cling film	Plastic wrap
Coriander	Cilantro
Corn	Wheat
Cornflour	Cornstarch
Courgette	Zucchini
Crayfish	Crawfish
Crisps	Chips
Crystallised	Candied
Cutlery	Silverware or place setting
Demerara sugar	Light-brown sugar

There's no shortage of top-quality eating

Superb food is on the menu at Café Bellagio

Desiccated coconut	Shredded coconut
Digestive biscuit	Graham cracker
Double cream	Heavy cream
Essence (e.g. vanilla)	Extract
Golden syrup	Corn syrup
Grated, fried potatoes	Hash browns
Grilled	Broiled
Icing sugar	Confectioner's sugar
Jam	Jelly
Ketchup	Catsup
King prawn	Shrimp
Main course	Entree
Measure	Shot
Minced meat	Ground meat
Off-licence	Liquor store
Pastry case	Pie shell
Pips	Seeds (in fruit)
Plain/dark chocolate	Semi-sweet or unsweetened chocolate
Pumpkin	Squash
Scone	Biscuit
Shortcrust pastry	Pie dough
Single cream	Light cream
Soda water	Seltzer
Soya	Soy
Sorbet	Sherbet
Spirits	Liquor
Sponge finger biscuits	Ladyfingers
Spring onion	Scallion
Starter	Appetizer
Stoned (cherries, etc.)	Pitted
Sultana	Golden raisin
Sweet shop	Candy store
Take-away	To go
Tomato purée	Tomato paste
Water biscuit	Cracker

Shopping

English	*American*
Bumbag	Fanny pack
Chemist	Drug store
Ground floor	First floor
Handbag	Purse
High Street	Main Street
In (Fifth Avenue, etc.)	On
Jumper	Sweater
Muslin	Cheesecloth
Suspenders	Garters
Tights	Pantyhose
Till	Check-out
Trainers	Sneakers

L'Atelier de Joël Robuchon

Trousers	Pants
Underpants	Shorts
Vest	Undershirt
Waistcoat	Vest
Zip	Zipper

Money

English	*American*
Bill	Check
Banknote	Bill
Cheque	Check
1 cent	Penny
5 cents	Nickel
10 cents	Dime
25 cents	Quarter

General

English	*American*
Air steward(ess)	Flight attendant
Anti-clockwise	Counter-clockwise
At weekends	On weekends
Autumn	Fall
Behind	In back of
Camp bed	Cot
Cinema	Movie theater
City/town centre	downtown (not the run-down bit!)
Coach	Bus
Cot	Crib
Diary (appointments)	Calendar
Diary (records)	Journal
Doctor	Physician
From ... to ...	Through
Lift	Elevator
Long-distance call	Trunk call
Nappy	Diaper
Ordinary	Regular, normal
Paddling pool	Wading pool
Post, postbox	Mail, mailbox
Pram, pushchair	Stroller
Queue	Line, line up
Tap	Faucet
Toilet	Restroom (public) Bathroom (private)

The Four Seasons on the Strip

RESORT-HOTELS

The biggest and the best hotels and how to choose the right one for you

Bugsy Siegel started it all and Howard Hughes, the famously reclusive billionaire, lent an air of respectability to the city, but modern Vegas is really a reflection of the dream of one man: Steve Wynn.

Steve Wynn, Las Vegas's modern-day casino mogul, opened the dazzling Mirage Hotel 1989. It was the first major hotel to be built on the Strip in 16 years. With a $630m price tag, dolphin pool, white tiger habitat, man-made volcano and elaborate swimming pool, it set a new standard and sparked off a massive building rush. Wynn, went on to build the pirate-themed Treasure Island and upmarket Italianate Bellagio before selling out and starting a brand-new project over at the Desert Inn. Between 1989 and 2004 a host of themed resorts, inspired by Wynn's success, erupted along the strip and turned Las Vegas into a true adult fantasyland.

Historians will no doubt see 2005 as another important year in the city's development. Wynn's first solo project – Wynn Las Vegas – opened to a fanfare of publicity after one of the most tightly guarded developments the city has ever seen. Instead of having an über-fantasy conjuration like Luxor, Excalibur and Circus Circus, or destination fantasies like Mandalay Bay, Paris or Venetian, the Wynn Las Vegas was simple luxury. Its opening also coincided with another hotel 'gold rush' of building after a period of relative dormancy. MGM/Mirage's massive City Center, the transformation of the old Aladdin into Planet Hollywood, and a raft of newcomers is all a move away from ritzy, gaudy and themed to cool, modern and trendy.

Recent years have also seen a sharp increase in lodging costs. The Las Vegas Visitor and Convention Authority says the average lodging expenditures per night in 2003 were $81.43, but in 2006 they had bounced to $107.12! And despite the thousands of new rooms coming available in 2008 and 2009, rooms will likely still be tight, with rising prices.

BRITTIP

The biggest problem the major resort-hotels have is registering guests – a 30-minute wait is not unusual at busy times!

In this chapter

The magic line-up

To really appreciate the sight of the glittering spectacles that are both resorts and attractions in their own right, it's best to fly into Las Vegas so you can get a bird's eye view as you land at McCarran International airport – either that, or take a fun helicopter flight. However, it's just as fascinating from the seat of a car.

As you come out of the airport you turn right on Las Vegas Boulevard and soon you'll pass the South Seas paradise of Mandalay Bay on your left, before spotting the daunting pyramid of the Luxor and the castle-like vistas of Camelot at Excalibur. At the new Four Corners of Las Vegas on the Strip, you will see the Tropicana to your right. Before you've had time to let out a gasp of amazement, you'll be passing the lion of MGM Grand, opposite the towers of New York-New York and its famous Big Apple landmarks. The Monte Carlo is next on the left, a fine re-creation of the ritzy Place du Monaco, then there is the edifice of City Center rising to the skies. Planet Hollywood (originally the Aladdin) is on the right, followed by the Eiffel Tower in Paris – but don't forget to glance left for a swift look at the Italian village setting of the Bellagio.

Now you've reached the old Four Corners, the original section of the Strip that was home to Bugsy Siegel's Flamingo, and here you'll see the majestic Caesars Palace with its Greco-Roman ramparts on the left. Opposite the Forum Shops at Caesars is the modern Flamingo Hilton.

The lobby at the Four Seasons

Then, further north on the right, is the Japanese-inspired Imperial Palace opposite the posh Polynesian resort of the Mirage and its erupting volcano. If arriving any time after 4pm, Treasure Island's *Sirens of TI* could well be in action, but don't forget to look right to see the spectacular Venetian with its re–creation of St Mark's Square and the Doge's Palace.

BRITTIP

Internet access through the TV is now available pretty much as standard in the major resort-hotels. Think around $6 for two hours or around $10 for 24 hours (plus tax!).

Soon, on the left is the circus-dome shape of the Grand Slam Canyon and Circus Circus, a family resort on the theme of a travelling circus. The rose citadel of the Wynn Las Vegas is tantilisingly screened by a large man-made hill and ranks of cool evergreen trees. After that is the spire of the Stratosphere Hotel, the tallest free-standing tower in America.

BRITTIP

For a complete list of all dining options – both fine dining and casual – available in each of the resort hotels see page 126.

Choices, choices! It's an amazing line-up – and it's all thanks to money and the making of it. But where do you choose to stay? There are three schools of thought, depending on your budget and your interests.

Resort-hotels

Undoubtedly, for the best time ever, stay in one of the main resort-hotels – all of which are featured in this chapter. The good part is if you stay and play at the same place you will get the most in convenience (no time-eating drives in Las Vegas traffic), attractions and night-time thrills. However, they are also pricey. For instance, rooms can often be had at the Venetian for $149 midweek, but on a busy convention day the *minimum* room price often soars to $750/night! Then the gambling minimums and odds are also more expensive in these posh surroundings. Still, for many, being able to have the ultimate experience makes the budget less important, especially since the resorts do have a number of different price ranges.

On a budget on the Strip

For the budget conscious, a great option is to stay at one of the many budget establishments on the Strip, downtown or on the locals' Boulder Highway Strip area where budget casinos offer clean and cheap rooms with great gambling odds. They then make the trip into the Strip area to enjoy the attractions and shows along the expensive real estate. While cheaper, the hotels are definitely NOT memorable and you spend a lot of time travelling back and forth.

BRITTIP

The term 'the Strip' was coined by a former Los Angeles police captain in 1938. Guy McAfee said the stretch of road with its brightly lit hotels and casinos reminded him of Hollywood's Sunset Strip, another mecca for night owls!

Strip resorts

A third option is to stay in Strip resorts for a delightful stay and for the attractions. Then for those intent gamblers, take a trip down to Fremont Street where the loose slots and advantageous gambling odds give you much longer play on your gambling budget.

Making your choices

To try to make your life easier – for both choosing a hotel and for seeing them as the attractions they are – I've given a full run-down of their facilities and roughly how much it costs for a room with two people sharing.

I have not given the major resorts a rating for the simple reason that they are aimed at different types of people, so a comparison would not really be appropriate. Also, do remember that in Las Vegas, as in no other city on earth, supply and demand vary greatly and the differences are reflected in hugely fluctuating room prices. My notes on booking your hotel room in Chapter 13 give a more detailed picture of how to find a room not only at the inn of your choice, but also at the right price.

BRITTIP

One tradition left over from the old mob-run casino days is the '$20 room upgrade'. When you check in, you'll need to show the desk clerk your passport and a credit card. When you do, add a $20 bill (as a tip) and say 'Am I eligible for any *complimentary* room upgrades?' If there are any better rooms available, be they larger or perhaps with a lovely view of the Strip, the desk clerk will book you into one at the cost of your original reservation. If they can't, because the hotel is booked full or some other reason, the desk clerk will apologise and return the $20 to you. It usually works, and I've often been able to stay in rooms costing several hundred dollars more than I paid for!

Major resorts on the Strip

Bellagio

Based on an entire village in northern Italy, this truly is a treat for romantics!
Location: The Strip at the corner of West Flamingo.
Theme: Upmarket, romantic Italian lakeside village.
Cost: $1.6b, plus $375m in 2005 for the new Spa Tower.
Web: bellagiolasvegas.com.
Reservations: 702 693 7111.
Fax: 702 693 8585.
Rooms: 3,005.
Room rates: From $179 Mon–Thurs; from $259 Fri–Sun.
Restaurants: 7 fine dining options including the award-winning Picasso, Prime Steakhouse and Le Cirque, and 8 casual eateries including the Shintaro sushi bar and the Petrossian Bar for caviar.
Nightlife: Upmarket nightclub, Light.
Show: Cirque du Soleil® theatrical circus spectacular, *O*.

The Bellagio at sunset

BRITTIP

Room rates are a rough guide only as they can vary wildly. If there's a large convention booked to stay at the hotel of your choice, rates can easily rise by $200 or more. Do your homework before booking your flights – see page 251 for details of good websites to check.

Attractions: The Fountains of Bellagio, the Conservatory and Botanical Gardens and the Bellagio Gallery of Fine Art.
Chilling out: 6 outdoor pools; 4 spas; 40 private cabanas in a Mediterranean courtyard setting.
Shopping: Bellagio Esplanade filled with designer shops including Prada, Chanel, Giorgio Armani, Tiffany & Co., Hermes and Gucci.
Other amenities: 2 wedding chapels; a salon for facials, manicures and pedicures; Spa Bellagio with a spa suite, steam rooms, 14 treatment rooms and an exercise room.

One of Las Vegas' largest luxury mega-resorts, its 'signature' show is the free Fountains of Bellagio – a $30m aquatic spectacle created by colourful, soaring fountains in a synchronised water ballet accompanied by lights and soaring music by Copland and Strauss, and famous renditions by Celine Dion and Elton John. Another enjoyable freebie is the Conservatory and Botanical Gardens. The Conservatory is a 55ft/17m high, glass-ceilinged edifice with floral displays that reflect the seasons and major American holidays. Each display is planned a year in advance to ensure the necessary flowers, plants and trees are available. The Bellagio is also home to its own art gallery, which houses travelling exhibitions of exceptional art.

The real crowd-puller of the hotel is *O*, the show by the world-famous Cirque du Soleil®. A special $70m theatre, modelled on the Paris Opera House, was built as a permanent home for the theatrical acrobatics and breathtaking stunts that make Cirque shows so amazing. The nightclub, Light, combines style with first-class service and a great ambiance, and has attracted the likes of Courteney Cox, Charlie Sheen, Tobey McGuire, Daryl Hannah, Owen Wilson and Matt LeBlanc.

Queen guest room at the Bellagio

BRITTIP

If you want to experience the vibes of the Bellagio without paying to stay, check out the sophisticated new Caramel Lounge. Have a drink, take the weight off your slingbacks and just watch the beautiful people while the band plays in the background. You may even spot a celeb or two!

From each of the many rooms are panoramic views of the 8.5acre/3.4ha lake, classical gardens, elegant pools and landscaped grounds filled with fountains, waterfalls and pools.

The restaurants range from casual bistros to the gourmet restaurants Le Cirque and Picasso, which are among the most successful and popular in Las Vegas. When you have a spare moment (and a spare million), try browsing round the esplanade lined with Chanel, Armani, Gucci, Prada and Tiffany boutiques, before taking afternoon tea – one of the more affordable pleasures at the Bellagio!

Caesars Palace

Originally designed for high rollers, it's still posh but is now accessible to all and should at least be on your must-see list.
Location: On the Strip at the famous Four Corners with Flamingo.
Theme: Greco-Roman empire.
Web: caesarspalace.com.
Reservations: 702 731 7110.
Fax: 702 731 7172.
Rooms: 3,340 in 5 towers: Augustus, Centurian, Forum, Roman and Palace.
Room rates: From $200 Mon–Thurs; from $260 Fri–Sun.

Restaurants: 5 fine-dining establishments including fabulous newcomers Guy Savoy and Bradley Ogden, plus 808 and Hyakumi. The Forum Shops at Caesars Palace is home to 5 more upmarket restaurants including the famous Spago, Chinois and The Palm, plus 9 casual dining outlets including the Cheesecake Factory and Planet Hollywood. One of the greatest budget eateries you'll find on the Strip is the Cypress Street Marketplace, just outside the Colosseum's ticket office.
Nightlife: Cleopatra's Barge and Pure, which has become hot with the young Hollywood crowd, and Shadow Bar live music lounge.

BRITTIP

If you want to smoke in your hotel room, you must specify you want a smoking room, both when you book and when you check in. Even if you do get a smoking room, the ashtray may be hidden away in a drawer.

Shows: Its 4,100-seat Colosseum spotlights world-class entertainers such as Bette Midler, Elton John and Jerry Seinfeld. It also hosts outdoor events in the Roman Forum.
Chilling out: Garden of the Gods pools and Quo Baths and Spa.
Shopping: Appian Way in the hotel, plus the fabulous Forum Shops.
Other amenities: 6 wedding chapels, 3 late-night lounges with live music, plus an outdoor amphitheatre, spa, salon and golf through Cascata Golf Course.

The first-ever hotel of Las Vegas to be entirely based on a theme, Caesars Palace opened in 1966, specifically aiming at big-money gamblers. Although it allows more ordinary mortals to enter its palatial doors these days, the emphasis is still very much on luxury and opulence. The Palace underwent a $600m expansion at the turn of this century, which included building the 17-storey Palace Tower, a Garden of the Gods outdoor area, with pools and landscaped gardens, and a wedding chapel.

Throughout the 85acre/34ha resort are spectacular fountains, majestic cypress trees, gleaming marble statues and beautiful landscaping. The Garden of the Gods area has three outdoor swimming pools inlaid with marble and granite, adjoined by two whirlpool spas and

BRITTIP

Be warned – there are no mini bars in your rooms – the hotels want you drinking downstairs where you can gamble, too! Nor are there any tea or coffee-making facilities, so remember to buy water or orange juice for yourself in the morning.

rimmed by lush gardens. There are also three floodlit tennis courts and an intimate outdoor amphitheatre.

The massive Colosseum quickly became a Strip landmark when it opened. Specifically built to house Celine Dion's *A New Day* one-woman show, the 4,100-seat, state-of-the-art venue can also be adapted to accommodate headliners and host major boxing events. Celine Dion has closed her show and been replaced by an extravaganza headlined by singer/actress/comedienne Bette Midler.

The hotel has joined the ranks of other major Strip properties in providing more adult-orientated entertainment and its Shadow Bar – right in the centre of the casino – is one of the places to visit during a stay in Vegas. A relaxed, comfy lounge by day, by night it is home to topless dancers who perform sexy routines behind backlit screens. There is also a secluded adult area for 'European sunbathing' for those who wish to go topless.

All of the rooms have Jacuzzi tubs and the latest fax/phone gadgetry, while the fabulous Forum Shops are also known as the Shopping Wonder of the World (see page 86). If you want to see how the other half lives, take a wiggle on down to the posh baccarat and VIP high-roller areas. You never know, you may just get a proposal of sorts!

The poker room at Caesars Palace

Circus Circus

A great-value, family-fun destination with some surprisingly good restaurants.
Location: The Strip between West Sahara and the Convention Center.
Theme: Circus carnival featuring the world's largest permanent circus.
Web: circuscircus.com.
Reservations: 702 734 0410.
Fax: 702 734 5897.
Rooms: 3,770 plus an RV park.
Room rates: From $55 Sun–Thurs; from $110 Fri and Sat.
Restaurants: Despite its emphasis on good prices, Circus Circus has a host of good eating outlets and 2 of its fine dining options – the Steakhouse and Stivali's Ristorante – consistently win awards for great food. There are also 5 casual eateries including a Mexican, 24-hour café and deli.
Attractions: Free circus acts, IMAX® theatre and Adventuredome theme park.
Chilling out: 3 swimming pools.
Shopping: 40,000sq ft/3,720sq m promenade with fun shops.
Other amenities: The surprisingly stunning Chapel of the Fountain wedding chapel; Année of Paris Beauty Salon (702 731 3201 for appointments).

BRITTIP
The American Automobile Association's coveted Five Diamond Award has only been given to two Las Vegas hotels: the Bellagio and the Four Seasons. The AAA's Four Diamond Award has been given to Mandalay Bay, the Venetian and Las Vegas Hilton.

The bright lights of Circus Circus

The owners of Circus Circus were the second operators to build a theme casino on the Strip. It originally opened in 1968 as the world's largest permanent circus tent plus casino but without any hotel rooms. Now it has three towers housing nearly 3,800 rooms, three major gambling areas, a whole raft of shops and some major family attractions. Inspired by the turn-of-the-century circuses that used to visit towns throughout America, it aims its services directly at the cost-conscious family market.

During the 1990s, Circus Circus had started to become seriously worn from years of gamblers and herds of kids. However, recently MGM/Mirage has dumped untold millions into the property and today it is a comfortable place. Part Circus tent and part renaissance fair, it can also be a quirky place.

BRITTIP
Circus Circus is so popular with families that it can seem that you're surrounded by wall-to-wall kids!

The Circus Arena appears in the *Guinness Book of Records* as the world's largest permanent circus and covers 120,000sq ft/11,160 sq m with a 90ft/27m high tent-shaped roof. The Carnival Midway is a circus-themed amusement arcade and its centre stage is where free half-hourly shows are presented from 11am to midnight by top circus acts, from high-wire daredevils to flying trapeze artists, acrobats, magicians and jugglers.

BRITTIP
Circus Circus provides rooms with roll-in showers that have been designed for the disabled. It also has its own phone line for the hearing impaired: 1-800 638 8595.

The Circus Circus theme park – the Adventuredome – is a fully enclosed 5acre/2ha elevated theme park, which is climate-controlled to provide temperatures of 21°C/70°F all the year round. This first-

BRITTIP
Las Vegas hotels are not known for their fantastic rooms. Unless you're paying top dollar for rooms at the Venetian, Wynn, Four Seasons or Bellagio, they are fairly plain affairs with few facilities.

An executive suite at Circus Circus

ever Las Vegas amusement park has been improved over the years and now has thrilling rides in a canyon-like setting (see Chapter 10).

If you're a novice and fancy a flutter on the Strip, this is the place to try out your luck on the roulette wheels as it has three casinos covering 107,500sq ft/1,000sq m. You can then move on to a high-stakes poker game elsewhere (we can dream, can't we?).

Excalibur

Great for family fun at reasonable prices, it should also be on your must-visit list.
Location: The Strip at West Tropicana.
Theme: King Arthur and the Knights of the Round Table.
Cost: $290m.
Web: excalibur.com.
Reservations: 702 597 7777.
Fax: 702 597 7040.
Rooms: 3,991 including 72 suites.
Room rates: From $91 Mon–Thurs; from $131 Fri–Sun.

Restaurants: 2 fine-dining options, the Steakhouse at Camelot and Sir Galahad's Prime Rib House, and a further 3 casual options.
Nightlife: One of the newest and hottest night clubs on the Strip is Octane.
Attractions: *Tournament of Kings* dinner show, live music in Minstrel's Lounge; free fire-breathing dragon show; strolling entertainers; 2 magic-motion cinemas; *Thunder from Down Under*, one of the hottest male strip shows in town.
Chilling out: Pool area that can hold 800 guests, with 2 heated pools, a 25-seat spa, waterfalls, water slides, snack bar and cocktail bar, open 9am–7pm daily (subject to seasonal change).
Shopping: Medieval Village.
Other amenities: The Royal Treatment Spa and Fitness Center; links to 6 challenging golf courses including Bali Hai, Resort Pines, Royal Links and Stallion Mountain Golf Club; Kristina's Salon open 7 days a week and also specialises in bridal parties (702 597 7255); 2 wedding chapels on a light and airy medieval theme (truly not an oxymoron in this case!).

BRITTIP

Beat the queues! You can fast track your check-in by filling out the King's Express form in advance or by going to one of the self check-in kiosks on arrival to get your keys instantly.

BRITTIP

Don't miss the medieval-costumed staff at the Excalibur, where entertainers wander around playing medieval trumpets!

The beautiful spires of the Camelot-style entrance building are set between two huge castle-like towers that house the 4,000-odd rooms at this family-orientated resort. Make no mistake, though, the free Dragon Battle that takes place every hour on the hour 10am–10pm to draw the crowds has the sole purpose of inviting you in to part with your cash in the 100,000sq ft/9,300sq m casino. But there are plenty of other free entertainments to keep you amused as you wander round the Medieval Village of shops and restaurants, from the strolling entertainers to the free variety acts on the Court Jester's Stage from 10am every day.

You can eat dinner and see the *Tournament of Kings* at either 6pm or 8.30pm any day of the week, or dance to live music at the Minstrel's Lounge. The

Excalibur at night

house of fun also has six restaurants and parking is free and relatively accessible by Las Vegas standards.

Four Seasons

Provides an oasis of elegance – predominantly for business people – as the first non-gambling hotel-cum-retreat on the Strip.
Location: The Strip, just south of the Mandalay Bay.
Theme: Understated luxury.
Web: fourseasons.com/lasvegas.
Reservations: 702 632 5000.
Fax: 702 632 5195.
Rooms: 424 including 86 suites.
Room rates: From $270 Sun–Thurs; from $370 Fri and Sat.
Restaurants: 3 restaurants and lounges including the Verandah Bar and Lounge, Charlie Palmer Steak Lounge and Pool Bar.
Chilling out: Pool and health and fitness club (and the ONLY hotel in Las Vegas to provide those facilities free and exclusively to guests).
Other amenities: A wedding chapel, plus facilities to wed in 3 of the most amazing suites in Las Vegas.

Although the guestrooms of the hotel are located on floors 35 to 39 of the Mandalay Bay, the Four Seasons is a separately functioning hotel. The first hotel in recent history to open on the Strip without massive theming, it is also the only one without a casino and one of only two with a five-diamond rating in Las Vegas.

The real beauty of the hotel comes in its divine suites, where spaciousness, supreme elegance and to-die-for views reign supreme. The Four Seasons is most famous for its Specialty Suites with 180-degree views of the glistening Strip and glistening desert. With the added bonus of separate lounge and dining areas filled with sumptuous furnishings, these suites were designed to provide the ultimate safe haven from the never-ending ker-chink, ker-chink of Las Vegas's casinos!

Ostensibly geared up to business people – it is the only hotel in Las Vegas to have a corporate rate – it still attracts tourists, many of whom are dedicated followers of the Four Seasons brand. While guests have access to all the facilities of the Mandalay Bay, they have their own exclusive facilities, too, starting with the private drive and entrance, and the casino-free, super-cool, gleaming lobby plus the lavishly landscaped private pool (where attentive staff are on hand to give you a cooling

The pool at the Four Seasons

Evian spritz!), two whirlpools and an exclusive health and fitness club.

BRITTIP

Don't worry if you arrive at the Four Seasons without your swimsuit or shorts and fall in love with its tranquil pool; the hotel can provide disposable swimsuits.

The restaurants – including celebrity chef Charlie Palmer's Steak Lounge – have been building up a regular band of loyal locals as well as guests of the hotel. Nor are they overpriced. The Verandah has a set $9 two-course or $21 three-course meal. At the Four Seasons it's all about understated elegance, darlink!

The Spa at Four Seasons is open 8am–7pm and features Jamu Asian spa rituals, which blend exotic ingredients with ancient traditions that work on both your inner and outer body. There are 16 elegant treatment rooms and a large steam room. Signature treatments (trust me, you have to try at least one) include the Jamu meditative massage, Zen garden massage and Four Seasons four-layer facial. Can you think of any reason why you would ever want to leave this paradise?

BRITTIP

You've got more chance of getting a room – and cheaply – at the resort-hotels if you go between Monday and Thursday.

BRITTIP

The Four Seasons has been ranked the Best Business Hotel in Las Vegas by America's *Travel & Leisure* magazine. Its spa was also ranked 13 of all top hotel spas in North America and Canada.

Luxor

Ancient Egyptian theme resort at good-value prices.
Location: The Strip between Tropicana and Reno.
Theme: Ancient Egypt.
Cost: $375m, plus a $240m expansion.
Web: luxor.com.
Reservations: 702 262 4444.
Fax: 702 262 4452.
Rooms: 4,408.
Room rates: From $69 Mon–Thurs; from $160 Fri–Sun.
Restaurants: 5 fine-dining experiences including Fusia, the award-winning Isis and the divine Sacred Sea Room, plus 5 casual eateries including a food court, deli and La Salsa Mexican grill.
Nightlife: Ra nightclub and Nefertiti's Lounge for live music and dancing.
Shows: Comedian Carrot Top and the adult revue *Fantasy* (formerly Midnight Fantasy).
Attractions: Adventure rides in IMAX® cinemas at the Pharoah's Pavilion.
Chilling out: 4 swimming pools and relaxing Jacuzzis in a luxurious oasis setting; the Oasis Spa; access to golf at 4 different courses.
Shopping: Giza Galleria promenade plus shops in the Pharoah's Pavilion.
Other amenities: Spa for over 18s only; wedding chapel.

BRITTIP

One company now owns the Mandalay Bay, Luxor and Excalibur and has built a monorail linking all three. There are also well-signposted walkways between them. The walkway from the Excalibur to its neighbouring rival, New York-New York, is NOT signposted but can be found just outside the main entrance.

For us Brits this is the hotel that is synonymous with Las Vegas extravagance, and staying in the fabulous replica of a pyramid is up there on your must-do list. With its trademark beacon of light that can now be seen from outer space (along with the Great Wall of China), the hotel is one of the most tastefully executed theme resorts in the middle-market sector. You enter the beautiful structure through a life-size replica of the great Temple of Rameses II, which takes you directly into the casino (funny that!) where 120,000 sq ft/11,160 sq m of gambling space houses slot and video machines, gaming tables, a sports book, poker and keno.

BRITTIP

The trick to finding a moment's peace and quiet in the Luxor is to head for the Sacred Sea Room, reached via the lobby lift. From its floor-to-ceiling windows, you can watch the hustle and bustle outside while enjoying some delicious seafood.

Even if you don't want to have a flutter, there's plenty to do as the Pharoah's Pavilion, one floor above the casino, is filled with shopping and attractions that include eight IMAX® movies – an IMAX® ride film, a virtual reality roller-coaster, and The Tomb & Museum of King Tutankhamun. On the show front, Carrot Top, a wacky entertainer who delights crowds with his idiosyncratic gadgets and sometimes coarse humour, draws great crowds, while the adult topless revue, *Fantasy*, keeps people out late. The hotel is also home to an all-night club called Ra, after the Egyptian God, which has a stage, dance floor, bars, cigar lounge and a 110-seater sushi and oyster bar.

The main lobby at the Luxor

To get to your room, you'll travel on the elevator at a bizarre 39-degree angle, while there are shops selling Egyptian antiquities, gemstones, charms and limited-edition art, and one of the hotel's many fine restaurants, Isis, is consistently voted among the top ten restaurants in America.

BRITTIP Make sure you have lip balm with you all the time as the constant air conditioning in the hotels really dries out your lips.

Chill out in one of the attractive swimming pool areas or pay $20 ($25 to non-hotel guests) for a day Spa Pass, which includes use of the hot and cold whirlpools, steam bath, dry sauna, fitness centre and a complimentary fruit juice or mineral water.

Mandalay Bay

A luxury resort filled with must-see shows, must-eat-at restaurants and some of the coolest nightlife venues in town.
Location: The Strip, just south of West Tropicana Avenue (entrance off Hacienda Drive).
Theme: South Sea Islands.
Cost: $950m.
Web: mandalaybay.com.
Reservations: 702 632 7777.
Fax: 702 632 7013.
Rooms: 3,700.
Room rates: From $99 Sun–Thurs; from $139 Fri and Sat.

BRITTIP The Mandalay's wave pool is generally closed for maintenance from around the end of October to March.

Standard suite at the Mandalay Bay

Restaurants: Fine dining restaurants include the new The Mix (with lounge), Restaurant rm and Fleur de Lys, the famous Aureole and Trattoria del Lupa, plus the new 3950 seafood and steakhouse Stripsteak and Shanghai Lily, venue of one of the most exclusive nightclubs on a Wednesday evening. Casual dining experiences include the Russian-themed Red Square, plus 2 live music outlets – the House of Blues and Rumjungle.
Nightlife: House of Blues, Rumjungle, Beach outdoor island stage, Coral Reef lounge and Ivan Kane's Forty Deuce strip club.
Shows: Headliners and Broadway productions on a rotating basis.
Attractions: Shark Reef; the *Mama Mia!* musical show.

BRITTIP Never use the phone in your hotel room – you'll be charged a small fortune.Get an international phone card before you go instead.

Chilling out: Sand-and-surf beach and the lazy river ride.
Shopping: Selection of shops on the South Seas theme, selling everything from cigars to Bali treasures.
Other amenities: Spa Mandalay; 2 wedding chapels.

Aimed at a slightly more sophisticated traveller than its sister property, the Luxor, it's still excellent value for money and well worth forking out that bit extra for.

For starters, it's one of the few hotels on the Strip where you don't have to walk through the casino to get to your room and, secondly, many of the rooms have massive soaking/Jacuzzi tubs plus a separate shower. A large number also have fabulous views down the entire Strip and, despite being the nearest hotel to the airport, you don't hear a peep out of those planes thanks to some pretty nifty double glazing.

Dan Aykroyd's House of Blues, the first of which opened on Sunset Strip in Los Angeles, has a home here. The live music venue is drawing such crowds that you need to book at least four weeks in advance. And if you just can't get enough of the blues, then ask for a room on the 34th floor of the hotel – it's filled with House of Blues-themed guestrooms.

Among the numerous upmarket restaurants are two celebrity-chef hot spots: Charlie Palmer's Aureole, and Trattoria del

The stunning MGM Grand

Lupo, owned by Wolfgang Puck, one of the most influential chefs in the US. The Mix offers amazing views of the Strip from its lofty spot, while it also has a wonderful chill-out lounge. In addition, there's Red Square, the Russian-inspired homage to vodka and caviar. Celebrities have their own vodka lockers, but the less well-to-do can try the frozen ice bar where there are more than 100 frozen vodkas and infusions, Martinis and Russian-inspired cocktails. You can also dine on an extensive selection of caviars or Russian classics.

Try Rumjungle for some dinner and dancing. Here the food and drinks are turned into works of art from a flaming wall to cascading waterfalls, while volcanic mountains of rum and spirits rise before you at the illuminated bar. Many of the sizzling meals are cooked over a giant open fire pit for that authentic South Seas flavour, while dancing is to Latin, Caribbean and African beats until the small hours.

It's not all fast-paced at the Mandalay, though, as there are plenty of ways to unwind in the 11acre/4.5ha tropical water environment. Try out the city's first sand-and-surf beach, take a dip in one of the many swimming pools or just go for a lazy river ride. You can now also get a day pass to the spa or opt for one of the many excellent massages, body treatments or facials.

On the site of the Mandalay Bay is its cousin property, THEhotel, which has an additional 1,117 suites in 43 stories of upscale and secluded sanctuaries.

BRITTIP

While most fine dining establishments close around 10pm or 10.30pm, all the major resort-hotels have at least one café that's open round the clock (24/7) and many others that stay open late.

MGM Grand

Massive resort hotel that is good fun for the whole family, yet provides plenty of adult entertainment.

Location: The Strip at the new Four Corners with East Tropicana.
Theme: The City of Entertainment.
Cost: Originally $1b, plus a $950m expansion and theme transformation.
Web: mgmgrand.com.
Reservations: 702 891 7777.
Fax: 702 891 1030.
Rooms: 5,034.
Room rates: From $90 Mon–Thurs; from $180 Fri–Sun.
Restaurants: Michelin-starred chef Joël Robuchon has created Joël Robuchon at the Mansion, while other new arrivals include Michael Mima's Seablue and the Japanese Shibuya. Other stalwarts remain, including Nobhill, Emeril's, Craftsteak and Tiamma; and 8 casual outlets including the Rainforest Café.
Nightlife: Studio 54 nightclub, Tabu ultra-lounge and Teatro cocktail bar.
Shows: *Kà* by Cirque du Soleil®; sporting events and major concerts in the Grand Garden Arena (seats 16,325); smaller gigs in the 650-seat Hollywood Theater; plus the *Crazy Horse Paris* adult show (formerly *La Femme*).
Attractions: Arcade centre with high-tech virtual reality games; the free Lion Habitat; the Youth Activity Center.
Chilling out: Grand Pool and Spa.

Other amenities: 2 wedding chapels; access to golf at Shadow Creek.

The MGM Grand is so huge it can be all things to all people. It is easy to get lost in the array of opportunities to eat, drink and generally be merry. In recent years, there has been a shift away from the old-style family-orientated entertainments to a more adult-based scene, yet it still has a high-tech arcade and a Youth Activity Center where parents can drop 3–12-year-olds off and go party.

BRITTIP
If you're staying at the MGM Grand or New York-New York, then head to the south baggage area at McCarran airport to check in while waiting for your luggage to come off the plane. For an extra fee you can even take the direct shuttle to your hotel.

The hotel is famous for staging headliner shows and big fights in its Grand Garden Arena and Hollywood Theater.

In an effort to cater to the adult market, the hotel opened Tabu, an ultra-lounge, while the Studio 54 nightclub has a more raunchy twist with Dollhouse night when grown-ups get to dress beautiful 'dolls' in outfits of their choice, and Zuri supplies a 24-hour drinking spot.

The 6.6acre/2.7ha Grand Pool and Spa complex features five pools, lush landscaping, a lazy river, bridges, fountains and waterfalls, and many rate MGM Grand's pool offerings as the best in Vegas. Meanwhile you can check out your cardiovascular rating in the state-of-the-art fitness centre at the spa. Afterwards, there are no end of eating choices available with a total of 17 fine and casual dining outlets, and if you wish you can even pop out to the neighbouring United Artists Showcase cinema.

The rooms, especially the suites, are very good for the price, with each one having artwork of Hollywood movies and celebrities of the past. A great game is to walk down your hallway trying to put names to the famous faces mounted on the walls.

It has also added 'cousin' towers for the Signature at MGM Grand and Skylofts, which offer another 1,441 luxury suites for those looking for the most pampered of settings.

The volcano at the Mirage

BRITTIP
Speed up your check-out times by taking advantage of the check-out systems available on many of the hotel's TVs. DO check the bill thoroughly, though, before paying, as mistakes can occur, and always resolve any queries before leaving the hotel.

Mirage

An elegant taste of paradise, yet within reach of most budgets.
Location: The Strip, between Flamingo and Spring Mountain.
Theme: Polynesian, South Seas oasis.
Cost: $730m.
Web: mirage.com.
Reservations: 702 791 7111.
Fax: 702 791 7446.
Rooms: 3,044.
Room rates: From $109 Mon–Thurs; from $179 Fri–Sun.
Restaurants: 6 fine dining experiences including the award-winning Onda and Renoir restaurants, plus 4 casual options.
Nightlife: The hopping JET nightclub, plus a superb lounge scene for live music at the Japonaisa Lounge, the Onda lounge, the Beatles Revolution lounge, Baccarat. Shows: Cirque du Soleil's® Beatles tribute, *Love*™; Danny Gans, entertainer of the year; plus a roster of visiting acts.
Attractions: The Secret Garden Dolphin Habitat, White Tiger Habitat, Tropical Rainforest Bar and outdoor Dolphin Bar.
Chilling out: 2 pools and cabanas in a lush, tropical setting; the new Bare pool area allows 'European-style' sunbathing.
Shopping: The Street of Shops promenade.
Other amenities: spa and salon – spa access is free when you book a treatment,

BRITTIP

One of the most unusual experiences Las Vegas has to offer is available at the Dolphin Habitat, where you can learn the art of being a trainer.

otherwise $20; the hotel has a link with Shadow Creek Golf Course.

The entrance garden surrounds you with a mass of foliage and waterfalls that cascade over 50ft/15m rocks to the lagoon below before you reach the Mirage signature volcano. This erupts every few minutes, spewing smoke and fire 100ft/30m above the water. The reception area is a tropical rainforest, filled with 60ft/18m high palm trees, more waterfalls, banana trees and tropical orchids, kept in perfect condition with natural sunlight and a computerised misting system. Behind the check-in desk is a massive coral reef aquarium that is home to sharks, puffer fish and angel fish, swimming among the buildings of a sunken city. The forest provides the delightfully exotic setting for Kokomo's, one of the Mirage's top-notch restaurants, serving steaks and seafood.

The Mirage became the latest Las Vegas resort to host a Cirque du Soleil® fantasy, when in 2007 it opened *Love*™. The Beatles' old studios, Abbey Road, provided the digital recording masters to make the music as real as possible.

When it opened in 1989, the Mirage's theme of a Polynesian island oasis was a taste of the big things to come in Las Vegas, and it has stood the test of time. Once host to the famous *Siegfried & Roy* magical show of illusions featuring tigers, lions, leopards and other animals, the habitat for the dolphins remains. It has become an educational and research facility and it is possible to spend a day with a trainer. The Secret Garden, where you can see white lions, and the vast Dolphin Habitat were built to create public awareness of the plight of endangered animals.

Accommodation ranges from luxurious standard rooms to opulent bungalows with their own private garden and pools, and eight two and three-bedroom private residences. Admission to the luxurious day spa and fitness centre costs $20, but is free if you book any one of the pampering treatments.

Monte Carlo

Posh-but-worth-it hotel with great chilling-out facilities.
Location: The Strip just north of West Tropicana.
Theme: Re-creation of the Place du Casino in Monte Carlo.
Cost: $344m.
Web: montecarlo.com.
Reservations: 702 730 7777.
Fax: 702 730 7250.
Rooms: 3,261.
Room rates: From $80 Mon–Thurs; from $150 Fri–Sun.
Restaurants: 2 fine-dining outlets including the famous André's, and 4 casual eateries including the 210-seat food court.
Nightlife: Monte Carlo Pub & Brewery nightclub and Houdini's live music lounge
Shows: Lance Burton, Master Magician; Gabriel Iglesias, comic.
Chilling out: 21,000sq ft/1,950sq m pool area with waterfalls, spa, children's pool, wave pool and rafting down the Easy River.
Shopping: Street of Dreams promenade.
Other amenities: A wedding chapel; health spa and exercise room.

The Monte Carlo at dusk

BRITTIP

Skip the expensive buffet at the Monte Carlo and go for one of the gourmet restaurants instead.

This elegant, upmarket resort hotel is so popular that it is hard for British travel agents to find you a room here. Modelled on the famous Place du Casino in Monaco, the emphasis is definitely on providing an elegant and refined atmosphere in which to part with wads of cash in the casino. Massive chandeliers, marble flooring, ornate fountains and gas-lit promenades all go towards setting the elegant tone. After a hard day seeing the sights, make sure you get back in time to make full use of the water facilities, which include a heated spa, children's pool and wave pool that re-creates both the sound and feel of ocean surf waves.

Resident entertainer Lance Burton is one of the top magicians in America and produces some of the most spectacular illusions in the world.

The Monte Carlo Pub & Brewery not only offers an excellent selection of beers, but also offers live music and dancing with a DJ and live music from a band kicking off around 9pm most nights. Houdini's Lounge is a more intimate affair, offering classic piano and sultry live music from Thursday to Sunday.

New York-New York

The most electrifying club scene in Vegas!
Location: The Strip at West Tropicana.
Theme: The Big Apple – doh!
Cost: $460m.
Web: nynyhotelcasino.com.
Reservations: 702 740 6969.
Fax: 702 740 6920.
Rooms: 2,033.
Room rates: From $89 Mon–Thurs; from $129 Fri–Sun.
Restaurants: 5 fine-dining restaurants include Gonzalez Y Gonzalez and Gallagher's Steakhouse, and 8 casual dining outlets include 3 in the ESPN Zone
Nightlife: Great range of bars including Coyote Ugly, Nine Fine Irishmen, the Bar at Times Square and the Big Apple Bar.
Shows: *Zumanity*, the adult-themed Cirque du Soleil® extravaganza.
Attractions: Manhattan Express™ roller-coaster ride; ESPN Zone.
Chilling out: Outdoor pool with 3 relaxing whirlpools.
Shopping: Numerous gift shops in the Central Park area.
Other amenities: Wedding chapel; spa and fitness centre.

Dubbed the 'greatest city in Las Vegas', the resort's façade re-creates the Manhattan skyline with 12 of its most famous skyscrapers from the Empire State Building to the Statue of Liberty, along with a

Just like the Big Apple – New York-New York

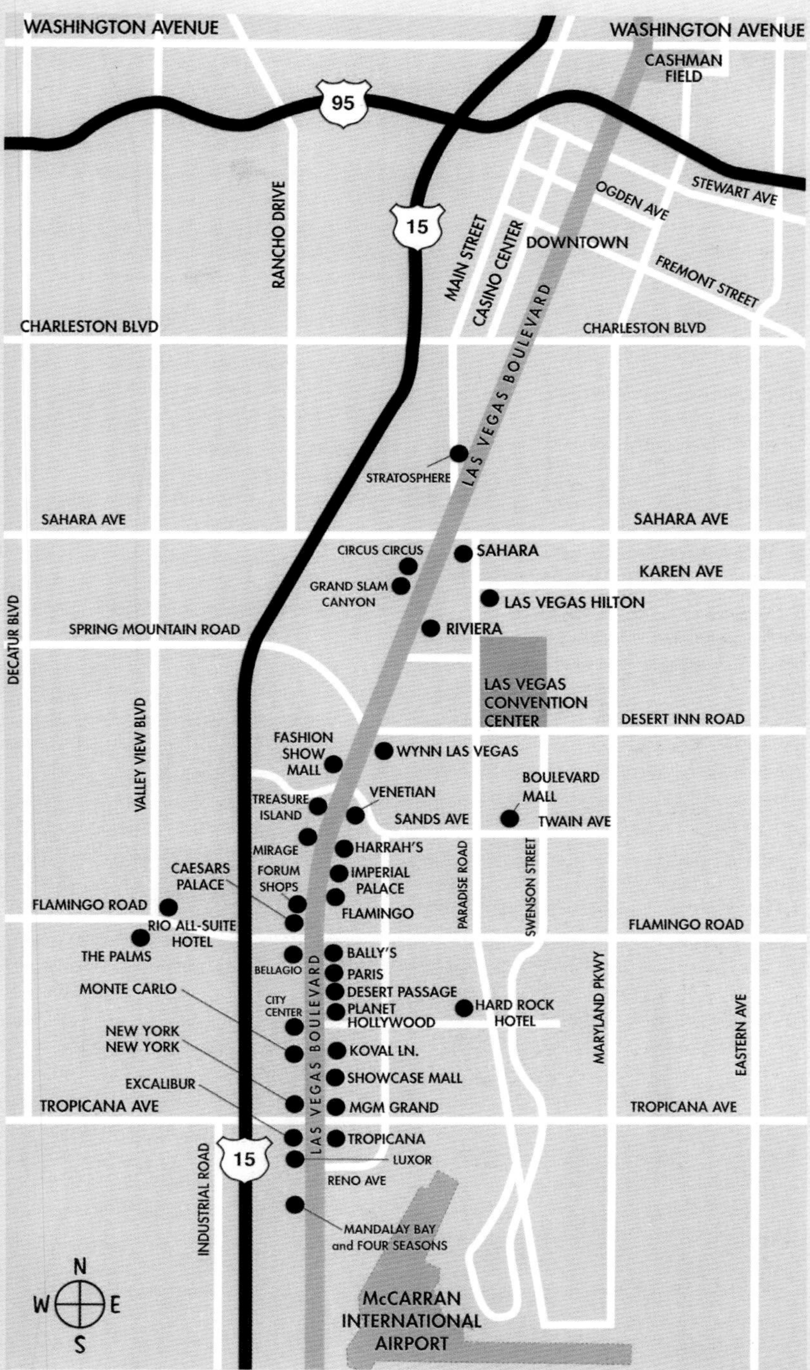
WASHINGTON AVENUE
WASHINGTON AVENUE
CASHMAN FIELD
95
STEWART AVE
OGDEN AVE
15
RANCHO DRIVE
MAIN STREET
CASINO CENTER
DOWNTOWN
FREMONT STREET
CHARLESTON BLVD
CHARLESTON BLVD
LAS VEGAS BOULEVARD
STRATOSPHERE
SAHARA AVE
SAHARA AVE
CIRCUS CIRCUS
SAHARA
KAREN AVE
GRAND SLAM CANYON
LAS VEGAS HILTON
DECATUR BLVD
SPRING MOUNTAIN ROAD
RIVIERA
LAS VEGAS CONVENTION CENTER
DESERT INN ROAD
VALLEY VIEW BLVD
FASHION SHOW MALL
WYNN LAS VEGAS
BOULEVARD MALL
TREASURE ISLAND
VENETIAN
SANDS AVE
TWAIN AVE
MIRAGE
HARRAH'S
CAESARS PALACE
FORUM SHOPS
IMPERIAL PALACE
PARADISE ROAD
SWENSON STREET
FLAMINGO ROAD
FLAMINGO
FLAMINGO ROAD
RIO ALL-SUITE HOTEL
THE PALMS
BALLY'S
BELLAGIO
PARIS
MONTE CARLO
DESERT PASSAGE
CITY CENTER
PLANET HOLLYWOOD
HARD ROCK HOTEL
MARYLAND PKWY
NEW YORK NEW YORK
KOVAL LN.
EXCALIBUR
SHOWCASE MALL
EASTERN AVE
TROPICANA AVE
MGM GRAND
TROPICANA AVE
TROPICANA
LAS VEGAS BOULEVARD
15
LUXOR
INDUSTRIAL ROAD
RENO AVE
MANDALAY BAY and FOUR SEASONS
N
W
E
S
McCARRAN INTERNATIONAL AIRPORT

BRITTIP

It's a good 10-minute walk through shops and casinos to get to the New York-New York's roller-coaster ride, but it's well worth the trek!

300ft/90m long replica of Brooklyn Bridge and a Coney Island-style roller-coaster called Manhattan Express™. From the food and the architecture, to the sights and sounds of America's capital city, this Las Vegas resort re-creates the energy and vibrancy of New York – then adds the Central Park casino!

Part of the MGM Mirage – whose empire includes the MGM Grand, Mirage, Bellagio and Treasure Island – entertainment is an important façet of the hotel, while Cirque du Soleil's® *Zumanity*, has turned into a long-running success.

The ESPN Zone, a sports-themed dining and entertainment complex with more than 165 TV screens so you don't miss a moment's action, also continues to be very popular. The Studio Grill offers classic casual American grub in a sports-themed environment, The Screening Room provides multi-game viewing, direct audio control for all televised games around two 14ft/4m screens and a dozen 36in/90cm video monitors with tiered seating, while the Sports Arena has more than 10,000sq ft/ 930sq m of interactive games.

However, it is the bar scene with its fun entertainment and live music that puts the 'party, party, party' atmosphere into New York-New York. Top of the pile is Coyote Ugly, which is based on a Southern-style bar, complete with gyrating female bartenders atop the bar. No fancy drinks here, just shots and beer. Anyone who asks for a water or soda are welcomed to a shower of water sprayed over the entire crowd! Then there is the Big Apple Bar, a hot live-music joint with speciality drinks and the Bar at Times Square, where you can sing along to tunes played by two pianists. The party-style ambiance is continued into the dining area Gonzalez y Gonzalez, a New York Mexican-style café famous for its tequilas.

Chilling-out facilities include a pool area with patio chairs for the cool cabanas. The new restaurant sets a lively vibe, while other fun elements include volleyball, poolside chair massages and a sound system. The spa is open daily 6.30am–7pm, and golf is provided through Primm Valley Golf Course.

Paris Las Vegas

Paris Las Vegas

A tribute to the French capital, from the undersized Eiffel Tower to the Arc d' Triomphe.
Location: The Strip, south of East Flamingo.
Theme: Capital of France!
Cost: $785m.
Web: parislasvegas.com.
Reservations: 702 946 7777.
Fax: 702 967 3836.
Rooms: 2,916.
Room rates: From $125 Sun–Thurs; from $230 Fri and Sat.
Restaurants: 8 fine-dining establishments include the popular Eiffel Tower Restaurant, the wonderful Ortanique and Mon Ami Gabi, with outside dining right on the Strip, plus 3 casual eateries including the poolside Le Café du Parc.
Nightlife: Fabulous ultra-lounge Risqué, plus Napoleon's and the Eiffel Tower lounges.
Attractions: Observation deck on the Eiffel Tower; the Le Rendez-Vous Lounge on the 31st floor offers drinks with a fab view of the Strip. Paris has developed itself into one of the finest adult entertainment stops in Las Vegas: start with the long-running version of the Mel Brooks musical *The Producers*, Anthony Cool's stunning magic show, and the sexy topless revue *Oh La La*; add some cool lounges like Risqué and you have a wonderful night for adults only.
Chilling out: Roof-top swimming pool in a manicured French garden setting; tennis courts.

BRITTIP

For a complete low-down on getting married in Las Vegas, see Chapter 8, Going to the Chapel.

Ah Sin at Paris Las Vegas

Shopping: French shops in the resort's Rue de la Paix district.
Amenities: 2 wedding chapels; Paris Spa by Mandara; golf is offered at the Cascata Golf Club.

Bringing to life the ambience and spirit of the French capital, this theme resort opened in the autumn of 1999 with replicas of the Eiffel Tower, Arc de Triomphe, Paris Opera House and the Louvre. The 34-storey hotel tower is fashioned after the famous Hôtel de Ville. Like the Mandalay Bay and Venetian, the Paris is aimed at the more sophisticated traveller, with prices – by Las Vegas standards, at least – to match.

The hotel is home to one of the city's chicest ultra-lounges – Risqué – plus Napoleon's, a gorgeous champagne and jazz bar, while the lounge at the new Le Rendez-Vous Lounge provides some of the best views in the city at a nominal fee.

All the restaurants – in true French fashion – provide wonderful food, while Ah Sin quickly became a popular spot for both its delicious Asian cuisine and outdoor patio dining overlooking the Strip.

There is a caveat, though. While so many aspects of this resort are wonderful, the service can be poor and prices are on the expensive side. It can feel as though you are really in Paris! Well, maybe not. Look out for signs such as L'Hôtel Elevators and Le Service Captain. On top of this, all the staff have been trained to say 'bonjour' and 'merci' but can't actually understand a word of French. Of all the resorts, this is the one that comes off with the thinnest veneer.

Planet Hollywood

A well-priced mega resort now home to some of the most adult-orientated entertainments on the Strip.
Location: The Strip on the corner of Harmon Avenue, south of the Paris resort and almost directly opposite the Bellagio.
Theme: The outrageously popular Planet Hollywood formula of film styling and memorabilia.
Cost: $1.4b in 2000, plus $100m in 2006–2007.
Web: planethollywoodresort.com.
Reservations: 702 736 7114.
Fax: 702 736 7107.
Rooms: 2,567.
Room rates: From $109 Sun–Thurs; $229 Fri and Sat.
Restaurants: 8, headlined by the Japanese offerings of Koi and the popular Chinese-fusion food of PF Changs. The lone holdover from the Aladdin days is the Spice Market Buffet, one of the best buffet values in Vegas. Plus the Miracle Mile shopping area has more great dining with Pampas Churrascaria and Trader Vic's.
Nightclubs: The celebrity attraction Extra Lounge, and the Heart Bar.
Shows: 7,000 seat Theater for the Performing Arts and the more intimate Showroom.
Attractions: The Magic show of Hans Klok and the international stage favourite *Stomp Out Loud*.

Heart Bar at Planet Hollywood

Chilling out: 2 6th-floor outdoor terrace and swimming pool areas overlooking the Strip.
Shopping: The Miracle Mile – once The Desert Passage at the Aladdin – is a massive shopping area with more than 140 shops and 6 fine-dining restaurants including hot city favourites the Commander's Palace from New Orleans, Sevilla, Bice and Anasazi, plus six casual eating outlets.
Other amenities: Luxurious 32,000sq ft/ 2,980sq m spa; two wedding chapels.

Seemingly born under an unlucky star, Planet Hollywood is hoping that her original (and unlucky) life as the Aladdin is behind her and she can look forward to a profitable future by mixing Hollywood Glamour with Vegas Sin.

Having opened in 2000, the Aladdin had one of the bumpiest rides of any of the major resort hotels in recent time. Of course, it didn't help that the project went massively over budget, nor that the opening was postponed for five months, nor that when it did finally open there weren't enough hotel rooms ready for all the reservations taken. So much for a 'grand' opening!

BRITTIP

If you don't want to walk miles to your hotel room, request one near to the lifts. These hotels are massive and rooms can be a considerable distance from the lifts!

The lobby at Planet Hollywood

The Aladdin was bought by Planet Hollywood, Starwood Hotels and Bay Harbor in the bankruptcy courts for $637m in 2004. A further $100m was spent on renovations that changed the facade, improved the casino and added restaurants, a 1,300-seat showroom and a 500-seat TV studio.

Planet Hollywood has also worked on her contacts in the entertainment industry to

The *Pulp Fiction* suite at Planet Hollywood

The pool at the Stratosphere

attract crowds of celebrities on a daily basis. Extra is a popular television show of big-name interviews and gossip mongering, and it has set up its headquarters in the newly minted Extra Lounge. They bring in a daily influx of beautiful people who willingly glad hand and pose for photos with their adoring fans.

A programme to improve guest facilities means that rooms now come with marble bathrooms with oversized bathtubs, and in-room personal computers.

The old Elemis Spa is now renamed the Planet Hollywood Spa by Mandara. The old version had won Leading Spa Resort in Southwest United States by the World Travel Awards in 2005 and 2006 so hopefully the world-class indulgences remain despite the name change.

Stratosphere

Extremely good-value hotel with some of the best gambling odds on the Strip.
Location: At the northern end of the Strip.
Theme: Tallest building west of the Mississippi.
Cost: $550m.
Web: stratospherehotel.com.
Reservations: 702 380 7777.
Fax: 702 383 5334.
Rooms: 2,444.
Room rates: From $39 Mon–Thurs; from $89 Fri–Sun.
Restaurants: 2 fine-dining experiences including the revolving Top of the World Restaurant on the 106th floor, plus 5 casual dining outlets.
Nightlife: Polly Esthers, Crazy Armadillo Oyster Bar, Images Lounge, Top of the World Lounge and Tequila Sky Bar.
Shows: *American Superstars* and *Bite*.
Attractions: Highest observation tower in America, world's highest roller-coaster and world's highest thrill ride, Big Shot!
Chilling out: Beach Club 25 and pool and recreation deck; Roni Josef Salon Spa.
Shopping: The Tower Shops.
Other amenities: A wedding chapel, state-of-the-art video arcade.

Stratosphere has paid the price for being located at the most northern point of the Strip – just that little bit too far from the rest of the action and in a little seedier part of town. Having faced bankruptcy, then received an injection of capital to provide a raft of new amenities, the Stratosphere finds itself offering party-time products in an environment that always looks as if it needs a lick of paint.

The Stratosphere

In its favour, though, are some real crowd-pleasers. XScream, Big Shot! and the High Roller attract the roller-coaster thrill seekers. Those with a less robust constitution can enjoy the observation deck in the tallest building in the city and enjoy a drink as the bar gently circles so you can see every dramatic view.

The restaurant scene is one of the hotel's biggest hits. Its Top of the World Restaurant provides great food and an incomparable view of the Strip. The Crazy Armadillo, a fun oyster bar with live entertainment daily and singing and dancing shooter girls and bar staff, is a boon, as is the Tequila Sky Bar with its 'flair' bartenders and tequila shots. Roxy's Diner is another fun place. Set in the 1950s, it provides classic all-American dishes, while the waiters and waitresses sing and dance along to the rock 'n' roll music.

The headliner for the nightclub scene is the new Polly Esther's, a popular nightclub chain that brings disco balls, Doc Martens and DeLoreans to the floor, opened in 2007. This complex is actually four nightclubs in one: Polly Esther's salutes the funky '70s, Culture Club brings back the '80s, Nerve Ana embraces the '90s, while the ultra-lounge Suite 2000 pounds with current club music.

Beach Club 25 was the first of the 'European-style sunbathing' facilities in Las Vegas. It is a popular, secluded adult environment with table tennis, fitness equipment, water volleyball and fun parties, with fantastic views of the Strip from its 25th-floor location. It is also incredibly popular with cast members of the topless *Bite* show who frequent the facilities to perfect their tans and allow the males to drool.

The unmistakable Treasure Island

The coffee shop at Treasure Island

Another chill-out zone is provided on the eighth floor of the tower block. The 67,000sq ft/6,030sq m pool and recreation deck offers a huge pool, oversize spa, waterfall and private cabanas.

The competitively priced rooms are among the cheapest on the Strip, although they aren't quite as good a value as first blush. The otherwise budget-priced hotel charges a sometimes pricey 'resort fee' on top of your hotel bill, which makes the value go from amazingly cheap to merely very good. But the amazing odds available in the casino make it the best place to try out your newfound skills on the tables (see Chapter 7)!

Treasure Island

It's kept the family-style brand, but is now offering a more adult package of entertainments.

Location: The Strip at Spring Mountain Road.

Theme: Robert Louis Stevenson's novel *Treasure Island*, as only Vegas can do.

Web: treasureisland.com.

Reservations: 702 894 7111.

Fax: 702 894 7446.

Rooms: 2,891.

Room rates: From $69 Mon–Thurs; from $109 Fri–Sun.

Restaurants: 4 fine-dining including sushi spectacular Social House, Isla Mexican Grill, the Tuscan eatery Francesco's plus 4 casual eateries.

Nightlife: Tangerine nightclub, Mist Bar, Isla Tequila Bar, Breeze Bar and Kahunaville Party Bar with live entertainment.
Shows: Cirque du Soleil's® *Mystère* and the *Sirens of TI* sea show.
Chilling out: Tropical paradise pool with private cabanas.
Shopping: The Pirate's Walk shopping promenade.
Other amenities: 2 wedding chapels; spa and beauty salon.
Built by Steve Wynn, who was also responsible for the Mirage and the Bellagio (before selling up to create Wynn Las Vegas), the owners MGM Mirage have gradually steered the resort away from families to provide a more adult-orientated destination.

BRITTIP

If you plan to see the *Sirens of TI* show at Treasure Island, arrive early to grab a prime spot as crowds build quickly.

The free *Sirens of TI* show is a steamy affair, with wanton sirens tempting buccaneers in a wild, outdoor sea battle four times nightly every 90 minutes starting at 7.30pm. While you can see it from Las Vegas Boulevard, it is best viewed from the Tangerine Lounge. And while Cirque's *Mystère* show continues to wow audiences twice nightly, there is a much more adult selection of bars. Tangerine nightclub is all about daiquiris and steel drums by day, before turning into a steamy club with burlesque show at night. Many of the staff only wear what is painted on their bodies.

The Kahunaville Party Bar is a tropical hotspot with eclectic music and flair bartenders that turn the venue from restaurant to party central until 3am every morning.

The Venetian

Luxurious recreation of the romantic city of Venice, and a favourite with celebrities and CEOs alike.
Location: The Strip at East Spring Mountain Road.
Theme: Renaissance Venice.
Cost: $1.2b, plus $275m Venezia Tower.
Web: venetian.com.
Reservations: 702 414 4100.
Fax: 702 414 4805.
Rooms: 4,049 suites, plus another 3,025 in the familial Palazzo next door.
Room rates: From $179 Sun–Thurs; from $299 Fri and Sat.

A stunning view of the Venetian

Restaurants: 12 fine-dining establishments throughout the hotel and Grand Canal Shoppes, including the new AquaKnox, Bouchon and Tao, plus 6 casual dining outlets.
Nightlife: Tao and Vivid nightclubs, V Bar and La Scena Lounge.
Shows: Andrew Lloyd Webber's *Phantom of the Opera*, Blue Man Group, Comedians Gordie Brown and Wayne Brady.
Attractions: Madame Tussaud's and Guggenheim Hermitage Museum.
Chilling out: Pool deck with private cabanas, with also the new Tao Beach, the latest Las Vegas entry in 'European-style' sunbathing.
Shopping: Grand Canal Shoppes.
Other amenities: A massive wedding chapel, which can be divided up into three; and Canyon Ranch Spa Club – one of the most luxurious on the Strip.

Here you will find replicas of everything that Venice stands for, from the Doge's

BRITTIP

For a truly romantic wedding, you can get married on the Ponte al di Piazza bridge overlooking the Venetian's St Mark's Square.

Palace to St Mark's Square, the Grand Canal and Rialto Bridge, all re-created in the finest detail by sculptors with the help of two Italian historians to 'ensure the integrity of the design and architecture'. In fact, its beauty and style is only matched by its service, which has established the Venetian as one of the most successful resorts on the Strip.

For many years the one thing missing at the Venetian was first-rate entertainment, but no more. The Venetian spent a raft of money to develop a dazzling theatre for a lavish production of Andrew Lloyd Weber's *Phantom of the Opera*. Then they wooed the staggeringly popular Blue Man Group from the Luxor and now have popular comedians Gordie Brown and Wayne Brady with separate shows.

The Venetian has a host of bars, lounges and restaurants that will help make your nights memorable. The flagship is Tao, both a fabulous Asian restaurant and a nightclub, with a 40ft/12m long outside terrace, giving spectacular views of the Strip, and go-go dancers. The swanky V Bar, based on LA's sophisticated Sunset Room, continues to be popular, as does La Scena Lounge. The Venetian is the king of upscale Las Vegas dining with no less than 12 top restaurants, starting with Emeril Legasse's Delmonico's Steakhouse, and including magical eateries like Pinot Brassiere, AquaKnox and B&B Ristorante.

The pool deck is based on a Venetian garden and includes a swimming pool, three spa pools and ornate gazebos. It is highly prized as a remarkable location for wedding receptions.

If you need refreshing, try the Canyon Ranch Spa Club, next to the 5acre/2ha pool deck, which has private cabanas and is modelled on a Venetian-style garden. The state-of-the-art spa, beyond a shadow of a doubt the best in Las Vegas, features massage and treatments, a 40ft/12m rock-climbing wall, Pilates studio, spinning gym, therapeutic Watsu pools and Canyon Ranch Café.

The centrepiece of the main shopping mall, known as the Grand Canal Shoppes, is the reproduction of Venice's majestic Grand Canal and St Mark's Square and for a price you can even take a romantic gondola ride. There are actually two places you can take a gondola ride –

Overlooking the Venetian

along the Grand Canal but also outside the main entrance by the massive edifice of the Doge's Palace. The ride in front is special, as all the gondoliers are accomplished singers who sing romantic Italian songs while they take you through the tunnels of the front waterways. Our boatman confided he was from Italy and studied at Julliard, and was working until he could find a job at one of Las Vegas' shows. There is nothing like an Italian song to fire the flames of romance! Also, there are a number of eateries along St Mark's, making it a great place to have a coffee or lunch, and watch Las Vegas-Venice pass by.

Another in the line of 'cousin' properties, the Palazzo opened in 2007 next door to the Venetian to add another 3,025 luxury suites spread over 50 floors to the mix.

Wynn Las Vegas

The new last-word in luxury, glamour and elegance.
Location: The Strip at Spring Mountain Road.
Theme: Understated glamour.
Cost: $2.7b.
Web: wynnlasvegas.com.
Reservations: 702 770 7100.
Fax: 702 7670 1571.
Rooms: 2,359 rooms, 270 parlour and salon suites, 45 executive suites, 36 1 and 2-bedroom fairway villas, 6 private-entry villas.
Room rates: from $209 Mon–Thurs; from $409 Fri–Sun.
Restaurants: 10 including Okado and Daniel Boulud's Brasserie, plus The Buffet Nightlife: Lure ultra-lounge and La Bête.
Shows: The $13m *Le Rêve* and the Monty Python musical *Spamalot*.
Shopping: High-scale promenade with designers such as Chanel, Manolo Blahnik, Dior, Louis Vuitton, Cartier, Gaultier, Oscar de al Renta, Jo Malone and Graff.
Other amenities: 3 wedding chapels; spa and salon.
Golf: the only hotel on the Strip with its own golf course, the 18-hole course has been designed by Tom Fazio.

Steve Wynn decided on a complete change of tack with his new resort. He snapped up the elegant but failing Desert Inn and its 215acre/87ha site for a mere $275m. He then went back to the drawing board for 18 months before announcing plans for the *Le Rêve* (the dream) in 2002. Eventually, it evolved into Wynn Las Vegas, hands-down the provider of the finest, most elegant, most luxurious service in a hotel casino. Proof is the Wynn Las Vegas is the only hotel-casino in the world to have been awarded both Mobil five-star and Diamond AAA five-star ratings.

A budget of $13m alone was given for the fantastic new *Le Rêve* production (all that remains of the original name for the hotel), which was created by Franco Dragone, the man behind so many Cirque du Soleil® spectaculars. *Le Rêve* is now unquestionably the swankiest show in Sin City.

And golfers will be delighted by the 18-hole golf course designed by Tom Fazio, in conjunction with Wynn himself, that requires no trip out of town, only a greens fee of $500 per round.

While there is no theme to this resort, it is designed with the inspiration of Steve Wynn's love of the Impressionist painters. The original name, Le Rêve, comes from a well-loved Picasso painting, while much of the decoration of the hotel lobby and casino are based on Matisse colours and themes. None of the resort's facilities can be seen from the Strip and only those who journey up the long driveway will get to see the 50-storey, curved tower covered in bronze glass that is this new hotel.

BRITTIP

Steve Wynn has brought another first to the city: the hotel's Oscar de la Renta store is the only Oscar boutique in the world.

Being the new last word in luxury, guest rooms provide a jaw-dropping spectacle in themselves. Executive suites come with floor-to-ceiling glass that spans the entire room from wall to wall, over 26ft/8m, to give breathtaking views of the Strip and the mountains surrounding the desert floor of the city. In all you get 933sq ft/187sq m in which to swing an army of cats (if you so

Wynn Las Vegas

wish) and facilities include separate bathrooms for him and her – his with glass-enclosed shower, hers with soaking tub, and both equipped with LCD TVs and over-sized Turkish towels. The living area is home to a sofa, console, coffee table, plus dining room table and chairs. And as you jump into the king-size bed you can snuggle into 320-count European linens before picking up the controls for the curtains and TV. In-room services include massage, manicure, pedicure and hair styling.

If you ever wish to leave your suite, then the resort's buffet is one of the best in town – with 17 live-action exhibition cooking stations and a sumptuous array of dishes, redefining the notion of buffet dining. As you would guess, food is toe-curlingly excellent with places like Corso Cocina, Daniel Boulud's Brasiere and Okada. Nightlife offered by Lure ultra-lounge and La Bête. The Lure ultra-lounge is a casual, yet chic, affair where cocktails, champagne and spirits flow from 10pm–4am nightly and La Bête (French for 'the beast') is another casual yet chic establishment where the music is pumped out from 10pm–4am from Thursday to Saturday.

The following morning allow your body a chance to recover in the spa, which offers 45 treatment rooms for massage, body treatments, facials and hydrotherapy. There are also separate his and hers facilities with showers, steam room, sauna and whirlpool for ultra comfort and privacy.

Resort-hotels off the Strip

Hard Rock Hotel

A big hit with models and celebrities, plus trendy young things.
Location: 4455 Paradise Road.
Theme: Rock 'n' roll.
Web: hardrockhotel.com.
Reservations: 702 693 5000.
Fax: 702 693 5010.
Rooms: 670.
Room rates: From $99 Mon–Thurs; from $259 Fri–Sun.
Restaurants: 3 fine-dining experiences, including the famous Nobu, and 3 casual establishments, including the Mexican Pink Taco, which is great for outdoor seating.
Nightlife: The Joint live gig venue, Body English the Nightclub, Center Bar, Viva Las Vegas Lounge, Poolbar & Poolspa and Pink Taco Bar.
Chilling out: Beach Club and Rock Spa.
Other amenities: Golf is offered through Walters Golf.

BRITTIP

Right next to the Hard Rock Hotel is the amazing Ice nightclub, with state-of-the-art special effects and 4,000sq ft/372sq m of dance space.

A truly trendy hangout and an instant hit when it opened at the end of the 1990s, it has remained a mecca for celebs and the

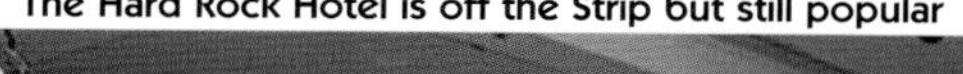

The Hard Rock Hotel is off the Strip but still popular

Las Vegas Hilton

beautiful people despite new competition in the guise of The Palms. Its restaurants are some of the best in town and in 2005 three won a total of four Epicurean Awards, including Best Japanese Restaurant for Nobu, Best New Restaurant off the Strip for Simon Kitchen & Bar, and Best Mexican Restaurant for Pink Taco.

Definitely not for the faint-hearted, there is a strong adult vibe at this resort. In addition to the very raunchy nightlife scene, the Beach Club (open to hotel guests only) has become a haven for 'some of the most beautiful bodies in Las Vegas'. With palm-shaded sandy beaches and blue water lagoons, the grass-shack cabanas (with phone, fridge and misting system!) are highly sought after. Every Sunday is a hard-partying, adults-only pool party which has become a Las Vegas tradition. After a hard day by the pool, if you need a little more R&R, try the Rock Spa to prepare you for a night of partying.

You can even get your gaming and pool lounging at the same time, with Hard Rock Café's Poolside Blackjack.

Each room in the fairly recent guest tower features French doors that open with views over the hotel's pool, the Strip or surrounding mountains. Rooms have leather headboards on king- or queen-sized beds, parchment and iron lamps, stainless steel bathroom sinks and various musical touches such as curtains with a musical instrument motif and framed photos of rock legends including Jimi Hendrix and Janis Joplin.

Las Vegas Hilton

Filled with conventioners, it now has a lively night scene.
Location: Paradise Road and Karen Avenue (behind the Strip).
Web: lvhilton.com.
Reservations: 702 732 5111.
Fax: 702 732 5584.
Rooms: 3,174.
Room rates: From $69 Mon–Thurs; from $155 Fri–Sun.
Restaurants: 5 fine-dining restaurants including the delightful Andiamo and the Japanese Benihana, plus 4 casual eateries including the Magarita Grille.
Nightlife: The ever-popular The Nightclub, plus Space Quest Bar and The Cantina cocktail bar.
Shows: Cabaret Center Stage for headliners, Barry Manilow, *Menopause the Musical* and *Star Trek: The Experience*.
Chilling out: pool, spa, tennis courts.
Shopping: 2 promenades.

Las Vegas Hilton

Skin Pool Lounge at The Palms

BRITTIP

When Elvis first appeared in Las Vegas at the Last Frontier Hotel on the Strip in 1956 he was a flop. He didn't return until 1969 when he mostly appeared – to great acclaim, of course – at the Las Vegas Hilton.

An understated elegance pervades what is ostensibly an upmarket hotel resort for business people attending one of the over 20,000 annual conventions held in Las Vegas. For them, its location near the Convention Center is perfect, but it's about a 12-minute walk to the Strip, so it's a little off the beaten track for real tourists. Fortunately, the tram has a stop right outside the Convention Center to whisk you away to the wilder parts of Sin City.

Salon suite at The Palms

The rooftop recreation deck includes a health club, massive swimming pool, six floodlit tennis courts and a putting green, while The Nightclub has all the latest high-tech nightlife gadgetry and is one of the in places to be seen. The hotel is home to one of the most exciting theme entertainments in Las Vegas: *Star Trek: The Experience*. Here are Klingons, Tribbles, Quarks Bar, rides and everything that would make a Trekkie swoon.

The Palms Casino Resort

A sultry boutique resort, which has rapidly established itself as the city's top place to party, attracting both the hip and the famous.
Location: Flamingo Road, west of the Strip, close to the Rio All-Suite Hotel.
Theme: Sophisticated adult playground.
Cost: $265m, plus $600m.
Web: thepalmslasvegas.com.
Reservations: 702 942 7777.
Fax: 702 942 7001.
Room rates: From $149 Sun–Thurs; from $189 Fri and Sat.
Rooms: 455 deluxe rooms.
Restaurants: include Nine from Chicago, Little Buddha Café from Paris, the upmarket Alizé, Garduños Mexican restaurant and the Blue Agave Oyster and Chile Bar.
Nightlife: This is club city, a long list of popular hotspots including the Playboy Club, Rain in the Desert Nightclub, Moon Nightclub and Ghost Bar, an indoor-outdoor lounge.

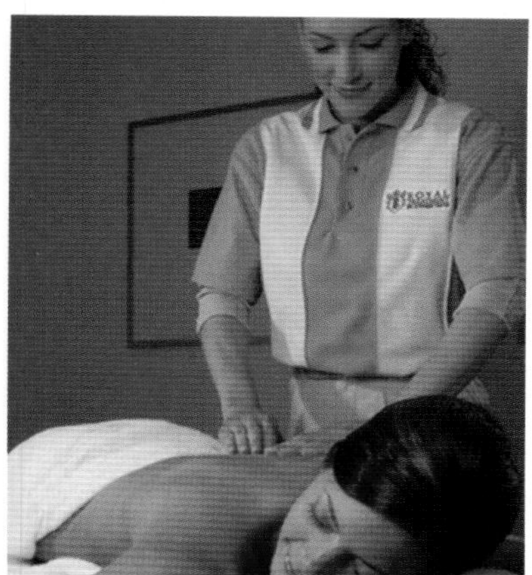

All resort-hotels offer spa facilities

Attractions: The Brenden Theater Complex, a state-of-the-art 14-screen cinema complex; a drive-in betting shop; and two Bachelor Suites for stag parties and hen nights.
Chilling out: Skin Pool Lounge.
Other amenities: 20,000sq ft/1,860sq m, 3-storey spa featuring candlelit yoga classes and fun and fruity body treatments.

BRITTIP

Just to give you an insight into VIP prices: a private room at The Palm's Rain Nightclub goes from $300 to $1,000 a night!

Having opened to a fanfare of glory in 2001, the Texas-based Malouf family targeted celebrities from the outset and the hotel is now the home of the Cine Vegas Film Festival, thus ensuring its status as one of the most star-laden hotels in Las Vegas.

The original 455 rooms – a mere drop in the ocean for this city – is being added to with a whopping $600m expansion programme that will include a 347-room Fantasy Tower, 2,200-seat showroom, 50-storey condo hotel and spa and a new pool in 2008 or 2009. The planned Hardwood Suite is clearly targeted at the money-is-no-object end of the market. To be housed in the new tower, the two-level 10,000sq ft/900sq m party room will have its own indoor basketball court (the new must-have!), scoreboard, pool table, poker table and dance floor, among many other facilities. As it is, revellers can choose between bungalows, 'Playpen Suites' or 'Hugh Hefner's Skyloft' for ultimate party hospitality.

The Palms quickly became one of the most coveted private party spots in Las Vegas and its Real World Suite has already been used to host events for Leonardo DiCaprio, Avril Lavigne and Mark Wahlberg. Ordinary mortals need not miss out on the fun as the hotel also has two Bachelor Suites, fitted out with dance poles (think Jamie Lee Curtis in *True Lies*!), a wooden dance floor and sophisticated sound system. The ultimate playrooms, perfect for both stag parties and hen nights, they're decked out in 1960s retro colour patterns, a mirror wall made up of fragmented squares of glass to create the effect of a disco ball, the same type of mirror above the bed, an LED lighting system and plasma TV screens.

BRITTIP

If good service is important, then The Palms could be the place for you as the Malouf family is famous for excellent hospitality.

In the meantime, punters flock to what is still just a bijou gem due to its huge array of entertainment amenities.

The award-winning Rain Nightclub, located on the casino level, is a multi-storey, multi-environment nightclub and concert. It combines performances by international headliners, with an ultra-cool dance club (see page 147) and private event facility, and comes with some amazing special effects including fog, haze, 16ft/5m fire plumes and 3ft/1m fireballs, while the bamboo dance floor is surrounded by a computer-programmed river of water with dancing jets and fountains. Ghostbar is a vibrant open-hour lounge on top of the 42-storey hotel tower, which has already won plaudits as a hot nightspot.

Superior room at The Palms

This resort hotel also has a fantastic line-up of restaurants that cover upmarket, steaks, casual and bistro-style dining. Top of the pile is the Alizé, the latest and probably swankiest offering from Las Vegan gourmet masterchef and restaurateur André Rochat. Named after the gentle wind that runs along the Mediterranean, it offers a French Riviera-style dining experience in an amazing glass atrium with aquamarine glass walls that provides spectacular views of the city. VIP tables are in front of the windows and secluded from the rest of the dining room by a curved glass partition. Rochat has won a clutch of awards for his distinctive restaurants.

The Skin Pool Lounge set a new trend in exotic oasis indulgence with relaxation pools, chaise longues, four bars, billiard tables, outdoor swings, poolside blackjack and trampolines. You can even hire one of the private cabanas that come with TVs, fridges, telephones and VIP amenities, while DJs spin tunes day and night and food can be ordered from the Nine Steakhouse. The whole area is only open to hotel guests during the day, but is turned into a voyeuristic club at night (see page 149).

Rio All-Suite Hotel

Proving there is life beyond the Strip, the Rio is an entertainment city in its own right.

Location: 3700 West Flamingo.
Theme: Tropical paradise.
Cost: $200m expansion.
Web: riolasvegas.com.
Reservations: 702 252 7777.
Fax: 702 253 6090.
Rooms: 2,563 suites.
Room rates: From $80 Sun–Thurs; from $159 Fri and Sat.
Restaurants: 6 fine-dining restaurants include city favourites Antonio's, Buzios and Fiore Steakhouse, plus the Gaylord Indian Restaurant, while 7 casual eateries include the funky VooDoo Café.
Nightlife: Great spots include the new Flirt lounge, BiKiNi nightclub, Voodoo Lounge and I-Bar ultra-lounge.

BRITTIP

The Rio may be off the beaten track of the Strip, but if you're near Harrah's, take the free shuttle bus between the two hotels – you don't have to be a guest of either to get a ride.

Rio All-Suite Hotel

Poolside waterfalls at the Rio

Shows: The amazing Penn & Teller, musical comedy *The Scintas*, Tony & Tina's Wedding and Chippendales.
Attractions: Masquerade Show in the Sky; Lucky Strike Bowling Alley.
Chilling out: Sand beach and outdoor recreational area, plus Rio Spa and Salon
Shopping: Masquerade Village.
Other amenities: 3 wedding chapels; golf is available at the Rio Secco Golf Course.

The Rio is consistently voted the best-value hotel in America and has some of the finest restaurants in Las Vegas: Gaylord Indian Restaurant, Antonio's Italion Ristorante, Amada's Asiana. Its buffet is second to none. It is also home to the city's first Wine Cellar Tasting Room, which has the world's largest collection of fine and rare wines, along with an array of tasting accessories.

The Masquerade Show in the Sky allows guests to ride aboard fantasy floats that glide above the crowds in a Mardi Gras-style fiesta of music and dance. This is an adult-orientated show with topless girls for the evening performances, while the hotel has generally shifted in a more raunchy direction with the opening of the sexy BiKiNi nightclub and two chi-chi lounges for grown-ups: Flirt and the ever-popular VooDoo Lounge.

During June and July it is impossible to get a room here, as it hosts the annual World Series of Poker (see page 167) and poker pros and addicts descend on it in droves.

Outside, the Ipanema Beach comes with real sand beaches at the edge of a tropical lagoon, complete with waterfalls, plus four nautical-shaped swimming pools and five jacuzzi-style spas. Here you can bask in the sun or order a variety of services including personal massages, poolside cocktails and food.

When it comes to weddings, the Rio does it in style. An entire floor of the Masquerade Tower has been given over to wedding facilities including two chapels and two themed, 1,200sq ft/112sq m honeymoon suites and reception areas.

Other resort-hotels

The following hotels still have their place in the city's hall of fame, but cannot compete with the big shots!

Imperial Palace

Friendly, reasonably priced hotel in prime location.
Location: The Strip at West Flamingo.
Theme: Japanese.
Web: imperialpalace.com.
Reservations: 702 731 3311.
Fax: 702 735 8578.
Rooms: 2,700.
Room rates: From $66 Mon–Thurs; from $140 Fri–Sun.
Restaurants: 9.
Show: Legends in Concert.
Attractions: A collection of over 250 antique and collectible cars.
Chilling out: Olympic-size swimming pool with waterfall and heated spa.
Other facilities: A wedding chapel; the only 24-hour medical facility on the Strip, (phone direct on 702 735 3600).

When the reviews of Las Vegas accommodation are given, the Imperial Palace hardly takes centre stage, it has reasonable prices and good gambling odds. The resort is home to a collection of vintage and special-interest cars and has a good-value full-service spa. It holds a Hawaiian-style Imperial Luau complete with Polynesian fire dancers, roast pig and unlimited piña coladas and mai tais!

Imperial Palace casino

Garden room at the Tropicana

Tropicana

Exotic chilling-out environment for grown-ups.
Location: The Strip at Tropicana.
Theme: Tropical paradise island.
Web: tropicanalv.com.
Reservations: 702 739 2222.
Fax: 702 739 2469.
Rooms: 1,875.
Room rates: from $79 Mon–Thurs; from $160 Fri–Sun.
Restaurants: 8, including Pietro's and Mizuno's.
Nightlife: Celebration live music lounge and Tropics karaoke lounge.
Shows: *Folies Bergère, Xtreme Magic* starring Dick Arthur, Comedy Stop and Titanic – The Artefact Exhibition.
Attractions: Live poolside entertainment.
Chilling out: Water park.
Other amenities: A wedding chapel; the Tropicana spa.

The Tropicana has a colourful Caribbean Village façade, while its 'signature' is a spectacular laser light show on its Outer Island.

The beautiful pool at the Tropicana

The 12,000sq ft/1,080sq m main pool is the centre of the summer action with its bar and swim-up blackjack games. There's also a swim-up bar, next to which sliding glass doors partition off a 1,500sq ft/135sq m heated indoor pool, one of the only indoor pools in Vegas, surrounded by lush tropical garden views. There is also an adults-only lagoon pool and a garden pool, while over 60 varieties of trees, ground cover, foliage and flowers create explosions of colour.

There are a lot of reasonably priced entertainment options here, especially the Comedy Stop, a traditional comedy club, and Titanic – The Artefacts Exhibition, with more than 300 artefacts from the doomed cruise liner.

Staying in Henderson

Just a 17ml/27km drive from the Strip, Henderson is a small but important location for two gorgeous hotels overlooking the brilliant blue waters of Lake Las Vegas. Ultra-romantic settings with wonderful water-based amenities, they're a great place to base yourself if you want to escape the maddening kerchink, kerchink of slot machines yet be within easy reach of the city's fun-filled attractions.

Ritz-Carlton Lake Las Vegas

An ultra-romantic, deluxe desert retreat-style resort that is still conveniently close to the hustle and bustle of Las Vegas.
Location: MonteLago Village, 1610 Lake Las Vegas Parkway, Lake Las Vegas Resort, Henderson.
Theme: Classic, sophisticated elegance.
Web: ritzcarlton.com/en/Properties/LakeLasVegas/Default.htm.
Reservations: 702 567 4700.
Fax: 702 567 4777.
Rooms: 349.

Room rates: From $155 Mon–Thurs; from $210 Fri–Sun.
Restaurants: A main restaurant, plus poolside dining and a lobby lounge serving food.
Nightlife: Firenze Lobby Lounge with live music.
Chilling out: Pool and gardens, beach and water activities.
Other amenities: Spa Vita di Lago; access to 2 golf courses; 3 wedding chapels.

Four Seasons lead the way, followed by the Hyatt Regency, now the upper-crust Ritz-Carlton group has opened a fabulous new hotel right on the sandy shores of the beautiful Lake Las Vegas. Just a short ride from the Las Vegas Strip, this is the perfect place to get the full deluxe desert resort treatment but still have easy access to the delights of Sin City.

An integral part of the MonteLago Village, guests at the hotel can stroll from their rooms over a quaint stone bridge, fashioned after Florence's Pontevecchio, to find themselves in an olde worlde area filled with shops, restaurants and the new Casino Monte Lago. The landscaped grounds provide a series of scenic walkways and cycling trails around the lake's shoreline, or guests can take to the waters in canopied water taxis, sailing boats or kayaks.

BRITTIP

The Ritz Carlton now offers the best of both worlds: a gambling-free environment but with adjoining casino. The separately run Casino Monte Lago sits next to the hotel, adjacent to The Village at Monte Lago, an upscale shopping complex.

A relaxed but elegant Mediterranean ambience is reflected in the arched doorways, clay tile roofs, interior courtyards and the palette of sun-washed colours that are reflective of European waterside towns and lakeside villas. The rooms live up to the high Ritz-Carlton standards and come with top-notch Frette bed linen, oversized marble bathrooms and a casual yet classy decor. Many of the rooms also have private balconies that look over the vine-covered trellises, shaded loggias, water features, white sand beach and heated swimming pool. There are also 35 suites and two whopping 2,400sq ft/ 223sq m suites.

The fabulous Medici Café and Terrace is set in an incredibly romantic courtyard with pretty Florentine gardens for outdoor dining and views over the lake. Elegant yet relaxed, you can have breakfast and lunch here, while it turns into a fine-dining experience for dinner.

The luxurious, 30,000sq ft/2,790sq m Spa Vita di Lago is the first spa in America to offer treatments from Italy. La Culla is the signature treatment, inspired by age-old water and desert treatments, and is a multi-sensory experience which includes a steam, skin treatment, facial and massage while bathed in fragrance, light and sound. Describing itself as a wellness and beauty oasis, Spa Vita offers fitness facilities, Pilates, yoga, wellness and beauty consultations plus a range of skin treatments and massages.

The hotel has ties with the Falls Golf Club, a Tom Weiskopf-designed, 18-hole course with waterfall, canyons and stunning views of the Las Vegas Strip, plus Reflection Bay Golf Club, designed by Jack Nicklaus and ranked the number one golf course in Las Vegas by *Where* magazine.

Top budget hotels

There are also a host of inexpensive hotels that follow the Las Vegas tradition of cheap hotels, food and drinks to draw the budget-conscious gambler. You will never gush about the rooms, but many have an engaging character sometimes missed in the massive resorts. If you want to experience Las Vegas and want to spend less money on your hotel room and more on the sights and fun, then here are some good places to consider.

Spa at the Ritz-Carlton

El Cortez

Mobbed-up hotel getting a new life.
Location: Fremont Street and North Sixth, one block from Las Vegas Boulevard
Web: elcortezhotelcasino.com.
Reservations: 702 385-5200.
Room rates: From $29 Mon–Thurs; from $59 Fri–Sun.
Restaurants: 4 including 2 awesome value options, Roberta's Steakhouse and Kitty's Café.

Many experienced Las Vegas travellers might raise their eyebrows at the inclusion of El Cortez. This was one of Bugsy Siegel's first properties and was long known for its great promotions, cheap lodging and fantastic gambling odds as well as mouldy carpets, smoky and dilapidated rooms and a clientele of wheelchair-bound octogenarians spending their pension cheques. That time is history. A $12m renovation in 2007 to go along with the development of the East Freemont Street Entertainment District has made the old girl into a freshly scrubbed belle of the ball.

The room rates are still wonderfully low, but the rooms are astonishingly comfortable. Kitty's Café and Roberta's Steakhouse also put out the best cheap food you will ever find anywhere.

The best part is getting rooms in the oldest part of El Cortez. There are no lifts to these rooms, only narrow stairs, but here Bugsy Siegel lorded over his early Las Vegas empire, and it has been said that more than one card shark had his hands broken, or some mob swindler met a bloody end here.

Fitzgerald's

Friendly, reasonably priced hotel in downtown Las Vegas.
Location: Fremont Street.
Web: fitzgeraldslasvegas.com.
Reservations: 702 388 2400.
Room rates: From $39 Mon–Thurs; from $79 Fri–Sun.
Show: *Country Superstars Tribute* and Larry G. Jones, Man of a Thousand Voices
Restaurants: 4.

In the centre of the Fremont Street Experience, 'the Fitz' is the tallest building downtown, and if you get the right room you can have a dazzling view of the best of Las Vegas. Try the '$20 upgrade' (see page 27) to get a south-facing corner room on an upper floor.

It has its own 40,000sq ft/3,716sq m casino, is easy walking to all the downtown activities, is just two blocks to catch 'the Deuce' bus to the Strip, and three blocks to the East Fremont Street Entertainment District. Rooms are clean and comfortable, if nothing special. This is also a place very popular with Brit and Aussie

El Cortez

Room at the Sahara

tour groups, and after a few days listening to the Yanks mangle the language, you'll be happy to hear a familiar accent.

Palace Station

One of the best-value hotels in Las Vegas.
Location: I15 at West Sahara.
Web: palacestation.com.
Reservations: 702 367 2411.
Room rates: From $29 Mon–Thurs; from $59 Fri–Sun.
Attractions: Soundtrax, a 175-seat music venue.
Restaurants: 7.
Chilling out: Two pools and a Jacuzzi.
Other facilities: Free shuttle to the airport and the Strip for guests with room keys.

Station Casinos own eight 'locals' casinos in the Las Vegas area. They don't particularly cater to tourists, but to local gamblers. This means they offer great deals, and you can get a room at an unbelievable price, plus the brand offers an aggressive marketing campaign of special freebies for customers. I've often stayed for free here; in fact, the most I've ever paid is $12 a night for two people. Again, the rooms are nothing to write home about, and the casino is extremely smoker-friendly, so non-smoker unfriendly, but the free shuttle to the Strip is a huge boon.

Sahara

Traditional Las Vegas.
Location: The Strip at West Sahara.
Theme: African desert oasis.
Web: saharavegas.com.
Reservations: 702 737 2111.
Fax: 702 791 2027.
Room rates: From $43 Mon–Thurs; from $89 Fri–Sun.
Restaurants: 6 including the House of Lords Steakhouse and NASCAR Café.
Shows: *Matsuri*, The Platters/Drifters/Coasters, the Amazing Jonathan Mind-reading Show, Trent Carlini – The Musical History of Elvis.
Attractions: NASCAR Racecar museum and display; SPEED – The Ride.
Chilling out: Beautiful pool with cabanas.
Sahara is one of the oldest properties on the Strip and it is steeped in history. The likes of Elvis Presley, Dean Martin and Frank Sinatra played here, and it shows on the photos along the walls of Las Vegas in the good old 'mobbed-up days'. The Sahara is a bit tired now and run down, with constant rumours of it being sold and either torn down or renovated into a new spectacular. Now it is a smoky, inexpensive place to stay on the Strip.

Coming soon

2006 and 2007 was a calm before the storm, as few new resort behemoths opened in the Las Vegas area. The hurricane hits in 2008 with a legion of new properties expected to open before the end of the decade.

As far as size, MGM/Mirage's City Center is opening in early 2008. While primarily a slavishly wealthy condo community, it also will include the über-luxurious condo/hotel Vdara, another massive casino, upscale shopping and entertainment, even more nightlife (as if Vegas needs more) plus family-friendly areas like bowling alleys and games rooms.

The Grand Hyatt Corporation will make its entrance into Sin City in 2008, with the opening of The Cosmopolitan, one of the few independently owned, operated and privately financed developments on the Strip.

Palace Station

BRITTIP

You cannot register at any hotel with a casino if you are under the age of 21 – nor can you gamble if you are under 21.

Owners of the Cosmopolitan, which will be superbly located in the mid-Strip, have taken more than a leaf or two out of the very successful Palm's book and are clearly focusing on attracting a youthful, celeb-driven clientele. Plans include two high-rise hotel and condo-hotel towers, providing around 3,000 luxury rooms, suites and condo-hotel residences, a shopping mall, fine-dining restaurants, 1,800-seat theatre, 500-seat cabaret, 50,000sq ft/4,650sq m spa, salon and fitness centre, and multiple nightclub venues. The Cosmo Beach Club, with its 5acre/2ha pool deck, will not only overlook the Strip, but will offer activities from dawn until dusk.

Meanwhile, Donald Trump has his $500m, 1,282-unit Trump International Hotel and Tower, which is on schedule to be completed in 2008.

Another newcomer to the city, Olympia Gaming, has begun to develop a $750m Southern Highlands casino resort and retail destination at the most southern end of the Las Vegas Strip. Just a stone's throw from the airport, the 100acre/40ha site is being developed to provide a luxury, mixed-use destination for visitors and locals alike. By the time each of the phases has been completed it is expected that $2b will have been spent on the resort.

And not to be left behind, Steve Wynn, having completed his epic, has looked to the next stage. In April 2007 the venerable Stardust was felled in a massive explosion complete with lights, fireworks and gawking crowds to make room for Encore, a $1.4b, 2,000-room resort on 20acres/8ha next to Wynn Las Vegas, with a completion date scheduled for late 2008.

The New Frontier was sold in 2007 with plans to raze that to make way for another major resort casino. Industry observers also believe that the Riviera will be knocked down to make way for new casino resorts before the end of the decade.

Whatever happens, the somewhat quiet (by this city's standards) period from 2000 to 2006 has been replaced by a new scramble to cash in on the ever-increasing success of the city. The personal rivalries between each of the city's main players will no doubt work themselves out through ever taller, ever grander, ever swankier, ever more adult resorts, shows and nightclubs. If nothing else, this truly is what the city is about!

Marble statues outside Caesars Palace

3 SHOWTIME

All the best shows from major productions to adults only

It has long been a Las Vegas basic that if you keep the customers entertained they will happily slap money on to the gaming tables. As they years have passed, the entertainment offerings have grown from scantily clad show girls to headliners like Elvis Presley and Frank Sinatra, and to a modern entertainment scene that rivals, and often surpasses, anything you might find in London, New York or even Los Angeles.

The top shows here are the incredible, mind-boggling, gravity-defying multi-million-dollar Cirque du Soleil® extravaganzas for which auditoriums have been purpose built up and down the Strip. Adding to the already hugely successful *Mystère, O, Zumanity* and *Kà, Le Rêve* at Wynn Theatre has been created by one-time Cirque director Franco Dragone, and the latest instalment of the Cirque franchise is *Love,* which opened in 2007 for a budget of more than $100m. Plus, the Sahara opened *Matsuri*, which is an impressive show of acrobatics and visual displays, although not in the same league as the Cirque offerings.

Classic Las Vegas showgirls

In this chapter

Stage plays are also the rage in Las Vegas these days. Many resorts have spent lavish amounts on Broadway hits like Andrew Lloyd Weber's *Phantom of the Opera*, Monty Python's *Spamalot*, *The Producers* and *Mama Mia!* and others that play to packed houses. This is Vegas, though, so there are changes. Most of the plays offered are a shorter version than the originals, in fact *Phantom* in Las Vegas is a full 20 minutes shorter than the show in New York or London. Keep them happy but out there gambling, right?

There is a glut of high-profile magicians – think Penn & Teller, Lance Burton and Steve Wyrick – more intellectually challenging stand-up acts such as the irrepressible Rita Rudner and a raft of rip-roaringly funny impersonators.

Of course, where Las Vegas sets itself apart from the rest is with its entertainment

BRITTIP

If you are flexible and don't mind waiting until the last minute, you can save lots of money on show tickets. There are many half-price ticket stands along the Strip and Fremont Street and shows that aren't overbooked will sell tickets through these dealers at cut rates to put bums in the seats. You can often get tickets for shows at 50% off by buying a ticket on the day of the performance from one of these shops. But sorry, this won't do for hard-to-find tickets, so Cirque extravaganzas are rarely available this way.

blockbusters. Celine Dion ended her wildly popular *A New Day* in February 2008, to be replaced by singer/actress Bette Midler. But you have huge shows by Elton John, Barry Manilow and others that keep packing them in.

If there is a downside to the spectacles and headliners, it is undoubtedly the ticket prices, which have skyrocketed during the last decade. A single ticket will quickly hit the $100 mark and rise steeply to more than $200. So for something a little kinder on the pocket, make the most of the lounge music scene. Nowhere does it better than Las Vegas. And when you've done all that there is, of course, those adult revues. As the city's motto goes: 'What happens in Las Vegas stays in Las Vegas' – unless, of course, you take the video camera!

In previous years, some prices included sales tax. Alas, as part of the rise in costs almost all tickets prices require you to add 7%.

There are other acts that are booked on a one or two-night basis and you can check these out before you go at: vegas freedom.com (the city's official website with details of all current shows), lasvegas.com (a comprehensive section on shows, comedians, regular local acts and live music venues) and vegas.com (a great place for show tickets). Also bear in mind you can visit ticketmaster.com to book more mainstream events.

Guide to ratings: *** pure brilliance; **** fantastic; *** a great show; ** poor value for money.**

BRITTIP

Want to know why you pay so much to see some of these Las Vegas shows? Michael Flatley got $250m to take his production to The Showroom at the Venetian until 2007, while it is reported that Celine Dion signed a $100m contract with Caesars Palace to appear at the Colosseum for three years.

***O* at the Bellagio**

Major productions

Kà

Kà Theater, MGM Grand, 702 891 777, ka.com
The circus-based Canadian performance company Cirque du Soleil® is noted for making visually stunning productions. Las Vegas is its playground and the magnificent *Kà* is the standard bearer for the MGM Grand. Each show has a theme, *Kà* has fire. The main subplot revolves around fire's dual powers both to destroy and create.

Essentially a tale of duality, *Kà* tells the epic story of separated twins who set out on a perilous journey through challenging landscapes, such as a mysterious sea shore, menacing mountains and foreboding forests, to fulfil their shared destinies. What makes it different from all the astonishing acrobatic performances available in other Cirque shows is that this production (a mere snip at $165m!) also incorporates the thrills and action of different martial arts forms from all over the world, plus amazing innovations in puppetry, multimedia and pyrotechnics.
Rating: ***** Breathtaking stunts that dazzle to the max.

Boat in a storm at *Kà*

Shows: Fri–Tues 7.30pm and 10.30pm.
Tickets: $69, $99, $125 and $150, all plus tax.

Something for nothing

Don't miss the amazing – and free – Fremont Street Experience in downtown Las Vegas. In addition to the multi-million dollar electronic light and sound show, which takes place in the enclosed, traffic-free pedestrian mall, the city also provides five blocks of street performers and live music. Street performers abound. Live bands usually perform at stages on First Street and Third Street Tues–Sat and the Fremont Street Experience takes place every hour on the hour from 7pm to midnight. Call 702 678 5777 for information, visit vegasexperience.com or just head downtown in the evening.

Most spectacular new entrant in the category of free shows is *Azure* at Silverton Hotel & Casino, 702 914 8557, silvertoncasino.com. An underwater fantasy show, all the action takes place inside a 120,000gall/545,530l saltwater aquarium as mermen and mermaids execute innovative choreography among the 4,000 fish and stunning coral. Shows run hourly on the hour Wed–Fri 5–10pm, Sat 2–10pm and Sun 1–7pm.

You can get into the carnival spirit at the Rio All-Suite Hotel by either watching or taking part in the Masquerade Show in the Sky. This fantastic parade, which takes place high above the casino floor, is an extravaganza of floats and dancers in exotic costumes with an adult twist. Daily shows at 3, 4, 5, 6.30, 7.30, 8.30 and 9.30pm are free, or you can pay $9.95 to don an exotic costume and ride on one of the main floats. You have to buy them in person at least one hour before the show and they do sell out! Call the Rio for more information on 702 252 7776.

Treasure Island's free show is also worth a mention. *The Sirens of TI* re-creates the age-old battle of the sexes between mermaids and pirates nightly at 7, 8.30, 10 and 11.30pm. Viewing is on a first-come, first-served basis, but guests at the hotel get exclusive VIP viewing access.

Other free shows include fiery illusion stunts in *Lumineria* at Caesars Magical Empire, daily 11am–4.30pm, and free circus acts in the Main Arena of Circus Circus from 11am until midnight every day.

LOVE

The Beatles LOVE Theater, Mirage, 702 352-0197, mirage.com
Unveiled in 2007, The Beatles *LOVE* grew out of a mutual admiration between the late George Harrison and Cirque founder Guy Laliberté. This is a different Cirque show compared to the others in Vegas. Here they have taken the original master recordings from the Abbey Road Studios and, instead of the traditional Cirque acrobatic wonders, have melded a celebration of modern marvels as rollerbladers and skateboarders fly and twist in youthful energy. There are still the dazzling sound and visual effects you would expect of a Cirque display, but mixed with a rawer emotion.
Rating: **** A Beatles Love-fest only Cirque du Soleil® and X-Games could produce.
Shows: Thurs–Mon 7.00pm and 10.00pm.
Tickets: $69, $93.50, $99, $125 and $150 plus tax.

Mystère

Treasure Island, 702 894 7722, treasureisland.com
The first of the Cirque du Soleil's® Las Vegas marvels, *Mystère* takes you on a journey through time that allows the supreme athletes to show off their strength and extraordinary flexibility with a mesmerising aerial bungee ballet, a precision performance based around Chinese poles and an awe-inspiring trapeze act. This is the most acrobatic of all the Cirque shows, and the most circus-like, It is also truly state-of-the-art theatre. The show originally cost $20m to stage and should definitely be on your must-see list.
Rating: ***** You'll want to go back again and again.
Shows: Sat–Wed at 7.00pm and 9.30pm, Sun at 4.30pm and 7.00pm.
Tickets: $60, $75 and $95 including tax.

Stunning displays at *Mysterè*

BRITTIP

At all of the Cirque shows, including Dragone's *Le Rêve*, try to be in your seats by 20 minutes before curtain up. There is always a comedic pre-show show as cast members go out into the audience and do humorous bits with unsuspecting victims. Maybe you!

O

Bellagio, 702 693 7722, bellagio.com
If you've ever been lucky enough to see the Cirque du Soleil® troupe in action, you'll know what makes these artists so special. The 70-odd cast of dancers, acrobats, actors, clowns, comedians and musicians may represent age-old talents of an old-style circus (without the animals), but that is where any similarities with the past comes to an end. *O*, like all the shows performed by the troupe, is a surrealist celebration of trapeze, dance, high-flying acrobatics and humour. In this case though, every act is performed in, on and above water in a $70m theatre that was developed specifically for the Bellagio resort and Cirque du Soleil®.

BRITTIP

If you're trying to decide between *Mystère* and *O*, most people find *Mystère* more accessible. *O*, although brilliant, is more ethereal.

O takes its title from the phonetic spelling of the French word for water – *eau*. The story takes you on a 90-minute voyage of the history of theatre in the trademark Cirque style with daring displays of aerial gymnastics, high-flying trapeze numbers, synchronised swimming, fire-eating, mind-boggling contortions, clowns and high-diving stunts.
Rating: ***** Breathtaking.
Shows: Wed–Sun at 7.30pm and 10.30pm.
Tickets: $93.50, $99, $125 and $150 all plus tax.

Le Rêve

Wynn Theater, Wynn Las Vegas, 702 770 9966, wynnlasvegas.com
Franco Dragone, former creative collaborator with Cirque du Soleil® – responsible for top-selling shows such as *Saltimbaco, Mystère* and *La Nouba* – set up his own production company Dragone in 2000.

Provocative and erotic *Zumanity*

Now he has returned to Las Vegas to create a world of dreams for another epic at Steve Wynn's Wynn Resort. What sets this work apart is not only the visually stunning performances themselves, but also the design of the theatre, which means that no one sits more than 42ft/13m from the main stage.

The main aim was to allow people to forget the world as they entered the dream-like realm of the theatre and this is achieved through a set that seems to owe more to the form of a temple than a stage. The dream-like quality is enhanced by a bank of digital windows that change displays from statues to clouds to birds as effortlessly as the performers execute feats of impossibility (to the ordinary mortal) in front of you. This is, without doubt, the most visually stunning show in Las Vegas.
Rating: ***** Thrilling perfection.
Shows: Thurs and Sun at 7.00pm and 9.30pm, Fri at 8.30pm and Sat 8.00 and 10.30pm.
Tickets: $99, $119 and $159 for true luxury of seating in overstuffed chairs with chocolate-dipped strawberries and a bottle of champagne for two, plus tax of course.

Zumanity

New York New York, 866 606 7111, nynyhotelcasino.com
Billed as the provocative, erotic, adult side of the Cirque du Soleil®, this show combines the usual amazing Cirque stunts, acrobatics and high-flying – only this time with a sensual, passionate and sometimes raunchy twist. There is also a feel of an old Parisian cabaret here. The cast of 50 performers and musicians blend erotic rhythm with dance with ribald comedy to create a world in which inhibitions are discarded.
Rating: ***** Sensual and stunning
Shows: Wed–Sun at 7.30pm and 10.30pm
Tickets: $65, $85, $95 and $105 including tax; dinner packages available at an extra $35 per person.

BRITTIP

Love birds wanting a romantic night out will adore the Love Seats and Duo Sofas that have been specially created in New York-New York's new theatre – custom-built for Cirque's over-18s-only *Zumanity*.

Bette Midler

Colosseum at Caesars Palace, 702 731 7208, caesarspalace.com
When Celine Dion finished her record-breaking three years at Caesars Palace, who was going to replace this magical entertainer? The answer is the talented singer, comedienne and actress Bette Midler, whose worldwide *Kiss My Brass* concert tour had impressed Harrah's execs. Her debut set for February 2008 promises more of the *Kiss My Brass* act, but with more 'gals, gags and the best song catalogue in America'.
Rating: Unrated, but we expect it to be terrific.
Shows: Every day except Monday and Thursday, 7.30pm.
Tickets: $117, $162, $197, $272 plus tax.

Bette Midler at Caesars Palace

Elton John's The Red Piano

Colosseum Showroom, Caesars Palace, 877 4 ELTONJ or 1-888 435 8665, ticketmaster.com
Elton will be performing his musical extravaganza at least through 2008 during periods when Bette Midler takes a break from her new show. Britain's most enduring export performs with his band members in a brilliant production directed by renowned photographer David LaChapelle. Rumour has it that Elton and Caesars are discussing an extension, with a heavier performance schedule for the master showman.
Rating: **** Eternal showman Elton at his best.
Shows: Check in advance.
Tickets: $100, $175 and $250 plus tax.

Toni Braxton Revealed

Flamingo, 702 733 3333, harrahs.com
International singing sensation and eight-time Grammy winner Toni Braxton exploded on to the Vegas scene with her steamy extravaganza. The music is hot, the dance and choreography sizzling, the wardrobe steaming and her unique voice dazzling in a superb production.
Rating: ***** Hot, Hot. Hot!
Shows: Every day except Mon and Sun, 7.30pm.
Tickets: $69–109 plus tax.

BRITTIP
To get a better deal on the major shows, pick up as many of the visitor magazines as you can and look through for discount coupons and two-for-one specials.

Toni Braxton at the Flamingo

V – The Ultimate Variety Show

V Theater at Miracle Mile, 702 260 7200, vtheshow.com
This is traditional old Las Vegas entertainment when Dean Martin would be performing and suddenly Sammy Davis Jr would show up and perform a few numbers. There is a core of show entertainers plus a plethora of talented acts who perform elsewhere on the Strip through the week, so no two shows are ever the same. When it first started, the acts were sometimes a hodgepodge, and you could get some real rotten tomatoes in the mix, but over the years the booking has improved so every show includes a breathtaking combination of magic, special effects, death-defying stunts and wild comedy. *V* has become a Las Vegas icon.
Rating: ***** Top-notch entertainment.
Shows: nightly at 7.30 and 9pm.
Tickets: $65 and $76 for VIP package, which includes line pass, preferred seating and an autographed poster; $33 for children plus dinner packages available, all prices plus tax.

V – The Ultimate Variety Show

The Blue Man Group at the Venetian

Other productions

Blue Man Group

Blue Man Group Theater, Venetian, 702 262 4400, blueman.com
The off-the-wall, off-off-Broadway production, which has been surprising, terrifying and entertaining theatre-goers in New York, Boston and Chicago, has become a Las Vegas staple. Mainstream this isn't. Throughout the black stage the three 'blue men' explore the world with both a child-like innocence and social incompetence. Here, plastic pipes and breakfast cereal are musical instruments and toilet paper is a signal for a riotous party. Children delight in it, even though it is not a 'children's show'. As an adult, you either love this show or hate it; there is no in between.
Rating: **** Delightfully kooky.
Shows: Mon, Tues, Fri, Sat 7pm and 10pm; Wed, Thurs, Sun 8pm.
Tickets: $71.50, $93.50 and $121 plus tax.

The Blue Man Group

ICE: Direct from Russia

Versailles Theater, Riviera, 702 794 9433, rivierahotel.com
This is cool entertainment based on the works of the famous Moscow Ice Circus and it brings 42 of Russia's most disciplined and athletic performers to an ice rink in the desert to entertain. Skating on thin blades are clowns, acrobats, animal acts and mimes interspersed with gloriously beautiful and romantic on-ice performances and breathtakingly aerial acrobatic displays.
Rating: **** A cool difference to the Las Vegas entertainment scene.
Shows: Sat–Thurs 8pm.
Tickets: $59.95, $69.95 plus tax.

Master magicians

Lance Burton, Master Magician

Lance Burton Theater, Monte Carlo, 702 730 7160, monte-carlo.com
Lance Burton has been running at the Monte Carlo for six years and he just keeps going on. The reason is he just is the finest magician-entertainer in town. Dubbed a World Champion Magician by his fellows, Burton's show involves classic feats of levitation, Houdini-style escapes and mysterious disappearing acts, all done with the flair and pazzazz expected of modern-day magicians. It all starts with the illusion that won him the Grand Prix at the Federation International Society of Magique.
Rating: **** Two hours of awe-inspiring, rib-tickling entertainment.
Shows: Wed–Fri at 7pm, Sat and Tues at 7pm and 10pm.
Tickets: $66.50 and $72.55 including tax.

Lance Burton at the Monte Carlo

Penn & Teller

Penn & Teller

Calypso Showroom, Rio All-Suite Hotel, 702 252 7776, riolasvegas.com
The famous duo have one of the funniest and most tantalising shows around. They are defiantly proud as they take many traditional magic tricks and expose their secrets to the audience. Then they stun you with a dazzling magical extravaganza, all the while making you hold your sides in pain from the laughter.
Rating: ***** Both riveting and funny.
Shows: Wed–Mon at 8.30pm, Sun at 2pm and 8.30pm.
Tickets: $75, $85 plus tax.

Xtreme Magic starring Dick Arthur

Tiffany Theater, Tropicana Resort, 702 739 2411, tropicanalv.com
With the departure of Siegfried & Roy, it was only a matter of time before someone else mixed big cats with magical illusion. In this mesmerising show, beautiful blue-eyed Bengals, African black leopards and a pure white snow tiger appear out of nowhere.
Rating: **** Truly entertaining.
Shows: Sun–Thurs at 2pm and 4pm.
Tickets: $31.90, $37.40 plus tax and surcharge.

BRITTIP

Shows generally last 90 minutes and there are no intervals. You can take drinks into shows in plastic containers.

Great nightlife at the Sahara

Magical comedy

The Amazing Jonathan

Congo Room, Sahara, 702 737 2515, saharavegas.com

Two-time winner of the Best Comic Magician of the Year by the World Magic Awards, Jonathan may not be well known to British audiences, but he is famous in America for his razor-sharp wit and bizarre illusions. Dubbed the Freddy Krueger of Comedy, he has his own TV show and has a long string of TV appearances.

Rating: ***** Crazy, wild, hilarious – don't miss it!

Shows: Fri–Tues at 10pm.

Tickets: $44.95 and 54.95 plus tax and tip.

The Mac King Comedy Magic Show

Comedy Cabaret, Clint Holmes' Theatre, Harrah's Las Vegas, 702 369 5111, harrahs.com

Mac King spent his summer holidays doing a two-person magic act with fellow college student, the now legendary Lance Burton, before taking his show on the road. Along the way he has made a name for himself as a talented magician with an off-beat, witty twist, and has appeared on shows such as *The World's Wildest Magic, An Evening at the Improv, Penn & Teller's Sin City Spectacular* and *Comic Strip Live*. Surprisingly, discounted tickets are regularly available for his show, and he is a fixture on the *Las Vegas Adviser*'s list of Top Ten Las Vegas Values.

Rating: ***** Great fun and excellent-value entertainment.

Shows: Tues–Sat at 1pm and 3pm.

Tickets: $24.95 plus tax.

Stand-up comedy

Rita Rudner

Harrah's Las Vegas, 702 740 6815, ritafunny.com

It's rare that a woman makes it to the top in Las Vegas without taking her clothes off, yet the multi-talented Rita has done just that. She stands on the stage in a long, classically leggy dress making wry, quirky comments on everything from relationships to family and cleaning women. She was named Las Vegas Comedian of the Year five years running. She moved her show from New York-New York to Harrah's Las Vegas, and the shows keep selling out.

Rating: ***** Comedic genius.

Shows: Every day except Thurs and Sun at 8pm.

Tickets: $54 plus tax.

Rita Rudner

George Wallace

Flamingo Showroom, Flamingo Las Vegas, 702 733 3333, flamingolas vegas.com
Wallace began his career as a comedy writer for *The Redd Foxx Show* and made a big splash on *The Big Laugh Off*, one of America's top stand-up competitions. His humour is based on making observations about everyday life – a type of comedy that had been selling out venues all over North America before he arrived in Las Vegas.
Rating: *** Great fun.
Shows: Tues–Sat at 10pm.
Tickets: $59.95 and $75 plus tax and fees.

Impressionists

American Superstars

Broadway Showroom, Stratosphere, 702 380 7711, stratospherehotel.com
Another testimony to the huge success of the long-running *Legends in Concert* is this celebrity-tribute extravaganza. Here you can see stars such as *Men in Black*'s Will Smith strut his stuff Big Willie Style and a full line-up of the Spice Girls, alongside impressionist favourites Michael Jackson, Madonna and Gloria Estefan.
Rating: *** Fun, but not as good as *Legends*, this is for real fans of *Stars in their Eyes*!
Shows: Wed, Fri and Sat at 6.30pm and 8.30pm; Sun, Tues and Thurs at 7pm.
Tickets: $39.25 plus tax.

George Wallace at the Flamingo

Danny Gans

Danny Gans Theater, Mirage, 702 792 7777, mirage.com
Singer, comedian, actor and impressionist Danny Gans portrays everyone from Prince to Sinatra. After wowing locals and tourists alike with his range of 300 voices at the Rio, he has had his own theatre built for him at the Mirage and is still always a sell-out.
Rating: **** Sure-fire winner.
Shows: Tues–Wed and Fri-Sat at 8pm.
Tickets: $100 including tax.

There's plenty of great nightlife at the Mirage

Legends in Concert is on at the Imperial Palace

Downtown Gordie Brown

Gordie Brown Theater, Venetian, 702 414 9000, venetian.com/gordie.aspx
One of the Venetian's latest thefts from another casino (this one from downtown's Golden Nugget) provides a must-see fusion of comedy, impressions and music. Gordie Brown's oddball humour is fresh, funny and edgy. Over 16s only.
Rating: **** Hilarious.
Shows: Fri–Wed at 7pm.
Tickets: $64, $74 plus tax.

La Cage

Mardi Gras Plaza on the third floor of the Riviera, 702 794 9433, theriviera.com
Frank Marino stars as Joan Rivers in the quicksilver world of lipstick, high heels, nine-button evening gloves and put-down lines to die for in this upmarket drag show that wins the hearts of even the most conservative theatre-goers. La Cage is the longest running show in Las Vegas.
Rating: *** Great fun and good value for money.
Shows: Every night except Tues at 7.30pm.
Tickets: $55 plus tax and fee.

BRITTIP

Arrive early for La Cage to get good seats and get your drinks before you go inside as they're not served inside the showroom.

Legends in Concert

Imperial Theater, Imperial Palace, 702 794 3261, imperialpalace.com
Here's a neat way to see all your favourite music stars from Elton John to Madonna, Michael Jackson to Elvis, the Beatles to Liberace. The look- and sound-alikes truly have 'stars in their eyes' and together put on one of the most highly rated and popular shows in town.
Rating: *** Great impersonations let down a little by a lack of exciting choreography.
Shows: Mon–Sat at 7.30pm and 10pm.
Tickets: $49.95–59.95 adults, $34.95–44.95 for 2–12-year-olds plus tax.

BRITTIP

Many shows are now offering the option of dinner and show packages including *Zumanity*, Rita Rudner, *Legends in Concert*, Clint Holmes, *Skintight* and the Improv Comedy Club. Check at the time of booking.

The Second City

Second City Theater, Flamingo Hilton, 702 733 3333, flamingolasvegas.com
A well-known sketch and improvisation comedy first formed in Chicago in 1959 and now famous for both its rehearsed skits and on-the-spot creations – many sparked off by ideas from the audience. This was

the group that originally inspired the *Saturday Night Live* television series, which is why Martin Short and Jim Belushi, among many other American comedians, have made surprise appearances.
Rating: **** Pure entertainment.
Shows: Thurs–Tues at 8pm, plus Fri–Sat at 10.30pm.
Tickets: $49.45 plus tax and fees.

Comedy clubs

Comedy Stop

Tropicana, 702 739 2714, comedystop.com
Part of a highly successful comedy club franchise, every night is two shows with four established comics. Plus, there are always loads of coupons floating around Sin City for a $5 discount off the entrance, which is one reason *Comedy Stop* is a fixture on the *Las Vegas Advisor*'s Top Ten Value list.
Shows: Nightly at 8pm and 10.30pm.
Tickets: $19.95 including tax and one drink.

Improv Comedy Club

The Improv, Harrah's Las Vegas, 702 369 5000, harrahs.com
Recently voted Best Comedy Club in the *Las Vegas Review Journal* by readers and critics for its stand-up routines by up-and-coming stars of comedy.
Shows: Tues–Sun at 8.30pm and 10.30pm.
Tickets: $24.95 plus tax; dinner packages available at $55.

Bill Robbins at the Riviera Comedy Club

Riviera Comedy Club

Mardi Gras Plaza on the first floor of the Riviera , 702 794 9433, rivierahotel.com
A nightly line-up of top stand-up comedians and comedy acts, many of whom have appeared on American TV.
Shows: Nightly at 8.30pm and 10.30pm.
Tickets: $17.95 plus tax and handling fees; VIP seating, queue passes and dinner/show combinations available.

Check out the Comedy Stop website for the latest shows

Headliner showrooms

Celebrity Room: Bally's, 702 739 4567 for information, times and reservations. Headliners include Liza Minnelli and Penn & Teller.
Circus Maximus: Caesars Palace, 702 731 7333, caesarspalace.com. Recent acts include Huey Lewis and the News, Earth, Wind and Fire and Tony Bennett.
Circus Maximus Showroom: Caesars Palace, 702 731 7333, caesarspalace.com. Since its gala opening in 1966, Judy Garland, Frank Sinatra, Diana Ross and Liberace have headlined here. More recent stars include David Copperfield, Liza Minnelli, Julio Iglesias and Celine Dion.
The Colosseum at Caesars Palace: Caesars Palace, 1-888-702 3544, caesarspalace.com. When Celine is not in action, the massive auditorium is used for major headliner shows.
Congo Room: Sahara on the Strip, 702 737 2515, saharavegas.com. The Drifters, the Platters and the Coasters have headlined here.
Grand Garden Arena: MGM Grand on the Strip, 702 891 7777, ticketmaster.com. The biggest venue in Las Vegas regularly hosts major concerts and sporting events. This is where Holyfield met Tyson for their heavyweight champion title clash and where top-notch performers like Sting, Elton John, Bette Midler, Gloria Estefan, Phil Collins and Billy Joel play when they're in town. The 16,325-seat venue has also hosted the Professional Bull Riders Championships and national league hockey. Tickets are likely to cost anything from $100.
Hilton Theater: Las Vegas Hilton, 702 732 5755, lvhilton.com. Headliners include Johnny Mathis and Barry Manilow.
Hollywood Theater: MGM Grand, 702 891 7777, mgmgrand.com. The MGM's more intimate venue (a mere 650 seats) is still big enough to attract such names as Smokey Robinson, Gladys Knight, Tom Jones and Wayne Newton.
Mandalay Bay Events Center: Mandalay Bay, 702 632 7580, mandalaybay.com. Steely Dan, Ricky Martin and REO Speedwagon have all appeared here recently.
Orleans Showroom: The Orleans, 702 365 7075, orleanscasino.com. Recent headliners include the Everly Brothers, Air Supply and Frankie Avalon.

Dinner shows

Tony and Tina's Wedding

Calypso Showroom, Rio All-Suite Hotel, 702 252 7776, riolasvegas.com

This comedy dinner show takes you on a romp through a classic American-Italian wedding as Anthony Nunzio Jr marries Valentina Lynne Vitale. The satire begins with the announcement of the wedding, then members of the audience join in the entire event from wedding ceremony to rowdy reception complete with Italian buffet dinner – allowing for plenty of improvisation along the way!

Rating: **** Great fun.
Shows: Nightly at 7pm.
Tickets: $79.08 plus tax.

Dragon Knight at the Tournament of Kings

Tournament of Kings

King Arthur's Arena at the Excalibur, 702 597 7600, excalibur.com

Central to this re-creation of a knights' battle are the laser lights, fireworks and clouds of billowing water vapour that give the production an air of mystery and magic. The musical begins when Merlin grants a young boy's wish to be a knight by transporting him back to the Middle Ages and transforming him into the White Knight of Kent. Along the way he meets King Arthur and Queen Guinevere and battles with the treacherous Dark Knight to win a princess's hand in marriage. The trick to seeing this show is to finish off your dinner before you become engulfed in water vapour!

Rating: **** One of the top shows – good for horses, feasts and magic!
Shows: Nightly at 6pm and 8.30pm.
Price: $58.24 plus tax.

Adults only on the Strip

Watch out if you go down to the big theme resorts today, for you're more and more likely to find topless shows in what were once considered family-friendly hotels. Of course, adult shows have always been a facet of Las Vegas entertainment, but never quite so blatantly on the Strip. Is it a reflection of waning interest in traditional shows – unlikely – or just another cleverly disguised attempt to get punters into gambling dens? Your guess is as good as mine, but either way, here they are.

Bite

Theater of the Stars, Stratosphere, 702 380 7711, stratospherehotel.com

A topless revue loosely based around a vampire 'story' of sin, sex and seduction. The Lord Vampire, aided by a coven of sultry dancers, goes on a search for the perfect female specimen to make the queen of the night. The story is told through the classic rock songs of the '70s, '80s and '90s. Best shock/surprise of all: members of the audience are chosen to become part of the erotic adventure.

Rating: **** Once bitten, you'll be going back for more!
Shows: Fri–Wed at 10.30pm.
Tickets: $45.95 including tax and tip.

BRITTIP

You must be over 21 to see any of these adult shows, with the exception of *Jubilee!* for which you must be over 18. For *Thunder From Down Under* 18–20-year-olds must be accompanied by an adult.

Afternoon shows

The Mac King: Comedy magic show. See review and details on page 67.
Xtreme Magic: Starring Dick Arthur. See review and details on page 66.

The Folies Bergères

Tiffany Theater, Tropicana, 702 739 2411, tropicanalv.com

A turn-of-the-last-century Parisian music hall is the scene for the opening and final acts of the longest-running show in Las Vegas, a tribute to France's early nightclubs that has been entertaining crowds since 1957. This constantly adapting version combines award-winning production numbers from past *Folies* shows with new production sequences, dazzling costumes and scenery and, of course, the famous Folies showgirls, who perform amazing feats in their high-kicking numbers.

BRITTIP

Choose your seat with care at *Folies* – it can be hard to see from some of the long tables and the plastic seats are uncomfortable after a while.

Rating: *** Well done, but more old-style revue than new spectacle.
Shows: Mon, Wed, Thurs and Sat at 7.30pm (covered) and 10pm (topless). Also topless Tues and Fri at 8.30pm.
Tickets: $44.95 for table seating and $54.95 for booth seating both plus tax.

Stardust showgirls

There's great entertainment at Ballys

Jubilee!

Jubilee Theater, Bally's, 702 739 4567, ballyslv.com
A lavish, seven-act tribute to American music, with topless showgirls and scantily clad guys. From the roaring twenties to the rock 'n' roll era of Elvis, it also features a seductive Sampson and Delilah sequence, a master magician who makes a 26ft/8m long helicopter appear, and a spectacular sinking of the *Titanic* in which 2,000galls/ 9,100l of water flood on to the stage. Just to give you some idea of the scale of its lavishness, more than 1,000 costumes are worn by the cast of 100 dancers and singers, while 70 different sets and backdrops and about 100,000 light bulbs are required to create the enchanting spectacles.
Rating: **** Lavish, wonderful over-the-top production numbers.
Shows: Sat–Thurs at 7.30pm and 10.30pm.
Tickets: $55 to $74 including tax.

Skintight

Main Showroom, Harrah's Las Vegas, 702 369 5111, harrahs.com
This adult revue has everything – dance, music, comedy, hilarious skits – plus über-fit babes and guys.
Rating: **** Good entertainment.

BRITTIP
You can now get a behind the scenes look at the world of *Jubilee!* Showgirls conduct tours every Mon, Wed and Sat at 2pm. Tickets $10 if bought with a show ticket, or $15.

Shows: Mon–Wed and Sat at 10.30pm, Fri at 10pm and midnight, and Sun at 7.30pm and 10.30pm.
Tickets: $49.95, dinner packages $75 plus tax.

BRITTIP
Like a show both men and women can enjoy? *Skintight* is an excellent option as it's the only semi-naked revue to include both male and female dancers.

Showgirls

Crazy Girls Sexiest Topless Revue

The Mardi Gras Pavilion, Riviera Hotel, 702 794 9433, theriviera.com
Updated version of the classic topless revue with music, dance, song and comedian Stuart May.
Rating: *** Enjoyable.
Shows: Wed–Sun at 9.30pm.
Tickets: $34.95 plus tax; VIP seating and dinner/show combinations are available.

Crazy Girls are on at the Riviera

The Chippendales is a great show for a girls' night out

BRITTIP The early evening performances of *Folies Bergères* and *Showgirls of Magic* are the only two adult shows that are NOT topless.

Fantasy

Pharaoh's Theater, Luxor, 702 262 4400, luxor.com
Featuring singing, dancing and a lot more besides in an outrageous and provocative topless revue.
Rating: **** Filled with sexy ladies.
Shows: Tues, Thurs and Sat at 8.30pm and 10.30pm, Wed and Fri at 10.30pm, Sun at 8.30pm.
Tickets: $59 including tax.

MGM Grand's Crazy Horse Paris

Crazy Horse Paris Theater, MGM Grand, 702 891 7777, mgmgrand.com
Billing itself as a show that 'celebrates beautiful women and the art of the nude', all the 12 dancers are members of the original Crazy Horse dance troupe from one of the hottest popular nightspots in Paris. This is the same show that used to be called *La Femme*. It has just reverted to the same name used in Paris.
Rating: *** Entertaining but pricey.
Shows: Wed–Mon at 8pm and 10.30pm.
Tickets: $59 including tax and programme.

Crazy Horse Paris finale

Showgirls of Magic

Parisian Cabaret, Hotel San Remo, 702 597 6028, sanremolasvegas.com
Now for something a little different: topless showgirls doing magic – and it works. In between, the dancers put on some enjoyable routines.
Rating: **** Enjoyable.
Shows: Tues–Sun at 8pm and 10.30pm.
Tickets: $39 plus tax including two drinks.

Girls' night out

Chippendales – The Show

Club Rio, Rio All-Suite Hotel, 702 252 7776, playrio.com
One of the loudest of the all-male revue shows, which leaves very little – a floss-thin G-string – to the imagination. Think motorcycles, beds and a giant computer monitor and imagine über-fit men writhing all over them and you'll build up a good picture of what's in store. Prepare to get your best screaming voice ready!
Rating: ***** Polished perfection.
Shows: Thurs–Tues at 8.30pm plus 10.30pm Fri and Sat.
Tickets: $39.95 to $49.95 for the Sky Lounge.

Booking tickets in advance

By and large you should have no problem getting tickets to see most of the shows, and you can usually buy them in advance by phone or in person at the hotel's theatre box office. Just bear in mind that getting show tickets in Las Vegas depends on the time of year, the day of the week and whether there is a huge convention in town. For details of the best times to visit see The Best Times to Go (page 18). In all cases, phone ahead to confirm show times, dates and prices as these are subject to change without notice. You can find out exactly who will be performing – including the big top-billing stars during your visit to Las Vegas – by visiting the Las Vegas Convention and Visitors' Authority's official website at vegas com. Many of the major tour operators will also be able to book tickets in advance for the major shows or you can try attraction specialists Keith Prowse (01232 232425, keithprowse.com). Most shows are now available through Ticketmaster – just visit ticketmaster.com.

Thunder from Down Under

Merlin Theater, Excalibur, 702 597 7600, excalibur.com

Once a trio of Aussie beefcakes, this troupe has expanded to a cast of nine breathtaking hard bodies. However, the troupe remains one of the best all-male entertainers in town – largely because they don't take themselves seriously and because they like to include members of the audience in the show. Watch out if you get pulled on stage, you could find yourself murmuring 'Oh baby' into a microphone in your best Meg Ryan-faking-it voice!

Rating: ***** Just … WOW!

Shows: Sun–Thurs 9pm, Fri–Sat 9pm and 11pm.

Tickets: $39.95 or $49.95 for VIP seating plus tax.

BRITTIP

If you've paid extra for VIP seating to see the knights shed their armour, it still pays to arrive 45 minutes early as seats are on a first-come first-served basis.

Cinemas

Brenden Theaters

The Palms, 4321 West Flamingo Road, 702 507 4849, brendentheaters.com

A state-of-the-art, 14-theatre cinema complex at this ultra-hip hotel resort. The brainchild of Johnny Brenden, grandson of the legendary Mann's Chinese Theater developer in Hollywood, LA, it has wall-to-wall curved screens, THX digital sound and stadium seating with comfortable, high-backed rocking chairs, plus love seats. Brenden Theaters has fast become the hottest Cineplex in town and now hosts many film premières with post-première parties at The Palms' Little Buddha restaurant.

Crown 14 Theaters

Neonopolis, 450 East Fremont Street, 702 383 9600

Movies at the Crown 14 usually begin around noon and go on until 11pm with midnight showings on Fri and Sat.

BRITTIP

If you head to the Crown 14 cinema complex, park free at the Neonopolis car park.

United Artists Showcase

Showcase Mall, 3785 Las Vegas Boulevard South, 702 740 4911

Still the only cinema on the Strip, you may have a hard time finding it as it's tucked down the side of the MGM Grand complex next to the parking garage. Parking is free if you keep your cinema ticket for validation.

Johnny Brenden

BRITTIP

With so much to see and do, it's unlikely you'll have time to go to the movies, but there are two advantages: you get to see a film before it hits our shores and you can guarantee not to hear the sound of slot machines! Tickets cost around $10.

Bonanza of musicals

There's a growing trend for Broadway shows to be staged at some of the classier theatres. Of course, we get them all in London as well now, but there's a big difference between something being available on our own doorstep – and actually seeing it. Here is a selection of the venues and their offerings at the time of going to press.

Mama Mia!

Mandalay Bay Theater, Mandalay Bay, 702 632 7600, mandalaybay.com
The smash hit musical based on the songs of Abba, Mon–Sat.

Spamalot has been a great success

Hot venues

Here are some other venues worth checking out for their edgier vibe.

House of Blues: Mandalay Bay Resort, 702 632 7600, ticketmaster.com

A massive array of acts covering everything from gospel to blues, jazz and even country.

The Joint: Hard Rock Hotel, 702 693 5066, hardrockhotel.com

Attracts the likes of Crosby, Stills and Nash, Jet, Garbage, Danzig and Sigur Ros.

Mandalay Bay Beach: Mandalay Bay Resort, 702 632 7580, ticketmaster.com
A great location for enjoying acts such as the Doobie Brothers.

Menopause the Musical (MTM)

Shimmer Caberet, Las Vegas Hilton, 800-222 5361, lvhilton.com
An international sensation that has landed in Las Vegas. A musical comedy inspired by 'a hot flash and a bottle of wine', it is a celebration of all women over 40 who have survived life.

Phantom of the Opera

Paris Opera House, Venetian, 702 414 9000, venetian.com
A lavish production of Andrew Lloyd Webber's classic show in a dazzling recreation of the Paris opera house.

The Producers

Les Theatre des Arts, Paris Las Vegas, 702 946 4567, ticketmaster.com
The uproarious Mel Brooks musical comedy, a story of two shady stage producers trying to make the worst stage play ever, and failing hilariously!

Spamalot

Wynn Theater, Wynn Las Vegas, 702 770 9966, ticketmaster.com
The story of Monty Python's search for the holy grail on stage, although the cost of putting on this stage production is many times more than the original movie hit.

4 SHOPPING

Everything from top designer malls to discount shopping outlets

The wild success of the opening of the Forum Shops gave the business community an epiphany. People come to Las Vegas to spend money – and not just on gambling! Since then, Sin City merchants have outdone themselves in piling on one new shopping experience after another, each new mall and store more wildly successful than the last! In fact, Las Vegas is now an international mecca for high-end merchandise. In past eras, a hot producer would first think about opening a new store in London, or Paris, New York or Los Angeles. No more – it's on to Vegas!

So shopping addicts beware: Las Vegas can do serious damage to your credit cards! But then the Las Vegas malls do it in such style and with so much 'free entertainment' attached, it's hardly surprising we can't resist. The trend for providing more and more shopping continues and over the last few years so many major American department stores have opened in the city that it now rivals, and perhaps surpasses, New York and San Francisco for upscale shops.

There are endless retail therapy opportunities

In this chapter

Major shopping malls: At the top of the pile is the **Fashion Show Mall**, which spent $1b to turn itself into the largest shopping destination on the Strip attracting more than 10 million visitors every year. The title of biggest and best used to belong to the **Forum Shops at Caesars**, which set new standards for shopping malls when it opened in the 1990s. It's still an excellent shopping destination and remains an attraction in its own right. Other high-end shopping malls can be found at the **Grand Canal Shoppes** at the Venetian. Apart from the Fashion Show Mall, best by far for a rounded shopping experience, with more mid-range shopping, is the **Miracle Mile Shops** (previously known as Desert Passage) at Planet Hollywood. There's also the **Hawaiian Marketplace**.

Discount shopping: Designer junkies got a great shot in the arm with the opening in August 2003 of the **Las Vegas Premium Outlets** right in the heart of downtown. There are many other discount outlet shopping malls, too, including the Factory outlet district, so it really is possible to leave Las Vegas with your overdraft intact!

Hotel shopping: Each of the major resort-hotels has its own range of shopping opportunities, topped by the Via Bellagio at the Bellagio.

Fashion Show Mall

Location: 3200 Las Vegas Boulevard South, at Spring Mountain Road, just north of Treasure Island and opposite the site of the Wynn Resort.
Tel: 702 784 7000 (information) or 702 369 8382 (concierge desk).
Web: thefashionshow.com
Open: Mon–Sat 10am–9pm and Sun 11am–7pm.
Parking: Underground car park is accessible via Spring Mountain Road and Fashion Show Drive North, then take the escalators to the shopping level, or use the North and South parking decks accessible from Industrial Road West, then follow the signs; there is also complimentary valet parking available at three points around the mall.
Attractions: The only mall in America with seven major US department stores under one roof: Neiman Marcus, Saks Fifth Avenue, Macy's, Dillard's, Robinsons-May, Bloomingdale's Home and Nordstrum, plus a further 240 shops; plus the Cloud and the Great Hall with its stage and fashion show runway.
Cafés and restaurants: The main restaurants include the Spanish Café Ba Ba Reeba!, the Capital Grille Steakhouse, Maggiano's Little Italy and RA Sushi Bar Restaurant; plus a raft of casual dining options include California Pizza Kitchen, Cinnabon, Mariposa at Nieman Marcus and Bloomingdale's B-Café.
Services: Cashpoints (ATMs) and phone booths, where you can use a pre-paid phone card, are dotted around the mall and there's a foreign currency exchange centre; the Concierge Desk can supply directions, concert tickets and show reservations, multilingual brochures, golf tee times and special event information.

For those who are serious about shopping, this is the place to come. Following a massive renovation and expansion programme, the Fashion Show Mall doubled in size within a few short years of opening and in the process turned itself into an entertainment experience as well.

BRITTIP

Maggiano's Little Italy restaurant is a dazzling dining room on the second floor of the Fashion Show Mall, with great views of Wynn Las Vegas across the Strip. It also has a pianist in its lounge during dinner.

Interior at the Fashion Show Mall

Hard to miss is the Cloud structure, which rises 20 storeys above the Strip, and is nearly 500ft/152m long, providing a much-needed shaded area during the day and a giant image projection surface at night. Below it is the 330ft/100m long Media Bank with four extraordinarily sized LED screens that are used to broadcast videos and events inside the mall and around the city.

The Great Hall, a 72,000sq ft/ 6,696sq m pedestrian plaza, is home to both the elevated Food Court overlooking the plaza and the Strip, and the 28sq ft/2.6sq m stage and 80ft/24m retractable runway, which is now used for fashion shows and other events.

Save as you go

Before you start to browse around the shops, join the Premier Shopper Club by going to the Customer Service Center and filling out the form or using the Smart Shopper Pavilion touch screen. Once you have been accepted, you can browse through the website and pick up a startling array of money-saving coupons from the stores. You can also find out about all the latest promotions and activities going on at each of the stores. As a club member, you will automatically be entered into free prize draws simply by swiping your card at the Smart Shopper Pavilion! There are many other bonuses, but most are really aimed at people living in America.

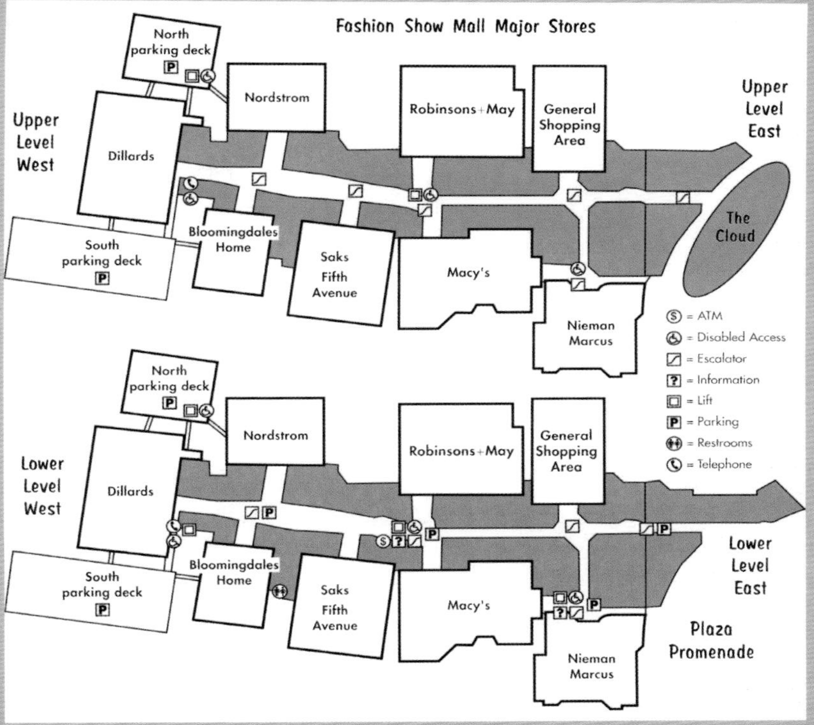

BRITTIP

While Fashion Show Mall closes any time 8–9pm, the main restaurants stay open until around 11pm or midnight, while Café Ba Ba Reeba!'s bar stays open until 2am on Sat and Sun nights.

The show must go on!

There are now seven major anchors to the mall – the most in any American mall and the only one to have all the main department store brands in one location: Macy's, Dillard's, Nieman Marcus, Nordstrum, Bloomingdale's Home, Saks Fifth Avenue and Robinson's-May. There are over 240 other shops, too. Here is a rundown of beauty boutiques, women's stores, men's stores, shoe shops and electronic outlets.

BRITTIP

Always take a bottle of water with you on a shopping trip – the air con will have you dropping before you finish shopping!

Accessories

Bally of Switzerland: 702 737 1968, wbally.com Shoes, clothes and accessories with a strong modern look in bold colours.
Banana Republic: 702 697 2011, bananarepublic.com High-quality men's and women's clothes and accessories.
BCBG Max Azria: 702 737 0681, bcbg.com Shoes, handbags, accessories and clothing with clean, simple lines by the award-winning American designer who has a loyal Hollywood following.
Carolee: 702 734 3080, carolee.com Stylish jewellery, handbags, gifts and bridal accessories.
Claire's Boutique: 702 650 9006, claires.com Accessories for every occasion and for women and girls of all ages – you'll always be sure to find what you're looking for here, be it earrings or a tiara!
Cole Haan: 702 731 3522, colehaan.com Hand-crafted, leather shoes and boots for

men and women, plus handbags, wallets and casual outerwear.
Misako: 702 735 3255 Trendy, affordable handbags and accessories.

Clothes for women

A Pea in the Pod: 702 893 8484, apeainthepod.com Trend-setting and sophisticated maternity fashions.
Abercrombie & Fitch: 702 696 0832, abercrombie.com Classic and casual clobber for the young at heart.
Ann Taylor: 702 734 8614, anntaylor.com America's leading retailer for stylish, professional yet feminine women's clothing.
Ann Taylor Loft: 702 731 0351, anntaylorloft.com Casual branch of Ann Taylor, offering co-ordinating, easy-to-wear pieces.
Aqua Beachwear: 702 732 7301, aquabeachwear.com High style for the beach or pool.
Arden B: 702 735 0090, ardenb.com Everything from dressy to casual wear for sophisticated yet fashion-savvy women.
Banana Republic: 702 697 2011, bananarepublic.com High-quality men's and women's clothes and accessories.
BCBG Max Azria: 702 737 0681, bcbg.com Shoes, handbags, accessories and clothing with clean, simple lines by the award-winning American designer who has a loyal Hollywood following.
Beachworks: 702 767-6930, beachworksshops.com Everything to make you the hottie poolside.
bebe: 702 892 8083, bebe.com Curve-hugging street clothes.
Betsey Johnson: 702 735 3338, betseyjohnson.com Funky frocks in flowing fabrics with hippie-inspired detailing and beaded embroidery.
Caché: 702 731 5548, cache.com Specialising in high-end fashion designers from Europe and America, many of whom are exclusive to the boutique.
Chico's: 702 791 3661, chicos.com High-end designer boutique famous for amazing service.
The Coach Store: 702 759 3451, thecoachstore.com America's leading accessories store offering good quality, classic yet modern styles. Every mall needs one!
Diesel: 702 696 1055, diesel.com Innovative Italian-style denim.

BRITTIP
One of the things the Americans do brilliantly is smart-yet-casual outfits at great prices for career women.

The superb Fashion Show Mall

The perfect place for that unique outfit

Everything But Water: 702 734 7946, everythingbutwater.com Designer labels right up to size 24.
Express: 702 737 8999, expressfashion.com Ultra-hip fashion clothes almost straight off the catwalk.
Fitelle: 702 731 0411 Sexy, stylish Parisian fashions.
Fossil: 702 369 3986, fossil.com High-quality watches and apparel.
Fredericks of Hollywood: 702 893 9001, fredericks.com Fun, flirty bras, panties and corsets.
French Connection: 702 369 0852, frenchconnection.com Contemporary fashion.
GAP: 702 796 0010, gap.com Clothing, accessories and personal care products for both men and women.
Guess: 702 691 2541, guess.com A worldwide brand famous for jeans, stylish denim outfits and accessories for women, men and children.
Hot Cats: 702 796 1870, hotcats.com Up-to-the-minute styles for men, women, boys and girls sold in an entertaining atmosphere.
J Crew: 702 731 2060, jcrew.com A wide range of clothes, shoes and accessories for women, men and children.
Jessica McClintock: 702 733 4003, jessicamcclintock.com Contemporary collections from a designer famous for romantic special occasion clothes for women and girls.
LaCoste: 702 796 6676, lacoste.com Classic sporting apparel.
Lillie Rubin: 702 731 3042, lillierubin.com In town for a wedding? Then here's the perfect location to pick up women's cocktail and evening formal wear.
Lucky Brand: 702 369 4116, luckybrandjeans.com Classic American denim gear for women and men.
Paul Frank: 702 369 2010, paulfrank.com Quiksilver, Puma and Diesel.
Rampage: 702 732 0478, rampage.com Everything from casual weekend kit to trendy clubwear, professional women's clothing and accessories, plus aromatherapy oils and bath products.
SoHo Collections: 702 732 4849 Up-to-the-minute hair accessories and clothing from trendy New York outlets including French Concept, Jesse USA, Anopia and Kosjuko.
Still: 702 696 1209 High-quality fashion.
Talulah G: 702 737 6000, talulahg.com A hip boutique chain.
Tommy Bahama's: 702 731 6868, tommybahama.com Fun-yet-chic Bahama-inspired fashion plus shoes, ties, bags, belts and accessories.
Victoria's Secret: 702 737 1313, victoriassecret.com Sexy lingerie and accessories.
Villa Moda: 702 733 6776, villamoda.com Italian goods, such as Versace, for women and men.
Wet Seal: 702 796 0344, wetseal.com Contemporary clothes and accessories for those who lead active lifestyles.
White House: 702 697 0427, whitehouse.com Romantic and feminine clothing in black and/or white only.
Zara: 702 733 6868, zara.com Well-priced Spanish fashion outlet.

Fossil at the Fashion Show Mall

Clothes for men

Abercrombie & Fitch: 702 696 0832, abercrombie.com Classic and casual clobber for the young at heart.
Aqua Beachwear: 702 732 7301, aquabeachwear.com Nike, Speedo, Nautica, Tommy Hilfiger, DKNY and Calvin Klein swimwear.
Bally of Switzerland: 702 737 1968, bally.com Shoes, clothes and accessories with a strong modern look in bold colours.
Banana Republic: 702 697 2011, bananarepublic.com High-quality men's and women's clothing and accessories.
The Coach Store: 702 759 3451, thecoachstore.com America's leading accessories company offering good quality, classic yet modern styles.
Cole Haan: 702 731 3522, colehaan.com Hand-crafted, leather shoes and boots for men and women, plus handbags, wallets and casual outerwear.
Express Men: 702 737 8999, expressfashion.com Innovative, savvy fashion.
French Connection: 702 369 0852, frenchconnection.com contemporary fashion.
GAP: 702 796 0010, gap.com A leading retailer offering clothing, accessories and personal care products for both men and women.
Guess: 702 691 2541, guess.com A worldwide brand famous for jeans, stylish denim outfits and accessories for women, men and children.
Harris & Frank: 702 737 7545 The finest men's suits, sports coats and sportswear from a shop famous for service and tailoring.

Even the decorations are amazing

Hollister: 702 696 0480 hollisterco.com Cutting-edge casual clothing for teenagers.
Hot Cats: 702 796 1870, hotcats.com Up-to-the-minute styles for men, women, boys and girls sold in an entertaining atmosphere.
J Crew: 702 731 2060, jcrew.com A wide range of clothes, shoes and accessories for women, men and children.
Kuhlman Lifestyle: 702 894 9505 Well-priced quality styles for the modern man.
LaCoste: 702 796 6676, lacoste.com Classic casual clothing.
Leather by Michael Lawrence: 702 697 0062 A massive assortment of leather jackets, belts and bags.

Evening at the Fashion Show Mall

Lucky Brand: 702 369 4116, luckybrandjeans.com Classic American denim gear for women and men.
No Fear: 702 792 3327, nofear.com Young men's casual and lifestyle clothing and accessories.
Paul Frank: 702 369 2010, paulfrank.com Great brands such as Puma, Diesel and Quiksilver.
St Croix Knit: 702 794 4333, stcroixshop.com Fine sweaters, knit shirts and outerwear for men, all hand finished and guaranteed.
Tommy Bahama's: 702 731 6868, tommybahama.com Fun-yet-chic Bahama-inspired fashion plus shoes, ties, bags, belts and accessories.

Health and beauty

Aveda: 702 733 6660, aveda.com Natural and organic hair products.
Bath & Body Works: 702 693 5944, bathandbodyworks.com Natural beauty and skincare products.
The Body Shop: 702 737 1198, thebodyshop.com All-natural hair and skincare products and make-up.
Crabtree & Evelyn: 702 732 3609, crabtreeandevelyn.com Renowned British toiletry and home fragrance company.
Fashion Nail: 702 699 9958 Full-service nail salon for women and men.
GNC Live Well: 702 651 9090 Featuring a create-your-own hair and skin product bar.
H2O Plus: 702 893 1332, h2oplus.com With its own line of more than 300 natural products for the whole family.
L'Occitane En Provence: 702 369 1286, loccitaine.com High-end French company that specialises in using natural ingredients to create skincare, essential oils, perfumes and home fragrances.
Omni Chemists Pharmacy & Drug Store: 702 731 1162 Exotic products.
Regis Hair Stylists: 702 733 1400, regishairstylists.com One of the largest and most experienced hair salons in the world.
Victoria's Secret Beauty: 702 796 0110, www2.victoriassecret.com/beauty Modern, sexy fragrances, cosmetics and bodycare.

BRITTIP

The Fashion Show Mall's Café Ba Ba Reeba! and the Capital Grille restaurants became an instant hit when they opened in 2005. See Chapter 5 for full reviews.

Music and electronics

Bang & Olufsen: 702 731 9200, bang-olufsen.com Stylish and high performance sound systems, loudspeakers, telephones, audio and video systems.
Brookstone: 702 650 2048, brookstone.com An assortment of products in an environment in which customers are encouraged to try out products.
EB Games: 702 737 1733, ebgames.com The latest PC entertainment, plus accessories and products.
Futuretronics: 702 387 1818, futuretronics.com High-end innovative electronics from Sony, Bose, Nokia, Panasonic and more.
The Sharper Image: 702 731 3113, sharperimage.com Innovative gifts and gadgets for the whole family.

BRITTIP

Just remember that American videos are not compatible with the VHS system used in the UK. DVDs are only compatible if you have a multi-region DVD player.

Shoes

Aerosoles: 702 796 4144, aerosoles.com Stylish and comfortable affordable footwear for women.
Aldo: 702 735 5590, aldoshoes.com French-based men's and women's fashion shoes.
Ann Taylor: 702 734 8614, anntaylor.com America's leading retailer for stylish, professional yet feminine women's clothing and footwear.

The Cloud at the Fashion Show Mall

The mall offers catwalk shows as well as shops

Ann Taylor Loft: 702 731 0351, anntaylorloft.com The casual branch of Ann Taylor, offering co-ordinating, easy-to-wear pieces and shoes.
Bakers: 702 737 0108, bakersshoes.com Well-priced sport and formal footwear, plus Baker's own tailored shoes.
Bally of Switzerland: 702 737 1968, bally.com Shoes, clothes and accessories with a strong modern look in bold colours.
Banana Republic: 702 697 2011, bananarepublic.com Quality men's and women's footwear.
BCBG Max Azria: 702 737 0681bcbg.com Shoes, handbags, accessories and clothing with clean, simple lines by the award-winning American designer with a loyal Hollywood following.

Macy's Las Vegas store

Boot Star: 702 682-0848, boot-star.com All things boots, including all the leather to make a cowboy or cowgirl strut.
Champs Sports: 702 893 0135, champssports.com Brand name athletic footwear.
Clarks England/Bostonian: 702 732 1801 Affordably priced European-style footwear plus belts, handbags and shoe-care products.
Cole Haan: 702 731 3522, colehaan.com Hand-crafted, leather shoes and boots for men and women, plus handbags, wallets and casual outerwear.
Easy Spirit: 702 693 4732, easyspirit.com Comfortable shoes in narrow and wide widths.
Footlocker: 702 369 0401, footlocker.com Athletic shoes and clothes for the whole family.
Footworks: 702 369 0048, footworks.com Casual footwear brands for women and children.
Guess: 702 691 2541, guess.com A worldwide brand famous for jeans, stylish denim outfits, shoes and accessories for women, men and children.
Johnston & Murphy: 702 737 0114, johnstonandmurphy.com America's leading outlet for high-end men's shoes and accessories.
Journeys: 702 732 0130, journeys.com Young, fashionable footwear.
Lady Foot Locker: 702 735 7030, ladyfootlocker.com Athletic shoes and clothes for women.

Nine West: 702 693 2904, ninewest.com From classics to modern-style footwear.
Nurielle: 702 733 0693, nurielle.com J Lo, Carmen Electra and Lil Kim are among the many divas who make a beeline for Alfie's high-heel designs.
Payless Shoe Source: 702 697 0280, payless.com Stylish shoes for the budget conscious.
Puma: 702 892 9988, puma.com Innovative sports brand.
Shiekh Shoes: 702 369 9911, shiekhshoes.com For teenagers.
Skechers: 702 696 9905, skechers.com Boots, shoes, sneakers and sandals.
Steve Madden: 702 733 2904, stevemadden.com Funky and trendy shoes and accessories for women and teens.
Stiletto: 702 791 0505 Eclectic boutique with a wide selection of designer styles, plus novelty handbags and accessories.
Wet Seal: 702 796 0344, wetseal.com Contemporary clothes, footwear and accessories for those who lead active lifestyles.

Cafés

Auntie Anne's: 702 791 0077 A wide variety of soft pretzels including cinnamon sugar, jalapeno and glazin' raisin, plus frozen drinks. Located on the upper level of the West Expansion between Bloomingdale's Home and Saks Fifth Avenue.
Bloomingdale's B-Café: 702 784 5400 An assortment of pastries, cakes, croissants and sandwiches. Located on the lower level of Bloomies.
Cento e Fanti Gourmet Market & Café: 702 732 1366 New York and Chicago-style pizzas, salads and pasta dishes.
Cinnabon: 888 288-7655, cinnabon.com Aromatic and delicious cinnamon rolls direct from the oven.

BRITTIP

The NM Café has a brilliant Happy Hour for Martinis and food, served nightly on the outdoor terrace overlooking the Strip.

NM Café: 702 731 3636 contemporary-style lunch and dinner cuisine in a fashionable yet casual setting. Located on the second level of Neiman Marcus. Open daily 10am–8pm.
Nordstrum E-bar: 702 784 1615 Open for coffee, smoothies, pastries, muffins, bagels and sandwiches. Located on the lower level next to Nordstrum's entrance. Open from 8.30am Mon–Sat and from 9.30am on Sun.
Nordstrum Marketplace Café: 702 784 1610 Salads, sandwiches, pastas, pizzas and an assortment of daily specials, plus a wide variety of drinks. On the third level of Nordstrum, you can even order food and drinks to take away.
Starbucks Coffee Company: 702 794 4010, starbucks.com Delicious speciality coffees plus pastries and puddings. On the lower level of the Fashion Show Mall opposite Bailey Banks.
Tropicana Smoothies and Swenson's Ice Cream: 702 699 9306 A massive selection of fresh fruit smoothies made with crushed ice and/or frozen yogurt or fruit sorbet. On the upper level of the West Expansion between Bloomies and Saks Fifth Avenue.

Restaurants

California Pizza Kitchen: 702 893 1370, cpk.com Part of one of America's leading casual dining chains, it features a wide variety of pizzas, pastas, salads, soups, sarnies, starters and desserts. Located on the lower level of the West Expansion next to Bloomies.

The mall is spectacular day and night

Maggiano's Little Italy: 702 732 2550, maggianos.com Lavish portions of southern Italian cuisine are served in a vibrant dining environment. Dishes range from homemade pastas to salads, prime steaks, fish and chicken.
Mariposa at Neiman Marcus: 702 731 3636, neimanmarcus.com A fine-dining establishment on the first floor of the upper crust department store. Serving Mediterranean cuisine with French, Italian and Asian infusions, it even has entrances on the Strip and at Spring Mountain Road. Open for lunch Mon–Sat 11am–3pm and for dinner nightly 5.30–10pm (11pm on Fri and Sat).
RA Sushi: 702 696 0008, rasushi.com An upbeat, lively restaurant where the music and the food are as hot as a dollop of wasabi. Japanese fusion cuisine is served here in a sleek and contemporary environment. Additions include a sushi bar, cocktail bar and lounge and upbeat music, with a weekend DJ spinning hot tunes and fresh mixes.

Forum Shops at Caesars

Location: Right next to Caesars Palace.
Tel: 702 893 4800.
Web: simon.com/mall/directory.
Open: Sun–Thurs 10am–11pm, Fri and Sat 10am–midnight; most of the restaurants are open throughout.
Parking: Either in the Caesars Palace free covered car park or make use of the valet parking in the underground traffic tunnel at Caesars Boulevard.
Stores: More than 160 stores, including Abercrombie & Fitch, DKNY, Gap, FAO Schwartz, Planet Hollywood, Louis Vuitton and Galerie Lassen.

Fountain at the Forum Shops

A huge range of shops at the Forum Shops

Attractions: Festival Fountain, Atlantis and the Great Hall shows, plus the aquarium.
Cafés and restaurants: Fine-dining outlets include Bertolini's, Chinois, the Palm and Spago, plus BOA Prime Grill, Joe's Seafood, Prime Rib & Stone Crab and Il Mulino New York; casual outlets include the Cheesecake Factory, Ferrara's Café, La Salsa, Planet Hollywood, Café Della Spiga, Segafredo Zanetti and Sushi Roku.
Services: Contact the hotel's concierge desk for wheelchair and buggy rentals and lost and found.

More than 22 million people – including 6.9 million non-Americans – visited the Forum Shops in 2006. Annual sales average more than $1,600 per sq ft of retail space, far exceeding America's national average of $300–400.

Heralded as the 'Shopping Wonder of the World', the Forum Shops are so amazing they should be on your must-visit list, even in the unlikely event you don't plan to do any shopping (yeah, right!). It was deliberately built as an entertainment mall and transports people back in time to the great Roman Empire era with architecture, materials and street lighting to match. Even the piazzas and streets are laid out in the traditional format of a Roman town. The entire mall is enclosed,

BRITTIP

All cafés and food outlets are open at the same time as the mall unless otherwise stated.

temperature-controlled and covered with a 'sky' that changes throughout the day from a rosy-mauve dawn to high noon, the fading gold of the afternoon, twilight and finally night-time with twinkling stars. It was a concept so successful it was copied by the old Desert Passage Mall, and parts of the Grand Canal Shoppes.

The original $110m complex, which opened in 1992, proved so successful that it was expanded and a further 35 stores and entertainment outlets opened in 1997. A second extension opened in the summer of 2000, adding another 240,000sq ft/ 22,320sq m to the existing 533,000sq ft/ 49,569sq m.

Fabulous features include a sweeping plaza with replicas of the fountains of Treviano Triton, a massive reflecting pool, dazzling skylight and amazing spiral escalator.

The Festival Fountain undertakes a seven-minute Tale of the Roman Gods show using music, sound effects, animatronics and special scenic projections every 90 minutes from 10am.

At the Great Roman Hall, Atlantis comes to life in a spectacle that has the gods unleashing their wrath on the ancient city. Fire, water, smoke and special effects are used to create a show in which the animatronic characters of Atlas, Gadrius and Alia struggle to rule Atlantis.

Surrounded by a massive saltwater aquarium, the mythical sunken continent rises and falls before your eyes. The Great Hall is surrounded by giant projection screens which, together with lasers and other special effects, help create the illusion that you are genuinely part of the action.

Another free show is the dive into the aquarium for maintenance and feeding, which takes place several times a day. Inside are sharks and schools of coral-reef fish.

Visit the website for all the latest details of the stores.

Accessories

Anthropologie: 702 650 0466, anthropologie.com
Brighton Collectibles: 702 933 1330, brighton.com
Christian Lacroix: christian-lacroix.com
Coach: 702 651 0363, coach.com
Corsa Collections: 702 733 9442
Davante: 702 737 8585, davante.com
Intermix: intermixonline.com
Judith Leiber: 702 792 0661, judithleiber.com
Kate Spade: 702 515 6075, katespade.com
Kenneth Cole: 702 794 2653, kennethcole.com
Louis Vuitton: 702 732 1227, vuitton.com
Marciano: marciano.com
Miss Sixty: misssixty.com
Montblanc: 702 732 0569, montblanc.com
Swatch: swatch.com
Tumi: 0800 783 6570, tumi.com
Vilebrequin: vilebrequin.com

Clothes for men

Abercrombie & Fitch: 702 731 0712, abercrombie.com
Agent Provocateur: agentprovocateur.com
AIX Armani Exchange: 702 733 1666, armaniexchange.com
Banana Republic: 702 650 5623, banarepublic.com
Bernini: 702 893 7786, bernini.com
Bernini Collections: 702 893 1786
Bobby Jones: bobbyjonesshop.com
BOSS Hugo Boss: 702 696 9444, hugoboss.com
Brooks Brothers: 702 380 3081, brooksbrothers.com
Christian Lacroix: christian-lacroix.com
Cuzzens: 702 732 1329
D & G: 702 732 9292
Diesel: 702 791 5927, diesel.com
DKNY: 702 650 9670,dkny.com
Dolce & Gabbana: 702 892 0880
Elie Tahari: elietahari.com

Boulevard entrance at Caesars Palace

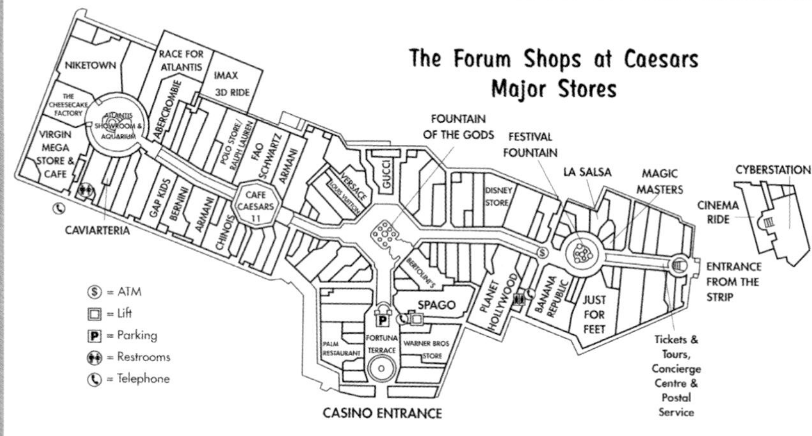

BRITTIP Most restaurants have long wait times to be seated, so make a reservation. Or better still, place your name with the maitre'd, and go shopping for an hour!

Emporio Armani: 702 650 5200, emporioarmani.com
Ermengildo Zegna: zegna.com
Etro: 702 792 3876, etro.com
Gap: 702 737 1550, gap.com
Guess: 702 727 1816, guess.com
John Varvatos: 702 939 0922, johnvarvatos.com
Just Cavalli: 702 893 0389, robertocavalli.net

BRITTIP Arrive early for the Atlantis shows as the crowds build up early and you'll want a good view of the sunken city.

Fountains at Caesars Palace

Kenneth Cole: 702 794 2653, kennethcole.com
Lacoste: 702 791 7616, lacoste.com
Loro Piana: loropiana.com
Lucky Brand Jeans: 702 369 2536, luckybrandjeans.com
Marc Jacobs: 702 369 2007, marcjacobs.com
Polo Ralph Lauren: 702 650 5656, polo.com
Roberto Cavalli: robertocavalli.com
Ted Baker: tedbaker.com
Theory: 702 643 7019, theory.com
Thomas Pink: 702 696 1713, thomaspink.com
Tommy Bahama's: 702 731 6868, tommybahama.com
Versace Jeans Couture: 702 796 7332, versace.com
Vilebrequin: 702 894 9460, vilebrequin.com

Clothes for women

Abercrombie & Fitch: 702 731 0712, abercrombie.com
Agent Provocateur: 702 696 7174, agentprovocateur.com
AIX Armani Exchange: 702 733 1666, armaniexchange.com
Ann Taylor: 702 794 0494, anntaylor.com
Anne Fontaine: 702 733 6205, annefontaine.com
Anthropologie: 702 650 0466, anthropologie.com
Banana Republic: 702 650 5623, banarepublic.com
bebe: 702 735 8885, bebe.com
Bobby Jones: bobbyjonesshop.com
Brooks Brothers: 702 380 3081, brooksbrothers.com

The entrance to Caesars Palace

CH Carolina Herrera: 702 894 5242, carolinaherrera.com
Christian Dior: 702 737 9777, dior.com
Christian Lacroix: 702 731 0990, christian-lacroix.com
D & G: 702 732 9292, dolcegabbana.com
Diesel: 702 791 5927, diesel.com
DKNY: 702 650 9670,dkny.com
Dolce & Gabbana: 702 892 0880, dolcegabbana.com
Emporio Armani: 702 650 5200, emporioarmani.com
Ermengildo Zegna: 702 369 5458, zegna.com
Escada: 702 791 2300, escada.com
Etro: 702 792 3876, etro.com
Gianni Versace: 702 796 7222, versace.com
Intermix: 702 731 1922, intermixonline.com
James Perse: 702 693 5482, jamesperse.com
Juicy Couture: 702 365 5600, juicycouture.com
Just Cavalli: 702 893 0389, robertocavalli.net
Lacoste: 702 791 7616, lacoste.com
Loro Piana: 702 369 0497, loropiana.com
Lucky Brand Jeans: 702 369 2536, luckybrandjeans.com
Marc Jacobs: 702 369 2007, marcjacobs.com
Marciano: 702 369 0322, marciano.com
MaxMara: 702 732 0900, maxmara.com
Miss Sixty: misssixty.com
Nanette Lepore: 702 893 9704, nanettelepore.com
Ron Herman: 702 699 5498, ronherman.com
Shauna Stein: 702 893 9786
St John: 702 893 0044, stjohnknits.com
Tadashi: 702 733 6071, tadashicollection.com
Ted Baker: 702 369 4755, tedbakercollection.com
Theory: 702 643 7019, theory.com
Thomas Pink: 702 696 1713, thomaspink.com
Tommy Bahama's: 702 731 6868, tommybahama.com
Valentino: 702 737 7603, valentino.com
Versace Jeans Couture: 702 796 7332, versace.com
Victoria's Secret: 702 765 5425, victoriassecret.com
Wolford: 702 866 2666, wolford.com

Health and beauty

Anthropologie: 702 650 0466, anthropologie.com
Bath & Body Works: 702 796 4902, bathandbodyworks.com
Estee Lauder: 702 737 9011, esteelauder.com
Fresh: 702 631 5000, fresh.com
Kiehl's: 702 784 0025, kiehls.com
MAC Cosmetics: maccosmetics.com
Truefitt & Hill: 702 735 7428, truefittandhill.com
Victoria's Secret: 702 765 5435, victoriassecret.com

Jewellery

Bvlgari: 702 734 2001, bulgari.com
Chopard: 702 862 4440, chopard.com
David Yurman: 702 862 4440, davidyurman.com
De Beers: 702 650 9559, debeers.com
Fred Paris: 702 650 0090, fred.com
Harry Winston: 702 933 7370, harrywinston.com
Hyde Park: 702 794 3541, hydeparkjewelers.com
Intermix: 702 731 1922, intermixonline.com
Judith Ripka: 702 792 5900, judithripka.com
Landau: 702 737 7117, landaucostume.com
Michal Negrin: 702 737 1735, michalnegrin.com
Montblanc: 702 732 0569, montblanc.com

A superbly elegant shopping experience

The galleries at the Forum Shops

Opals & Gems of Australia: 702 696 1882
Swatch: 702 734 1093, swatch.com
Tiffany & Co: 702 644 3065, tiffany.com
Tourneau: 702 732 8463, tourneau.com
Vicci: 702 734 3008, vicci.com

Music and electronics

Brookstone: 702 734 8400, brookstone.com
Peter Lik Photography: 702 836 3110, peterlik.com
Sony Style: 702 697 5420, sonystyle.com

Shoes

a. testoni: 702 735 7732, testoniusa.com
Bally: 702 893 7718, bally.com
Bobby Jones: 702 413 6313, bobbyjonesshop.com
Donald J. Pliner: 702 796 0900, donaldjpliner.com
Giuseppe Zanotti: 702 866 0055, giuseppezanotti.com
Jimmy Choo: 702 691 2097, jimmychoo.com
Kate Spade: 702 515 6075, katespade.com
Kenneth Cole: 702 794 2653, kennethcole.com
Louis Vuitton: 702 732 1227, vuitton.com
Moda Scapa: 702 696 9786, salvatory.com
Shoooz at the Forum: 702 734 7600, shoooz.com
Stuart Weitzman: 702 369 9222, stuartweitzman.com
Taryn Rose: tarynrose.com
The Walking Company: 702 792 8400, thewalkingcompany.com

Stationery, cards, books and gifts

Anthropologie: 702 650 0466, anthropologie.com
Brookstone: 702 734 8400, brookstone.com
Essentials at The Forum: 702 866 1207
Forum Collections
Forum Gifts & Sundries: 702 734 0678
Kate Spade: 702 515 6075, katespade.com
Magnet Maximus: 702 369 0195
Montblanc: 702 732 0569, montblanc.com

Speciality shops

Antiquities: 702 792 2274, antiquities.com
Baccarat: 702 693 6877, baccarat.com
Brookstone: 702 734 8400, brookstone.com

Style and choice abound

Stylish courtyard at the Forum Shops

Burberry: 702 731 0650, burberry.com
Caesars: 702 731 7851
Casa Fuente: 702 731 5051, cigarfamily.com
Christian Dior: 702 737 9777, dior.com
Chrome Hearts: 702 893 9959, chromehearts.com
Coach: 702 651 0363, coach.com
Corsa Collections: 702 733 9442, corsacollections.com
Custo Barcelona: 702 893 0015, custo-barcelona.com
Davante: 702 737 8585, davante.com
Elie Tahari: 702 732 2454, elietahari.com
Elysium Gallery: 702 369 1888, theartofelysium.org/gallery
Emilio Pucci: 702 735 7731, emiliopucci.com
Fabergé: faberge.com
Fendi: 702 893 2616, eluxury.com
Field of Dreams: 702 792 8233, fieldofdreams.com
Galerie Lassen: 702 731 6900, lassenart.com
Galleria di Sorrento: 702 369 2085, gdsorrento.com
Georg Jensen: 702 369 2424, georgjensen.com
Gucci: 702 369 7333, gucci.com
Houdini's Magic Shop: 702 866 0010, houdini.com
Ice Accessories: 702 696 9700, iceaccessories.com
Jay Strongwater: 702 732 4448, jaystrongwater.com
Judith Leiber: 702 792 0661, judithleiber.com
La Perla: 702 732 9820, laperla.com
Lalique: 702 731 2155, lalique.com
Longchamp: longchamp.com
Louis Vuitton: 702 732 1227, vuitton.com
Montblanc: 702 732 0569, montblanc.com
Niketown: 702 650 8888, nike.com
Planet Hollywood Superstore: 702 369 6001, planethollywood.com
Playboy: 702 851 7470, playboy.com
Roman Times: 702 733 8687
Saint Andrews Golf Shop: 702 837 1234, saintandrewsgolfshop.com
Salvatore Ferragamo: 702 933 9333, salvatoreferragamo.it
Scoop NYC: 702 734 0026, scoopnyc.com
The Art of Peter Max: 702 644 7070, petermax.co,
Tod's: 702 792 1422, tods.com
Tumi: 0800 783 6570, tumi.com
West of Santa Fe: 702 737 1993, westofsantafe.com

Toys and games

FAO Schwarz: 702 796 6500, faoschwarz.com

Cafés

Breath Oxygen Bar: 702 258 4202
Cafe Della Spiga: 702 731 7110
Café Express: 702 893 4045
Fat Tuesday: 702 369 3265
Forum Café: 702 734 0951
Stage Deli: 702 893 4045, arkrestaurants.com
Vosges Haut-Chocolat: 702 836 9866, vosgeschocolate.com

Spago is a Wolfgang Puck outlet

BRITTIP

The Forum is home to a super-trendy nightclub OPM. Sitting above Wolfgang Puck's, Chinois, the Latin jazz and house sounds will keep you dancing until the wee small hours.

Restaurants

BOA Prime Grill: 702 733 7373, boasteak.com
Cheesecake Factory: 702 792 6888, cheesecake-factory.net
Chinois: 702 737 9700, wolfgangpuck.com
Il Mulino New York: 702 492 6000, ilmulinonewyork.com
Joe's Seafood, Prime Steak & Stone Crab: 702 792 9222, http://icon.com/joes
La Salsa: 702 735 8226, lasalsa.com
Planet Hollywood: 702 791 7827, planethollywood.com
Spago: 702 369 6300, wolfgangpuck.com
Sushi Roku: 702 733 7373, sushiroku.com
The Palm Las Vegas: 702 732 7256, thepalm.com
Trevi Italian Restaurant: 702 735 4663, trevi-italian.com

Miracle Mile Shops

Location: Wrapped around Planet Hollywood with entrances on the Strip and Harmon Avenue.
Tel: 888 800 8284.
Web: miracle mileshopslv.com
Open: Sun–Thurs 10am–11pm. Fri and Sat 10am–midnight.
Parking: Free parking available at Planet Hollywood.
Attractions: Rainstorm in Merchants' Harbor every hour on the hour Mon–Thurs and every half hour on Fri and Sat; plus live entertainment from musicians in the courtyards.
Cafés and restaurants: Fine-dining outlets include Asia Lombardi's Romagna Mia and Pampas Churrascuria Brazilian Grill; the casual options are Aroma D'Talia Blondies, La Salsa Cantina, Merchants' Harbor, Oyster Bay, Todai and trader Vic's.

You'd never know this was once the Desert Passage under the old Aladdin. Where once was a façade of a Moroccan shopping fantasy, now it has been completely ripped away as part of a $100m make-over to the new Miracle Mile Shops. The exterior 1001 Arabian Nights theme was taken down in 2007, replaced by the new, Rodeo Drive hipness of the Miracle Mile Shops. The interior's North African Sky, Morocco Gate, mosaic tiles and Aladdin trading seaport themes are being renovated in stages through 2008. In its place are tall windows and floor-to-ceiling heavy glass doors with brushed steel accents, and flat-screen monitors offering directions and advertisements.

All that will remain are the shops and the Merchant Harbor Rainstorm – a refreshingly pleasant affair where you stand 'dockside' as rain falls from the sky accompanied by rolls of thunder and crashes of lightning. However, even this will be changed over to a new design by 2008, although plans as of 2007 were not finalised.

As most things, the change has good and bad. The old Desert Passage was dark, poorly signed and easy to get lost in.

Wolfgang Puck's Chinoise

Galleria di Sorrento at the Forum Shops

Bebe Sport at the Miracle Mile

The modern Miracle Mile is brighter and smarter to the eye. However, the old incarnation veritably oozed character and shopping fantasy, and at least that part will be missed.

Also because of the change, as of 2007 the list of shops was in a bit of a flux, several leaving, a few expanding and many new ones supposedly opening their doors in the later part of 2007. Here is the best guess at the 2008 roster of stores.

Clothes and accessories for women

Alpaca Pete's Slippers and Sweaters: 702 862 8297, alpacapetes.com
Ann Taylor Loft: 702 732 2248, anntaylorloft.com
BCBG Max Azria: 702 735 2947, bcbg.com
bebe: 702 892 0406, bebe.com
Bebe Sport: 702 733 8999, bebe.com
Ben Sherman: 702 688 4227, bensherman.com
Betsey Johnson: 702 731 0286, betseyjohnson.com
Bettie Page: 702 636 1100, bettiepage.com
Bikini Bay: 702 699 5597
Caché: 702 699 5448, cache.com
Carlo Ferre Leather Collection: 702 450 9777
Chico's: 702 732 2816, chicos.com
Crazy Shirts: 702 893 7780, crazyshirts.com
Frederick's of Hollywood: 702 893 9001, fredericks.com
French Connection: 702 733 6420, frenchconnection.com
Front Row Sports: 702 733 6420, fronrtrowsports.com
Gap: 702 862 4042, gap.com
GapBody: 702 862 4042, gap.com
H&M: handm.com
Herve Leger: 702 732 4529, herveleger.com
Hilo Hattie: 702 733 6900, hilohattie.com
Lucky Brand Jeans: 702 733 6613, luckiebrandjeans.com
Marciano: 702 659 9928, marciano.com
Max Studio: 702 732 2592, maxstudio.com
Metropark: 702 650 7200, metroparkusa.com
Mimi Mango: 702 650 2295
Napoleon: 702 733 6005, napoleonfashions.com
Parallel: 702 732 4489
Roxy: 702 731 1521, roxy.com
Santiki: 702 699 9106, santiki.com
Sisley: 702 733 3080, sisley.com
Stash Clothing: 702 794 0003, stashclothing.com
Tommy Bahama: 702 731 3988, tommybahama.com
United Colors of Benetton: 702 731 2317, benetton.com
Urban Outfitters: 702 735 0058, urbanoutfitters.com
Victoria's Secret: 702 735 3174, victoriassecret.com
West Coast Wraps: 702 731 1805
White House/Black Market: 702 732 2562, whiteandblack.com

Clothes and accessories for men

Alpaca Pete's Slippers and Sweaters: 702 862 8297 alpacapetes .com
Ben Sherman: 702 688 4227 bensherman.com
Carlo Ferre Leather Collection: 702 450 9777
Crazy Shirts: 702 893 7780, crazyshirts.com
French Connection: 702 733 6420, frenchconnection.com
Front Row Sports: 702 733 6420, frontrowsports.com
GAP: 702 862 4042, gap.com
GapBody: 702 862 4042, gap.com
H&M: handm.com
Hilo Hattie, The Store of Hawaii: 702 733 6900, hilohattie.com

Get the latest at Benetton

Luxury shopping at the Grand Canal Shoppes

Lucky Brand Jeans: 702 733 6613, luckiebrandjeans.com
Metropark: 702 650 7200, metroparkusa.com
Napoleon: 702 733-6005, napoleonfashions .com
Quicksilver: 702 731 1521, quicksilver.com
Shaunz: 702 792 5255, shaunz.com
Stash Clothing: 702 794 0003, stashclothing.com
Stash Men's: 702 893 0010, stashclothing.com
Tommy Bahama: 702 731 3988. tommybahama.com

BRITTIP

Of all the Strip resort-hotel shopping malls', the Miracle Mile Shops is the only one with direct entrances on the Strip – i.e. you don't have to walk through a casino to get to it!

Gandini at the Grand Canal Shoppes

Urban Outfitters: 702 735 0058, urbanoutfitters.com

Plus there will be several score more restaurants and speciality stores by January 2008.

Besides shopping, Miracle Mile is host to the Variety Theater, which means it is one of Las Vegas's entertainment hot spots. The performance line-up is tantalising, headlined by *V – The Ultimate Variety Show* and supported by Nathan Burton, *Comedy Magic*, *Marc Savard: Mesmerized* (a comedy hypnosis show), *Fab Four Mania* (a Beatle's tribute show), and Popovich Comedy Pet Theater (a hilarious animal act). Perhaps the most daring is *Stripper 101* – a class for the ladies where they can learn striptease moves and how to pole dance.

Just a few steps away are the entertainment options of Planet Hollywood, which includes *Stomp Out Loud* and the *Magic of Hans Klok*. This makes Miracle Mile a great way to spend a day shopping, eating, taking in a show followed by some late-night dancing or gambling.

Grand Canal Shoppes

Location: The Venetian.
Tel: 702 414 4500.
Web: thegrandcanalshoppes.com
Open: Sun–Thurs 10am–11pm, Fri and Sat 10am–midnight.
Parking: Parking at the Venetian; valet parking available.
Cafés and restaurants: Fine dining is unparalled here with one fantastic place

after another. Recent additions include B&B Ristorante, well hyped offering from renowned chef Mario Battaglia and famous winemaker Joseph Bastianich, continue with dazzling stalwarts like the incomparable Delmonico's, Canaletto, Canyon Ranch Café, Postrio, Tsunami Asian Grill and Zeffirino Ristorante; casual dining is at Taqueria Canonita and Tintoretto's Bakery, while you can listen to live music at Tao.

This is another luxurious shopping environment that has been specifically created to provide entertainment as well as retail outlets. As you enter from the Strip, you are greeted by extravagant vaulted ceilings adorned with images reminiscent of Italy's great pointed palazzos.

Along the streets of this recreated 15th-century Venice are high-fashion luxury boutiques, national branded stores of America, and entertainment retailers. After wandering past some of these shops you arrive at the huge space called St Mark's Square from where you can take a gondola ride – just like those on Venice's fabled canals – and enjoy the illusion created by decorated second-storey balconies.

Posh stores include Burberry, Jimmy Choo, Mikimoto, which is famous for its pearls, and Oliver & Company, the latter filled with men's fashions by Ralph Lauren, Donna Karan, Giorgio Armani and Borrelli. Other retailers include Ann Taylor, Banana Republic and bébé. Interesting one-off shops include Il Prato, which sells authentic Venetian masks, Ripa di Monti for Venetian glass and collectibles, and Sephora beauty emporium.

The whole process of browsing or parting with your cash is made sweeter by the entertainments, with jugglers showcasing their talents along the cobblestone walkways and the glass blowers demonstrating their craft in St Mark's Square.

Hawaiian Marketplace

Location: 3743 South Las Vegas Boulevard, just south of Harmon Avenue and in front of the Polo Towers.
Tel: 702 795 2247.
Open: Hours vary, but generally are 10am–11pm.
Parking: A small car park is available next to the market or you can try the Polo Towers public car park.
Attractions: Free daily shows by an animatronic bird show in the Enchanted Forest every hour; and Thurs–Sat Team Aloha puts on extended shows that include singing, dancing, fire-knife dancers and live bird shows.
Cafés and restaurants: Indian Tamba, Zinger's hamburger joint, a Chinese buffet at China Star.

While the outdoor market is still popular, with several dozen thatch huts and carts of vendors selling a wide range of shirts, mobile phone accessories and tourist memorabilia, the interior of this $175m centre is dead, including most of the restaurants. The story goes that one group of investors bought out almost all of the interior stores, then promptly went bankrupt. A shame, as this was a pleasant shopping experience. It still is, but on a much smaller scale. Until the owners get the problems sorted out, there is little reason for a special trip, but if you are near the MGM Grand/Planet Hollywood area, it is worth stopping by.

Grand Canal – Las Vegas style

Las Vegas Premium Outlets

Location: 875 South Grand Central Parkway, downtown Las Vegas, just off Interstate 15.
Tel: 702 474 7500.
Web: premiumoutlets.com
Open: Mon–Sat 10am–9pm, Sun 10am–8pm.
Parking: Free and immediately outside the village.
Cafés and restaurants: Auntie Anne's Soft Pretzels, China Pantry, Dairy Queen/Orange Julius, The Great Steak & Potato Co., Italia Express, Japan Café Grill, Makino's, Starbucks Coffee and Subway.
Services: Go to the management office to collect a map to see the full layout; there you can also rent a pushchair, wheelchair, get a trolley, arrange for international shipping and buy international phone cards; three sets of WCs; three cashpoints (ATMs), foreign currency exchange; telephones.
Additional services: Attraction tickets, dinner and show reservations and sightseeing tours available through the Allstate Ticketing/Showtickets.com located in the kiosk in front of Timberland at suite 1901.

Discount shopping in Las Vegas took a turn for the better with the arrival of Chelsea Premium Outlets' latest village – the $95m Las Vegas Premium Outlets. Run by the same people who run Woodbury Common in New York, this is one of the best discount outfits in America. Each of their village-style settings is picturesque, well laid out and fully serviced by food and drink outlets and plenty of toilets.

On top of that, it provides high-end designer gear at 25–65% of the original price on a year-round basis, while also running fabulous sales with even cheaper prices – generally held on the major American holidays and over Christmas.

However, with its open design, and paucity of shade, it can be an uncomfortable experience trudging around on very hot or very windy days.

To get to Premium Outlets by car, take Interstate 15 northbound, then take Exit 41B Charleston Boulevard, southbound, and exit at Charleston Boulevard. This will take you on to Martin Luther King Boulevard. Turn left into Charleston Boulevard and left again into Grand Central Parkway. If you are going by taxi, there's a pick up behind Ann Taylor at Suite 1201 and a drop off between Adidas and Brooks Brothers, suite 1701.

Las Vegas Outlet Center

Children's stores

Carter's, The Children's Place, Disney Store Outlet, K*B Toy, Little Me, OshKosh, Strasburg Children, Stride Rite Keds Sperry.

Clothes for men and women

A/X Armani Exchange, Adidas, Ann Taylor Factory Store, Anne Klein, Banana Republic Factory Store, Bass, Benetton, Bezene, Bernini, Big Dog Sportswear, Billabong, Brooks Brothers, Calvin Klein, Charlotte Russe, Chico's, Dolce & Gabbana, Dress Barn, Ecko Unlimited, Eddie Bauer, Elie Tahari, French Connection, Front Row Sports, Geoffrey Beene, Guess, Haggar Clothing Co., Hurley, Izod, Jockey, Jones New York, Kenneth Cole, L'eggs Hanes Ball Playtex, Lacoste, Leather by Michael Lawrence, Levi's, Lids for Less, Limited Editions for Her, Liz Claiborne, Maidenform, Maternity Works, Max Studio, Nautica, Nike, Oakley Vault, PacSun, Perry Ellis, Polo Ralph Lauren, Puma, Quiksilver, Rave, Reebok, Rip Curl, Rue 21, Sarar, St John Company Store, Theory, Timberland, Tommy Hilfiger, Van Heusen, Volcom, White House/Black Market, Wilsons Leather.

Health and beauty

The Cosmetics Company Store, Crabtree & Evelyn, Designer Fragrances, L'Occitane, Lancome, Perfumania, Perfumes 4U, Vitamin World.

Jewellery and accessories

Claire's Accessories, Coach, Crescent Jewelers, Fossil, Leather by Michael Lawrence, The Luggage Factory, Movado Company Store, Samsonite, Seiko The

TV merchandise at Television City in the MGM Grand

Company Store, Sunglass Hut, Sunglass Icon, Time Factory Watch Outlet, Totes Sunglass World, Ultra Diamonds, Wilsons Leather Outlet, Zales The Diamond Jewelry Outlet.

Shoes

Adidas, Aerosoles, Bass, Clarks Bostonian, DC Shoes, Ecco, Factory Brand Shoes, Hush Puppies, Johnston & Murphy, Journeys, Kenneth Cole, Liz Claiborne Shoes, Naturalizer, Nike, Nine West, Puma, Rack Room Shoes, Reebok, Robert Wayne Footwear, Skechers, Stride Rite Keds Sperry, Timberland, Two Lips Shoes, Vans.

Speciality items, gifts and homeware

Book Warehouse, Bose, The Fudgery, Fuzziwig's Candy Factory, Harry and David, Kitchen Collection, Le Gourmet Chef.

Cafés and restaurants

Auntie Anne's Soft Pretzels , China Pantry, Dairy Queen/Orange Julius, The Great Steak & Potato Co, Italia Express, Japan Cafe Grill, Makino Seafood & Sushi Buffet, Starbucks Coffee, Subway.

Factory outlet district

Just a short trip south of the MGM Grand along the Strip is the district of factory shops where many famous brand names are sold at 20–70% discounts. First stop is the Belz Factory Outlet World at the corner of Las Vegas Boulevard South and Warm Springs Road. Here, the 625,000sq ft/ 58,125sq m mall is home to a permanent laser show plus 140 outlet stores that include Nike, OshKosh, Off 5th, Saks Fifth Avenue and Levis.

A mile/1.6km further south is the open-air Las Vegas Factory Outlet Stores of America that has a huge range of shops from men's and women's clothing to bookstores and shoe shops. Both are open Mon–Sat 10am–8pm and Sun 10am–6pm.

Hotel shopping

In addition to the major shopping parades featured at different hotels, earlier in this chapter, here is a full guide to the shops available in each of the major resort hotels. Some offer high-end items – such as the Paris Resort – while many provide shopping that fits in with the theme of the hotel.

Bally's Hotel

Bally's Avenue Shops, 702 736 4111
More than 40 stores from jewellery to fashion, plus men's and women's hair salons, an ice-cream parlour and a place to have your photo taken in costumes from the 1800s.

Open seven days a week. Most shops open at 9am, closing times vary.

Giorgio Armani at the Bellagio

Via Bellagio

The Bellagio

Via Bellagio, 702 693 7111
The tenants of the Bellagio's shopping 'mall' – a street which winds its way from the hotel down to the Strip – fit in perfectly with the elegant surroundings. Prada, Georgio Armani and Chanel cater to the Bellagio's well-heeled clientele, as does Tiffany & Co, the epitome of subdued shopping style.

Open seven days a week. Most stores open at 10am, closing times vary.

Caesars Palace

Appian Way, 702 731 7110
Despite its proximity to the Forum Shops at Caesars, Appian Way is a fair-sized corridor winding through the hotel and connecting the Roman, Palace and Centurion Towers, which is filled with some of the most exclusive shops and finest salons in the world.

Shops include Ancient Creations, filled with high-quality jewellery and rare coins and artefacts; Cartier; Le Paradis jewellery store; Venus Salon for hair, nail, make-up and skin services; Cottura for hand-painted ceramics; Galerie Michelangelo filled with fine art; Emperors Essentials for Caesars logo merchandise; Piazzas Del Mercato for sportswear, perfumes, golf collections and spa products; Godiva Chocolatier; Colosseum Cigars, Bernini Couture; Cuzzens for men's clothing; Paul and Shark for men's sportswear; Carina for women's designer clothes, shoes and accessories; and Paradiso for swimwear.

Open seven days a week from 10am, closing times vary.

BRITTIP

If you are having trouble finding a parking spot, try the valet parking at the side entrance of Polo Towers and you'll be just steps away from the Hawaiian Marketplace.

Circus Circus

Circus Circus Shops, 702 734 0410
Want a break from high-falutin', designer-by-the-dozen, serious shop-till-you-drop malls? Then, head to the hotel's 40,000sq ft/3,783sq m shopping promenade. You won't find Dior's latest must-have sunglasses, but you will find a whole lot of laughs in shops such as Nothing But Clowns (yup – they come in all shapes and sizes!), Houdini's Magic Shop, Circus Kids and LYSONSPL8 for fun licence plates. Also pretty handy are the off-licence, newsagent and gift shop. Circus Circus also is a frequent host of liquidation sales, where overstock jeans and other merchandise from national chains are heaped in massive boxes and sold at pennies on the retail dollar.

Open seven days a week from 10am, closing times vary.

Excalibur Hotel

Excalibur Shoppes, 702 597 7777
Fantasy shops on the medieval theme include the Excalibur Shoppe, Castle Souvenirs, Gifts of the Kingdom, Spirit Shoppe, Dragon's Lair and Desert Shoppe, which sell everything from swords and suits of armour to Excalibur merchandise.

Open seven days a week from 10am, closing times vary.

Las Vegas Hilton

Hilton Shops, 702 732 5111
Don't forget to pick up your Star Trek souvenir merchandise and other goodies at the Hilton shops.

Open seven days a week from 10am, closing times vary.

Tesorini Jewelry Store at the Bellagio

Shopping hints and tips

Duty free: Buy your booze from US liquor stores – they're better value than airports, but remember your allowance is 1 litre of spirits and two bottles of wine.

Measurements: The Americans still work in feet and inches, which is great for anyone over the age of 30!

Sizes: Clothes sizes are one size smaller in America, so a dress size 10 in the US is a size 12 in the UK. It means you can travel out in a size 12 and come back in a size 10! It is the same for men: a jacket size 42 is the English size 44. But it's the opposite with shoes: an American size 10 is our size 9.

Taxes: In all cases you will have to add local taxes on to the cost of your goods. In Nevada this adds 7.5% on to the final price.

UK shopping allowances: Your duty-free allowance is just £145 and given the wealth of shopping opportunities in Las Vegas, you're likely to exceed this, but don't be tempted to change receipts to show a lesser value as the goods will be confiscated and you'll face a massive fine. In any case, the prices for some goods in America are so cheap that even paying the duty and VAT on top will still work out cheaper than buying it in Britain. Duty can range from 3.5% to 19% depending on the item. Computers are charged at 3.5%, golf clubs at 4%, cameras at 5.4% and mountain bikes at a massive 15.8%. You pay this on goods above £145 and then VAT of 17.5% on top of that.

The Luxor

Giza Galleria, 702 262 4444

The Galleria contains 18 shops selling everything from King Tut's souvenirs to ice cream and sweets. Other shops include the Scarab Shop for hieroglyphic T-shirts and sweatshirts, Innerspace for limited-edition Egyptian collections, and the Logo Shop selling everything from Luxor key chains to stuffed animals and glassware. Exclusive is the exciting women's clothing store that has everything from business outfits to cutting-edge designer gear.

Open seven days a week from 10am, closing times vary.

Mandalay Bay

Mandalay Bay Shops, 702 632 7777

A selection of tropically themed shops to match the hotel, selling everything from Bali art to fine cigars, children's and designer clothes, imported rum, toys, rare coins, swimwear and jewellery.

Open seven days a week from 10am, closing times vary.

MGM Grand

MGM Grand Avenue, 702 891 3300

The City of Entertainment has fun and exclusive shops that provide something for everyone from fine jewellery to men's, women's and children's fashions. You can browse through the luxurious shops along Studio Walk, visit Star Lane Shops on the lower level of the main lobby, or explore the shopping outlets located throughout MGM Grand. Studio Walk is a magnificent 115,000sq ft/10,695sq m shopping promenade located between the casino and the gardens and is designed to look like a Hollywood sound stage, while each of the shops and restaurants has been inspired by some of Hollywood's legendary buildings and landmarks. Star Lane Shops has a variety of outlets in a fun and colourful shopping arcade.

Open seven days a week from 10am, closing times vary.

Fornarina at the Mandalay Bay

The Mirage

The Street of Shops, 702 791 7111
An exclusive collection of designer boutiques offering everything from unique gifts to beautiful jewellery and designer clothes in a sophisticated Parisian/Italian boulevard setting. Designers include DKNY, Moschino and La Perla, while there are also souvenir shops for Siegfried and Roy and Cirque du Soleil.

Open seven days a week, Sun–Thurs 10am–11pm, Fri and Sat until midnight.

Monte Carlo

Monte Carlo Shops, 702 730 7777
Boutiques include a small convenience store, sweet shop, flower shop and the Lance Burton Magic Shop with demonstrator shows.

Open seven days a week from 10am, closing times vary.

New York-New York

Soho Village, 702 414 4500
Provides a limited number of stores but still a fun experience. The village is set against a background of New York landmarks and includes both Greenwich Village and Times Square.

Open seven days. Most Stores open at 10am, closing times vary.

Paris Resort

Le Boulevard, 702 946 7000
High-end shops in their own Rue de la Paix district. Here quaint cobblestone streets and winding alleyways lead you to French boutiques selling wine and cheese, flowers and designer clothes.

Open seven days a week 10am–10pm.

Rio All-Suite Hotel

Masquerade Village, 702 252 7777
The $200m Masquerade Village is actually a combination of shopping, dining, entertainment and gaming woven together by the ongoing carnival atmosphere of the hotel's Masquerade Show in the Sky (see page 53). Here you can stroll down 200-year-old Tuscan-tiled streets filled with boutiques selling designer gear, such as Armani, Versace, Gucci, Rolex and Torras.

Open seven days a week from 10am, closing times vary.

Stratosphere Hotel

Tower Shops, 702 380 7777
Visitors pass through themed street scenes reminiscent of Paris, Hong Kong and New York on their way to the Broadway Showroom and lifts to the Observation Deck. More than 50 shops include Bernini Sport, Aerosoles, Swatch, Perfumania, Marshall Rousso and Haagen Dazs.

Open Sun–Thurs 10am–11pm, Fri and Sat until midnight.

The Tropicana

Atrium Shopping, 702 739 2222
Selection of shops and services such as shoeshines and boutiques.

Open seven days from 10am, closing times vary.

Wynn Las Vegas

Wynn Las Vegas, 702 770 7100
Home to the only Ferrari Maserati dealership in the city, Steve Wynn's wonderful new resort has a clutch of top designer boutiques, including Chanel, Manolo Blahnik, Dior, Louis Vuitton, Cartier and Gaultier, plus the first-ever Oscar de la Renta outlet.

Open seven days from 10am, closing times vary.

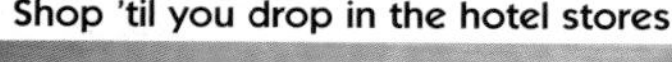

Shop 'til you drop in the hotel stores

5 RESTAURANTS

Your choice of the best restaurants and eating places in town

Food, glorious food abounds in Las Vegas from the classiest gourmet restaurants to the cheap and cheerful diner and from relaxed lounge-style settings to trendy bistros. Not so long ago, the city was most famous for its 99-cent shrimp (i.e. giant prawn) cocktails and the amazing all-you-can-eat buffets and not a lot else in the dining department. But, like every other aspect of Las Vegas, things have changed as a result of the massive influx of bright young professionals from California and a surge in sophisticated visitors looking for something more than a bit of casino action.

The resorts have gone far afield to woo top chefs of every country and discipline to open dazzling eateries. While most resorts or hotels worldwide are happy if they have one, or perhaps two, world-class restaurants, the Las Vegas resorts collect them like some do postage stamps. The Venetian can make a case of having at least 12 four- or five-star eating houses of distinction on their property. Most of the other grand resorts have a half-dozen each. The king of Las Vegas food must be

Fusia is just one of many superb restaurants

In this chapter

BRITTIP

Do not assume that because you can smoke anywhere you like in casinos that the same goes for the restaurants. All hotel restaurants are completely non-smoking.

the iconic celebrity chef Wolfgang Puck, who has no less than six restaurants covering Sin City, including a Wolfgang Puck Gourmet Express at McCarron airport!

But while the classy restaurants have taken over the headlines, with $777 kobe beef hamburgers and $421 white truffle lobsters, there still resides quality cheap eats if you know where to look. You can still get a complete steak dinner for $4.95 at the Ellis Island Casino, and a huge presentation of shrimp downtown at Golden Gate for a mere 99 cents, and a massive steak and eggs breakfast 24-hours a day on Boulder Highway's Arizona Charlie's. Many places retain the 'Midnight Menu' for late revellers and gamblers where filling breakfasts and sandwiches can be had for a pittance after midnight.

Obviously, space dictates that I cannot list all the restaurants on offer, so I have provided information on what are considered to be the finest restaurants in each category. They're all popular, though, so book a table in advance. I have also included a good smattering of extremely well-priced cafés – some of which are open 24/7 – and plenty of non-resort restaurants with enduring appeal.

We have included as many websites as possible. In some cases, you can go direct to the restaurants web page. In other cases, it is quicker to go to the main resort-hotel page, then select the dining option, rather than key in a long URL.

Price codes

Per head for a three-course meal and one drink:

$ = under $40
$$ = up to $80
$$$ = $81 and over!

Aureole at the Mandalay Bay

American restaurants

Aureole

Mandalay Bay, 702 632 7777, mandalaybay.com/dining/aureole.aspx
Charlie Palmer, famous for his New York Aureole, has been enticed to open a second outlet, this time in Las Vegas. The New York restaurant is consistently voted number one for American cuisine by the Zagat survey and Charlie was awarded Best Chef by the James Beard Foundation in 1997. For this restaurant, a four-storey wine tower has been created and wine stewards strap on harnesses to be hoisted up the tower to make their wine selections. Open daily 5.30–10.30pm. **$$$**

Bradley Ogden

Caesars Palace, 702 731 7110, caesarspalace.com
Putting farm-fresh American cuisine at the top of the agenda has earned famous Bay Area chef Bradley Ogden a clutch of awards. Having started at San Francisco's renowned Campton Place Hotel, Ogden opened his first restaurant outside California at Caesars and immediately picked up Best New Restaurant 2004 by the James Beard Foundation. An incredible line-up of tastes and textures is included in dishes such as Maytag blue cheese soufflé with candy-stripe beets and chilled asparagus soup and Mascarpone lemon cream for starters. Main courses include: steamed Alaskan halibut with Maine lobster, basil vinaigrette, asparagus and parsley froth; Columbia river wild king salmon with sautéed shrimp, black olive gnocchi, arugula, California morels and oregano croutons; and slow-roasted Muscovy duck with endive leaves, purple artichokes, polenta and rhubarb. Open daily 5–11pm. **$$–$$$**

Buccaneer Bay Club

Treasure Island, 702 894 7111, treasureisland.com
One of the best American restaurants in town with a series of nooks and crannies that give a bird's-eye view of the spectacular pirate show outside. You can tuck into lobster bisque, salads, duckling and shrimp. Specials are offered every night and the chef is happy to prepare special orders. The soufflés are the signature desserts of the restaurant. Open daily 5–10.30pm. **$$$**

BRITTIP

For a bird's eye view of the pirate ship action outside Treasure Island, book yourself a window seat at the Buccaneer Bay Club.

Cheesecake Factory

Forum Shops at Caesars Palace, 702 792 6888, thecheesecakefactory.com
Famous for its extensive menu – there are more than 250 items plus nearly 30 specials – this is more of a place to people-watch than expect gourmet cuisine, yet the food is delicious too. Portions are huge, but please find some room at the end for a serving of their excellent, and imaginative, desserts. Open 11.15am–11:30pm (until 12.30am Fri and Sat) Sunday brunch 10.15am–2:00pm. **$**

FIX

Bellagio, 702 693 7111, fixlasvegas.com
The menu, designed to offer the best in classic American fare, focuses on simply prepared, top-quality fish, meat and poultry, cooked to order on a wood-burning grill. The longer-than-usual opening hours allow for both pre-show and après-show dining, while the bar and lounge offer a full menu of speciality cocktails. Open Sun–Thurs 5pm–midnight; Fri and Sat 5pm–2am. **$-$$**

Nero's

Caesars Palace, 702 731 7731, caesarspalace.com
Nero's specialises in dry-aged prime beef, tender chops and fresh seafood – all artistically presented. House specials include grilled lamb chops on crispy polenta with baby greens and garlic; grilled swordfish with sweet potato purée, herb-roasted onion, pea shoots and lemon aioli; and halibut pan-roasted in lobster oil with braised baby artichokes, steamed clams and saffron couscous. The menu changes according to the season but favourites include crab cakes; carpaccio of beef with shaved Parmesan; and salad of frisée, fennel and roasted red peppers and truffle aioli. Open daily 5.30–11pm. $$$

Pegasus

Alexis Park Hotel, 375 East Harmon, 702 796 3353
Pegasus offers gourmet dining in a classy environment. Dishes include freshly made pastas, beef, pork and fresh fish that come with delicious vegetables. Open daily 6–11pm. **$$**

Tableau

Wynn Las Vegas, 702 248 3463, wynnlasvegas.com
The hotel's signature restaurant, open for breakfast, lunch and dinner, is to be found in a light, airy atrium setting with poolside views. Chef Mark LoRusso, who perfected his culinary skills first at Aqua in San Francisco, then at the Bellagio version, showcases American ingredients prepared with French flair. Breakfast 8–10.30am; lunch 11.30am–2.30pm; dinner 5.30–10.30pm. **$**

Tommy Rocker's Cantina & Grill

4275 Industrial Road, 702 261 6688, tommyrocker.com
It's unlikely you'll be visiting Tommy's unless you're coming here for the music, as it's a little off the beaten track. What will surprise you though, will be the half-decent, well-priced, largely American grub that allows you to enjoy the live music and DJ well into the night. **$**

Asian restaurants

Ah-Sin

Paris Las Vegas, 702 739 4111, parislasvegas.com
A new type of dining experience with Japanese sushi, Chinese noodle specialities and a host of favourite cuisines from the Pacific Rim, all prepared by chefs at stations around the dining room. Service begins with a ritual hand-washing ceremony that includes the pouring of pure water scented with jasmine oil. Open Wed–Sun 5.30–10.30pm. **$$**

BRITTIP

Ah-Sin is right next door to the Risqué ultra-lounge (see page 143) where you can relax on the plush couches while tucking into dessert.

Classic American fare at FIX

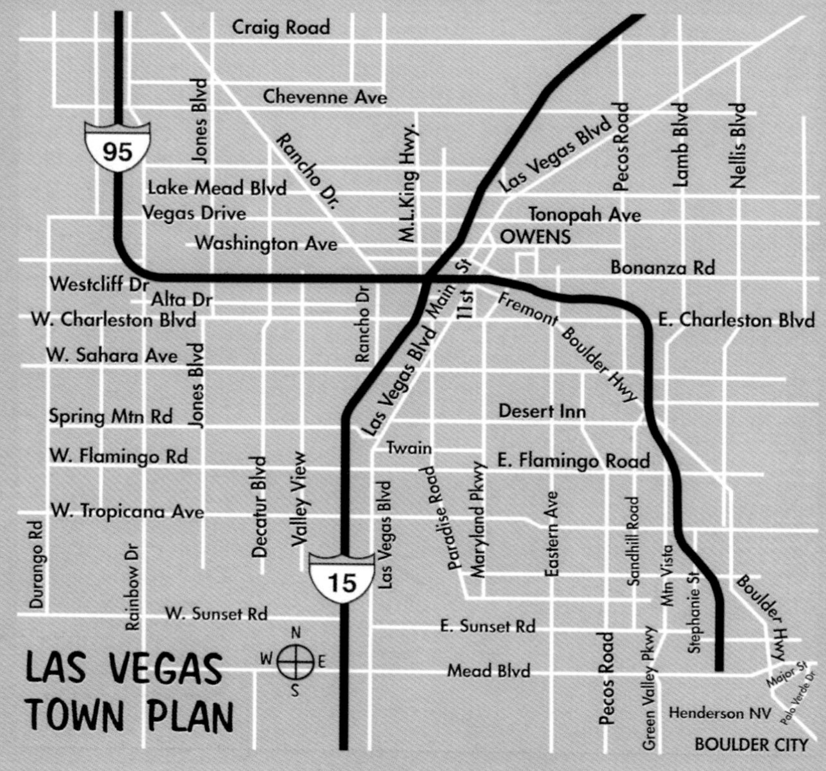

Asia

Miracle Mile Shops, 702 794 2582, asianightclublv.com
The newest eatery on the scene, this part-nightclub, part-restaurant offers fusion oriental food for the Hollywood Hip. **$$**

Bamboo Garden

4850 West Flamingo Road, 702 871 3262
Popular spot for locals who love the delicious range of unusual dishes at the very reasonable prices. It looks modest enough, but the friendly staff provide excellent service and dishes include: cream of seafood soup; Mongolian lamb; firecracker beef; emerald shrimp; and Peking duck with Mandarin pancakes. Open Mon–Sat 11am–10.30pm. **$$**

Chin Chin

New York-New York Hotel, 702 740 6969, nynyhotelcasino.com/restaurants
In a restoration of New York Chinatown, you'll find everything from the Pacific Rim to Szechuan and Cantonese food. Open daily 11am–11pm. **$$**

Chinois

Forum Shops at Caesars Palace, 702 369 6300, wolfgangpuck.com
Celebrity chef Wolfgang Puck's second outlet in Las Vegas provides dream cuisine from China, Japan and Thailand. The menu features sushi, sashimi, wok-fried and grilled seafood, poultry and meats with fresh, high-quality ingredients and homemade desserts. You have a choice of settings, too – you can dine at the sushi bar, in the 'outdoor' café or the dramatic dining room. Open 11am–midnight. **$$**

HoWan

3145 Las Vegas Boulevard South, 702 733 4547
Beautifully decorated with tapestries and antiques, and a fish and seafood tank, while the costumed staff provide an excellent service. Many Asians eat here and enjoy tucking into house specialities

Best views in the valley

Eiffel Tower Restaurant: Paris Resort (page 110).

Firenze Lobby Lounge: Ritz-Carlton Lake Las Vegas (page 124).

Japengo: Hyatt Regency Lake Las Vegas (page 118).

Kiefer's Atop the Carriage House: East Harmon Avenue (page 107).

Medici Café and Terrace: Ritz-Carlton Lake Las Vegas (page 55).

Mix: Mandalay Bay (page 111).

Mon Ami Gabi: Paris Resort (page 113).

PF Chang's China Bistro: Planet Hollywood (page 126).

Tao: The Venetian (page 105).

The Top of the World: Stratosphere (page 122).

VooDoo Café: Rio All-Suite Hotel (page 107)

such as minced squab and crackling shrimp, steamed fish, lobster and seaweed with cabbage and bean curd soup. Open daily 6–11pm. **$$$**

Pearl

MGM Grand, freephone 1-877 793 7111, mgmgrand.com/dining
A stylish, upmarket Chinese-meets-Western restaurant based on Cantonese and Shanghai specialities. The largely seafood dishes include both Maine and Australian lobsters, shark fin and lobster spring rolls and Sian bouillabaisse. An added bonus is the trolley with a range of fine Chinese teas – for a good pick-me-up, try green tea. Open 5.30–10pm. **$$–$$$**

Shanghai Lilly

Mandalay Bay, 702 632 7409, mandalaybay.com/dining/shanghaililly.aspx
Classic Cantonese and Szechuan dishes using only the finest ingredients make this one of the best places to enjoy Eastern cuisine. Open 5.30–11pm. **$$$**

Tao

Grand Canal Shoppes at the Venetian, 702 388 8338, http://venetian.com/tao.aspx
The amazing $20m complex of nightclub and restaurant specialises in Hong Kong Chinese, Japanese and Thai cuisines. Chef Sam Hazen's creations include everything from Kobe beef to traditional Peking Duck, all prepared by master chefs from across Asia. How popular is it? It is by far the most successful privately owned restaurant in the USA, having twice the revenue of the second ranked (Tavern on the Green in New York City) Open Sun–Thurs 5pm–12am, Fri and Sat 5pm–1am. **$$–$$$**

Thai Spice

4433 West Flamingo Road, 702 362 5308
A friendly restaurant that attracts a lot of the local Asians and tourists alike. Tuck into traditional Thai food from fish cakes to noodles, Thai-spiced beef and pepper-garlic pork. Open Mon–Thurs 11.30am–10pm, Fri and Sat until 11pm. **$**

Todai Seafood & Sushi Buffet

Miracle Mile Shops, 702 892 0021, todai.com
More than a sushi buffet, Todai offers Japanese, Chinese and Korean cuisine alongside salads, rice and noodle dishes and, of course, a full range of fresh sushi. Open daily for lunch 11.30am–2.30pm and for dinner 5.30–9.30pm. **$–$$**

Tsunami

Venetian, 702 414 1980, venetian.com/tsunami.aspx
Taking its inspiration from Pan-Asian flavours, Tsunami offers delicious food from Japan, China, Korea, Thailand and Guam alongside sushi, makimono and nigiri. Open 11am–11pm weekdays and 11–12am weekends. **$**

Bistros and brasseries

Bouchon

The Venetian, 702 414 6200, venetian.com/bouchon.aspx
World-renowned chef Thomas Keller, named America's best chef by *Time* magazine, is the sole recipient of consecutive Best Chef awards from the prestigious James Beard Foundation. It

Pearl at the MGM Grand

opened in 2004 in the beautiful Venezia Tower and is one of the finest restaurants in Las Vegas.

An extensive selection of bistro classics is added to by raw seafood and seafood platters, including lobster, oyster, shrimp, mussels and crab. Fabulous main courses include: roasted leg of lamb with flageolets beans in a thyme jus; pan-seared prime flatiron served with maître d'hôtel butter and French fries; and roasted chicken with garlic-braised Swiss chard and pommes sarladaises. Salivating stuff! Open for breakfast 7–10.30am; Sat and Sun for lunch 11.30–2.30; 5–11pm for dinner. **$$–$$$**

Daniel Boulud Brasserie

Wynn Las Vegas, 702 248 3463, wynnlasvegas

World-renowned chef Daniel Boulud, who for many years was the chef at New York's Le Cirque before opening his own restaurant, Daniel, in New York, teamed up with fellow award-winning chef Philippe Rispoli to create a classic French brasserie at Wynn's super resort. The laid-back environment – where you can choose to dine indoors or by the lake outside – is the perfect place to enjoy everything from typical bistro fare to caviar and champagne. Signature dishes include: beefsteak tomato with fromage; blanc tarte pissaladière with onion, anchovies and black olives; crispy pork belly with lentils and frisée; and spicy mustard fricassee of Dover sole amandine. Open 5.30–12.30pm. **$$**

Pinot Brasserie

Venetian, 702 414 4100, venetian.com/pinot.aspx

Famous Los Angeles chef Joachim Splichal brings his Pinot concept to the city. The food is delightful and service is spot on. It looks out over the Venetian gardens and the Venezia Tower's pool area, giving the lunch crowd a lovely view. Open daily 11am–11pm. **$$**

The dining room at Sensi

Most romantic spots

Alex: Wynn Las Vegas (page 108).

Alizé: The Palms (page 109).

André's: South 6th Street (page 109).

Daniel Boulud Brasserie: Bellagio (page 106).

Eiffel Tower Restaurant: Paris Resort (page 110).

Gaylord Indian Restaurant: Rio All-Suite Hotel (page 112).

Jasmine: Bellagio (page 108).

Le Cirque: Bellagio (page 109).

Ortanique: Paris Resort (page 40).

Peppermill Café and Lounge: The Strip (page 125).

Picasso: Bellagio (page 116).

Postrio

Venetian, 702 414 4100, venetian.com/postrio.aspx

Based on Wolfgang Puck's San Francisco bistro, which serves up American food with Asian and Mediterranean influences, the menu is changed seasonally. House specialities include: gourmet pizzas; foie gras terrine with fennel, haricots verts and walnut toast; grilled quail with spinach and soft egg ravioli; and Chinese-style duck with mango sauce and crispy fried scallion. By the way, Postrio has been named one of the 10 best restaurants in the world by *Hotels* magazine. Open daily 11am–11pm. **$$**

BRITTIP

If you love people-watching, then make the most of Postrio's patio dining area, which gives a great view of the beautiful people who flock to the Venetian.

Sensi

Bellagio, 702 693 7111, bellagio.com

With carved stone, earthy hues, mirrored chrome and waterfalls, Sensi offers a delightful environment in which to discover delicious dishes based around Italian, Asian, seafood and grilled recipes all using quality fresh ingredients. Open daily for lunch 11am–2.30pm and dinner 5.30–10.30pm. **$$**

Cajun/Creole restaurants

Big Mama's Soul Food Kitchen

Utopia Center, opposite Rue de Monte Carlo, 702 597 1616, bigmamas-ribshack.com
Good, honest food at rock-bottom prices. Known for its gumbo, fried catfish and barbecue dishes. For a slice of real New Orleans food, try a piece of pecan pie. Open Mon–Thurs 11am–9pm, Fri and Sat 11am–10pm, Sun 12 noon–8pm. **$**

Big Al's Oyster Bar

New Orleans Hotel, 702 365 7111
Get a flavour of New Orleans-style dining with this Cajun/Creole restaurant with a Bayou oyster bar. Opt for oysters and clams on the half-shell with various oyster shooters from the bar, or choose from a range of southern specials including gumbo, Jambalaya pasta, steamed clams, bouillabaisse and Voodoo mussels. Open Sun–Thurs 11am–midnight, Fri and Sat until 1am. **$**

Emeril's New Orleans Fish House

MGM Grand, 702 891 1111, mgmgrand.com/dining
A real must-visit restaurant if you want to experience celebrity chef Emeril Lagasse's New Orleans blend of modern Cajun/ Creole cooking. Tuck into seared Atlantic salmon served on a wild mushroom potato hash with herb meat juices and a spicy onion crust or grilled fillet of beef with Creole oyster dressing and homemade hollandaise sauce. Open 11.30am–2.30pm and 6pm–11pm. Next door is the seafood bar, a walk-up style of eatery featuring fresh shellfish and seafood specials. **$$**

A brilliant eating experience at Rumjungle

Kiefer's Atop the Carriage House

105 East Harmon Avenue, 702 739 8000
This place has one of the best views of the Strip, which you can look down at while you dine on delicious Creole food from Louisiana at reasonable prices. Open 7–10am and 5–11pm and until midnight Fri–Sun. **$$**

VooDoo Café

Rio All-Suite Hotel, 702 252 7777, riolasvegas.com
Superb Cajun and Creole dishes in an elegant New Orleans setting, the view of the Strip is one of the best in town. Specials include: blue water seafood platter for starters; the ménage à trois of filet mignon, lobster and prawns for entrée; and bananas foster for dessert. Open 5–11pm. **$$**

Caribbean restaurants

Rumjungle

Mandalay Bay, 702 632 7777, mandalaybay.com/dining/rumjungle.aspx
Here food and drink become the artistic environment with a dancing firewall of food that turns into a soothing wall of water, and volcanic mountains of rum and spirits that rise up behind the illuminated bar. The menu is tropically inspired and many of the dishes are cooked over a giant open fire pit. After your meal you can dance to Latin, Caribbean and African beats until the wee small hours. Open 5pm–4am. **$$**

BRITTIP

Rumjungle is one of the best all-rounders in town. It serves superb food, is famous for its wide selection of rums, has great live music and a fabulous atmosphere that attracts the hip and the celebs alike.

Caviar restaurants

The Petrossian Bar

Bellagio, 702 693 7111, bellagio.com
A lavish bar next to the resort's dramatic entrance with its walkway overhung by beautiful cypress trees. It specialises in everything from afternoon tea to caviar, champagne and smoked salmon. Open 12pm–12am and until 1am weekends. **$$$**

Red Square

Mandalay Bay, 702 632 7777, mandalaybay.com/dining/redsquare.aspx
Check out the extensive caviar selection or try out the menu of updated Russian classics at the frozen ice bar, where you can choose from a selection of more than 100 frozen vodkas and infusions, Martinis and Russian-inspired cocktails. Open 5.30–12am. **$$$**

Chinese restaurants

Empress Court

Caesars Palace, 702 731 7110, caesarspalaace.com
Empress Court has a watery theme with a large, salt-water aquarium at the entrance to reflect the waters of its cuisine – the more unusual Hong Kong dishes. Chinese furniture such as chow tables, tea tables and altar tables in ebonised wood or aged silver leaf add an authentic feel to the room. Open Thurs–Mon 6–11pm. **$$$**

Jasmine

Bellagio, 702 693 7111, bellagio.com
Chef Philip Lo, an originator of nouvelle Hong Kong cuisine, creates contemporary and classic Cantonese, Szechuan and Hunan dishes in a delightfully romantic setting overlooking the Bellagio lake and gardens. Dishes include: Maine lobster dumplings with ginger sauce; minced squab in lettuce petals; crystal Florida stone crab claws; garlic beef tenderloin; and imperial Peking duck. Open 5.30–10pm. **$$**

Lillie Langtry's

Golden Nugget Hotel, 129 Fremont Street, 702 386 8831
Provides downtown gamblers with delicious and exotic Cantonese dishes in a brightly decorated setting with great service. The Great Combination Plate is a favourite starter, before moving on to black pepper steak, stir-fried shrimp or lemon chicken. Open 5–10.30pm. **$**

Stylish dining at Jasmine

The Mandarin Court

1510 East Flamingo Road, 702 737 1234
Designed as a replica of a Peking palace, this is something of a landmark locally. However, it is an excellent place to go to get far from the madding crowds and enjoy delicious traditional Chinese food at good prices. It is also notable for serving its trademark sweet and sour dishes until 4am! **$$**

Wing Lei

Wynn Las Vegas, 702 248 3463, wynnlasvegas.com
This Asian delight is an elegantly casual Chinese restaurant with a dramatic yet sumptuous décor that owes much to the colour schemes of French-influenced Shanghai. Executive chef Richard Chen oversees the masterful mix of refined Cantonese, Shanghai and Szechwan cooking styles that feature: wok-fried Szechuan Kobe beef; Peking duck for two (served tableside); Mongolian lamb; and beef chow fun and abalone fried rice. Open 5.30–10.30pm. **$$**

English restaurant

Sir Galahad's

Excalibur, 702 597 7777, excalibur.com/restaurants
This place serves up traditional English roast beef and Yorkshire pudding in its English castle setting with staff in dress reminiscent of King Arthur's day. The house speciality is basically prime rib, but you'll also find chicken and fish on the menu if you don't fancy tucking into the main meal, which is served from a large, copper cart. Open Sun–Thurs 5–10pm and Fri, Sat and holidays 5pm–midnight. **$**

French restaurants

Alex

Wynn Las Vegas, 702 248 3463, wynnlasvegas.com
Chef Alessandro Stratta, winner of the James Beard Foundation's Best American Chef, South-west, brings a taste of the French Riviera to the desert oasis of Las Vegas. And what better setting in which to tuck into roasted monkfish or Tuscan-style pork with stewed tomatoes than in the outdoor seating area? If you find it hard to make a choice from the wide-ranging choices, then go for the 'tasting menu' and tuck into tiny courses of carpaccio of red

prawns, sea scallops with white asparagus and foie gras ravioli. Open Tues–Sun 6–10pm. **$$$**

Alizé

The Palms, 702 951 7000, andrelv.com
Las Vegas' very own celebrity chef and restaurateur, André Rochat, who also owns his own restaurant called André, has created a gourmet dining experience in the trendy Palms hotel. Winner of the Best Gourmet Restaurant in the *Las Vegas Review Journal*'s 2003 Best of Las Vegas awards, delicious entrées include sautéed Muscovy duck breast and market-fresh seafood. This is a top-of-the-pile dining experience, which includes the classic French sorbet between courses for cleansing the palate, a cheese trolley and an extensive wine list. Open Sun–Thurs 5.30–10pm, Fri and Sat until 10.30pm. **$$–$$$**

André's

401 South 6th Street, 702 385 5016, andrelv.com/original
André's has been serving up delicious gourmet food to locals and tourists alike for nearly two decades. Just one block off the Strip, the restaurant is housed in one of the early homes of Las Vegas – dating all the way back to 1930! The menu changes all the time, but mouthwatering offerings include: chartreuse of Muscovy duck, stewed in Merlot with portabella mushrooms and spring vegetables; sautéed prime fillet of beef with green peppercorn and cognac cream sauce; baked zucchini, gratin dauphinoise and baby carrots anglaise; and Maine lobster. Open nightly 6–10pm. **$$$**

Aristocrat

850 South Rancho Drive, 702 870 1977
Another well-established and fine French restaurant that is filled with locals and tourists. Tuck into classics such as: mussels in white wine; beef Wellington; filet mignon; or any of the fresh fish specialities that are changed daily. Open for lunch weekdays 11.30am–2pm and dinner daily 6–11pm. **$$**

Le Cirque

Bellagio, 702 693 7111, www,.bellagio.com
Elizabeth Blau, who has been with the Maccioni family's famous flagship restaurant in New York for more than a decade, re-creates its gourmet French dishes with great aplomb, while the views of the Bellagio's famous fountains lend it more than a touch of elegance. Open 5.30–10pm. **$$$**

Celebrity chef restaurants

Aureole: Charlie Palmer (page 102).

Border Grill: Mary Sue Milliken and Susan Feniger aka Too Hot Tamales (page 109).

Bradley Ogden: Bradley Ogden (page 102).

Daniel Boulud: Daniel Boulud (page 106).

Delmonico Steakhouse: Emeril Lagassé (page 119).

Drai's: Victor Drai (page 116).

Emeril's New Orleans Fish House: Emeril Lagassé (page 107).

Fleur De Lys: Hubert Keller (page 110).

Guy Savoy: Guy Savoy (page 111).

Il Fornaio: Luigi Bomparolo (page 114).

Joël Robuchon: Joël Robuchon (page 110).

Le Cirque: Elizabeth Blau (page 109).

Mesa Grill: Bobby Flay (page 122).

Michael Mina: Michael Mina (page 120).

Mix: Alain Ducasse (page 111).

Olives: Todd English (page 116).

Picasso: Julian Serrano (page 116).

Pinot: Joachim Splichal (page 106).

rm Seafood: Rick Moonen (page 121).

Simon Kitchen: Kerry Simon and Elizabeth Blau (page 129).

Trattoria del Lupo, **Chinois**, **Postrio**, **Spago** and **Wolfgang Puck's Café**: Wolfgang Puck (pages 115, 104, 106, 112, 126).

Alizé is André Rochat's restaurant

Eiffel Tower Restaurant

Paris, 702 739 4111, www,parislasvegas.com
The signature dining experience of the new resort hotel is set 17 storeys up on the Eiffel Tower replica and has stunning views of Las Vegas' glittering golden mile. The softly lit ambience includes a romantic piano bar where you can enjoy a glass of champagne or an entire meal while absorbing the views, or try the full gourmet experience in the restaurant. Dinner Sun–Thurs 5.30– 10.30pm, Fri and Sat 5.30–11pm. Bar and lounge menu 5.30–11pm. Light meals 11am–3pm. **$$$**

Fleur de Lys

Mandalay Bay, 702 632 7777, mandalaybay.com/dining/fleurdelys.aspx
A beautiful offering at the Mandalay Bay gives Hubert Keller the chance to show off his signature French cuisine in Las Vegas. Starters include: ocean baeckeoffe with Maine lobster; crab cake; lobster bisque; leeks and wild mushrooms; and smoked salmon ravioli with guacamole. Mains include: slow-roasted Alaskan king salmon with hazelnut crust, leeks, duck comfit and black Perigord truffle vinaigrette; roasted sea bass with chicken jus flavoured with passion fruit; and filet mignon with braised oxtail tortellini. Open 5.30–10.30pm. **$$**

Fleur de Lys at the Mandalay Bay

Frogeez on 4th

Bank of America Center, 300 S 4th St, 702 380 1122
André Rochat and Mary Jane Jarvis of André's fame provide another fine dining experience downtown. The menu and wine lists are short but sweet, while the atmosphere – particularly with live music at weekends – is always good and the bar is jumping on a Friday night. Open 11am–11pm. **$**

Joël Robuchon at the Mansion

MGM Grand, 702 891 7777, mgmgrand.com/dining
France's Chef of the Century, and the first chef to win three consecutive Michelin stars, has been lured to the MGM Grand, providing a counter service setting in which you can watch your dinner being prepared before your eyes. Tapas and entrées include: fresh tomato and king crab; asparagus with Oscetra caviar; fresh scallop with lemon and seaweed butter; pan-fried sea bass with lemongrass foam and stewed baby leeks; and sautéed veal chop with vegetable taglierini flavoured with pesto. Open 5.30–10.30pm. **$$**

Les Artistes Steakhouse

Paris, 702 739 4111, parislasvegas.com
A wide choice of gourmet dishes include the signature Scottish pheasant brushed with tarragon mustard sauce and served with red-bliss potatoes; and lime oil-brushed swordfish with basil garlic mashed potatoes. Desserts include classics such as crème brûlée and raspberry clafoutis. Open 5.30–10.30pm. **$$$**

Mon Ami Gabi

Paris, 702 946 7000, parislasvegas.com
A Parisian-style café set in the Louvre façade of the Paris hotel. It is on the Strip and you can even opt to sit outside. Open 11.30am–3pm and 5–11pm Sun–Thurs, 5–midnight Fri and Sat. **$$**

BRITTIP

As in every other American city, top-notch, gourmet restaurants have prices to match, particularly with bottles of wine that can easily cost $200 each, so take care when making your choice!

Pamplemousse

400 East Sahara Avenue, 702 733 2066, pamplemousserestaurant.com
Like all the top French restaurants, this small but elegant establishment is pricey – but it's worth it. House specialities include: roast duckling in red wine and banana rum sauce; and veal medallions in cream sauce; plus a huge selection of fresh seafood according to the season from mussels to monkfish and salmon. Open daily 6–11pm. **$$$**

Restaurant Guy Savoy

Caesars Palace, 702 731 7110, caesarspalace.com
The famous French restaurateur, winner of three Michelin stars and Chef of the Year, France in 2002, has opened his first restaurant in America in Caesars Palace. Run by his son and protégé Franck Savoy, the new restaurant takes pride of place on the second floor of the hotel's Augustus Tower, offering delightful views of the Roman Plaza. **$$–$$$**

Fusion restaurants

Fiore Rotisserie and Grille

Rio All-Suite Hotel, 702 252 7702
One of the best restaurants in town, with great food, service and prices that won't break the bank! It has an eclectic range of dishes from chilled, roasted aubergine with balsamic vinaigrette and pesto, to spaghettini with pastrami duck breast and cabbage for starters, and Black Forest ham with shiitake mushrooms to Gulf red snapper sautéed with fennel and mushrooms. Cigar lovers will be pleased to note that the restaurant has an excellent selection and a special cigar patio where you can imbibe coffee and cognac. Open for lunch weekdays only 11.30am–2pm and dinner nightly 6pm–midnight. **$$**

Fusia

Luxor, 702 262 4000, luxor.com/dining
A delightful blend of tastes and textures is served in a series of generously portioned appetisers, such as: satay beef skewers served in spiced tempura rings, drizzled with sweet cilantro sauce and spiked with a zesty mango papaya salsa; spiced Indonesian crab stack; and Fusia Nigiri-style sushi. Open daily 6–11pm. **$**

Little Buddha

The Palms, 702 942 7778, littlebuddhalasvegas.com
Based on the award-winning Buddha Bar and restaurant in Paris, this stylish eatery serves up both Pacific Rim and Chinese dishes with a French twist. There are three dining areas, all decorated in an opulent East-meets-West style, plus a sushi bar. Open Sun–Thurs 5.30–10.45pm, Fri and Sat until midnight. **$**

BRITTIP
Little Buddha offers poolside dining during the summer season and is one of the best places in town to spot a celeb or two.

Mayflower Cuisinier

Sahara Pavilion, 4750 West Sahara at Decatur Boulevard, 702 870 8432, mayflowercuisinier.com
One of the most highly rated restaurants in Las Vegas and consistently appears in the Zagat Top 10. Here you will find Mongolian/Chinese cuisine served Californian style in a casual, but elegant environment. Book ahead for a table at weekends. Open weekdays only 11am–3pm, Mon-Sat 5–10pm. **$$**

Mix

Mandalay Bay, 702 632 7777, mandalaybay.com/dining/mix.aspx
With its cutting-edge interior and fab views of the Strip, Mix is the perfect place to enjoy wonderful fusion cuisine. Think roasted Maine lobster 'au curry' with coconut basmati rice; bison tenderloin with sauce au poivre; seared rare tuna with prosciutto shavings, and Colorado rack of lamb with Mediterranean condiment. Open 6–11pm. **$$**

Superb fusion food at Fusia

Nobhill

MGM Grand, freephone 1-877-793 7111, mgmgrand.com/dining
Renowned chef Michael Mina, who created Aqua in San Francisco and at the Bellagio, has created this popular restaurant to reflect the stylish San Francisco neighbourhood scene. Most of the American-Asian fusion dishes use ingredients from the Bay area around the city and include: beef Wellington; rich lobster pot; fish carpaccio; and roasted rack of Hop Sing market pork. Open 5.30–10.30pm. $$-$$$

BRITTIP

Men are advised to wear a jacket for dining at the sophisticated Nobhill restaurant – named after the famous Nob Hill in San Francisco.

Spago

Forum Shops at Caesars Palace, 702 369 6300
This is one of celebrity chef Wolfgang Puck's famous outlets in Las Vegas and, as with all his other establishments in Los Angeles, is a popular place for celebs and local movers and shakers. You'll find everything from pastas to salads and seafood. Open for dinner Mon–Thurs 6–10pm and until 10.30pm Fri–Sun. The separate café is open for lunch Sun–Thurs 11am–11pm, Fri and Sat until 1am. **$$**

Roy's

620 East Flamingo Road, 702 691 2053
Fusion is the name of the game in a restaurant that serves up European-style dishes with an Asian and Pacific flavour. Open Sun–Thurs 5.30–10pm, Fri and Sat 5.30–11pm. **$**

Fine Indian food at the Gaylord

Hawaiian restaurants

808

Caesars Palace, 702 731 7731, caesarspalace.com
Chef Jean-Marie Josselin, owner of the award-winning A Pacific Café restaurant in Hawaii, brings a whole new combination of flavours to titillate the palate of Las Vegas natives and visitors alike. Signature dishes are based on the freshest seafood available and organic Hawaiian produce fused with Thai, Japanese, Chinese, Italian, Indian and French flavours to create a unique dining experience. Chef de Cuisine Wesley Coffel prepares the lamb, beef, chicken and veal dishes. Open Wed–Sun 5–11pm. **$$$**

Kahunaville

Treasure Island, 702 894 7111, kahunaville.com
A tropical restaurant setting complete with tiki torches and plants, this features Hawaiian dishes such as teriyaki ginger steak, Hawaiian pork tenderloin and coconut shrimp. It also doubles as a supper club with live entertainment, and there is a great choice of margaritas, coladas, beers and wine. Open daily at 8am; lunch 11am–4pm, dinner 4–10pm. The bar is open 11am–3am. **$**

Indian restaurant

Gaylord Indian Restaurant

Rio All-Suite Hotel, 702 777 7777, riolasvegas.com
A romantic setting with authentic Indian artefacts in which to enjoy tandoori and Mughlai-style dishes from the creators of the award-winning San Francisco restaurant. One of its main features is the Combination Dinners, in which you can choose different starters and entrées for an all-inclusive price. Lunch buffet Fri–Sun11.30am–2.30pm; dinner every day 5–11pm. **$**

Irish restaurant

Nine Fine Irishmen

New York-New York, 702 740 6969, ninefineirishmen.com
In a town where everything is copied it was only a matter of time before an 'authentic' Irish pub with drink, food, music and entertainment opened its doors. And where better than the New York-New York

Restaurants with live music

Crazy Armadillo: Stratosphere (see page 117).

Drai's: Barbary Coast (see page 116).

Eiffel Tower Restaurant: Paris Resort (see page 110).

Frogeez on 4th: Downtown (see page 110).

House of Blues: Mandalay Bay (see page 152).

Jazzed Café: University District (see page 126).

Kahunaville: Treasure Island (see page 112).

Harley Davidson Café: Southern end of Strip (see page 123).

N9ne Steakhouse: The Palms (see page 120).

Ortanique: Paris Resort (see page 40).

Rumjumgle: Mandalay Bay (see page 107).

Tommy Rocker's Bar & Grill: 4275 Industrial Road (see page 152).

VooDoo Café: Rio All-Suite Hotel (see page 107).

hotel, evocative of the city that is home to so many Irish-Americans. Dishes have been created by nine of Ireland's top chefs, though the name is based on the lives of nine Irishmen from the 19th century. Open from lunch 11am–3am. The bar is open Sun–Thurs 11am–3am, Fri and Sat 24 hours. **$–$$**

Italian restaurants

Al Dente

Bally's Hotel on the Strip, 702 739 4656
Contemporary Italian cuisine served in a bright setting with plenty of favourites from bruschetta to gourmet pizzas, antipasti, spinach and chicken dishes. Open Tues–Sat, 6–11pm. **$$**

Antonio's

Rio All-Suite Hotel, 3700 West Flamingo Road, 702 252 7777, riolasvegas.com
This, like all the Rio restaurants, makes an excellent choice, this time for those in search of a delicious Italian meal. Dishes include osso bucco, pork loin, lobster and chicken. Open nightly 5–10.30pm. **$$**

B&B Ristorante

Grand Canal Shoppes, The Venetian, 702 266 9977, thegrandcanalshoppes.com
Celebrity chef Mario Batali, winner of the 2005 James Beard Foundation Chef of the Year Award and the genius behind several intensely popular New York restaurants brings his genius to the Venetian along with friend and expert wine maker Joseph Bastianich. It is wine and Italian cooking that 'captures the soul of an Italian grandmother dancing the tango with pop rock hipsters'. Open daily 5–11pm. **$$$**

Battista's Hole in the Wall

4041 Audrie Lane, 702 732 1424, battistaslasvegas.com
Classic Italian fare served in a fun and friendly atmosphere that makes it a great eating place for locals and tourists alike. Open for dinner only 6–11pm. **$$**

Bartolotta Ristorante di Mare

Wynn Las Vegas, 702 248 3463
Paul Bartolotta, winner of the James Beard Foundation's Best American Chef Midwest award, has fresh seafood flown in daily from fish markets in Europe for his casual yet vibrant restaurant that offers outdoor seating near the lake and gardens. Alongside the signature seafood dishes are classic Italian specialities such as homemade pasta dishes. Open 11.30am–2.30pm and 5.30–10.30pm. $$

Bertolini's

Forum Shops at Caesars Palace, 702 735 4663, bertolinis.net
A sidewalk-style café inside the exquisite Forum Shops in the piazza surrounding the Fountain of Gods. Outside you can watch the world go by, but inside there are quieter seats to be found. Pastas and rice dishes, pizzas, soups and salads, chicken and fish. Open Sun–Thur 11am–11pm, Fri and Sat 11am–12am. **$**

Bartolotta serves great seafood

Onda's Wine Lounge

Casa Nicola

Las Vegas Hilton, 702 732 5664, lvhilton.com/dining
Specialises in fine northern Italian specialities in a beautiful setting. The exhibition kitchen gives customers the chance to watch chefs preparing the fresh pastas, pastries and sauces. Open 5.30–11pm. **$$**

California Pizza Kitchen

3400 Las Vegas Boulevard South, 702 791 7111, cpk.com
Part of a growing national chain that highlight 'California Fusion' food, which serves mostly delicious pizzas with mouthwatering selections of fresh ingredients. Think Chocolate Pizza and Thai Chicken Pizza. Open Mon–Thurs 11am–midnight, Fri and Sat until 2am. **$**

Canaletto

Grand Canal Shoppes, the Venetian, 702 414 4100, thegrandcanalshoppes.com
Based on a concept by Il Fornaio's Larry Mindel, classics include homemade ravioli filled with fresh Maine lobster in a lobster cream sauce topped with shrimp. Open Sun–Thurs 11.30am–11pm, Fri and Sat until midnight. **$$**

Chicago Joe's

820 South 4th Street, 702 382 5637, chicagojoesrestaurant.com
Chicago Joe's is an ageless Las Vegas standard and is famous for its Italian sauces. Try the cream garlic dressing with one of the many delicious salads, Mexican Gulf shrimp and Maine lobster. Open Tues–Fri 11am–10pm, Sat 5–10pm. **$**

Francesco's

Treasure Island, 702 894 7111, treasureisland.com
Filled with artwork by celebrities including crooner Tony Bennett, the menu here includes fresh pastas, antipasti, Mediterranean-style seafood and signature freshly baked breads. Open daily 5.00–10.30pm. **$**

Il Fornaio

New York-New York, 702 740 6969, ilfornaio.com
Superb re-creation of an Italian restaurant from New York's Little Italy neighbourhood. Here you'll find classic Italian cuisine and signature breads, rolls and pastries from the in-house bakery. By the way, most of the waiters migrated to Las Vegas from New York when the hotel opened, so the accents are real! Open Sun–Thurs 7.30–10.30am and 11.30–midnight; Fri and Sat until 1am. **$$**

Onda

Mirage, 702 791 7223, mirage.com/dining
Regional Italian and new American cuisine inspired by Todd English and served up in an elegant setting. Open 5.30–11pm. **$$$**

Sergio's Italian Gardens

1955 East Tropicana Avenue, 702 739 1544, sergiosrestaurant.com
Consistently rated as one of the best Italian restaurants in town, Sergio's has a delightful garden with Roman columns. Dishes include calamari, Belgium endive salad, sautéed veal and filet mignon Rossini. Open Mon–Fri 11.30am–2.30pm, and nightly 5.30–11pm. **$$**

Trattoria del Lupo

Mandalay Bay, 702 632 7777, mandalaybay.com/dining/trattoria.aspx
Another of celebrity chef Wolfgang Puck's six eating outlets in Las Vegas, this one is pure Italian with traditional recipes cooked in pizza ovens and wood-burning rotisseries. The interior was designed by Adam Tihany, who has re-created a typical small, secluded piazza in Milan with views of pasta, meats and bakery production areas. Open 5.30–11pm. **$$**

Venetian

3713 West Sahara Avenue, 702 876 4190
No, not the hotel, but a similarly named restaurant that still stands out a mile due to the exterior and interior murals. When it opened in 1955 it was the first place to serve pizza in Las Vegas! It still does a roaring trade serving everything from pizza to pasta and plenty of other delightful dishes in between, all at great prices. Open for dinner 4–10pm. **$**

Japanese restaurants

Benihana Village

Las Vegas Hilton, 702 732 5821, lasvegashilton.com
Japanese fantasyland in an enchanting garden setting complete with thunder and lightning storms, lush flowers, flowing ponds and an authentic Torii Arch. There are two restaurants to choose from – the Hibachi where skilled chefs chop, slice and grill your food tableside and the Seafood Grille, where delicious delicacies are the order of the day. You can enjoy drinks and Oriental hors d'oeuvres in the Kabuki Lounge while your table is prepared. Open daily 5–11pm. **$$$**

Hamada's Asiana

Rio All-Suite Hotel, 702 777 7777 x 2770, riolasvegas.com
The waitresses are dressed in kimonos, which gives this restaurant a touch of authenticity. The main dining room features classics such as beef sukiyaki, shabu-shabu and seafood yosenabe. A second dining room, the Teppan Room, is where food is prepared in front of you by knife-wielding chefs. Delicious dishes are made up from shrimp, lobster, steaks and marinated chicken. It also has a sushi bar. Open Sun, Mon, Thurs 5–11pm, Fri–Sat 5pm–12am. **$$**

BRITTIP

If you want an early evening appetiser, head for the Hamada's cocktail lounge, where you can get little plates of deep-fried tempura and sushi with your drinks.

Hyakumi Japanese Restaurant and Sushi Bar

Caesars Palace, 702 734 6116, caesarspalace.com
Home to award-winning executive chef Hiroji Obayashi. For dinner you have a choice of three set-price menus that include a four-course feast of appetisers, miso soup, salad and main course at $64–74 or à la carte dishes that include beef, chicken or fish teriyaki, yakitori, shrimp and vegetable tempura. The sushi bar also has a fabulously large selection of delicacies. The main restaurant is open Tues-Sun 6–11pm, the sushi bar stays open Fri and Sat until midnight. **$$$**

Nobu

Hard Rock Hotel, 702 693 5000, hardrockhotel.com
Chef Nobu Matsuhisa's ground-breaking temple of Japanese cuisine with Peruvian influences has already set unmatched standards of excellence in Los Angeles, New York and London. Nobu Las Vegas has been hugely successful for the Hard Rock Hotel. Dishes include squid pasta, miso-infused cod and creamy, spicy, cracked crab. Open daily 6–11pm. **$$$**

Shibuya

MGM Grand, 702 891 7777, mgmgrand.com/dining
An expansive and spectacular environment forms the perfect backdrop to this stylish offering, which takes its name from the Tokyo district of Shibuya. Featuring freshly prepared ingredients and exquisite sushi, the restaurant also boasts one of the widest sake selections available anywhere in America. Open Sun–Thurs 5.00–10pm and Fri and Sat until 10.30pm. **$$–$$$**

Shibuya at the MGM Grand

Shintaro

Bellagio, 702 693 7111, bellagio.com
Authentic sushi, teppanyaki and pan-Asian tasting menus are served in a sleek, California-inspired dining room with expansive views of the fountains of Bellagio. The popular sushi bar is highlighted by a dramatic, kaleidoscopic display of live jellyfish. A large selection of Japanese beers and sakes are always on offer. Open daily 5.30–10pm. **$$**

Sushi Roku

Forum at Caesars Palace, 702 7333 7373, caesarspalace.com
A tranquil background creates a serene environment in which to tuck into delicious California sushi and modern Asian cuisine. Setting a new standard in sushi bar dining, the vast menu of sushi is augmented by salads, hot and cold appetisers and an extensive selection of entrées. **$–$$**

Teru Sushi

Las Vegas Hilton, 702 732 5111, lvhilton.com/dining
Teru Sushi features more than 40 types of fresh sushi shipped daily from the west coast and prepared by a licensed sushi chef. Reservations are not required. Open Tues–Sat 5.30–10.30pm. **$–$$**

Mediterranean restaurants

Corsa Cucina

Wynn Las Vegas, 702 248 3463, wynnlasvegas.com
Chef Stephen Kalt's stylish dishes feature traditional and contemporary Italian and Mediterranean specialties, with signature dishes of roasted monkfish, lamb shank tagine and lobster ravioli. The large dining room has delightfully comfy red leather booths and canopied windows. Open for lunch daily 11.30am–2.30pm, dinner Sun–Thurs 5.30–10.30pm, Fri and Sat until 11pm. **$$**

Drai's

Barbary Coast, on the Strip at East Flamingo, 702 737 7111
Run by ex-Hollywood producer Victor Drai, this is one of the most popular venues in town among the locals. Tuck into a fusion of French and Mediterranean food to the background sounds of live jazz and blues. Winning dishes include seared jumbo scallops with citrus ginger sauce, crispy duck comfit and seven-hour leg of lamb. Open nightly 5.30pm–1am. **$$**

Best local restaurants

André's: French (page 109).
Aristocrat: French (page 109).
Mamounia: Moroccan (page 118).
Mayflower Cuisinier: Asian (page 111).
Pamplemousse: French (page 111).
Venetian: Italian (page 115).

Olives

Bellagio, 702 693 7111, bellagio.com
Todd and Olivia English bring their famous Boston Olives to Las Vegas with Mediterranean-style dishes in a lively café setting. Open 11.30am–11pm. **$$**

Picasso

Bellagio, 702 693 7111, bellagio.com
Julian Serrano, who dazzled diners at San Francisco's Masa, brings his trademark Spanish-tinged French cuisine to one of the world's most opulent settings for a restaurant – dine here and you'll be surrounded by $52m worth of Picasso originals and even some of the artist's ceramics. The menu changes nightly but usually includes Julian's foie gras in Madeira sauce or warm lobster salad with mangoes or potatoes. The views of the Bellagio's dancing fountains finish off a superb dining experience. Open Wed–Mon 6–9.30pm. **$$$**

Mexican restaurants

Blue Agave

The Palms, 702 942 7777
A fun, casual dining experience at the über-trendy Palms hotel, named after the plant that gives tequilas their flavour. The house specialities are oysters, seafood cocktails and pan roasts, plus a chilli bar with South American favourites. Open Sun–Thurs 11am–10pm, Fri and Sat until 1am. **$$$**

BRITTIP

For a real party atmosphere, head to the Blue Agave, where along with delish Mexican-based cuisine, there is a range of 150 tequilas and a whopping 350 different margaritas to choose from!

Border Grill

Mandalay Bay, 702 632 7777, mandalaybay.com/dining/bordergrill.aspx
Mary Sue Milliken and Susan Feniger, the duo known on American TV as Too Hot Tamales, are renowned for their Border Grill in Los Angeles and have now opened an outlet in the new all-jumping hotel, Mandalay Bay. Their bold and tasty Mexican dishes are served in a vibrant beachside setting. Open for lunch Mon–Fri 11.30am–5pm and Sat–Sun 11am–5pm; for dinner Sun–Thurs 5–10pm, Sat–Sun 5–11pm. **$$**

Cozymel's

Hughes Center, 355 Hughes Center Drive, 702 732 4833, cozymels.com
An upscale franchise restaurant serving spectacular seafood specials and delicious fajitas. Open Mon–Thurs 11am–10pm, Fri and Sat until midnight. **$**

Crazy Armadillo

Stratosphere, 702 380 7777, stratospherehotel.com/crazy.html
'Flair' bartenders, singing waiters, dancing waitresses and live music make this rowdy cantina-style eatery a fun place for food. House specialities include meatball soup, baby back ribs, salmon fajitas, tacos and oysters on the half-shell. Enjoy! Open 4–11pm. **$**

Garduños

The Palms, 702 942 7777, gardunosrestaurants.com
Part of a Mexican cantina chain, this restaurant serves authentic Mexican cuisine and has quickly become a firm favourite in Las Vegas. Margaritas are also available. Open Sun–Thurs 11am–10.50pm, Fri and Sat until 11.50pm. **$**

Gonzalez Y Gonzalez

New York-New York, 702 740 6455, nynyhotelcasino.com/restaurants
A great spot to soak up the atmosphere of the hotel's outdoor courtyard with lanterns and Spanish piñatas, this serves authentic Mexican cuisine at reasonable prices. Open Sun–Thurs 11am–11pm, Fri and Sat until midnight. **$**

BRITTIP

The real secret of Gonzalez Y Gonzalez is the long list of margaritas, which can even be served by the yard!

Guadalajara Bar and Grille

Palace Station Hotel, 2411 West Sahara Avenue, 702 367 2411
A 24-hour joint famous for its 99-cent margaritas. It may be a little off the beaten track, but you'll still need to make a reservation! Lunch is served 11am–5pm, dinner 5pm–11am. **$**

Isla Mexican Kitchen & Tequila Bar

Treasure Island, 702 894 7111, treasureisland.com
Chef Richard Sandoval offers traditional Mexican cuisine with a modern twist. Innovations include the roving guacamole cart armed and ready with freshly made guacamoles. Dishes include: grilled Mexican spiced chicken breast with corn dumplings; crispy red snapper with cactus salad; and Isla sirloin with mashed potatoes and chimichurri sauce. Tacos, enchiladas, tamales and burritos all get a modern twist, with ingredients such as battered rock shrimp and wild mushrooms. The Tequila Bar features an impressive selection of tequilas plus margaritas, sangrias and other Mexican cocktail favourites. Open daily from 4–11pm. The bar and lounge is open daily from 11am–2am. **$$**

Margaritagrille

Las Vegas Hilton, 702 732 5111, lvhilton.com/dining
An incredibly popular party-time destination, yet still one of the best Mexican restaurants in town. Specialities include enchiladas, spicy burritos, chimichangas, crispy tostadas and tacos as well as the chef's own sizzling fajitas. You can also get delicious fresh fruit margaritas from the salsa bar. Open daily 11.30am–3pm and 5–11pm. **$**

Inside Olives at the Bellagio

Margarita's Mexican Cantina

Frontier Hotel on the Strip, 702 794 8200
Classic Tex-Mex food from burritos to tacos, enchiladas and chimichangas. The tortillas are freshly prepared and come with the usual salsa, guacamole and bean dips. Open Sun–Thurs 10.30am–10pm, Fri and Sat 10.30am–11pm. **$**

Pink Taco

Hard Rock Hotel, 702 693 5000, hardrockhotel.com
A trendy restaurant offering celebrated Californian chef Tacho Kneeland's fresh and modern taste on Mexican classics. Choices include tamales nachos, quesadillas, tacos and a whole range of tequilas – served the traditional way, natch! Open Sun–Thurs 11am–10pm, Fri–Sun 11am–midnight. **$$**

Viva Mercado's

3553 South Rainbow, 702 871 8826, vivamercadoslv.com
Regularly wins the local daily paper's poll for best Mexican restaurant in town. That is due to delicious food including chilli relleno, carnitas and Mexican-style steak at great prices. Open Sun–Thurs 11am–9.30pm, Fri and Sat 11am–10.30pm. **$**

BRITTIP

Be warned: although Las Vegas is a 24-hour city, most of the top-notch restaurants close as early as 10pm or 10.30pm.

Craftsteak at the MGM Grand

Moroccan restaurants

Japengo

Hyatt Regency Lake Las Vegas, 702 567 1234
A real Moroccan affair, this superb restaurant focuses largely on products from the sea and even includes a sushi bar that has been rated the best in the Las Vegas valley by the Zagat survey. Best of all, though, are the amazing views of Lake Las Vegas and the mountains. Open daily 6–10.30pm except Sun. **$$**

Mamounia

4632 South Maryland Parkway, 702 597 0092
Delicious Moroccan dishes are served in a simulated Middle Eastern desert tent setting complete with low benches or pillows, costumed waiters and belly dancers. House specialities include all the Moroccan classics such as hummus, kefta, tabbouleh, briouats, cacik yoghurt dip, shish kebabs and couscous. Great value. Open daily 5.30–11.30pm. **$$**

Marrakech Restaurant

3900 Paradise Road, 702 737 5611
The oldest Moroccan restaurant in town taking the whole eating in the desert thing one stage further than Mamounia by expecting diners to eat with their hands! The house specialities include Moroccan-style chicken in a light lemon sauce and flambéed lamb brochette. Dinner features a belly-dancing show. Open daily 5.30–11pm. **$$**

Seafood and steakhouses

3950

Mandalay Bay, 702 632 7414, mandalaybay.com/dining
Contemporary-yet-classic steak and seafood cuisine served in a bold setting with high-back suede booths and red leather walls. Starters include Beluga caviar or escargot and lobster bisque, while entrées include orange duck, rack of lamb, New York strip steak, grilled swordfish and pan-seared Chilean sea bass. The speciality of the house is the innovative fresh white truffle and lobster macaroni cheese. Open 5–10.30pm. **$$$**

AquaKnox

Grand Canal Shoppes, the Venetian, 702 414 3772, grandcanalshoppes.com
Chef Tom Moloney, who honed his skills during 12 years with Wolfgang Puck, won Best New Restaurant in Vegas when his seafood extravaganza opened. Fresh seafood is flown in daily from around the world to provide a superb raw bar alongside wonderful dishes of filet mignon with truffle aioli, and grilled lobster with herb butter. Favourites include the fresh stone crab claws from Florida Keys; sweet shrimp cocktail; Louisiana prawns; jumbo lump crab cocktail; dry aged prime New York steak; and oven-roasted guinea hen. Open Sun–Thurs 12am–2.30pm, 5.30–11pm; Fri and Sat 11.30am–2.30pm and 5.30–11.30pm. **$$–$$$**

BOA Prime Grill

Forum Shops at Caesars Palace, 702 733 7373, caesarspalace.com
Think traditional lobster and steakhouse with a refreshing spin in a classic setting of leather seats and wooden and chrome finishings. Favourite dishes include a prawn cocktail spiced up with vodka-spiked cocktail sauce, prime-aged beef with a choice of eight sauces and four rubs including a sweet, homemade Worcestershire sauce, a sage sauce and a blue-cheese crust. Other specialities include ostrich fan filet; seared rare ahi tuna with romesco sauce; and fire-roasted aubergine Parmesan. Open Sun–Thurs 12pm–10pm and to midnight Fri and Sat. **$**

Burgundy Room

Lady Luck, 206 North 3rd Street, 702 477 3000
If you want to get away from expensive gourmet rooms, then the Burgundy serves up classics like beef Wellington and steak au poivre in an attractive setting at reasonable prices. Open daily 5–10pm. **$$**

Búzio's

Rio All-Suite Hotel, 702 252 7697, riolasvegas.com
Probably one of the best seafood restaurants in town – not just because of its extraordinary selection of seafood dishes, but also because of its pricing policy – dinner will cost around $29 per person. This is another fine restaurant based at the Rio All-Suite Hotel and well deserves its appearance in the annual Zagat survey of top restaurants in Las Vegas. Open daily 11am–11pm. **$$**

Craftsteak

MGM Grand, 702 891 1111, mgmgrand.com/dining
Craftsteak was created by award-winning chef Tom Colicchio, founder of the critically acclaimed Craft restaurant in New York. The philosophy is simple: use the finest available produce and cook in such a way to allow the flavours of the ingredients to shine through. A classic steakhouse, there is a $39, three-course Market Menu available seven days a week. Open daily 5.30–10.30pm. Live music Tues-Thurs 8pm–midnight, Fri and Sat 9pm–1am. **$$–$$$**

BRITTIP

An added bonus of dining at Craftsteak is the live music. Pianist Shane Stephens sings a blend of jazz, soul and pop songs every night except Monday.

Delmonico Steakhouse

Grand Canal Shoppes at the Venetian, 702 733 5000, thegrandcanalshoppes.com
Emeril Lagasse's second outlet in Las Vegas features the food surprises that have made him famous. It seems to be on everybody's list of top steakhouses in the USA. Open daily 5.30–10.30pm. **$$$**

House of Lords

The Sahara, 702 737 2111, saharavegas.com/food/houseorlords
One of the longest-running steak shows in town, the House of Lords keeps putting out good food at a decent price. Favourites – alongside the famous New York strip steak, double lamb chops and roast prime rib of beef – include escargot, lobster bisque, stuffed portobella mushrooms and roasted crab cakes. Open Sun–Sat 5pm–10pm. **$$**

House of Lords at the Sahara

Prime's main dining room

Hugo's Cellar

Four Queen's, 202 Fremont Street, Downtown, 702 385 4011, hugoscellar.com

A popular choice with locals and visitors alike, so book ahead to get a table. Famous for its excellent wine list. Open daily 5.30–10.30pm. **$$**

Joe's Seafood, Prime Steak & Stone Crab

Forum Shops at Caesars Palace, 702 792 9222, caesarspalace.com

This popular destination at the Forum Shops offers both classic and modern-day dishes using fresh seafood flown in daily from around the world. Specialities include Madagascar shrimp, Nantucket Cape scallops, fresh Alaskan king crab and Copper River salmon. A 16oz bone-in filet mignon, served with side dishes including hashed brown potatoes, grilled tomatoes, creamed spinach and coleslaw keeps the meat-lovers happy. Open Sun–Thurs 4–11pm and until midnight Sat–Sun. **$$**

Michael Mina

Bellagio, 702 693 7111, wbellagio.com

Celebrity chef Michael Mina has replaced the top-notch Aqua with an even more amazing restaurant that has been drawing ecstatic plaudits for its innovative yet gourmet seafood dishes. Blending fresh ingredients from California, Britain and the Mediterranean, the incredible line-up of tastebud-tickling starters include savoury black mussel soufflé with saffron Chardonnay cream; seared sea scallops and foie gras with a rhubarb-lime compote and Thai coconut soup with Dungeness crab. First courses include the tempura langoustine with young ginger, pickled fennel, saffron aioli, green papaya and mango. Entrées include Angus beef filet mignon, tapioca-crusted black bass with toasted almonds and Chile garlic vinaigrette; Maine lobster pot pie and roasted whole Hudson Valley foie gras. Eat it and weep with sheer joy. Open daily 5.30–10pm, reservations advised. **$$–$$$**

Michael's

Barbary Coast, 3595 The Strip at East Flamingo, 702 737 7111

Despite its unprepossessing setting, this is the choice of Las Vegas high-flyers so tables are hard to get. The food is superb, but the prices match. For real foodies only. Open nightly 6–9.30pm. **$$$**

N9ne Steakhouse

The Palms, 702 933 9900, http://n9negroup.com

Another stylish offering from The Palms, the Chicago-style prime-aged steaks and chops are served in a sleek setting. Aside from the restaurant, a champagne caviar bar sits amid comfy suede-covered booths from where you can gaze at the changing colours of the ceiling or try to spot the celebs arriving at the glass-enclosed private dining room. Open Sun–Thurs 5–11pm, Fri and Sat 5–11.30pm. **$$**

Palm Restaurant

Forum Shops at Caesars Palace, 702 732 7256

Following on from the success of the New York restaurant, the Las Vegas version also appears in the Zagat Top 40. Famous for crab cakes, lobster, prime rib and the house speciality, charcoal-burnt steak. Open daily 5–11pm. **$$**

Prime

Bellagio, 702 693 7223, bellagio.com

Award-winning chef Jean-Georges Vongerichten uses only the highest-quality meats, seafood and chops to create a fine dining experience. Open daily 5.30–10.30pm. **$$**

Michael Mina at the Bellagio

Lakeside dining

Café Lago: Caesars Palace (see page 125).

Daniel Boulud: Wynn Las Vegas (see page 106).

Le Cirque: Bellagio (see page 109).

Japengo: Hyatt Regency Lake Las Vegas (see page 118).

Jasmine: Bellagio (see page 108).

Medici Café and Terrace: Ritz-Carlton Lake Las Vegas (see page 55).

Olives: Bellagio (see page 116).

Shintaro: Bellagio (see page 116).

SW Steakhouse: Wynn Las Vegas (see page 121).

rm Seafood

Mandalay Bay, 702 632 9300, mandalaybay.com/dining/restaurantrm.aspx
With two restaurants in one, New York chef Rick Moonen offers the R Bar Café on the ground floor and the gourmet Restaurant rm upstairs. Delicious offerings include abalone in butter with Pacific sturgeon caviar, mussel soufflé with green curry sauce, halibut with foie gras and melted leeks in a red wine emulsion, and butter-poached lobster with corn chowder. There is also a six-course tasting menu that will set you back just over $100. Open Sun–Sat 5–10.30pm. **$$–$$$**

Ruth's Chris Steakhouse

3900 Paradise Road, 702 791 7011 and 4561 West Flamingo Road, 702 248 7011, ruthschris.com
A chain of franchised steakhouses that started in New Orleans, these places have a reputation for serving prime meat on a sizzling-hot platter with butter. Other offerings include lamb, chicken and fish with delicious vegetables from sautéed mushrooms to creamed spinach. Open daily 4.30–10.30pm. **$$**

Seablue

MGM Grand, 702 891 7777, mgmgrand.com/dining
Another of James Beard award-winning chef Michael Mina's restaurants offers fish and shellfish flown in from around the world daily and prepared in two open-show kitchens. Custom-designed salads and innovative seafood mains include whole fish cooked over a wood-fired grill. Open 5.30–10.30pm. **$$**

Smith & Wollensky

3767 The Strip opposite the Monte Carlo next to the MGM Grand, 702 862 4100, smithandwollensky.com
Alan Stillman's New York steakhouse group's $10m free-standing, three-storey restaurant seats up to 600 diners in a catacomb-like series of rooms, niches and chambers. Open daily 11.30am–11pm. **$$**

SW Steakhouse

Wynn Las Vegas, 702 248 3463, wynnlasvegas.com
Eric Klein, winner of the Best New Chef 2004 award from America's *Food & Wine* magazine, has created a wonderfully eclectic menu based around a fusion of classic American steaks and Alsatian influences. Well known for his work at Spago and Maple Drive restaurants in Beverly Hills, Eric imbues the finest ingredients of beef, chops and fresh seafood with the wonderful flavours of Alsace. An elegant yet contemporary space, the restaurant offers the chance to dine outside overlooking the hotel's famous lake and mountain. Open 5.30–10.30pm. **$$**

The Steak House

Circus Circus, 702 794 3767, www.circuscircus.com/dining
An exception to every other rule at the family-friendly Circus Circus, this is definitely adult-friendly (the kids are running around the lobby outside) and serves some of the best steaks and seafood in town, making it one of the finest in its price range. Open for dinner daily from 5pm. **$$**

The Steakhouse at Camelot

Excalibur, 702 597 7777, excalibur.com/restaurants
Gourmet cuisine served in the Excalibur castle overlooking make-believe English countryside creates a truly wonderful eating experience. Epicureans will find everything they are looking for from a fine

The main dining room at rm Seafood

wine cellar to a cigar room, lounge and private dining chamber, while the casual ambience makes it a friendly place for anyone to enjoy a meal. Open 5–10pm and until 11pm Fri and Sat. **$$**

The Tillerman

2245 East Flamingo Road, 702 731 4036, tillerman.com/
One of the best places in town to get a fabulously fresh seafood dinner – and not at sky-high prices. Pacific salmon, Chilean sea bass and Florida snapper are some of the seafood platters on offer, while you'll also find steaks and pasta. Open daily 5–11pm. **$$**

BRITTIP

The Top of the World restaurant is one of the '10 Great Places to Pop the Question' according to America's wedding website, The Knot – theknot.com. Other locations include Paris and New York's Brooklyn Bridge.

The Top of the World

Stratosphere, 702 380 7711, topoftheworldlv.com
The name says it all! More than 800ft/240m up the tallest free-standing building in America, the Top of the World revolving restaurant makes a full 360-degree revolution every 70 minutes. Awarded the Best Gourmet Room award by the *Las Vegas Review Journal*, the top-notch food includes sizzling steaks and fresh fish and seafood, tasty salads and flaming desserts. Even if the food wasn't great, the view would be worth it all by itself. Open Sun–Thurs 5–11pm, Fri and Sat until midnight. **$$**

The Tillerman

Yolie's

3900 Paradise Road, 702 714 0700, yolies.qpg.com
A Brazilian steakhouse with large, wood-fired rotisseries that cook the meals in full view of the diners. The selection includes turkey, lamb, brisket, chicken, sausages and steak, plus side dishes of fried brown rice, potatoes and vegetables. Open 11.30am–11pm. **$$**

Southern restaurant

House of Blues

Mandalay Bay, 702 632 7777, mandalaybay.com/dining/houseofblues.aspx
Las Vegas' version of Dan Aykroyd's famous House of Blues on Los Angeles' Strip at the majestic Mandalay Bay is living up to its 'hot' reputation. You'll find every kind of dish from Southern to Creole and Cajun staples as well as wood-fired pizza and burgers. Gospel fans will enjoy the Gospel Brunch, which features live music and an all-you-can-eat Southern-style buffet. At other times of the week expect blues-inspired and other live music. Open daily 11am–3pm. **$$**

South-western restaurants

Chili's Grill and Bar

2590 South Maryland Parkway, 702 733 6462; 2520 South Decatur Boulevard, 702 871 0500; and 2751 North Green Valley Parkway, 702 433 3333, chilis.com
Mexican style with grills, sandwiches, steaks and fajitas at the three restaurants in this chain. **$$**

Mesa Grill

Caesars Palace, 877 650 5965, caesarspalace.com
Celebrity chef Bobby Flay turns down the heat on a range of South-western classics that can usually set your throat on fire. A contemporary approach means: smoked chicken and black bean quesadilla; and lobster and cod griddle cakes, with red cabbage slaw for starters. Main course signatures include: the 16-spices rubbed rotisserie chicken; whole-fried striped bass with five-pepper ginger sauce; and Flay's Cuban burger, sandwiched between slices

BRITTIP

Don't forget to check out your fun books and local magazines for great two-for-one deals.

of roast pork, cheese, ham and pickles. Open for lunch Mon-Fri 11am–2.30pm, brunch Sat and Sun 10.30am–3pm, and dinner daily from 5–11pm. **$$**

Theme restaurants

Allstar Café

3785 The Strip between Harmon and Tropicana, 702 795 8326
Cashing in on the trend of being rich and famous and then opening a restaurant are the tennis stars André Agassi and Monica Seles – and who can blame them? The food might not be brilliant, but it's a fun setting. Open Sun–Thurs 11am–11pm, weekends until midnight. **$**

ESPN Zone

New York-New York, 702 933 3776, nynyhotelcasino.com/restaurants
With flat-screen TVs throughout showing the latest sport action and a fully stocked bar, this is the place for sports fans to tip up. Food offerings include buffalo wings, burgers, garlic mashed potatoes and grilled steak with salad. Open Sun–Thurs 11.30am–11pm, Fri and Sat 11am–midnight. **$**

Hard Rock Café

4475 Paradise Road, 702 733 8400, hardrock.com/las vegas
Another chain theme restaurant that won't let you down in the memorabilia and food departments. You can even pick up a Hard Rock T-shirt or other souvenir to prove you've been there! Open 1–10pm. **$**

Harley Davidson® Café

The Strip at Harmon Avenue, 702 740 4555, harley-davidsoncafe.com
The second outlet that pays homage to the 100-year-old motorbike and is hard to miss with its 28ft/8.5m high, 15,000lb/6,800kg $500,000 Harley Davidson Heritage Softail Classic bike outside! Inside the 20,000sq ft/1,860sq m, two-storey café is a celebration of the free-spirit lifestyle of Harley Davidsons. And the food and drink lives up to it, too! You can sip on a range of cocktails with names such as Hill Climber, Rockin' Rita and Flat Tracker. Soak up the alcohol with fajitas, hamburgers, barbecue chicken, chillis, pasta or hot dogs. Open Mon-Thurs 11am–11pm, Fri-Sun 11am–midnight. **$**

Outdoor and patio dining

Bartolotta: Wynn Las Vegas (page 113).
Bertolini's: Forum Shops (page 113).
BOA Prime Grill: Forum Shops (page 119).
Bouchon: The Venetian (page 105).
Café Ba Ba Reeba: Fashion Show Mall (page 125).
Daniel Boulud: Wynn Las Vegas (page 106).
Gonzalez Y Gonzalez: New York-New York (page 117).
Sergio's Italian Gardens: Tropicana Avenue (page 114).
Mon Ami Gabi: Paris Resort (page 110).
Nine Fine Irishmen: New York-New York (page 112).
Olives: Bellagio (page 116).
Pink Taco: Hard Rock Hotel (page 118).
Simon Kitchen: Hard Rock Hotel (page 129).

Jimmy Buffett's Margaritaville

The Flamingo, 702 733 3302,, margaritavillelasvegas.com
For a themed night out with a difference, head to the great new Caribbean joint at the Flamingo where a three-story volcano erupts as it serves up delicious margaritas in the Volcano Bar. Spread over three levels, the restaurant has five bars and live music while steaks, seafood, hamburgers and Caribbean cuisine are served up with toppings such as pineapple-rum sauce. At

The chain restaurant Hard Rock Café

Rainforest Café

the top of the restaurant are two outdoor patios overlooking the Strip, one of which is home to the 12 Volt Bar, where live music is provided nightly on a theme of island and rock. Even if you don't plan to party the night away, do visit the bar if only to see the giant sails of the life-size Euphoria boat flying high! Open Sun–Thurs 11am–2am, Fri and Sat 10.45am–2.30pm (dinner served until midnight). **$**

Nascar Café

Sahara, 2535 South Las Vegas Boulevard, 702 734 7223, saharavegas.com/food/nascar-cafe
For lovers of the Las Vegas Motor Speedway or stock racing generally, this is the theme café to visit. A two-level offering with NASCAR merchandise, giant TV screens showing NASCAR races and authentic stock cars, the centrepiece is a Pontiac Grand Prix car that comes to life every hour, re-creating the excitement of being at the track. Dishes include Talladega tenders, supercharged chilli and dipstick fried cheese. Cocktails include battery acid and caution-flag margaritas. What fun! Open Sun–Thurs 11am–10pm, Fri and Sat 11am–11pm. **$**

Planet Hollywood

Forum Shops at Caesars Palace, 702 791 7827, planethollywood.com
A chain famous more for their décor than the food, the place is overrun with photos and costumes and other Hollywood mementos. It seems every square inch has a Klingon costume or Freddie Kruger mask. The menu includes gourmet pizzas, pastas, fish, burgers and more. Open Sun–Thurs 11am–11pm and until midnight Fri and Sat. **$**

Quark's Bar and Restaurant

Las Vegas Hilton, 702 697 8725, lvhilton.com/dining
Theme me up, Scotty! For an out-of-this-world meal try Quark's Bar and Restaurant in the Star Trek: Experience at the Hilton. Inspired by all things Trekkie, laser-style lights give an eerie glow to the metallic furniture, while costume-clad servers dish up offerings such as Isolinear chips and dips, Class M pizza, Glop on a stick (corn dog), Holy Rings of Betazed (onion rings) and the Final Frontier desserts. In reality, of course, it's just the standard burgers and steaks affair offered at most theme restaurants, but a real treat for Trekkies. Open Sun–Thurs 11.30am–10pm, Fri and Sat 11.30am–11pm. **$**

The Rainforest Café

MGM Grand on the Strip, 1-800 929 1111, mgmgrand.com/dining/rainforest-cafe.aspx
A real-life simulation of a rainforest complete with tropical rainstorms featuring thunder and lightning that boom and spark across the entire restaurant. It's an untamed paradise brimming with exotic tropical birds, animated elephants, leopards and gorillas and tropical trees. You enter the dining area by walking under a massive double archway aquarium filled with marine fish from around the world. The food, quite good by the way, consists of pastas, salads, sandwiches and delectable desserts. Open daily 11am–11pm. **$**

Lounge dining

Lounges are almost unique to Las Vegas. Relaxed yet stylish environments, they all provide live entertainment and in some cases delicious food. Here's a selection.

Coral Reef Lounge

Mandalay Bay, 702 632 7777, mandalaybay.com
Sushi bar cuisine provides delicious food while you listen to the nightly live music. Changes are being discussed for 2008, so you could find changes here. Open Sun–Thurs 11am–midnight, Fri and Sat until 1am. **$$**

Firenze Lobby Lounge

Ritz-Carlton Lake Las Vegas, 702 567 4700, wwwritzcarlton.com
For a light bite in a relaxing and romantic setting, this is the place to come. With views of the lake and beautiful art around the walls, you can enjoy hors d'oeuvres, desserts and soufflés before and after your

BRITTIP

For a moment of refinement, try afternoon Florentine tea at the Firenze Lobby Lounge. Fresh flower arrangements and a live pianist create the perfect setting in which to enjoy scones, sandwiches and savouries while taking in the view of Lake Las Vegas and the mountains.

meal. There's live music nightly plus an excellent selection of cocktails, champagne, brandy and liqueurs. Open 11am–midnight. **$$**

Peppermill Café & Lounge

2985 Las Vegas Boulevard South, 702 735 4177

For a taste of old-style Vegas hospitality, the Peppermill should be on your must-visit list. The food is excellent and portions are on the large side. Think burgers, sandwiches, steak, seafood and huge salads. While you're here, have a drink in the romantic lounge, which is famous for its fireplace, candlelit tables and comfy sofas. Open 24 hours. **$**

Cafés and diners

America

New York-New York, 702 740 6451, nynyhotelcasino.com/restaurants

A large, open restaurant with a few booths, serves classic casual American food such as roast turkey, meatloaf, pastas, salads and burgers. If all else fails to capture your imagination, try the all-day breakfast. Open 24/7. **$**

Binion's Coffee Shop

Binion's Horseshoe Hotel, 128 Fremont Street, 702 382 1600

Binion's gets cram–packed with downtown gamblers, so you have to pick your time to avoid long queues. Specialities include Benny Binion's Natural, considered to be one of the best-priced, most delicious breakfasts in town, and Binion's Delight, a hamburger platter with chips. Open 6–10.30pm. **$**

Bugsy's Deli

Flamingo Hilton, 702 733 3111

The gangster who created the Flamingo is remembered by the Hilton. The hotel has had a complete overhaul in the last few years and this cafeteria-style coffee shop and diner serves up eggs, hamburgers and roast beef sandwiches to your specifications, plus delicious piping-hot waffles. Good at any time of the day, but a great stop for breakfast. **$**

Cafe Ba-Ba-Reeba

The Fashion Show Mall, 702 258 1211, cafebabareba.com

The delicious combination of flavours that are the hallmark of Spanish tapas cuisine arrives on the Strip in a fun café. Using the freshest seafood, cheeses and vegetables, the speciality is the paella, while there is a wonderful variety of sangrias to choose from. Open for lunch Sun–Sat 11.30am–3.30pm; dinner Sun–Thurs 3.30pm–1am and Fri and Sat until 2am. **$**

Café Lago

Caesars Palace, 702 731 7845 (groups over 14), caesarspalace.com

Just to prove that the Bellagio isn't the only resort in town with water views, Caesars has opened this large café right by the Garden of the Gods Pool Oasis. Serving international dishes and American favourites throughout the day and night, it also offers live music with pianist David Osborne and other soloists in the evening. The one drawback, of course, is that enjoying the beautiful setting doesn't come cheap. Open 24 hours. **$$**

Café Michelle

1350 East Flamingo Road, inside the local mall, 702 735 8686

The place to go for plenty of cheap grub far from the madding crowd. The red-and-white checked tablecloths and Cinzano umbrellas over tables in the plaza create a European ambience, while you tuck into omelettes, crêpes, salads and seafood. **$**

Nascar Café for speedway fans

Cyber City Café

Target Shopping Center, 3945 Maryland Parkway at East Flamingo, 702 732 2001
Internet addicts will want to make the trip out to the University District on the east side of town to sit in the overstuffed sofas, drink copious amounts of coffee and check out their email for next to nothing. **$**

Enigma Garden Café

918 S Fourth Street, 702 386 0999
One of the best cafés downtown, it even has live music outside in the garden at weekends. During the summer it's open 24 hours a day (7am–10pm in winter). **$**

Fog City Diner

Hughes Center, 325 Hughes Center Drive, 702 737 0200
Simple diner food given a twist with Japanese-inspired mu shu burritos, first-class seafood and shellfish, plus soups and sandwiches. Open 11.30am–10pm. **$**

Jazzed Café

Napoli Plaza, 2055 East Tropicana in the University District, 702 798 5995
It's worth making the trek out to the east side of town to see how the locals live it up at the hippest café for miles. Check out one of the best wine lists and coffee selections in town, surrounded by dancers, who go for the dark ambience. Open Mon–Thurs 5pm–1am, Fri and Sat 5pm–3am, Sun 10am–2pm and 5pm–1am. **$–$$**

Jitters

2457 East Tropicana, 702 898 0056, wwwjitters.com
Jitters specialises in providing one of the biggest and best selections of coffees in town and even roasts its own beans on the premises! Apart from the coffee, you'll also get yourself a decent breakfast, lunch or dinner for under $10. Open 6am–7pm. **$**

Fine dining at Michael Mina

Mariposa Café

Paradise Plaza, 4643 Paradise Road, 702 650 9009
A real favourite with patrons of the nearby gay and lesbian clubs, this coffee shop is open 5pm–5am. **$**

Mr Lucky's

Hard Rock Hotel, 702 693 5000, hardrockhotel.com
The second of only two restaurants at the world's first rock 'n' roll hotel, this is a fun setting for a fun meal. You'll find excellent choices for breakfast, lunch and dinner, while afterwards you can check out the rock 'n' roll memorabilia in the hotel casino, including items once owned by stars such as the Supremes, Elvis and James Brown. Open 24 hours. **$**

Roxy's Diner

Stratosphere on the Strip, 702 380 7711, stratospherehotel.com
A fun place to experience a piece of 1950s America – everything from the decor to the uniforms and music pay homage to the rock 'n' roll era. Food includes chicken, fried steak with homemade gravy and Mom's meat loaf with fresh vegetables and real mashed potatoes. Drinks include thick, cold milkshakes in tall, frosted glasses. Open daily 12 noon–10pm. **$**

Wolfgang Puck's Café

MGM Grand, 1-800 929 1111, mgmgrand.com/dining
A brightly decorated café with mosaic-tiled booths around the open kitchenette – another of celebrity chef Wolfgang's five outlets in Las Vegas. Tuck into the usual eccentric array of Italian nosh and pizzas. Open daily 11am–11pm. **$**

Hotel restaurants

Many of the best restaurants that have been reviewed and listed are in the top resort hotels. To make life easier I have listed all the eating places at the main resort hotels in town. The hotels also have their own buffets!

Planet Hollywood

702 736 7114, planethollywood.com
PH has made a great turnover in her restaurants since changing from the Aladdin, with the lone exceptions of the Spice Market Buffet, which continues to be one of Vegas' best values, and PF Changs.

Best gourmet-style dining in a hotel

Alizé: The Palms (see page 109).

Aureole: Mandalay Bay (see page 102).

Búzio's: Rio All-Suite Hotel (see page 119).

Les Artistes Steakhouse: Rio All-Suite Hotel (see page 110).

Michael Mina: Bellagio (see page 120).

Onda: Mirage (see page 114).

Nero's: Caesars Palace (see page 103).

Prime: Bellagio (see page 120).

Top of the World: Stratosphere (see page 122).

Fine dining:

Koi	Japanese
Strip House	Steakhouse
Alfredo of Rome	Italian
Yolo's	Fusion
PF Chang's China Bistro	Chinese

Casual

Spice Market	Buffet
Starbucks	Coffee bar
Earl of Sandwich	Deli
Planet Dailies	American brasserie

Miracle Mile Shops at Planet Hollywood

Fine dining:

Pampas Churrascaria Brazilian Grill	Brazilian Grill

Casual:

Aroma D'Talia	Italian bistro
Blondies Sports Bar & Grill	Sports bar
Cheeseburger Las Vegas	American
Hawaiian Tropic Zone	Hawaiian
La Salsa Cantina	Mexican
Lombardi's Romagna Mia	Italian
Merchant's Harbor	Coffee house
Ocean One Bar & Grill	American
Oyster Bay	Seafood wine bar
Sbarro	Italian
Tacone Flavor Grill & Daquiri Bar	American
Todai	Japanese Seafood Buffet
Trader Vic's	Seafood

Bellagio

702 693 7111, bellagio.com

When the Bellagio opened at the end of 1998, it set a new standard both for hotels and for restaurants, and deliberately went out of its way to attract top celebrity chefs, including Elizabeth Blau, Julian Serrano and Todd English. All were a hit from word go and have remained popular ever since.

Fine dining:

Le Cirque	French
Picasso	Mediterranean
Michael Mina	Seafood
Circo	Tuscany
Prime Steakhouse	Steakhouse
Jasmine	Chinese
Shintaro	Japanese/Pan Asian

Casual:

The Buffet	Buffet
Café Bellagio	24-hour dining
Fix	American
Noodles	Asian
Olives	Mediterranean
Pool Café	Mediterranean
Sensi	Asian
Palio	Pastries and tea
The Petrossian Bar	Caviar

Caesars Palace

702 731 7110, caesarspalace.com

The resort is posh and the restaurants reflect that, serving top-notch and largely pricey meals. If you're feeling flush, you can do no wrong by trying any of the following establishments.

Fine dining:

808	Hawaiian
Bradley Ogden	American
Empress Court	Gourmet Chinese
Hyakumi	Japanese sushi bar
Nero's	Contemporary American
Restaurant Guy Savoy	French

Casual:

Augustus Café	24 hour bistro
Café Lago	24-hour snacks
Cypress Street Marketplace	Self-service

Circo at the Bellagio

The Steak House at Circus Circus

Forum Shops at Caesars Palace

The incredibly upscale Forum Shops have a tremendous number and range of dining options from celebrity chef to other upscale and more casual dining. In some cases you can even dine pavement style and watch the world go by.

Fine dining:

Bertolini's	Italian
BOA Prime Grill	Steakhouse
Chinois	Asian
Il Mulino New York	Italian
Joe's Seafood	Prime Rib & Stone Crab
The Palm	Steakhouse
Spago	American fusion

Casual:

Café Della Spiga	Café
Cheesecake Factory	American
Ferrara's Café	Patisserie
La Salsa	Mexican
Planet Hollywood	American
Segafredo Zanetti	Café
Sushi Roku	Sushi bar

Circus Circus

702 734 0410, circuscircus.com

The Steak House is one of the finest of its kind in town and is regularly honoured by local newspaper polls as the Number One steakhouse of Las Vegas.

Fine dining:

Steak House	American

Casual:

Barista Café	Coffee shop
Blue Iguana	Mexican
Stivali X-Press	Westside deli
The Pink Pony	24-hour café
The Pizzeria	Italian

Excalibur

702 597 7777, excalibur.com

Themes abound at the eating establishments of this resort that pays tribute to King Arthur's day. Sir Galahad's is a Tudor-style rib house, there's Italian cuisine in an Italian setting at Lance-A-Lotta Pasta and live music and country dancing at Wild Bill's Saloon.

Fine dining

Sir Galahad's Prime Rib House	English
The Steakhouse at Camelot	Gourmet dining overlooking the English countryside!

Casual

Regale	Italian Eatery
Sherwood Forest Café	24-hour bistro
Village Food Court	Fast food

24/7 Gems

All the following serve excellent grub at under $10 throughout the day and night. These are perfect locations to get a great breakfast after a big night out or stock up on carbs before you hit the town.

Liberty Café: 1700 Las Vegas Boulevard South, 702 383 0196. Just to prove good, old-fashioned grub works, here is an old-fashioned American drugstore with a counter. Famous for its monster breakfasts, it specialises in burgers and chicken-fried steak, while the retro drinks are a speciality. **$**

Monterey Room: Gold Coast Hotel, 4000 West Flamingo Road, 702 367 7111. Serving classic American grub throughout the day, plus great Chinese cuisine noon–5am, the Monterey is famous for its lunch and dinner specials. Lunch from $6.95 and dinners from $5.95 to $15.95. **$**

Pelican Rock Café: Castaways Hotel & Casino, 702 385 9123. Traditional American breakfasts include omelettes, waffles and pancakes, lunch soups, salads and sandwiches, while dinner offerings include steaks and burgers. This is one of the cheapest joints in town, still famous for its mega-cheap steak and egg deals. **$**

Ristorante dei Fiore: Hotel San Remo, 115 East Tropicana Avenue, 702 739 9000. Sounds posh, but this is a cheap-as-chips joint serving excellent American and international food. Locals love its prime rib dinner and steak and egg breakfast, both $4.95, which are served 24 hours a day. **$**

Four Seasons

702 632 5000, fourseasons.com/lasvegas

Fine dining:

Charlie Palmer Steak	American

Casual:

The Verandah	Eclectic

Hard Rock Hotel

702 693 5000, hardrockhotel.com

The rock 'n' roll memorabilia that adorns the first-ever hotel on this theme makes a visit to the casino a must – and while you're there you won't be disappointed by any of the dining establishments.

Fine dining:

AJ's Steakhouse	American
Mr Lucky's	Coffee shop
Nobu	Japanese

Casual:

Pink Taco	Mexican
Simon Kitchen & Bar	American
Starbucks	Coffee shop

Las Vegas Hilton

702 732 5111, lvhilton.com

The elegant resort-hotel has some fine restaurants. The prices are on the high side but then you are getting some of the best ingredients cooked to perfection and served in delightful settings.

Fine dining:

Benihana Village	Japanese
Casa Nicola	Mediterranean
Garden of the Dragon	Chinese
TJ's Steakhouse	Steaks
Teru Sushi	Japanese

Casual:

888 Noodle Bar	Asian
Fortuna	Wine Bar
Hacienda Margarita	Mexican
Paradise Café	24-hour diner
Quark's Bar & Restaurant	American
Quick Dine	Fast food

Luxor

702 262 4000luxor.com

Known for excellent food, nonetheless, at press time Luxor had announced that a number of their themed restaurants, including Pharoah's Pheast, would be receiving a make-over for 2008, so check out the latest information before you travel.

Fine dining:

Fusia	Fusion
Luxor's Steakhouse	American

Casual:

Back Stage Deli	Deli
Burger bar	American
Café Giorgio	Italian
Food Court	Self-service
La Salsa	Mexican grill
Nile Deli	Deli
Pharaoh's Pheast	Buffet
Pyramid Café	American

Mandalay Bay

702 632 7777, mandalaybay.com

The hotel is in the top-end bracket and aims directly at the more sophisticated traveller in search of fun. It has two cracking live music venues – House of Blues and Rumjungle – within a selection of celebrity chef restaurants.

Fine dining:

Aureole	American
China Grill	Chinese
Fleur de Lys	French
Mix	Fusion
Red Square	Caviar
rm Seafood	Seafood
Shanghai Lilly	Cantonese
STRIPSTEAK	American
Trattoria del Lupo	Italian

Casual:

Bayside Buffet	Buffet
Border Grill	Mexican
Burger Bar	American
the café	24-hour dining
Giorgio Ristorante e Café	Italian
Noodle Shop	Chinese
r.bar.café	Seafood
Red, White and Blue	French
Verandah	International

Live music:

House of Blues	Southern
Rumjungle	Caribbean

Wolfgang Puck's Trattoria del Lupo

Bargain specials

Las Vegas abounds in great food deals, especially at downtown casinos and those off-Strip casinos that cater to local gamblers. Here are just a few:

Ellis Island Casino (in the Café): $4.99 Steak Dinner includes a sirloin steak, baked potato, salad, vegetable and a drink. Look for 2-for-1 coupons you can use to buy two of these dinners for only $4.99. You have to ask for this special, as it is not on the menu (although there are notices at the blackjack tables).

California Casino: $6.99 Prime Rib Dinner includes a trip to a full salad bar, cooked-to-order prime rib, potato, vegetable and a cherries jubilee for dessert. California also has a great Midnight Special of an 8oz New York cut steak with potato and vegetable for $3.99 from 11pm–9am.

Gold Coast Casino Steak Dinner: $10.95 for a massive 16oz T-bone steak cooked to order with two sides and a beer!

Golden Gate: 99-cent Shrimp Cocktail gives you a mass of cold water bay shrimp served in a large tulip glass with a side of homemade cocktail sauce.

Stratosphere: Lucky's Diner has several midnight specials including a New York cut steak and shrimps with vegetables and choice of potato for $9.99 from midnight to 5am.

MGM Grand

702 891 7777, mgmgrand.com
Celebrity chefs Wolfgang Puck, Joël Robuchon and Emeril Lagassé all have restaurants here.

Fine dining:

Craftsteak	Steakhouse
Fiamma Trattoria	Italian
Joël Robuchon at The Mansion	French
L'Atelier du Joel Robinson	French
Nobhill	Californian
Pearl	Chinese
Seablue	Seafood
Shibuya	Japanese

Casual:

Diego	Mexican
Emeril's	New Orleans/Creole
Grand Wok	Asian
MGM Grand Buffet	Buffet
Rainforest Café	Bistro
Stage Deli	New York deli
Starbucks	Coffee shop
Studio Café	24 hours
Wichcraft	Deli
Wolfgang Puck Bar & Grill	Italian

André's is one of the finest restaurants in Las Vegas

Mirage

702 791 7111, mirage.com
You won't go wrong dining at any of the eateries here, and many offer fine food at mostly reasonable prices.

Fine dining:

Fin	Contemporary Chinese
Japonais	Japanese
Kokomo's	Seafood
Onda	Italian
Samba Brazilian Steakhouse	Steakhouse
Stack	American bistro

Casual:

California Pizza Kitchen	Californian
Caribe Café	24-hour coffee shop
Carnegie Deli	NY Deli
Cravings	Buffet
Dolphin Snack Bar	Café
Noodle Kitchen	Casual Chinese
Paradise Café	Café
Roasted Bean	Coffee shop

Monte Carlo

702 730 7777, montecarlo.com
Here you will find one of the best restaurants in town – André's – and three run by top Californian restaurateurs, Salvator Casola, his son Sal, and Chipper Pastron. Their Market City Caffé is an Italian eatery featuring fresh homemade bread and pasta dishes. The Dragon Noodle company features the Tea Bar with a range of exotic teas and the Golden

Bagel is a replica of a classic New York deli.

Fine dining:

André's — Gourmet French
Blackstone Steakhouse — American

Casual:

Café — Fusion
Dragon Noodle Co — Asian
Market City Caffé — Italian
Monte Carlo Brew Pub — Microbrews

New York-New York

702 740 6969, http://nynyhotelcasino.com

Each of the hotel's restaurants provides a themed dining experience based on the New York areas including Little Italy, Chinatown and Manhattan. The quality is good and the prices are reasonable.

Fine dining:

Chin Chin — Chinese
Gallagher's Steakhouse — Steakhouse
Il Fornaio — Italian

Casual:

America — 24-hour bistro
Coney Island Pavilion — Food court
ESPN Zone — American
Gonzalez Y Gonzalez — Mexican
Häagen-Dazs — Ice-cream parlour
Il Fornaio Panetteria — Italian
Nathan's Hot Dogs — New York street food
Nine Fine Irishmen — Irish
Schraff's Ice Cream — Ice-cream parlour
Studio Grill — American
Village Street Eateries — Fast food outlets

The Palms

702 942 7777, palms.com

The newest casino hotel on the block is also one of the hippest and has an excellent line-up of restaurants.

Fine dining:

Alizé — French
Garduños — Mexican
Little Buddha Café — French
N9ne Steakhouse — American
Nove Italiano — Italian

Casual:

24 Seven Café — American
Ben & Jerry's — Ice cream
Blue Agave — Oyster bar
Famiglia Pizzeria — Italian
Panda Express — Chinese
Vegas Subs — Deli

Paris

702 739 4111, parislasvegas.com

The Paris-inspired resort keeps the French theme in all of its dining outlets ranging from true gourmet to casual. The restaurants have gone from strength to strength and new ones have even opened in this successful resort-hotel.

> **BRITTIP**
> Delis originated in New York and are basically the American version of our sandwich bars, with a heavy Italian feel.

Fine dining:

Eiffel Tower Restaurant — Gourmet French
Le Provençal — Regional French
Les Artistes Steakhouse — Gourmet French
Mon Ami Gabi — Brasserie
Très Jazz — Caribbean

Casual:

Ah Sin — Asian
du Parc — Poolside bistro
JJ's Boulangerie — Pastries and salads
La Crêperie — Crêpes
Le Café Ile St Louis — French
Le Village Buffet — Buffet

Rio All-Suite Hotel

702 252 7777, riolasvegas.com

Many of the Rio's restaurants are consistently highly rated by the Zagat survey. This is one of the most successful off-Strip resort hotels and has a tremendous range of restaurants and casual dining options to satisfy its ardent fans.

Fine dining:

Antonio's — Italian
Búzios — Seafood
Fiore Steakhouse — Fusion
Gaylord India Restaurant — Indian
Hamada's Asiana — Asian

Casual:

All-American Bar — American
Beach café — Poolside dining
Café Martorano — Italian/American
Carnival World Buffet — Buffet
Mah Jong — Asian Noodle Bar

Village Street Eateries at New York-New York

Sao Paulo Café	24-hour diner
Sports Kitchen	American
Tilted Kilt	Irish-American Tavern
Toscano's Deli	New York deli
Village Seafood Buffet	Buffet
VooDoo Café	Cajun/Creole

Stratosphere

702 380 7777, stratospherehotel.com
The tallest free-standing tower in America houses the amazing revolving restaurant, the award-winning Top of the World. Then there is the 'fun 50s' Roxy's Diner in which servers are dressed in rock 'n' roll outfits, and the new Crazy Armadillo Oyster Bar and live music venue.

Fine dining:

Fellini's Ristorante	Italian
Top of the World	American

Casual:

Courtyard Buffet	Buffet
Lucky's Café	Diner
Naga Chinese Express	Chinese
Roxy's Diner	1950s America
Triple Crown	Deli

Live music:

Crazy Armadillo	Oyster bar

Treasure Island

702 894 7111, treasureisland.com
The resort tribute to the world of the Caribbean has some great restaurants.

Fine dining:

Buccaneer Bay Club	American
Francesco's	Italian
Isla	Mexican
Social House	Sushi
The Steakhouse	Steakhouse

Casual:

Ben & Jerry's	Ice-cream parlour
Buffet at TI	Buffet
Canter's Deli	Deli
Delicatessen	Deli
Kahunaville	Hawaiian
Starbucks Coffee	Coffee bar
Terrace Café	American

Tropicana

702 739 2222, tropicanalv.com
There is a distinctly tropical theme to many of the restaurants at this resort-hotel – with delicious food to match. After watching the high-roller baccarat players in action you won't go far wrong taking the time out to dine at any of these.

Fine dining:

Mizuno's	Japanese

Casual:

Garden Café	American
Island Buffet	Buffet
Java Java	Coffee bar
Legend's Steak & Seafood	American
Tuscany's Italian Café	Pizzeria

Venetian

702 414 4100, venetian.com
Aiming at the more sophisticated traveller and diner, this hotel has a host of celebrity-chef restaurants.

Fine dining:

AquaKnox	Seafood
B&B Ristorante	Italian
Bouchon	French bistro
Canaletto	Italian
David Burke	American
Delmonico Steakhouse	Steakhouse
Orchid Asian Cuisine	Asian
Pinot Brasserie	Gourmet French
Postrio	Fusion
Tao Asian Bistro	Asian
Valentino	Italian
Zeffirino	Italian

Casual:

Canyon Ranch Cafe	Healthy Food
Enoteca San Marco	Italian café
Grand Lux Café	American
Grill at Valentino	Italian
Noodle Asia	Noodles
Taqueria Cañonita	Mexican/American
Tintoretto bakery	Café

Try Mexican style at Isla

Getting the most out of buffets

- Generally, avoid breakfast buffets as you won't be able to walk for the rest of the day and the choice is not as good as at other times.
- A lot of buffets change from breakfast to lunch at around 11am. Arrive at 10.45am to pay the breakfast rate and get the lunch spread!
- Never, ever attempt more than one buffet a day or you will explode!
- Try to avoid peak lunch and dinner times or you'll find yourself standing in a queue for an hour and a half. At weekends, even going off-peak times, the queues can take 45 minutes.
- If the queues are long, take a good book or magazine to read – and opt for comfortable shoes!
- Always check out the local magazines for two-for-one coupons.

Grand Canal Shoppes at the Venetian

702 414 4500, thegrandcanalshoppes.com
Along with everything else about this resort hotel, the shops are beautiful and contain some wonderful restaurants.

Fine dining:

Canaletto	Italian
Canyon Ranch Café	American
Food Court	various
Postrio	Italian
Zeffirino Ristorante	Italian

Casual:

Taqueria Cañonita	Mexican
Tintoretto's Bakery	Deli

Live Music

Tao	Asian bistro

Buffets

These all-you-can-eat-for-little-bucks feasts are what Las Vegas used to be most famous for in the culinary stakes and they are still going strong. The mega-feasts date back to the 1940s when the owner of the El Rancho devised a plan to offer a

BRITTIP
Weird but true: at some buffets now you have to queue up to get a table after you've queued to get your food!

Tao

Midnight Chuck Wagon Buffet – 'all you can eat for a dollar' – and found the crowds rolling in. Other hotels quickly followed suit, introducing breakfast, lunch and dinner spreads, and the buffet boom was born. Now they are known as the gambler's revenge – a way to fill up on food for as little as $3 for breakfast to $15 for dinner – though some of the more upmarket, speciality buffets run to $30 a head.

BRITTIP
The buffets are constantly changing hours and prices. To see what the current best deals are, checkout lasvegasadvisor.com/buffets.cfm

You'll find buffets at just about every hotel on the Strip and downtown but both the choice and the turnover vary considerably. The Rio Suites has the biggest buffet, serving upwards of 12,000 hungry gamblers a day, but the queues are incredibly long!

For a Sunday brunch with a difference, try the Southern cuisine at The House of Blues. Sittings are at 10am and 1pm.

Round Table Buffet at the Excalibur

BRITTIP

If staying at the Rio All-Suite Hotel or playing in the casino, don't forget to use the VIP queue to get a head start on the crowds!

Buffets on (or near) the Strip

Buffet of Champions: Champagne brunch at the Las Vegas Hilton, $16.99, Sat and Sun 8am–2.30pm.
Carnival World Buffet at the Rio All-Suite Hotel: On West Flamingo, this is both the biggest and best. The food is laid out in separate kiosks that have different cuisines from around the globe such as American, Chinese, Japanese and Mexican. It's so impressive you'll want to go back again and again, but the long queues may put you off as this is a real favourite with locals.
Frontier: In the middle of the Strip, this is well worth queuing for.
Hooters: On Tropicana Avenue, just east of the Strip, this has a small but good buffet in an intimate atmosphere. Generally the queues are short here, as this is slightly off the beaten track, and the prices are excellent.
Imperial Buffet: Champagne brunch in the Imperial Palace, Sat and Sun 8am–3pm. $12.99.
Luxor Steakhouse: Champagne brunch, Sun 10am–3.30pm, $17.99.
Mirage: Champagne brunch, 8am–9.30pm, $20.50.
Stratosphere: At the northern end of the Strip, this has a wide selection of good quality food at very good prices.
Other buffets: Other places on the Strip that are worth going to but are a little more expensive are at the Mirage, Caesars Palace and Bally's. The Excalibur is one of the biggest and has costumed staff with Robin Hood-style trumpets to add to the atmosphere. The MGM Grand is also good but the queues are incredibly long.
Monte Carlo: Champagne brunch, 7am–3pm, sdults $18.95.
Palatium Buffet: Caesars Palace offers a champagne brunch, Sun 10.30am–3.30pm, adults $23.50.
The Steak House: Great champagne brunch, Sun 10am–2pm at Circus Circus, adults $32.95.
Sterling Brunch: At Bally's Hotel on the Strip, this is truly expensive ($65) but also truly worth it if you want to splash out on a great dining experience, 9.30am–2pm.
Treasure Island: Champagne brunch, 7.30am–3.30pm, $18.
Tropicana: Champagne brunch in the El Gaucho restaurant, 10.30am–2pm, adults $32. The hotel's Island Buffet also has a cheaper champagne brunch, Sat and Sun 10.30am–2.30pm. $16.25.
Village Seafood Buffet: Also at the Rio in the new Masquerade Village, this is more expensive than the norm (around $18) but offers an incredible selection of all the different types of seafood in the world.

Greater Las Vegas

If you really want to get the best out of a Las Vegas buffet then you need to travel downtown to the Garden Court Buffet at Main Street Station. While a bit on the smaller side, compared to the massive resorts, the champagne brunch is a mere $9.99 and the food is rated excellent.

In the opposite direction, the Feast at Boulder Station on the Boulder Highway provides an excellent stop on your way to or from the Hoover Dam. Here you'll find a good choice of quality foods ranging from tacos to pizzas and rotisserie chicken (champagne brunch a mere $9.95).

BRITTIP

For a Sunday brunch with a difference, try the Southern cuisine at the House of Blues. Sittings are at 10am and 1pm.

Luxor Steakhouse

6 BARS, LOUNGES AND NIGHTLIFE

Bars, lounges, nightclubs, live music venues and strip clubs

The word in Las Vegas nightlife is ultra-lounges! Over the last few years an erotic force of ultra-lounges has taken over Sin City with pounding music, dark corners with oversized couches, long queues vying to pass entrance across a velvet rope. Places like Lure, Pure, Ice, Jet, Tao, Light, Krave, Mix, Tryst and Trio are magnets for the movers, shakers, beautiful people and celebrities with their 'crews' who flock to where skin is flaunted, liquor flows and we little people fight for a glance at the rich and famous. A whole raft of VIP rooms, private booths and sky bars at many of the nightclubs command hundreds of dollars for access. Many of these places actually pay famous party animals fees to come and be seen, and notorious naughty girls Lindsay Lohan and Jessica Simpson reportedly get up to $10,000 for partying at some top clubs.

There is also a darker side to many of these power party joints. Ecstasy, the popular club drug of choice, is downed like candy in many of these places. Another open secret, which is pointedly not talked about lest it cut down on the numbers of visiting and near-naked young women, is that these are hunting grounds for those creatures who use 'date rape' drugs like GhB. So make sure that if you go to one of these ultra-lounges, you go with people you trust implicitly.

Enjoy a cocktail on your night out

In this chapter

Even though hotspots abound, you don't have to reveal all or spend a fortune to have a great night out in Sin City. Vegas now has many more nightclubs, lounges and bars where times are good, entertainment is great and prices are reasonable. Even better, most of them are conveniently located along the main drag of the famous Strip.

For those who really need a raunchy fantasy, there are many establishments both on and off Strip where beautiful bodies gyrate in nothing but the briefest of g-strings before panting customers clutching $5 bills. Not just males, either, as a swath of gin joints cater to the erotic fantasies of bachelorettes on holiday.

Many top nightspots start off as restaurants or bars early in the evening and transform into something altogether hotter around 10 or 11pm. Other venues are dedicated nightclubs, while live music can be found in the plethora of lounge bars – mostly at hotels and usually free, though the drinks are expensive! – and dedicated live music venues, where drinks are cheaper.

Here's a selection of all types of venues available to keep you well amused during your time in Vegas. As with the restaurants, it is usually quicker to go to the hotel-resort website, where appropriate, then follow the entertainment or nightlife link, rather than keying in a long URL.

Bars

Bar at Times Square

New York-New York, 702 740 6969, nynyhotelcasino.com/entertainment
The duo of pianists here are famous for trying to outdo each other and have become the best piano show in town. Give them a song and enjoy singing along in a cosy bar based on an old New York city pub. Open nightly from 8pm.

Big Apple Bar

New York-New York, 702 740 6969, nynyhotelcasino.com/entertainment
Happening venue known for its huge selection of one-of-a-kind speciality drinks. There are plenty of seats to relax in and to enjoy the live entertainers who perform on a stage that rises above the actual bar. Open nightly from 8pm, live music from 9.30pm.

Bar at Times Square

Big Apple Bar

Center Bar

Hard Rock Hotel, 4455 Paradise at Harmon, 702 693 5000, hardrockhotel.com
A flashy circle bar at the heart of the hippest hotel in Vegas, this is filled with the hottest babes in town flashing their cleavage and g-strings. Drinks are pricey but the people-watching is priceless. Celebs spotted here include Gwyneth Paltrow, Ben Affleck and the Backstreet Boys. The only downside, say insiders, are the desperados trying to hit on 'hot chicks' – you know you've been had when you hear the line, 'Are you a model?' Follow the party link on the website. Open 24 hours, seven days a week.

Centrifuge

MGM Grand, 702 891 7777, mgmgrand.com/nightlife
The newest bar at the MGM Grand near the Lion Habitat and Poker Room. Remixed Top-40 hits pump out of the speakers and drinks are served along the circular black bar. Twice an hour the music pumps up and the bartenders, male and female, ascend the bar for a hip-grinding dance to the delight of the crowd. Open daily 4pm–2am.

BRITTIP
You have to be over 21 to buy or drink alcohol in Las Vegas and may often be asked to produce photographic ID, so keep your passport with you.

Coyote Ugly is popular with celebs

Coyote Ugly

New York-New York, 702 740 6969, nynyhotelcasino.com/entertainment
This is by far the wildest bar in town. This is like the wild fraternity parties from *Animal House* you've seen on the movies, only like a Southern bar. Based on the New York namesake, this saloon with a dance floor is designed to look like a bar that has seen years of partying. The hot and sassy female bartenders are part of the entertainment – they have not only elevated pouring drinks to an art form, but also get on the bar for an act of sexy dance numbers and amazing stunts from fire-blowing to body shots. Once they've done their thing, female punters are invited to dance on the bar as well and even nail some of their undies on the Bra Wall of Fame. No fancy concoctions served here, only straight shots of liquor and beer. Open nightly 6pm–4am.

Crazy Armadillo's

Stratosphere, 702 380 7777, stratospherehotel.com/entertainment.html
A rowdy, south-of-the-border-style bar with 'flair' bartenders who juggle bottles and entertain the crowd as they mix the speciality margaritas. The house special is the Triple Armadillo made with Cuervo Gold tequila, Reposado tequila, Cuervo Tradicional tequila, Cointreau, sweet and sour, and lime juice. If that's not enough to give you alcohol poisoning, opt for the $20 Tequila Sampler, which offers five different tequila shots.

At the oyster bar you can try oyster shooters such as the Kamikaze Shooter, made from fresh oysters with Smirnoff vodka, triple sec and a splash of lime juice. Just remember: if you feel terrible in the morning you did it to yourself! Along with the singing and dancing Shooter Servers – waitresses who serve tequila shots from their shooter belts – there is also live entertainment nightly. Open nightly 5pm–5am.

Bar and club awards

Best for beautiful people: V-Bar, Venus, Tabu and Risqué.

Best for celeb spotting: Light, Ghost Bar, Tabu, Lure, Whiskey Bar and Rumjungle.

Best for cowboys: Gilley's.

Best party time: Coyote Ugly.

Best for salsa/Latin: Club Rio, Thursday nights.

Best Strip views: Curve, Mix Lounge, VooDoo Lounge, Hush, Pure.

Hippest: Shadow, Ghost Bar.

Hottest club in town: Tao Bar.

Swankiest: Whiskey Bar, Tabu, Ghost Bar and Light.

Wildest: Coyote Ugly, BiKiNis and Rumjungle.

Drai's

Barbary Coast at Flamingo, 702 737 7111
A smart-casual joint with some of the most expensive cocktails in town. Don't be put off by its location in the basement of the Barbary Coast Hotel. This is a plush bar with a quiet jazz combo playing and plenty of atmosphere. Open nightly 5.30–11pm.

A bar at the Flamingo

Gordon Biersch

3987 Paradise Road at Flamingo, 702 312 5247, gordonbiersch.com
Filled with beautiful people, this is one of the city's hottest pick-up parlours. Great brews, good food and live swing music make it a fun place to go. Open daily 11.30am–midnight and Tues–Sat until 2am.

I-Bar

Rio All-Suites Hotel, 702 777 6869, riolasvegas.com
The 'I' stands for Ipanema and this is a cool, quiet but erotic place. There are ten I-Girls – part model, part provocative dancer and part gifted mixologist – who serve up fruity drinks like Tropicana Hypnosis and Peachy Keen.

Monte Carlo Brew Pub

Monte Carlo, 702 730 7423, montecarlo.com
You can get meals, music and brews with live nightly entertainment from 9pm in the first microbrewery in a resort hotel. The DJs start spinning at 9pm, with live bands 9.30pm–2am. Open Sun–Thurs 11am–3am, Fri and Sat 11am–4am.

Red Square

Mandalay Bay, 702 632 7407, mandalaybay.com
The place to come for a spot of Russian firewater. Decorated to look like a former tsar's palace-turned-Communist Party HQ, drinks range from hardcore firewaters such as Red Army and Yubilev to shooters such as Stolichnaya (try saying that after two!) and a whole range of other vodkas. The other speciality of the house is the vast list of Martinis, for which the bar is famous. Open Sun–Thurs 5pm–2am, Fri and Sat 5pm–4am.

The stylish Petrossian Bar

Monte Carlo's Brew Pub

Petrossian Bar

Bellagio, 702 693 7111, bellagio.com
Those who enjoy the finer things in life should head to the chichi Petrossian. Champagne, smoked salmon, Petrossian caviar, vodka tastings and a choice of cigars are the order of the day here. Furthermore, it's all available 24/7.

> **BRITTIP**
> In the mood for quintessentially English afternoon tea? Then head to the Petrossian 2–5pm.

Shadow: A bar at Caesars Palace

Caesars Palace, 702 731 7110, caesarspalace.com
Right in the centre of the upmarket hotel's action, the ambience starts off relaxed enough but heats up when the nightly entertainment begins. Silhouetted dancers perform seductive routines behind backlit screens before venturing out to mingle with the crowd. If that's not your thing, watch the bartenders in action as they create speciality drinks such as Forbidden Fruit, Techno Rush, The Rave and Ultimate Explosion. There's no dance floor, but DJs

> **BRITTIP**
> Shadow Bar is the perfect place for a drink after a show and before hitting your chosen nightclub.

There's live entertainment at Zuri

spin a mix of house and hip-hop, while dancers perform Sun–Thurs 8pm–2am and Fri and Sat 7pm–3am. Open daily noon-4am.

Tilted Kilt

Rio All-Suite Hotel, 702 252 7777, riolasvegas.com
An Irish-American tavern with an extensive list of beers from around the world, plus billiards, darts and an eclectic menu featuring Drunken Clams and Sloppy Janes – a colossal sandwich spin-off of Sloppy Joes. Open daily 4pm–2am with happy hour 4–6pm.

Wine Cellar

Wine Cellar Tasting Room, Rio All-Suite Hotel, 3700 West Flamingo, 702 252 777, riolasvegas.com
The world's largest and most extensive collection of fine wines includes more than 600 different wines once only enjoyed by kings, presidents and the cultural elite. Open Sun–Thurs 3–11pm, Fri and Sat 3pm–midnight.

Zuri

MGM Grand, 702 891 1111, mgmgrand.com/nightlife
With live nightly entertainment this 100-seat bar just off the hotel's main lobby specialises in fruit-infused spirits such as frozen Woodford Reserve bourbon infused with peaches, cinnamon-infused vodka and speciality beers from around the globe. Open 24/7.

BRITTIP

If you've had a heavy night, try Zuri's For the Morning after the Night Before menu, which includes a variety of liquid brunch drinks and Bloody Marys!

Hotel lounges

One of the most wonderful things about Las Vegas is the lounge scene, a phenomenon that's unique to the city. Best of all, there is no entrance fee, although there may be a minimum drink order. The lounges all provide live music and just about every hotel has a good one.

Armadillo Lounge

Texas Station, 2101 Texas Star Lane, 702 631 1000
A real hit with the locals, thanks to the fair prices, this lounge is a happening place most nights of the week. Almost every musical style plays here from rock to blues, jazz, country and reggae. Phone the entertainment hotline for more information on 702 631 1001.

There's a great lounge at Planet Hollywood

BRITTIP Fancy a pit stop on your way up and down the Strip, but don't want to sit in a freezing cold, air-conditioned bar? Then head for the outdoor Ava Lounge or the poolside Dolphin Bar at the Mirage, where it's cool, not cold.

The Beatles REVOLUTION Lounge

Mirage, 702 692 8383, thebeatlesrevolutionlounge.com
Along with Cirque du Soleil®'s new Beatle's tribute show *LOVE*, the Mirage opened up this 60s retro lounge inspired by all things Beatles. It has a modern twist on 60's psychedelic décor, including viewing holes behind the bar inspired by a yellow submarine. Open nightly 6pm–4am.

Le Cabaret

Paris Las Vegas, 702 739 4111, parislasvegas.com
Designed to create the feeling of sitting outside in a garden area, you can sit under trees laced with twinkling lights while sipping your drinks and enjoying the live entertainment.

Caramel Lounge

Bellagio, 702 693 7111, bellagio.com
This is an excellent spot to enjoy a pre-show or late-night drink. Opaque marble tables, hand-blown glass sculptures, oversized round ottomans and leather sofas create an elegant and sophisticated setting for a trendy, yet relaxed lounge. It's all done on a theme of caramel – hence the name. Music ranges from the Rolling Stones to Frank Sinatra and the Beatles. The food menu includes the classic Las Vegas shrimp cocktail, pâté, smoked salmon and an assorted cheese plate, but the thing to go for here is the signature Martini served in chocolate and caramel-coated chilled glasses. Open nightly 5pm–4am.

The Caramel Lounge is an excellent nightspot

Skydeck at Ghost Bar

Fleur de Lys Lounge

Mandalay Bay, 702 632 7777, mandalaybay.com/entertainment
A cosy and intimate lounge with live music, it opens pre-dinner and provides an excellent spot for a late-night, post-meal nightcap.

Galleria Lounge

Caesars Palace, 702 731 7110, caesarspalace.com
An elegantly laid-back lounge in which to relax and enjoy a happy hour cocktail. Open 24 hours a day.

Ghost Bar

The Palms, 866 725 6768, http://ghostbar-las-vegas.n9negroup.com
A sultry indoor-outdoor lounge and sky deck on the 55th floor of The Palms, with 360-degree views of the glittering Las Vegas skyline, that has quickly become one of the hottest places in town. Decked out in silver, white, greens and greys, it has floor-to-ceiling windows, a 30ft/9m ghost-shaped ceiling that changes colour and custom-made ultra-contemporary lounge furniture including plastic egg-shaped chairs that would be perfect in a 1960s sci-fi show. Celebs such as David Schwimmer, Cuba Gooding Jr, Samuel Jackson and Mark Wahlberg have all enjoyed the private VIP lounge and the eclectic music. Miss it and miss out. Open nightly 8pm–4am.

The Lounge at the Mandalay Bay

Houdini's Lounge

Monte Carlo, 702 730 7423, montecarlo.com/entertainment
An intimate, understated but elegant lounge in which to enjoy a drink while listening to piano music. Live music is offered Thurs-Sun 10pm–1am.

The Lounge

Mandalay Bay, 702 632 7777, mandalaybay.com/entertainment
Slink into plush, club chairs, enjoy a match from the TV at the bar or get in a round at the billiards table.

Mist

Treasure Island, 702 894 7111, treasureisland.com
Another stylish yet casual lounge from the same people who created the Light nightclub (see page 145). Mist has state-of-the-art plasma screens, which are used for showing sporting events and music videos, while video poker is also available at the bar. Open daily 4pm–4am.

Mix Lounge

Mandalay Bay, 702 632 7777, mandalaybay.com/entertainment
Stylish lounge with breathtaking views of the Strip that sits alongside the hot new restaurant, the Mix.

BRITTIP
Martini is the drink of Las Vegas – and the best places for it are the Red Square at Mandalay Bay and Rain in the Desert at The Palms.

BRITTIP
Lounges may provide free music, but drinks can start at a pricey $5 and rise to an even more hefty $12 a hit – so sip, don't glug!

La Scena Lounge

Venetian, 702 414 4100, venetian.com
You won't escape the video games here, but you will enjoy the nightly entertainment of high-energy bands performing anything from rock 'n' roll to Motown, disco and Top 40 hits.

Seahorse Lounge

Caesars Palace, 702 731 7110, caesarspalace.com
Inspired by the most captivating elements of the sea world, a towering 1,700gall aquarium filled with seahorses announces your arrival at one of the most chilled lounges in town. Tuck into seafood appetisers and sip on champagne or any one of the speciality Martinis as you get a 360-degree view of Australian pot-belly seahorses.

Teatro

MGM Grand, 702 891 3695 for general information, 702 891 3650 for table or bottle service reservations, mgmgrand.com/nightlife
Not burlesque, not an ultra-lounge and not a nightclub. However, the emphasis at Teatro is very heavily weighted on the adult side. With the chichi atmosphere of an upmarket lounge, the clink-clink fizz of the champagne is served alongside go-go dancers, who strut their stuff on the bar. Later in the evening, the dark and secluded booths that line the perimeter wall are filled with huddles of mostly men intent on an up close and personal view of the dancers,

Teatro

who in the finest traditions of a strip club, expect to be decorated with dollar bills while boogying along to the acid jazz, urban, electronica and 1980s pop sounds spun by the DJs. Open Tues–Sat from 9pm.

Top of the World Lounge

Stratosphere, 702 380 7777, stratospherehotel.com/entertainment.html
A casino lounge on the 104th floor. Entrance to the Tower is $6, though you can avoid that by booking a table for dinner at the revolving restaurant (see page 122).

VooDoo Lounge

Rio All-Suite Hotel, 3700 West Flamingo, 702 252 7777, riolasvegas.com
The view of the Strip is fantastic and so are the bottle-juggling bartenders. Sit inside or outside on the terrace while sipping one of the many speciality drinks, such as the Witch Doctor, a mix of four rums and tropical fruit juices. Hot music plays nightly from 9pm. Open 5pm–2.30am.

BRITTIP
The lifts to the VooDoo Lounge and Café are on the second floor of the Masquerade Tower.

Whiskey Bar

Green Valley Ranch, 2300 Paseo Verde Parkway, Henderson, 702 617 7777. For concert tickets call 1-866-264 1818, greenvalleyranchresort.com
About a 30-minute drive from the Strip, this haven of old-style Hollywood charm is one of the places to see and be seen. The interior is elegant, but do step outside to enjoy the fantastic views. If you're here for the live music, then you'll see the magical surroundings anyway, as the Whiskey has a unique outdoor concert venue. Open Sun–Wed 5pm–2am, Thurs 5pm–3am, Fri and Sat 5pm–4am.

Non-hotel lounges

Fireside Lounge

The Peppermill Coffee Shop, 2985 Las Vegas Boulevard South, 702 735 4177, peppermilllasvegas.com/lounge
One of the swankiest and oldest surviving lounges with cosy booths, an intimate atmosphere and the famous fire pit – a circular fireplace surrounded by a pool of bubbling water. Recently named one of America's 10 Best Make-out Bars by *Nerve* magazine, this kitschy spot has attracted the likes of Sharon Stone and Joe Pesci. One of the quirks of the joint is that the waitresses – clothed in long black dresses split to the thigh – sit down at your table to take your order. Try the Scorpion, the giant-sized house special cocktail for two, a 64oz glass with six shots of various spirits, ice cream and two 2ft/60cm long straws! Open 24/7.

BRITTIP
It's worth making the trip out to Henderson to visit the Whiskey Bar for the views alone. Take your camera to record the valley during the day and the glittering lights of Las Vegas at night.

Patio at the VooDoo Lounge

Ice House Lounge

650 South Main Street, Downtown Las Vegas, 702 315 2570, icehouselounge.com
Not just a lounge, this is a new $5m, two-storey restaurant and gambling venue with two lounges featuring bar tops made of ice to keep drinks cold! The exterior has an art deco look with white stucco and LED lights that shine on the building and turn it different colours. Inside you can play video poker or watch sporting events and concerts and the like on any one of the 13 plasma screen TVs or the 100in/2.5m projection screen. The lounge interior has a retro feel with photos of old downtown Las Vegas and furniture from the 1960s. For a spot of outdoor dining, try the patios available on both levels; even better, the second floor patio has seating around a fireplace. Open 24/7.

Ultra-lounges

Is it a bar? Is it a music venue? Is it a nightclub? Is it a decadent den of iniquity? The new breed of nightlife in Las Vegas is called the ultra-lounge and it combines all of the above. Think luxurious decor, ultra comfy seating, sensuous music and a sense that anything goes and you'll start to build up a picture of the newest kind of scene on the block. Another element that marks an ultra-lounge out from a lounge or a nightclub is the relatively small dance floor – it's all about getting intimate, baby!

Best lounges for views

- Ghost Bar at The Palms (page 140)
- Top of the World at the Stratosphere (page 122)
- Voodoo Lounge at the Rio (page 142)
- Whiskey Bar at the Green Ranch (page 142)

Pure

Caesars Palace, 702 731 7873, caesarspalace.com
This insanely popular ultra-club was actually launched by a group of Hollywood personalities, thus it receives a steady stream of celebrities who draw locals and tourists in vast numbers. Inside is a 14,000sq ft/1.500sq m terrace that you can only reach through a shoulder-squirming, bottlenecked staircase, but which offers a magnificent view of the Strip. This is high-intensity partying with Hollywood royalty at its best. Open Tues, and Fri–Sun, 10pm–4am.

BRITTIP
Drink-drive penalties are severe and strictly enforced in the city so don't even think about it. Besides most of the best bars, lounges and nightclubs are around the Strip so you can either walk or take a taxi (see page 16).

Risqué

Paris Las Vegas, 702 946 4589, parislasvegas.com
On the second floor of the chic Paris hotel with dramatic views of the Strip, this ultra-lounge combines classic Parisian architecture with contemporary Asian style and discreet lighting elements in which to lounge or dance till dawn. An extension of the fabulous Ah Sin-restaurant (see page 103), you can indulge in late-night desserts here prepared by top pastry chef Jean-Claude Canestrier. What makes this place

Pure nightclub at Caesars Palace

so special, though, are the balconies, plush couches, ottomans, beds, lots of pillows and intimate, lighted dance floor. Open Wed–Sun 10pm–4am.

Tabu

MGM Grand, 702 891 7183, mgmgrand.com/nightlife

The MGM Grand's cutting edge nightclub for the ultra sophisticated beautiful people combines luxury with state-of-the-art technology and excellent service. The funky furniture, marble tops, wooden floors and gorgeous textiles are highlighted by saucy images of body parts that bounce off every surface with reactive imagery. The main room leads to two private rooms, one with a bar made of ice and metallic fabrics. Music goes from classic lounge tunes earlier in the night to more progressive vocals later in the evening. Champagne and vodka are the house specials. Open Tues–Sun from 10pm.

BRITTIP

Ensure yourself a reserved table at the trendy Tabu by ordering a bottle in advance of your visit, through the VIP services manager on 702 891 7129.

Tao

Venetian, 702 492 3960, venetian.com

Tao is not only a top restaurant but it also hosts what has become the hottest and sexiest ultra-lounge in Vegas. It is an odd mix of Oriental spirituality – with sensitive rock gardens, candles and waterfalls – with New York Modernism in the clean lines and colours. Just see the modernistic bar surrounded by hundreds of tiny Buddha statues and you will understand. It is also a hands-down favourite with celebrities and home to some of the most raucous parties in Sin City. Open Thurs–Sun, 10.30pm–5.30am.

Body English at the Hard Rock Hotel

The stylish ultra-lounge of Tabu

Hotel nightclubs

Body English

Hard Rock Hotel, 702 693 5555, hardrockhotel.com

The Hard Rock's hot nightclub is firmly aimed at the kind of Hollywood celeb who loves to enjoy the adult environment of Las Vegas at the weekend. With mirrored walls, Baccarat crystal chandeliers and rich leather booths, it screams high class, while a booth on the upper floor overlooking the dance floor will set back four people $300 for a bottle. Also upstairs is a VIP area offering an overview of all the action and a bar with standing room for ordinary mortals to mingle and watch the action.

BRITTIP

The Body English is discreetly tucked away from the Hard Rock crowds under The Joint and is entered via an easy-to-miss set of stairs.

Downstairs is the main dance floor, overhung with a huge crystal chandelier that changes colour throughout the evening. There is also a second bar, more booths and an ultra VIP area that is so discreet the occupants can see out but cannot be seen. The room has its own bar and is soundproof so those inside can choose their own music.

While you may not be able to access all places, women will love the ladies toilets – the club has one of the largest 'restrooms'

Cleopatra's Barge

in town, an elegant escape with large golden swan faucet fixtures. Open Fri–Sun 10.30pm–4am.

Cleopatra's Barge

Caesars Palace, 702 731 7110, caesarspalace.com
A theme offering from the Greco-Roman resort, this always popular club is housed in an ornate replica of the kind of craft that once transported royalty down the River Nile. Statues and centurions abound in the beautiful setting where live contemporary dance music is on the menu and drinks are served by luscious hand maidens in diaphanous Cleopatra costumes. Open Tues–Sun 8.30pm–4am.

Club Rio

Rio All-Suite Hotel, 702 252 7777, riolasvegas.com
A video wall surrounds the circular room of this club and a misting system keeps you cool when things get hot! Music includes Top 40 dance hits, 1980s music, Latin, hip-hop and house, while ladies get cheap drinks. Be warned: it's a popular haunt and is always crowded despite a strict no-jeans policy and white collared shirts for men. Open Wed and Fri 11.30pm– 3.30am, Thurs and Sat 10.30pm–4am.

The Dragon

Mandalay Bay, 702 636 7404, mandalaybay.com/entertainment
An ultra-hip after-hours club in the China Grill restaurant, which really gets going after 1am and always attracts a beautiful crowd. The 1960s design of the restaurant with fab sofas and dramatic lighting is a perfect backdrop for this exotic, multi-tiered club, which has a circular, granite dance floor. Open Wed only 11pm–4am.

Light

Bellagio, 702 693 8300, bellagio.com
Sexy and refined nightclub and lounge with chichi decor, excellent service and state-of-the-art electronics, based on the New York nightclub of the same name. On a par with Annabelle's in London, the 7,000sq ft/650sq m space includes cocktail bars and a lounge with 40 tables that can be pre-booked. DJs spin a mix of hip-hop and house, while go-go dancers do their thing. It's all about high-rollers and celebrities and it works – this is one of the best places in town to spot one! Celebs seen here include Leonardo DiCaprio, Tobey Maguire, Courteney Cox-Arquette, Lucy Liu, Matt LeBlanc and Sting. Open Thurs–Sat 10.30pm–4am.

BRITTIP
To avoid the long queues to get into Light, go before 11pm.

Club Rio

BRITTIP

Smart dress is essential to get into most nightclubs. Generally no trainers, denim or shorts are allowed, while baggy jeans are also banned and tank tops for men are a real no-no almost everywhere!

The Nightclub

Las Vegas Hilton, 702 732 5111, lvhilton.com
Showcases up-and-coming singers, while top resident DJs provide the kind of music that makes this another of the best nightspots in town. Dressing up to the nines is a must! Open Thurs–Sat 11pm–4am.

OPM

Forum Shops at Caesars, 702 369 4998
An ultra-modern club with a state-of-the-art light and sound show and DJs spinning progressive and funk music, say the name fast and you'll get its subversive meaning! The decor is a mix of West meets East with rich red fabrics and communal ottomans, while cocktail servers dressed in sensual Asian outfits appeal to the upmarket 'in' crowd. Upstairs from Wolfgang Puck's Asian-French Chinois restaurant, food is available until 3am. Open Thurs–Sun 10pm–6am.

BRITTIP

Las Vegas has no shortage of bias. Men pay more to get into nightclubs than women and many clubs charge out-of-towners double. Think anywhere from $10 to $30 for men and up to $20 for women. In fact, if ladies are prepared to work their charm, they can often schmooze their way in for free!

The Luxor pyramid looks stunning at night

The new hotspot, Pure

Pure

Caesars Palace, 702 731 7873, caesarspalace.com
One of the hot new nightclubs, the 36,000sq ft/1,215sq m nightclub offers three distinct areas over two storeys. The cream, white and silver decor of the main room contrasts sharply with the VIP-only Red Room with its plush fabrics, chandeliers and upholstered walls. A glass lift will then take you up to the terrace with its dance floor, private cabanas and tables that offer spectacular views of the Strip. The club also provides access to the new burlesque Pussycat Dolls Lounge (see page 154) Open Fri–Sun 10pm–4am.

Ra

Luxor, 702 262 4000, luxor.com/entertainment
Another all-nighter where you most definitely dress to impress, this is now one of the longest-running nightclubs in town. There are two enormous bars with a central dance floor surrounded by tables and booths for more privacy, while VIPs get

BRITTIP

Want to experience the VIP treatment? Well, money talks in Vegas. You don't need to be a celeb – you just need to hand over the dosh. You may have to part with at least $150–200 for a booth – could be worth it for the special treatment if you're with a crowd. Call in advance to check out the prices.

Purple Rain!

their own special area. There are also two cigar lounges, plus a sushi and oyster bar. Open Wed–Sat 10pm–6am.

Rain in the Desert

The Palms, 702 942 7777, palms.com
The massive multi-level Rain doubles as a nightclub and concert venue and is famous for its special effects, which include water, fire and fog. The back of the stage is flanked by a 16ft/5m, colour-changing water wall and the front by a rain curtain. You enter through a gold-mirrored mosaic tunnel and can either head straight for the elevated bamboo dance floor surrounded by a computer-programmed river of water or find a private booth with water sofas (only eight, so it's best to book one!). VIPs and the very wealthy can opt for one of the cabanas with mini-bars or a sky box with a private balcony on the third floor.

Food is available and appetisers include shrimp cocktail, smoked salmon canapés, crab cakes, tenderloin skewers with dipping sauce and full oyster and caviar menus. Drink specialities include a sake selection, premium tequilas, champagnes and Martinis. Open Thurs–Sat 11pm–5am.

Rumjungle

Mandalay Bay, 702 632 7777, mandalaybay.com/entertainment
Still one of the hottest clubs in town. A massive cocktail lounge featuring flaming walls and waterfalls, rum cocktails (natch!), flaming meat skewers and go-go dancers, it is home to the world's largest rum bar (85ft/26m long and 19ft/6m high). Celebs spotted here include Brad Pitt, Pete Sampras, Jimmy Smits and 'N Sync. The queues get long, so arrive early. And don't forget a trip to the restrooms, which are very similar to the unisex version in *Ally McBeal*. Open Tues and Wed 11pm–2.30am, Thurs–Sat and Mon 11pm–4.30am.

Studio 54

MGM Grand, 702 891 1111, mgmgrand.com/nightlife
A high-energy nightclub with state-of-the-art sound, video and lighting along with a troupe of live dancers. There are four separate dance floors and bars, an exclusive area for invited guests, plus the Rainforest Café, a giant show bar with video screens and music. Tuesday evening is Eden – Erotically Delicious Entertainer's Night – and Thursday is Dollhouse night when guests can dress up beautiful life-size 'dolls' in outfits from the club's reach-in closets. The dolls then serve as hosts in place of cocktail waitresses. Mon–Sat 10pm–5am.

Studio 54 at the MGM Grand

BRITTIP

Avoid queuing to get into the hippest nightclubs in town. Buy front-of-line tickets in advance from vegas.com.

SynCity, The Nightclub

Riviera Hotel, 702 794 9426, rivierahotel.com

'Bring only your temptation!' is the slogan of one of the newest nightclubs in town. With Dynamixx of the SynCity Mechanixx, flare bartenders create a true party atmosphere in a place where anything goes. Wild Women Wednesdays feature wild and crazy contests (women get in free and pay just $1 per drink all night), then there are Nuts and Bolts Thursdays and Fantasy Fridays, while every Saturday becomes New Year's Eve in SynCity, and Synful Sundays allow female entertainers free entrance. Wed–Sun 10pm–4am.

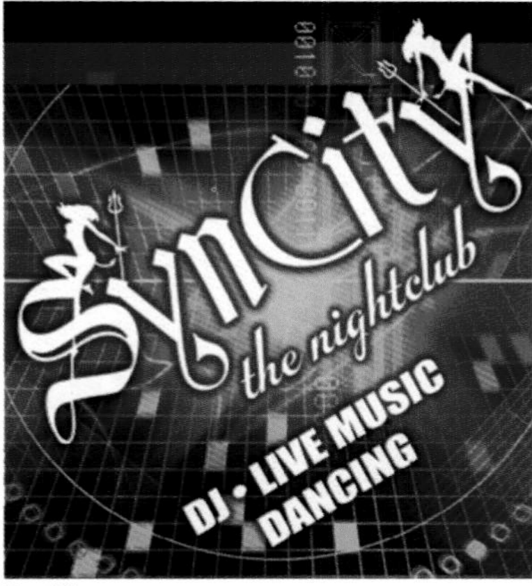

SynCity

Tryst

Wynn Las Vegas, 702 770 3633, wynnlasvegas.com

This could be the cause of the ultimate romantic moment and something like this could only be found at the lavish Wynn Las Vegas. This fiendishly luxurious nightspot has intimate seating under an open-air main room and a sizeable dance floor that ends at a 90ft/27m waterfall that falls under cunning mood lighting. Service and drinks are decadently wonderful – and costly. Cover charge sometimes applies. Open Thurs–Sun 10pm–4am.

Tryst

V Bar

Venetian, 702 414 3200, venetian.com

One of the coolest nightclubs in town, it is based on both the trend-setting supper club Lotus in New York and Los Angeles's swanky Sunset Room. An upscale lounge, it has opaque glass walls, double-sided leather chaises longues and subdued lighting. The focal point is a custom-designed oversized bed made of pearlised silver leather and hollowed in the centre to allow space for a table holding a selection of exotic cocktails. Top DJs spin wide range of heart-pumping tunes. Open daily 6pm–4am.

There are plenty of clubs to enjoy

BiKiNis Club

The View

Harrah's Las Vegas, 702 369 5222, harrahs.com
Located in the hotel's Range Steakhouse, it has spectacular views of the Strip. This is a comfortable, intimate place to dance, drink and dine after hours on a menu of appetisers, while DJs spin dance tracks from the 1970s to the present day. Open Thurs–Sat midnight–5am.

Whiskey Sky

Green Valley Ranch, 2300 Paseo Verde Parkway, Henderson, 702 617 7777, greenvalleyranchresort.com
An innovative nightclub with an 8acre/3ha backyard pool area with private cabanas, day beds and an outdoor bar with gambling tables. The nightclub is right next door to Whiskey Bar (see page 142). Open daily 4pm–4am.

Hotel beach clubs

BiKiNis Beach & Dance Club

Rio All-Suite Hotel, 702 252 7777, riolasvegas.com
A year-round indoor beach party with a South Beach-inspired design, the 11,000sq ft/1,020sq m dance club has a bar and even a shopping area. The real attraction is the sexy bikini and swimming-trunk-clad cocktail servers, bartenders, dancers and lifeguards, who use the beach showers to cool off after entertaining guests from the top of the lifeguard stands. A lava lounge offers old school and disco music from the 1970s and 1980s and there are four bars, but if you get desperate, just flag down one of the shot-toting cocktail servers. Sunday night fever with Boogie Knights. Open Thurs–Sun 9pm–4am.

Moorea Ultra Beach Lounge

Mandalay Bay, 702 632 7777, mandalaybay.com/entertainment
The Tahitian-style poolside club – decked out appropriately with tiki torches, cabanas and floating candles – is where the beautiful people go to party in their cossies late into the night. In previous years, this topless bathing area was considered risqué, but now that 'European bathing' has become so popular throughout Sin City, it has become almost blasé. Things can get pretty wild once the sun has set and the DJs come out to spin music for dancers, displayed on giant video screens.

Poolbar & Palapa

Hard Rock Hotel, 702 693 5000, hardrockhotel.com
Home to some of the naughtiest night scenes in town (and that's saying something), the Hard Rock's poolside paradise comes complete with swim-up blackjack, waterfalls and private cabanas in an Indonesian-style setting. There are Sunday Pool Parties that are only just short of the limit to becoming called orgies (and sometimes cross the line).

Skin

Skin Pool Lounge, The Palms, 702 942 7777, palms.com
By day a luxurious outdoor lounge with two pools, a lavender-shaded swimming pool and the Mermaid Cove – an elevated pool with portholes where mermaids swim after dark – plus private cabanas and fibre-optically lit water salons, four bars, billiard tables, outdoor swings, poolside blackjack, trampolines, massages and other spa services.

Come night-time in the summer, the lounge is transformed into one of the most spectacular outdoor nightclubs and concert venues in Vegas. It has a concert stage,

The Strip at night

two dance floors, including Plexiglass dance platforms where aqua go-go girls emerge from the depths of the lavender pool. An elevated pool-top dance floor allows you literally to dance on water. Atmosphere is added with amazing lighting and fog effects.

Along with the rest of The Palms' venues, this has become a fast hit with locals and visitors alike – a true haven of voyeurism for adults. And if you're hungry, poolside dining is provided by Nine Steakhouse and includes specialities such as sashimi and ceviche.

During the day, Skin is only open to hotel residents, but in the evening it is open to the public. Cover charges vary depending on the entertainment, while the beach party element is only on during the summer.

Non-hotel nightclubs

The Beach Las Vegas

365 Convention Center Drive, 702 731 1925, beachlv.com

One of the most happening venues in town. Maybe it has something to do with the bikini-wearing waitresses and muscle-bound bartenders. Rock 'n' roll fans will enjoy Wednesday's special night, while Thursday night is Almost Famous night, when live bands, garage bands and up-and-coming artists can show off their talents. Open 24/7.

BRITTIP

Visit The Beach website 24 hours in advance to organise free entry to the nightclub. Your name will be put on the guest list, but you will have to arrive before midnight.

The Beach is the place to party

Club Seven

3724 Las Vegas Boulevard South, 702 739 7744

Great restaurant and nightclub with a main dance floor with two bars, plus two smaller rooms and a sushi bar. The restaurant is swathed in elegant red and filled with swanky booths. The main nightclub has two bars – one featuring a glass top with roses and lights twinkling beneath – a circular dance floor and tiger-skin booths, while DJs spin house, hip-hop and dance music.

The club's main feature is its patio overlooking the Strip, which has a bar, couches and tables – a great spot for people-watching. Open Mon–Wed 11pm–2am, Thurs–Sat 11pm–5am.

Drink

200 East Harmon Avenue, 702 796 5519

The place to go for a fun, party atmosphere. Full of hip, young locals and tourists, it's a friendly place where you can

The bright lights of Vegas

Empire Ballroom

dance, drink and eat, too! If you can make it through the madding crowds, the VIP room above the cigar room is the place to go. Unheard-of drink combinations are served in babies' bottles, test tubes and small plastic buckets. Open Tues–Sat 8pm–5am.

Empire Ballroom

3765 S Las Vegas Boulevard, 702 492 3960, empireballroom.com
The Empire is the newest kid of the Las Vegas independent nightclubs, but it is fast gaining a reputation. In many places, managers limit top DJs on what type of music they can spin, but at Empire Ballroom the top DJs are flown in and told to do whatever they want. The result is a wild time when the music can send the crowd into hysteria.

Owners took over the long-empty Strip building that was once the home of the famous Utopia Club as a home for their creation. The Empire is all about deep reds and browns and overstuffed couches flanking a big dance floor that is always filled with gyrating bodies moving to edgy sounds. Open Tues–Wed 10pm–6am, Thurs–Sat 1am–6 am and Sun 10.30pm–6am.

Ice

200 East Harmon Avenue, next to the Hard Rock Hotel, 702 699 5528, icelasvegas.com
An amazing nightclub with five bars, a massive dance space, two DJ booths and a fog system. Not for the fainthearted, the scene is definitely on the lurid side, thanks to the heavy tribal rhythms, and favoured skimpy leather outfits and ultra-suggestive dance movements of the punters! Open Fri 10.30pm–5am, Sat 10.30pm–7am.

Plush Lounge & Lagoon

221 North Rampart Boulevard, 702 869 2335
A refreshing lounge and nightclub venue located off the Strip. The gorgeous interiors – designed to draw the beautiful people – include two dance floors, two bars and private VIP areas decked out in rich velvet. Or step outside and enjoy the pretty lagoon views from the terrace, which has its own couches, bed and bar. Enjoy half-priced drinks during the happy hours of 5-8pm, while the nightclub kicks in at 10pm, complete with go-go dancers and VIP bottle service. Open 7pm–12am Wed, 7pm–2am Thurs, 5pm–4am Fri and 7pm–4am Sat.

After hours

Alesium Afterhours at Seven

3724 South Las Vegas Boulevard, 702 992 7970
In the same venue as Club Seven, the crowd here is very friendly and relaxed, while the DJs continue the beat with dance, hip-hop and house music. Open Thurs–Sat 2am–9am.

AM at OPM

The Forum Shops at Caesars, 702 369 4998
The chichi OPM club is used for a great after-hours party on Fri and Sat 3am–8am.

HOB: Late night

House of Blues, Mandalay Bay, 702 632 7777, mandalaybay.com/entertainment
After the live music has finished, the DJs do their thing. Friday features 1980s music, Saturday is for the Boogie Knights disco and Sunday is a Service Industry Night. Open Fri–Sun 11pm–6am.

Dancing at Ice

Live music venues

House of Blues

Mandalay Bay, 702 632 7777, mandalaybay.com/entertainment
The legendary chain of restaurants-cum-live music venues and nightclubs provides an eclectic mix of music to serve all tastes. The venue, which can hold 1,900 people, plays host to every kind of band from rock to R&B, reggae, hip-hop, country, jazz and, of course, blues. A Sunday Gospel Brunch features the best of gospel music and a Southern-style buffet with seating at 10am and 1pm. Live blues Thurs–Sat. The 500-seater restaurant serves everything from the casual to the sublime including the classic Elwood sandwich (named after Dan Aykroyd's character in *The Blues Brothers*), Memphis-style ribs with Jack Daniels sauce, cedar plank salmon with watercress-jicama salad and voodoo shrimp served with rosemary cornbread.

BRITTIP
Don't hang around the bar at the House of Blues if you want to catch a good view of the band, as the low-lying ceiling will obscure your view.

The Joint

Hard Rock Hotel, Harmon Avenue, 702 226 4650, hardrockhotel.com
Famous for its cracking live music in a great rock 'n' roll environment. Phone for live music updates.

Tommy Rocker's

BRITTIP
Generally gig tickets go from between $20 and $80, but can rise to a staggering $1,000 a hit if you want to see the Rolling Stones, for instance, at The Joint!

Tommy Rocker's

4275 South Industrial Road, 702 261 6688, tommyrocker.com
A snazzy grill and cantina for a casual set who like to have fun. A greater selection of beers than most bars, while the rock music makes this a legendary, if extremely loud, live music joint! Open 24/7.

Stunning views from the House of Blues

Freemont Street offers five blocks of fun

Jazz

Napoleon's

Paris Las Vegas, 702 739 4111, parislasvegas.com
One of the best champagne bars in the city, with more than 100 varieties to choose from, it also has a full-service bar. So enjoy a glass of bubbly and sit back to soak up the smooth live jazz. The bar also has a fully-stocked cigar humidor and a carving station for fresh rolls piled high with steak, mustard-rubbed roast turkey and wine-braised pork loin. Open Sun–Thurs 4pm–2am, Fri and Sat 4pm–3am.

BRITTIP
Phone Napoleon's in advance to check Happy Hour times, when you get a complimentary carving station roll if you buy a drink.

Onda Lounge

Mirage, 702 791 7111, mirage.com
Just outside the Onda restaurant (see page 114), this is where you can sip wines by the glass or indulge in a cocktail while enjoying the live jazz. Open nightly 5pm–midnight.

Jazz Festival at the Fremont Street Experience

Downtown Las Vegas, 1 800 249 3559, vegasexperience.com
Go to the city during the last weekend in May and you'll enjoy the now annual free Jazz Festival that takes place throughout the five city blocks that make up the Fremont Street Experience.

Country and Western

Gilley's

New Frontier Hotel, 702 794 8434
For the true cowboy experience Las Vegas-style, head for Gilley's, which has become known around town for its amazing barbecue, great music – both live and by DJ – excellent service and the Gilley's Girls. On top of all this, you can try out the famous mechanical bull and take line-dancing lessons. On Friday and Saturday game (and brave!) girls can take part in the bikini bull-riding contest at midnight for $500 in cash and prizes. Sun–Wed bull rides 4–9pm (first ride free), the DJ starts at 7.30pm.

BRITTIP
Weird but true: women are allowed to 'entertain' men, but are not allowed entry to 'gentlemen's' clubs unless they arrive with a man!

Thursday is ladies' night with line-dancing lessons 7.30–8.30pm, free bull rides and drinks for $1 all night from 9pm. Thurs–Sat you can opt for the $10 all-you-can-drink draft beer after 9pm. The band starts at 10pm, when it costs $10 to get in.

Other Country and Western venues

Gold Coast Dance Hall: 4000 West Flamingo, 702 367 7111.
Idle Spurs Tavern: 1113 Rainbow Boulevard, 702 363 7718.
Saddle 'n' Spurs Saloon: 2329 North Jones, 702 646 6292.
Sam's Town Western Dance Hall: 5111 Boulder Highway, 702 456 7777 with free dance lessons.
Silverado Dance Hall: 5255 Boulder Highway, 702 458 8810.

Jazz at the Onda Lounge

Burlesque

Ranging anywhere from sexy through steamy and ribald to flat-out raunchy, sex sells, and the Las Vegas tradition of beautiful bodies reaches new levels as dancers and strippers from both sexes peel down to the very briefest of g-strings to panting crowds. The main admission prices may be reasonable, but guaranteed entry and the best seats in the house come with a hefty price tag.

Ivan Kane's Forty Deuce

Mandalay Bay, 702 632 9442, mandalaybay.com/entertainment

Modelled on a 1920s speakeasy and popular with the celebrity crowd, the Forty Deuce offers plush leather chairs, tiered seating and cocktail tables with sweet little lamps. The sultry atmosphere is created by the low-level lighting and the dark red hues and wooden decor. The club can hold just 300 people, so it pays to arrive early to bag a prime-viewing seat. The burlesque dancers strut their stuff magnificently before defrocking to their sexy undies. The club also has a boutique selling burlesque-inspired clothing.

Admission is $20, front-of-line (queue) admission $40, and a host of packages range $400–850. The $400 Naughty Package includes front-of-line admission for four guests, a guaranteed VIP table, one bottle of vodka, mixers and a 10% discount at Champagne Suzy. The $850 Premium Scandalous Package includes front-of-line admission for eight guests, a guaranteed VIP table, two bottles of premium vodka, mixers and a 10% discount at Champagne Suzy. Open Wed–Sun, 10.30pm–dawn.

Ivan Kane's Forty Deuce

X Burlesque at the Flamingo

Pussycat Dolls Lounge

Caesars Palace, 702 731 7873, caesarspalace.com

Inside Caesars' Pure nightclub, the famous Pussycat Dolls of Hollywood lore have re-created their sexy show in a bijou lounge decorated with celebrity guest Dolls Charlize Theron, Christina Aguilera and Paris Hilton. Clad in fishnet tights and leather bustiers, the Dolls sing, dance and generally tantalise their audience from the stage and swings that hang from the ceiling. At just three to five minutes long, shows are relatively short, but take place every 30 minutes from 10pm. The cover price varies constantly. Open Tues–Sat, 6pm–4am.

Tangerine

Treasure Island, 702 492 3960, treasureisland.com

Tangerine is the name and the funky, retro decor in orange and white includes fabrics draped over walls that glow with orange light while a bevy of burlesque dancers hop on the bar and strip from glitzy evening gowns to their lingerie several times a night. Of course, often the lingerie is merely painted on! The club has one of the hotel's best views of the Strip, plus the Siren Cove. During the day a steel drum band performs as daiquiris are served on the patio.

The nightclub is open Tues–Sat 9pm–4am, during which time there is live music. The patio is open Tues–Sat 10pm–4am, Sun–Mon 5pm–midnight. The Tangerine dancers perform every hour 10.45pm–1.45am. General admission $20, front of line $40, VIP packages including line passes for four and a table with two bottles of Absolut $550.

Showgirls at Bally's

Strip clubs

The sex industry is big business in Las Vegas and to prove it a raft of swanky new clubs has recently opened. Indeed the latest – Sapphire – cost $25m and is so upmarket you may even feel you've wandered into the lobby of a five-star hotel. Kid yourself not though, the club is purely about titillation with a spot of elegance thrown in! The following are the major topless clubs.

Club Paradise

4416 Paradis Road, 702 734 7990
One of the older-style clubs, but extremely popular thanks to its lack of seediness (which in Las Vegas equals classy!). It consists of a large room with a nightclub atmosphere, one main stage and two other dance floors, plus go-go type dance stages near the ceiling. The club also has a restaurant and VIP room. Open Mon–Fri 4pm–6am, Sat and Sun 6pm–6am. Cover prices: before 9pm $5 for women, $10 for men; after 9pm $10 for women, $20 for men; lap dance $20.

Sapphire Gentlemen's Club

3025 South Industrial Road, 702 796 6000, sapphirelasvegas.com
The newest, swankiest, largest club in town, at 71,000sq ft/6,600sq m, it is massive, and at peak times there can be up to 800 topless dancers entertaining the crowds. The huge, multi-layered central stage can be seen from any part of the club, while music includes a variety of dance and Top 40 hits. The three main bars are the Martini Bar, which has an enormous Martini glass as its centrepiece, Pete's Bar and the Off Broadway bar, generally used for private parties. Other facilities include the Stake restaurant, serving steaks, which has its own separate entrance, and VIP Sky Boxes, which allow clients to overlook the main dance floor from a private room. Cover prices: free 6am–6pm, then $10 for locals, $20 for non-residents. Lap dances $20; VIP lap dances $100 for three; an hour in the VIP area $400; Skybox $250 an hour including drinks, plus $500 an hour for lap dances. Open 24/7.

BRITTIP

If you really want to get up close – but not personal – the going rate for a lap dance is generally $20. VIP rates, usually for four dances in a private room, start at around $100

Burlesque dancers at Tangerine

Strip club etiquette

- First of all, in Las Vegas anyway, there is a distinction between a strip club and a gentlemen's club – the former offers full nudity and the latter topless only. Both have strict rules governing behaviour.
- While many strip clubs don't necessarily have a dress code, you won't get in if you look really scruffy or if you're drunk.
- If you try to touch one of the girls, you'll find yourself out on your ear pretty pronto.
- Have plenty of cash. The girls are not paid and work for tips only. It's a big no-no to take in the sights and not tip.
- Don't even think about sitting stage side without a wad for both drinks and tipping.
- While the dancers are working girls, they're not THAT kind of working girl. Prostitution is illegal in Las Vegas – ironic or what! – so don't even think about it. It's also not on to ask for a date or even suggest dinner.

Other topless-only clubs

Cheetah's Topless Lounge

2112 Western Avenue between West Oakey Boulevard and Sahara Avenue, 702 384 0074, cheetahsnv.com
One of the friendliest clubs, it puts a big emphasis on providing coverage of major sporting events. It has five intimate little stages and is a favourite with locals. Open 24/7. Cover price: $10.

Sapphire Gentlemen's Club

Glitter Gulch on Fremont Street

Crazy Horse Too

2476 Industrial Road at Sahara Avenue, 702 382 8003, crazyhorsetoo.com
Like Cheetah's, this club has been around forever, but is nowhere near as well laid out. There are only two stage areas and you'll have a long wait to get a ringside seat. Open 24/7. Cover price: $20 6pm–6am.

Girls of Glitter Gulch

20 Fremont Street between Casino Center and Main Street, 702 385 4774, glittergulchlv.com
Thanks to its location close to the Fremont Street Experience, this attracts a fairly touristy crowd. Open Sun–Thurs noon–4am, Fri and Sat noon–6am. Cover price: $20 1pm–4am.

Olympic Garden Cabaret

1531 Las Vegas Boulevard South at Wyoming Avenue, 702 385 8987, ogvegas.com
Once one of the largest topless clubs in Vegas – prior to the opening of Jaguar's and Sapphire's – the main room has several stages, while the second has two stages and a catwalk. An exotic male dance revue takes place in the VIP lounge upstairs. Open 24/7. Cover price: free before 6pm, $20 after 6pm.

Play It Again, Sam

4120 Spring Mountain Road, 702 876 1550, playitagainsams.com
A gentlemen's-style club with an almost restaurant-like atmosphere, booths and video poker machines, the intimate club features an all-you-can-eat gourmet lunch buffet. Open 24/7. Cover price: $10 after 7pm.

Scores

Pleasures

6370 Windy Road, 702 873 8800
Tucked away off the far south end of the Strip, it is easy to miss, but the joint has an accessible club-like atmosphere and a decent design that makes it the perfect pit-stop for the uninitiated. Open Mon–Sat 2pm–6am. Cover price: $20 after 10pm.

Scores Las Vegas

3355 South Procyon Road, 702 367 4000, lvscores.com
The famous New York gentleman's club has opened in Las Vegas and set a new standard in elegance and superior service in the space formerly known as Jaguars. There are three main stages and the chairs are particularly comfortable – an important factor when considering indulging in a lap dance. There are also three bars and VIP rooms. Open 5pm–8am daily. Cover prices: $20 before 8pm, $30 after 8pm.

Sin

3525 West Russell Road, 702 673 1700, singentlemensclub.com
One of the largest pleasure domes in town, the 40,000sq ft/3,728sq m building features an 18,000sq ft/1,683sq m topless nightclub with three stages, a VIP room, and hundreds of dancers. There is also a 3,500sq ft/327sq m sports bar. Open 24 hours daily. Cover price: $20.

The Spearmint Rhino

3344 Highland Drive, 702 796 3600, spearmintrhino.com
Considered one of the best strip clubs in town, it offers excellent dancers, seating options and a choice of stages. Open 24/7. Cover price: $20 non-residents.

Striptease

3750 South Valley View Boulevard, 702 253 1555
The 'cosy' atmosphere and its location just behind the Rio make this one of the most accessible strip clubs in town. Open 12pm–6am daily. Cover price: free before 6pm, $10 after 6pm, guests arriving by limo or taxi $20.

Total nudity

For classic dark and steamy, make for any of these old-time strip clubs, which all feature total nudity.

BRITTIP
Strip clubs that offer total nudity do not serve alcohol.

Can-Can Room

3155 Industrial Road, one block west of the Stardust Hotel, 702 737 1161, cancanroom.com
There are five stages and seven fantasy theme rooms. The club offers private

Las Vegas is a 24-hour city

BRITTIP

Some strip clubs do a big, hard-sell number on private dances. Do not feel you have to commit yourself to something that could easily cost $150 unless you are happy with the quality of the dancer.

dances in VIP bedrooms – at a cost of $150 for 30 minutes. Open 4pm–5am. Cover price: $20 non-residents (includes two drinks).

Déjà Vu Showgirls

3247 South Industrial Avenue, north west of the Fashion Show Mall, 702 894 4167, dejavu.com
Open Mon–Sat 11am–6am, Sun 6pm–4am. Cover price: $25.

Diamond Cabaret

3177 Highland Drive, north-west of the Fashion Show Mall, 702 731 2365
Open 5pm–5am daily. Cover prices: $20, $30 if arriving by taxi.

Leopard Lounge

3500 West Naples, a mile south of the Rio All-Suite Hotel off Polaris Road, 702 798 6939, theleopardlounge.com
Open daily 2pm–4am. Cover prices: free if arriving by personal transportation, $20 if arriving by taxi or limo.

Little Darlings

1514 Western Avenue, half a mile south of Charleston Avenue/Interstate 15 intersection, 702 366 1633
Open Mon–Sat 11am–6am daily. Cover prices: $10 for locals, $20 for non-residents.

Palomino Club

1848 North Las Vegas Boulevard, 500m south of the intersection with East Lake Mead Road, 702 385 8987
Open daily 5pm–5am. Cover prices: $15 for locals and women, $30 non-residents.

Palomino Club

Showgirl Video

631 South Las Vegas Boulevard in the downtown area, 702 385 4554
Open daily 8am–5am. Cover price: $1.

Talk of the Town

1238 South Las Vegas Boulevard, one block south of the intersection with East Charleston Road, 702 385 1800
Open daily 4pm–4am. Cover price: free with one-drink minimum ($10).

BRITTIP

Make sure you have plenty of singles ($1 bills) with you to tip the dancers!

7 GAMBLING

Everything you need to know about having a flutter without blowing all your cash

You've seen the erupting volcano, watched the fountains of Bellagio and witnessed amazing circus acts – all in the most opulent, best-that-money-can-buy settings. Now let's get down to the nitty gritty, the *raison d'être* of the city – the casinos.

Most of the Strip resorts have their casinos laid out in such a way that you can't fail to notice them even before you've got to your room. That is so you don't need to spend five straight hours taking a chance, but just hit a few dollars here and there to and from the show or dinner. It's no surprise really: you have to accept that there is only one reason for all the glamour and razzmatazz: the making of money – absolutely billions of it.

BRITTIP

Remember the golden rules of gambling: stick to your own limits and always, always quit while you're ahead!

The casinos want people to have fun and to know when to walk away because they want them to return again and again and again. That way, they know, the odds are that they'll always get their money back – and more besides! High-roller baccarat players, the very latest slot machines, state-of-the-art video gambling machines and sports betting are the big money-spinners, and you'll also find everything else from roulette to craps and poker to blackjack.

To this end, the industry has been working hard to make casinos more user-friendly by providing free lessons in easy-to-find locations. A move to put 'comps' (see page 172) on a more straightforward

In this chapter

Never let a small win dazzle you!

BRITTIP Money raised from gambling was used to buy uniforms, provisions and bullets for troops fighting us Brits during America's fight for independence from 1775 to 1783.

footing has led to the creation of loyalty cards by many establishments where the amount of money you spend along with the time you spend gambling generates points to put towards free meals, free rooms and free shows.

Whether you intend to spend $20 or $2,000 gambling, or just sit in one of the many bars and watch the action, all these factors mean you can have a fantastic time in Las Vegas without parting with huge amounts of money – as long as you follow the rules: stick to your own limits and always, always quit while you're ahead!

High-rollers

The casinos like to keep all their customers happy, but they go to extraordinary lengths to accommodate high-rollers (big betters) – and I mean HIGH! Baccarat, the game they tend to play, accounts for a massive 13% of casino takings. With its high-bet limits and liberal odds, baccarat is worth a cool $1b in gambling income worldwide and other Las Vegas casinos have been working hard to cash in. Bally's casino on the Strip has hired a high-roller expert to weed out the big fish – gamblers willing to bet $300,000 to $1m each hand – from the 'whales', who only bet around $250,000 a hand!

High-stakes poker is big business, too, and Las Vegas has been home to the World Series of Poker title for the last four decades. For 35 years, Binions Casino in the Fremont Street area hosted this gathering of card sharks. However, in 2005 Harrah's bought the rights to the WSOP and eventually moved it to the Rio Suites and Casino. This came as internet poker sites began to explode in popularity, and the WSOP exploded in size, besides being moved from May to a June–July setting.

High-rollers area at Caesars Palace

Casino at Planet Hollywood

The move included an increase in the number of events, and what was once a single poker tournament has reached a stunning series of 51 poker tournaments held over six weeks. The main event, a no-limit Texas Hold 'em tournament that costs a cool $10,000 just to enter, attracted over 8,200 contestants in 2007. The winner in 2006, Jamie Gold, took home a breathless $12,000,000 from a single tournament played over seven days. A set of laws enacted by the US Government which cut into the ability to transfer gambling money from US-based credit cards and bank accounts cut down on the 2007 WSOP event. The 2007 winner, Jerry Yang, overcame only 6,358 players and won a 'mere' $8,250,000.

The law

You must be over 21 to gamble in Las Vegas and under 18s are not allowed in arcades 10pm–5am during the week and midnight–5am at weekends. In a further move to appease the anti-gambling lobby, the city has passed a new law that bans under 18s from walking down or cruising the Strip after 9pm without a parent or guardian.

Gambling is for over-21s only

How to get in on the action

I remember the first time I visited Las Vegas, the bright lights were so overwhelming and the sheer scale of everything so overpowering that it seemed far too daunting to go into the casinos and play a game or two. Removing some of the mystique surrounding these games of chance is not to remove the magic of the setting, but it will give you the right kind of edge.

BRITTIP

When in a casino always remember that Big Brother is watching you! Mirrors or dark glass in the ceilings house cameras to record almost every square inch of the casino. In the old days, similar mirrors hid people who stood on catwalks to watch casino action to stop cheating by players or dealers.

When it comes to a weekend gambling spree, the average American will allow a budget of $200–500. When a touring Brit arrives in town, their budget of $100–200 is usually simply there to fritter away while downing complimentary drinks. If you do want to have a go, though, here is a guide to the different games, the rules and the best ways to place your bets, so that even if you don't win, you won't blow your entire budget straight away.

The aim of the game is to make your spending money last as long as possible while having fun – and, who knows, you may even come out a winner! Bear in mind that these tips are aimed at those people who are new to gambling as opposed to those looking for more detailed and advanced information. But I have included details of where you can go for further information and more in-depth advice.

The odds

There are two aspects to every game you play – the chance of you winning inherent in each game (the odds) and the rules designed to favour the house, including payoffs at less than the actual odds or predetermined payoffs, as in slot machines (the edge). It is because of this edge that, no matter how well you are playing or how much luck you seem to be having, the odds almost always favour the casinos, who'll win everything back in the long run. That's why when you've come to the end of a winning streak you should always walk away.

Table games with the best odds on winning or on reducing your losses are baccarat and blackjack (in fact, you can expect to win money if you are an accomplished 'card counter' in blackjack). Craps is not good, roulette is terrible and in keno you have about as much chance of winning as you do with our National Lottery. Of course, a keno bet is usually $1 or less, so you may not care.

The two games on which you can actually expect to win money are blackjack (if you are a skilled card counter) and poker (if you are better than the other players). The odd side to the coin, though, is that if you are not skilled, you will likely lose your coin quite fast.

As a general rule, the smaller casinos away from the Strip are what are known as the 'loosest' – they will offer the best returns on slot machines. For some time, the downtown casinos have been rated as the 'loosest slots in America' by the *Casino*

Have fun at the MGM Grand casino

Fun books and other freebies

Whether or not you intend to do any gambling, always check the casino cages for their free fun books. These will give free goes on slot machines, may entitle you to double a bet at the blackjack table or increase the value of a keno ticket. They will also be full of bargains on food and drink or offer discounts on souvenirs such as T-shirts. These books are also available from car rental agencies, hotels, motels and other locations in the city. Some tour operators – most notably Funway – have put together their own fun books, which include some fantastic deals on excursions and attractions.

The monthly *Las Vegas Advisor* gives subscribers lots of information on deals and freebies available in Las Vegas and sometimes includes valuable coupons or arranges special deals for subscribers. Write to the Las Vegas Advisor, Huntington Press, PO Box 28401, Las Vegas, Nevada 89126. Subscriptions are $54 a year, but you'll generally get back that cost in money-saving coupons the first day in Las Vegas, let alone all the other tips! Also, check out their website at lasvegasadvisor.com for up-to-the minute top bargains and information.

Player magazine. For instance, slot machines will give 95–99% return on your play. That means if you bet $1, you'll get 95–99 cents back over the long term if you win. Downtown, you have more chance of finding machines with a 98–99% return. Sometimes as part of promotions, a casino will offer a few slot machines that offer a 100–101% return! But then it is only one or two machines and they'll be available for only a short time.

BRITTIP

Be careful of places that have gaudy signs that say 'Loosest Slots'. Often they will have only one or two 99% machines in some hard-to-find corner, while the rest of the machines are 95% money-eaters.

The exception on the Strip is the Stratosphere, which has made a corporate decision to lure in punters with the promise of the best returns in town. Their deals include 100 times odds on craps, single-zero roulette, hand-dealt double-deck blackjack, double-exposure blackjack (where you see both the dealer's cards), 98% return on 100 $1 slots and more than 100% return on 100 video poker machines. But do bear in mind that there are only a certain number of the high-paying machines, so always check the returns on a machine before you play.

Limits

The table limits are an important consideration because the higher the minimum bet, the quicker you'll get through your money. Unless you're a serious gambler, you'll steer clear of baccarat. The minimum at most Strip resorts is $100! Cheapest, though, is New York-New York, which has games with minimum bets of $10. You can also play mini-baccarat at the Stratosphere with minimum bets of $5 per hand.

BRITTIP

Limits fluctuate. Minimum bets tend to be higher in the evening, at weekends and during special events. The Strip hotels all have higher minimums than downtown casinos.

Beachside Casino at the Mandalay Bay

Blackjack is one of the easiest games

Most Strip resorts have a minimum of $10 on blackjack. The cheapest are Circus Circus ($5), Excalibur ($5), Luxor ($5), Monte Carlo ($5), Stratosphere ($3) and Treasure Island ($3). In comparison, you'll find $2 blackjack tables aplenty and $1 roulette at casinos away from the Strip.

Table games

Baccarat

There is normally an aura of glamour surrounding this game as it tends to attract high-rollers and is usually played in a separate, often more refined, area, cordoned off and staffed by croupiers in posh tuxedos. But don't be put off by the glamour of it all. The mega-bucks, high-roller games will be played in special VIP rooms, so the areas you see really are for mere mortals! What's more, it is an easy game to play and offers the best chance of you beating the casino.

Generally, up to 15 players sit around a table where two cards from an eight-deck shoe are dealt to each of the players and to the bank (see Gambling lingo, page 166). You can bet either on you winning, the bank winning or there being a tie, but you are only playing against the bank, not the other players. Each time you win, the casino takes a commission, though not if you lose.

The idea is simple: you're aiming to get to a total of either eight or nine and the value of the cards are: ace to nine – face value; tens and face cards – zero. If the cards add up to more than ten, only the second digit is counted. For instance, if your hand contains a nine and a four, it adds up to 13 but is worth three as you drop the first digit from the total. In this case you'd ask the dealer for another card.

The house edge in baccarat is very low, which is why it is such an attractive proposition. The edge when betting on a bank hand is 1.17% (though that is increased by the fact that a commission is always paid to the house on with-bank bets) and the edge on a player is 1.36%.

A version that is becoming very popular is mini-baccarat. Basically it is the same game, but it is played around a table about the size of a blackjack table, with spaces for six or seven players.

Blackjack or 21

After baccarat, blackjack (or 21) is one of the easiest games to play and the rows of blackjack tables in casinos reflect the huge number of gamblers who play the game. The object is to get as close to 21 as possible without 'busting'. There can be up to six people around a table, all playing against the dealer.

Bets are placed first, then the dealer gives two cards to each player and himself, the first face down (known as the hole card), the second showing (upcard). Numbered cards count as their face value, face cards count as 10 and aces are worth either one or 11. You can either decide to stand with the two cards you received or take a hit (another card from the dealer) until you're happy with your hand or you go bust.

BRITTIP

In blackjack, avoid high minimum/low maximum tables like the plague – they'll eat up your bankroll in a very short space of time.

Table games at New York-New York

Card counters

You will probably have heard of card counters. These are people who basically keep a track of the low and high cards that are being played in blackjack to try to determine the likelihood of drawing a high or low card at a crucial moment – e.g. when you've got a 15, which is unlikely to be enough to win but you can't guarantee you'll get a six or under. There are many different forms of card counting, but the most simple is the one used with single-deck blackjack. Basically, 10, J, Q, K and Aces are worth minus one, while 2, 3, 4, 5 and 6 are worth one, and the other cards (7, 8, 9) have no value. Starting from zero, you count upwards and downwards according to the cards dealt. Generally you should bet the minimum when the score is negative (you're more likely to bust) and higher when the count is positive two or more.

It is not illegal to count cards but the casinos in Las Vegas frown on this misguided attempt by players to play the game well. They consider it an attempt to cheat them out of money and tend to refuse to let card counters into their casinos. This is why it's best to practise your technique in advance so you won't be noticed!

When all the players have finished, the dealer turns over his hole card and takes hits until his total exceeds 17. If the dealer busts, everyone around the table wins, otherwise only those whose hands are higher than the dealer's win. If the first two cards you are dealt total 21, then you've got what is known as a natural, i.e. a blackjack, and you automatically win. If both you and the dealer are dealt a blackjack, then it is a stand-off and no one wins.

As a general rule, if you have a hand without an ace against the dealer's seven or higher, you should take hits until you reach at least 17. Against the dealer's four, five or six, you can stand on a 12 or higher; if against the dealer's two or three, hit a 12.

With a soft hand (one which includes an ace), hit all totals of 17 or lower. Against the dealer's nine or 10, hit 18.

What gives the house the edge is that you have to play your hand first, so even if the dealer busts after you have, you're still a loser. But there are two ways to help you even the odds – you can double down or split pairs. If you feel you may have a good hand and will only need one more card, you double down – i.e. you double your initial bet and accept one extra card to complete your hand.

Swim-up blackjack at the Tropicana

If you are dealt a pair, you can opt to split them, thereby increasing your chances of winning. You separate the cards to create two hands, thereby doubling your bet, and draw extra cards for each hand. When splitting aces you are only allowed to take one extra card for each ace. If the next card is an ace, though, you can split again. The rule is always to split aces and eights.

A word about 'insurance'. When the dealer's 'show' card is an ace, you will be offered the chance to insure yourself against the dealer getting a blackjack to win 2–1 if the dealer holds a blackjack, so you break even. But it is not a good bet to make because even if you end up with a blackjack, you'll only get 2–1 on a bet that should pay 9–4.

Another way the casino gets an edge is by using a shoe containing six packs of playing cards. This makes busts less likely, which helps the dealer, who is forced by the rules to take more hits than the player. And blackjacks are also less frequent, another drawback as you get paid 3–2 for those.

If you want to learn more, call into the Gambler's Book Club (630 South 11th Street, 1 800 634 6243) where you'll find copies of just about every book ever written about blackjack, and experts on the game – including card counters – who are happy to answer questions. Also, most gift shops have blackjack strategy cards, playing card sized helpers that give the 'book' answer to when to hit and when to stand.

Always stick to your limit

Craps

We've all seen this game played down New York alleyways in gangster movies, now here's your chance to give it a go! Sadly it is one of the most complicated table games on offer, but it is also the one that produces the most excitement.

You join a game by standing anywhere around the table, start betting any time and wait for your turn to shoot. When rolling the dice you have to do it hard enough for them to bounce off the far wall of the table to ensure a random bounce. Basically, the shooter rolls a pair of dice that determine the outcome of everyone's bets. The first roll is called the 'come-out roll'. If it is a seven or an 11, the shooter and all those who bet with him or her win. If the shooter rolls a two, three or 12, that is craps and the shooter and all those betting with him or her lose. If the shooter rolls a four, five, six, seven, eight, nine or 10, he or she must roll the same number again to win. If the shooter rolls a seven before that number, he or she 'sevens out' and loses.

> **BRITTIP**
> Carry a sweater – the air con is deliberately chilly to put you off facing the desert heat outside.

There is a whole series of bets that can be made – with the most bizarre titles you could imagine – from 'pass lines' to 'don't pass', 'come' and 'don't come', 'field', 'big six' or 'eight', 'any craps', 'hard ways', 'bet the horn', 'any seven' and 'under or over seven'.

The odds on winning and payouts vary wildly.

Best bets: The **pass line**, where you are betting with the shooter, and the **don't pass line**, where you are betting against, pay even money. **Come** and **don't come** bets are the same as the **pass** and **don't pass** bets, with the same odds, but can only be placed after the first roll of the dice. The best bet of all is the **free odds**, which is only available to the above betters, but is not even indicated on the table. Once the point has been established by the first roll of the dice, you can make a bet equal to your original and get true odds (2–1 on the four and 10, 3–2 on the five and nine and 6–5 on the six and eight) rather than even money.

Poor bets: The **field**, where you bet that any number in the field, i.e. not five, six, seven or eight, will be rolled. If the numbers mentioned come up, you lose. **Place bets**, where you bet the four, five, six, seven, eight, nine or 10 will be thrown before a seven, sound like a good idea but the casino edge is so great that you should not consider any bets other than placing the six and eight.

> **BRITTIP**
> Many casinos have moving walkways that take you in but rarely take you out again!

The downright daft bets!: Big six and **big eight** bets on either the six or eight or both can be made at any time and either must appear before a seven is thrown to win. But the bet only pays even money so the casino's advantage is high. Worst bets of all are the **proposition** bets, which include the **hard ways** and **one-roll** bets. The casino's advantage is so great that you shouldn't even consider these.

Craps at the Thirsty Camel

Gambling lingo

Acorn	Player who is generous with tips
Ante	Money you bet in card games
Bank	Inventory of coins and chips on all table games
Big digger	Ace of spades
Book	Place where bets are made on sporting events
Boxcars	When a gambler rolls two sixes for a point of 12
Boxman	Craps table dealer who sits over the drop box and supervises bets and payoffs
Bumble puppy	Careless or inexperienced card player
Bust	Exceed the maximum score allowed, for instance 21 in blackjack
Buster	Term used for illegally altered dice
Casino cage	Secure area within the casino for banking services and casino operations
Casino boss	Person who oversees the entire casino
Comp	Free meal, gift, etc. (short for complimentary)
Coupons	Redeemable for nearly everything from a free meal to a free pull on a slot machine
Crossroaders	Card cheats who travel across America in search of games
Dealer	Person who conducts table games
Drop box	Locked box on 'live' gaming tables where dealers deposit your cash
Eye in the sky	One-way mirror used for surveillance of the casino area
Flat top	Slot machine with a fixed jackpot, as opposed to a progressive slot machine where the jackpot increases according to the amount of play
Frog skin	Old-time gamblers' name for paper money
Gaming	Las Vegas euphemism for gambling
Green	Gambling chip worth $25, also known as a quarter
High-roller	Someone who bets large sums of money
Hit me	What you say when you want another card from the dealer in a blackjack game
In red	If you get a free meal, your name will appear in red on the maître d's reservation list
Ladderman	The person who supervises baccarat games and has the final say over any disputes
Limit	Minimum and maximum bet, as decided by the casino
Loose	Term used to describe slot machines that pay out at the best percentages
Marker	IOU
Nevada lettuce	$1,000 bill
Pit	Area of the casino containing gambling tables
Pit boss	Person who oversees a number of table dealers
Red	Gambling chip worth $5, also known as a nickel
RFB comp	If the casino is impressed with someone's credit rating, they will arrange free room, food or beverages (RFB) during a hotel stay
Shoe	Contains the packs of playing cards used in blackjack and baccarat
Shooter	Person rolling the dice in craps
Snake eyes	Craps term used when the dice holder rolls a point of two
Soft hand	When you have at least one ace in your blackjack hand; it is counted as either one or 11 so you have two possible totals
Spoon	A device used by slot machine cheats
Stand	To refuse any more cards in blackjack
Stickman	Dealer who moves the dice around on a craps table with a hook-shaped stick
Table games	Everything from blackjack and baccarat to roulette
Toke or gratuity	Tip
Whale	Gambler who is willing to bet $250,000 a hand
Whip shot	In craps, the way of rolling the dice to hit the table in a flat spin so the desired numbers are on top when the dice stop rolling

The poker room at Beau Rivage

Roulette

This game has been growing in popularity in America since Europeans started visiting the city in greater numbers, but generally it does not carry very good odds even in the European version. The American roulette table has 36 numbers, plus a green zero and a green double zero – as opposed to the European wheel, which does not have the extra double zero (the only Strip exception is at the Stratosphere). This turns the roulette wheel into a game heavily tilted to the casino's favour.

You place chips on the game board, gambling that either a single number, any of a dozen numbers, a column of numbers, corner of four numbers, red or black, or odd or even numbers comes up on the wheel. After all the chips have been put down, the dealer sends a small metal ball spinning around the roulette wheel, which spins in the opposite direction. When the ball drops into one of the slots, the owner(s) of the chips in that slot collect(s).

BRITTIP

Exits from casinos are hard to find and even if you do see a signpost it won't be plain sailing getting there, as your way will be blocked by a maze-like arrangement of slot machines!

The lure is that if your number comes up you're paid at the rate of 35–1, but what makes roulette a poor game for strategists is that it basically involves blind luck. Best way to reduce the chance of losing is to stick to betting that the ball will drop on either a red or black number; and odd or even number of numbers 1–18 or 19–36. Worst bet is any one number. Other bets include groups of 12 numbers (2–1), groups of six numbers (5–1), groups of four numbers (8–1), groups of three numbers (11–1), groups of two numbers (17–1) and a group of 0, 00, 1, 2 and 3 (6–1).

Card games

Poker

For the real Wild West experience, this is a must! There are many variations, but most follow the same principles: all players play for themselves, paying a commission, or 'rake', from each pot (or a certain sum of money per half hour of play at high limits) to the casino, and a regular deck of cards is used. Before joining a game, always check with the dealer to find out the specific game being played.

In the past there were many different styles of poker games available. At the World Series of Poker tournaments, held at the Rio All-Suites, you can still play old-time poker games like seven card stud, Omaha which is favoured in most European casinos, deuce to seven and five card draw. But with the enormous increase in interest caused by the televised events of the World Poker Tour and the European Poker Tour, Texas hold 'em has become the game of choice in Las Vegas. In fact, it is almost impossible to find any other poker game.

Poker is a game that requires nerves of steel and the skill to know when to cut your losses and drop out. Professional poker players reckon that you'll have a pretty good idea of your chances by the time the first two cards have been dealt, and there are basic combinations that you need to have if you are going to continue.

Roulette is an easy game to understand

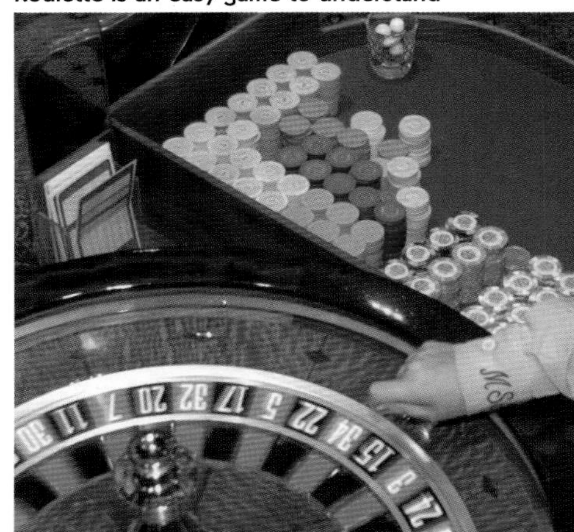

Texas hold 'em: This is the game of the high-stakes World Series of Poker and is now the most popular poker game in the world. There are two types of game offered: limit hold 'em, where there are only set amounts that can be bet at each betting round, and no-limit hold 'em, where you can bet any amount during any betting round, up to and including your entire stack of chips.

In both limit and no-limit there is a 'dealer button' which advances round the table at the start of each hand. It indicates which two players, called the 'big blind' and 'small blind', are required to make forced bets before any cards are dealt, so that there is some money on the table to fight for. Everybody is then dealt two cards face down and a round of betting starts. Obviously, the first two cards you're dealt are the most important and should be either a pair of aces, kings, queens or jacks or two high-value cards.

After the first round of betting, the dealer places three cards in the middle of the table, called 'the flop'. These are community cards that all players use, with the two cards in their hand, to make their best five-card poker hand. There is another round of betting. Then a fourth card is placed on the table by the dealer, 'the turn'. Another round of betting is made, then the last card is placed in the middle, 'the river'. There are now seven cards, two in your hand and five on the table. You use the best five cards of the seven to make your best five-card poker hand. The last round of betting ensues and when the last bet is covered or called, the dealer calls for the showing of hands and the highest one wins.

Most casinos now have poker rooms, where Texas hold 'em is offered. Most also hold a series of daily tournaments, where you play poker against other players. You keep playing until you have no more chips.

Most casinos have a high-limit salon

Usually 10% of the top-placing players get cash prizes, and the top prizes typically run into the thousands of dollars.

There are other poker games that are offered with the other table games, where blackjack and baccarat are offered.

Pai gow poker: Played with a deck of 52 playing cards plus one joker, which can be used only as an ace to complete a straight, a flush or a straight flush. Players are dealt seven cards which they arrange to make two hands – a low hand of two cards and a high hand of five. The cards are arranged according to high-draw poker rankings, i.e. the highest two-card hand is two aces and the highest five-card hand is a royal flush. The object is for both hands to beat the banker's hands.

Caribbean stud poker™: Played with a standard 52-card deck and no joker, it is the first casino table game to offer a progressive jackpot. You start by placing your bet in the box marked 'ante' and then have the option to bet $1 to enter the

'Dealertainers' – celebrity impersonator dealers – at the Imperial Palace

Slots accept any kind of cash!

progressive jackpot, after which all the players and the dealer are dealt five cards. None of your cards is exposed, though one of the dealer's is, but you cannot draw any more cards.

Now you have to decide whether to play or fold; in the latter case your ante is lost. To carry on playing, you have to wager double your ante in the box marked 'bet' to see the dealer's hand. If the dealer's hand is less than ace-king high, then he folds and automatically pays the ante bets at even money. The bet wagers are considered 'no action' and returned to the player regardless of their hand. If the dealer's hand is ace-king high or higher, then he calls all bet wagers. If the dealer's hand is higher than yours, he takes both the ante and the bet. If it's lower than yours, he pays the ante at even money and the bet according to the signposted rates, based on your hand. Regardless of the dealer's hand, if your hand qualifies for the progressive jackpot, you will win the appropriate amount for your hand (shared if there is more than one winner).

Let it ride poker™: In this game, you are not playing against the dealer or the other players but simply trying to get a good poker hand. To play, you place three equal bets as indicated on the table layout and then get three cards. After looking at your cards, you can ask for your first bet back or 'let it ride'. The dealer then exposes one of his cards, which becomes all of the players' fourth card. At this point you can either ask for your second bet back or again let it ride, after which the dealer exposes another card to complete the five-card hand. Winning hands are then paid according to the payout schedule.

BRITTIP

The average electricity bill for a large Las Vegas casino is around $3m a year!

Keno

This game originated in China more than 2,000 years ago but is basically a form of our lotto. You mark anywhere between one and 15 of the 80 numbers on the keno ticket, then place your bet with the keno writer. You then keep a duplicate ticket to match against the 20 numbers drawn by the casino at a set time. All the casinos have their own rules about winning combinations, so check before playing. The alternative to this game is throwing your money in a bin, but the lure is the massive payouts.

Slots

Las Vegas is home to the most sophisticated, state-of-the-art machinery in the world and gamblers get so mesmerised by the idea of their winning line coming up that they spend hours feeding money into these machines. But slot machines are such big business now that they account for around 60% of total casino earnings – and so fill a staggering amount of floor space in the casinos.

BRITTIP

Most of the newer slot machines have coloured lights on top to signify the machine's denomination. A red light means it's a 5-cent machine, green 10 cents, yellow 25 cents, orange 50 cents, blue $1 and purple $5.

Loose slots offer the best return

BRITTIP

Only play on machines that tell you the return and look for a 98–99% return on $1 slots.

Mechanical penny and nickel slot machines that took one coin at a time have been replaced by computerised dollar slot machines that can accept multiple coins simultaneously and now feature poker, keno, blackjack, bingo and craps. Some even accept credit card-style gambling and the linking up of machines has led to massive $10m-and-more jackpots. You can still play for as little as a nickel a go, but some slots now allow you to use $500-dollar tokens – usually in special VIP slot areas!

Progressive slots are machines that are computer-linked to other machines throughout the States and pay out incredible jackpots. One of the progressive slots is known as Megabucks, which is computer-linked to other machines in the state of Nevada. The CircusBucks progressives start the jackpot climbing at $500,000, but the most recent Super Megabucks starts climbing at $10m! What's more, gamblers can now phone a toll-free number to find out the current jackpot total on Megabucks and seven other progressive slot networks run by International Game Technology. The number is: 888 448 2946.

BRITTIP

The coin trays of slot machines are not anchored to the machine so that the money falls with a 'play-me' ting-ting-ting-ting!

Video games

These are basically interactive slot machines aimed directly at the new generation who grew up with computers and computer games. Multiple-use videos can offer up to 10 games with anything from poker to keno and blackjack, plus regular slot machines and are activated simply by touching the screen. Some machines even allow you to play for a $1m poker payout with a 25-cent bet! Another reason for the increase in popularity of video games is that you can play at your own pace, without pressure from dealers, croupiers or other players. The returns that you should be looking for on all the different games are as follows:

All-American poker: Also known as gator bonus poker. Go for machines that pay 8–1 on full houses, a flush and a straight.

Bonus deuces: Best machines are those paying 20–1 for a wild royal flush, 10–1 on five of a kind and straight flush and 4–1 on four of a kind and a full house.

Deuces wild: Look for a 5–1 payout on four of a kind, which is considerably better than 4–1 for four of a kind that you'll find on many of these video machines.

Double bonus poker: Find a 10/7 machine – one that pays 10–1 on a full house and 7–1 on a flush.

Flush attack: Do not play on a machine that needs more than three flushes to go into attack mode, and look for one that pays 8–1 for a full house and 5–1 on flushes (known as an 8/5 machine).

Jacks or better: Look for 9/6 machines, which pay 9–1 for a full house and 6–1 on flushes.

Joker wild: Kings or better. Look for a machine that pays 20–1 for four of a kind, 7–1 for a full house and 5–1 on a flush.

High-roller lounge at Treasure Island

The stylish casino at Monte Carlo

Sports betting

The race and sports book, as it is known, gives you the chance to bet on horse races and major sporting events. For horse races you can bet on a win (first place only), a place (first or second) and a show (first, second or third). Further bets include naming the first two horses in any order, naming the first two horses in the correct order or the horses that will win any two specified races.

Details of races, the horses and odds are displayed or you can read local newspapers, racing sheets and other publications before making up your mind. Then watch the action on closed-circuit broadcasts live from race tracks across America. The latest innovation in sports betting are proposals for a progressive prize MegaSports jackpot, where the final payout is determined by the amount of betting over a certain period. The prize pools will start at $1m.

The surge in televised coverage of sporting events in America has also created a surge in sports gambling. During one Super Bowl weekend (held every February), nearly 200,000 visitors flocked to Las Vegas to bet more than $50m on their favourite team and spent a further $50m in the city in the process! At Caesars Palace Race and Sports Book – the first to open in Las Vegas – they have a total of 50 different ways to part with your cash, including betting on the number of quarterback sacks or the total field goals.

Internet betting

Online casinos have exploded in popularity, especially those sites offering poker. Many different sites often have more than 10,000 punters playing at the same time, all in the comfort of their own homes. The casinos also offer home access to gambling on blackjack, craps, video poker, roulette, bingo and three-dimensional, interactive slot machines. In fact, many industry experts credit much of Las Vegas recent explosive growth to the internet. It is estimated that over 100,000,000 people gamble on internet sites worldwide (62,000,000 in the US alone!) and soon get the urge to give the lights of Vegas a try!

The race and sports book at the Mirage

Gambling lessons

Many hotels are linked to the Players Network, which you can access through the TV for tips on how to play different games, table etiquette and sports betting.

Ask for details of 'live' classes when you check in. Most casinos run them, but it is generally agreed that the Circus Circus casino is one of the friendliest environments in which to build up your confidence.

BRITTIP

Floral fragrances are pumped around selected slot machines, which increases play by up to 50%.

For tips on how to play all the different video poker machines, it is worth taking the trip to north-west Las Vegas for Bob Dancer's weekly lessons at the Fiesta Casino Hotel (2400 North Rancho Drive, 702 631 7000). Circus Circus offers free poker lessons at noon Mon–Fri in the poker room and, along with the Tropicana and Excaliber, offers low-bet games that are perfect for beginners! The Tropicana also offers baccarat games for beginners in a youthful yet sophisticated environment.

Comps

Many Vegas veterans are misty over the good old 'mobbed-up days' when the mob-owned casinos offered free drinks, cheap food and cheap or even free hotel rooms to draw in the punters. The new age of corporate casinos brought a waft of business managers who demanded all areas, including the hotel and restaurant sides, show a profit along with the gambling hall.

Most casinos still liberally hand out free drinks for gamblers. And you can still get comps on everything from free rooms to food, show tickets, front-row seats and limos, without being a high-roller. You just have to earn them.

Playing the slots at the Bellagio

Themed machines can be mesmerising

To qualify for a comp, you'll need a player's card, which you can request from the casino as soon as you arrive. Blackjack used to be the fastest way to get comps. Over the last two decades casinos began to recognise that slot machines were more profitable so they now offer their best comps for slot players. In fact, the old players cards are now as often referred to as 'slot club cards'.

BRITTIP

Savvy locals know that if they play at a slot machine that offers a 99% return on $1 slots, plus play with their slot club card to get comps from the casino (generally a 1–3% value), they can actually expect to beat the casino!

But while slots get the best comp values, some savvy blackjack players have learned some tricks to maximise their comps. As soon as you sit down at a table, ask to be 'rated', presenting your player's card to the pit boss. This effectively starts the clock on your play and the idea from this point is to make it look as if you're placing good bets for as long a period of time as possible, while reducing your risk of losing money by playing as little as possible.

Once the floorperson has walked away, bet as little as you can, depending on the table's minimum. Also, don't play every hand. If the dealer is on a winning streak, tell him or her you're going to sit things out until they've busted a couple of times. A natural break in a game is provided when

Table games at the MGM Grand

the dealer starts to shuffle and at this point you can whiz off (not forgetting your chips!) to another table out of your pit boss's jurisdiction, though you must always tell them where you're going. Then lay your chips on the table and chat to the dealer, making it look as if you're playing without actually making one bet. After an hour of 'play', take a break, asking the dealer to mark your seat.

About every half hour, the floor person normally comes around with a clipboard to check on play. Bump up your bets back to $25 while he's there.

BRITTIP

Part of the fun of a visit to Las Vegas is to check out all the different resorts and attractions. However, try to do most of your gambling at one casino to maximise your freebies.

It's a pleasant enough way of spending a few hours, but always remember the golden rule of never going beyond the amount of money you have given yourself to play with. Obviously, you'll need to walk around the casino for a while before you start playing so you know which pit bosses cover which tables. Thereafter, it will be down to your ability to act in a natural way!

Deception and subterfuge are not always necessary when it comes to earning freebies, though. Many of the casinos are so determined to foster good relationships with their customers that they have introduced loyalty cards, where the amount of play gives you points that can be put towards meals, rooms, shows or even getting cash back. Ask at your hotel, but the following are a few of the best.

BRITTIP

If you're a regular gambler or plan to gamble a lot when in Las Vegas, join a slot club and see what deals you're offered. Apart from free drinks, you may get a comp room or even free show tickets.

Club Magic: Slot players can join at the Las Vegas Hilton to win cash, comps and merchandise based on the amount of play.

Gold Chamber: With this slot and table club at the Luxor, you can get a 98.4% return on slot games, plus other comps.

Beachside casino at the Mirage

Island Winners' Club: At the Tropicana, this rewards slot, video poker and table-game players. Slot and video poker players can earn both comps and cash by inserting their club card into the slot machine. On average, about two hours of play on a dollar slot with maximum coins played on each 'pull' will earn about $10 cash back. Table-game players present their card to a floorperson to earn comp credits at blackjack, craps or roulette tables. Credits are based on the average bets and length of time you play.

Play Rio Card: This card, at the Rio All-Suite Hotel and Casino in Valley View Boulevard at Flamingo Road, will allow you to earn points during both slot and table play towards reduced-price or comp suites, comp dining or tickets to a show. Sign up at the Play Rio Center.

Players Club: In Las Vegas the most valuable club card has to be the MGM Mirage Players Club, because no less than 12 resorts and casinos belong to the brand. Everywhere you turn, it seems, you can either save money by using your card, or earn points to get something free later.

Total Rewards: The new Harrah's card you build up points at all Harrah's properties, especially valuable at Caesars Palace.

The casinos

As much imagination has gone into the decor of the casinos as in every other part of the resort-hotels.

Caesars Palace: caesarspalace.com At Caesars Palace Forum Casino you can take a break from gambling and have your photo taken with Caesar and Cleopatra as they stroll around with their royal entourage, while the west corridor is home to animatronic Atlantis statues!

Excalibur: excalibur.com/casino The Excalibur casino continues its theme with staff dressed in medieval costume and trumpet players blowing on horns straight out of Robin Hood.

Imperial Palace: imperialpalace.com/play.php If you're having trouble parking, then you can always place your bets at the new drive-up sports book at the Imperial Palace! In fact, more casinos would offer the same service but just don't have the space. The manager at the Imperial drive-up says business is always brisk – especially in summer when gamblers prefer to remain in their air-conditioned cars.

Las Vegas Hilton: lvhilton.com/casino The Las Vegas Hilton Casino is one of the most beautifully decorated, with marble, rich woods and tier after tier of crystal

Casino floor at the Excalibur

Third level at the Mandalay Bay beachside casino

chandeliers. The largest race and sports book is also to be found at the Hilton.

Luxor: luxor.com/casino At the Luxor you'll find a sumptuous setting surrounded by the Nile.

MGM Grand: mgmgrand.com/gaming If you want to see how the other half lives, take a sneak look into the VIP high-limit area at the MGM Grand. Here high-rollers rub cheeks with celebrities in a setting based on the elegance and style of the grand old casinos of Monte Carlo. Tall, classic columns, rose-coloured curtains and cherry wood and suede tables embroidered with the gold MGM Grand monograms are a real sight!

Race and Sports SuperBook: lvhilton.com/casino/superbook.shtml At the Las Vegas Hilton, this is the biggest in the city with an impressive array of more than 40 video monitors to screen nearly every major sporting event and race being televised in America at any time.

SpaceQuest Casino: lvhilton.com The new pièce de résistance is the SpaceQuest Casino where gamblers board a futuristic space station that orbits the earth, with space windows that create the illusion of circling the globe from sunrise to sunset.

Tropicana: http://tropicanalv.com/casino_slots.asp You can beat the heat of the summer at the Tropicana by swimming up to the blackjack table, open daily 9.30am–5pm. In the indoor area of the resort's indoor- outdoor swimming pool, up to 14 players sit on marble stools up to their hips in water. They play with plastic cards and use either chips or cash. The paper money is kept in mint condition by specially heated rotating drop boxes that dry the cash in less than 60 seconds!

BRITTIP

Many of the casinos have information on how to play the games on their websites.

Downtown casinos

Now home to the last neon signs of what used to be Glitter Gulch city, the downtown casinos are generally more friendly and relaxed, have cheaper-play slot machines, better returns and more comps. Regular visitors to Las Vegas may like staying at the ritzy, glamorous Strip hotels, but often enjoy a trip downtown to play on the nickel slot machines.

The casino at New York-New York

BRITTIP

So many people are so rude, the waitresses always remember the nice punters who tip in advance, and make sure they get their free drinks.

Binion's Horseshoe: 128 East Fremont Street, 1 800 937 6537, binions.com Once home to the world poker championships, this casino is famous for its single-deck blackjack and liberal rules, single-zero roulette, great odds-on crap, loose nickel and quarter machines and loads of comps. Binion's is also known for its friendly atmosphere.

Copper Mine at the Gold Spike: 40 East Ogden Avenue, 702 384 8444, goldspikehotelcasino.com This place has many old-time penny slots that are just perfect for people who hate to waste money.

Four Queens Hotel: 202 Fremont Street, 702 385 4011, fourqueens.com You'll find the world's largest regular slot machine at the Four Queens Hotel downtown. It is the size of a small motorhome and allows six people to play at the same time!

Gold Coast: 4000 West Flamingo Road, 702 367 7111, goldcoastcasino.com The karaoke bar at the Gold Coast is excellent for entertainment (locals dressed as stars such as Roy Orbison, Dean Martin and Elvis) and cheap drinks.

Golden Gate: 1 Fremont Street, 702 385 1906, goldengatecasino.net Another friendly establishment, this still serves up its famous 99-cent shrimp (i.e. huge prawn) cocktail.

Sam's Town: 5111 Boulder Highway, 800 851 1703, samstownlv.com The favoured haunt of locals is Sam's Town on Boulder Highway (going out towards the Hoover Dam). The free light and laser show is excellent and you'll find great odds on slots and video machines, and good comps.

Binion's Horseshoe has a friendly atmosphere

Smoking

In the last edition we predicted that smoking would not be banned from Las Vegas casinos. Two years later that has changed! New laws have made smoking in any building except casinos and smoke shops to be illegal, so now all restaurants, card rooms, gift shops and bars are smoke free. Many casinos are also considering smoking and non-smoking sections of their casinos, and there is a new push for tighter legislation which could compel smoking to become a permanent, outside experience.

Sam's Town

8 GOING TO THE CHAPEL

Getting married on any budget in the wedding capital of the world

Las Vegas has more chapels per square mile and more options on how you tie the knot than any other city in the world – and it's all so easy. Liberal state laws mean that Nevada is one of the few states that does not require a blood test and to get you quickly on your way to the altar as the Marriage License Bureau is open from 8am–midnight daily, including holidays.

If you do decide to go ahead, you'll be in star-studded company – this is where Elvis wed Priscilla, Frank Sinatra wed Mia Farrow, Jane Fonda wed Roger Vadim and Paul Newman wed Joanne Woodward. Others include Bruce Willis and Demi Moore, while Brigitte Bardot, Britney Spears, Bob Geldoff, David Cassidy, Richard Gere, Michael Jordan and Joan Collins all said 'I do' at a chapel in Las Vegas.

Getting married here is so simple that an amazing 110,000 get marriage licences here every year. The most popular day is Valentine's Day, closely followed by New Year's Eve, while the date 7 July 2007 (7/7/07) was considered lucky and a flood of weddings were booked for that day.

And you can do it all in such style. Dress up as a medieval prince and princess at the Canterbury Chapel in the Excalibur, allow an Elvis impersonator to wed you at Graceland Wedding Chapel, or try any of the other themes available from Star Trek to gangsters and rock 'n' roll. Then again, you could decide to make your vows before diving off a bungee-jump platform, soaring high above Las Vegas in a hot-air balloon or flying over the Grand Canyon. You can even stay in your car at the world's first ever drive-up wedding chapel or try the Tunnel of Love chapel at A Little White Chapel on the Strip.

In this chapter

BRITTIP

Avoid Valentine's Day unless you want to queue for four hours to get your licence!

It costs $55 for a marriage licence, which must be paid in cash, and $35 for the ceremony. A very basic package starts at $100, but the sky's the limit depending on where you wed, what you do and the accessories you choose.

The stunning setting at the Excalibur

The rules

- Both parties must go to the Marriage License Bureau. You'll find it on the 1st Floor, Clark County Courthouse, 201 Clark Avenue (702 671 0600 or visit co.clark.nv.us) and it's open Mon–Thurs 8am–midnight and continuously from 8am Fri–midnight Sun. (Once the licence has been issued it is valid for one year.)
- Minimum age for adults is 18. Those aged 16–17 must have either a parent present at the time the licence is issued or a notarised affidavit.
- Oddly enough, identification was never required to get married in Vegas until 1 January 2008. Now you have to have your passport with you.
- If you have been divorced, you will need to specify the date, city and state/country when it became final.

The good news is that while many of the high-profile marriages may have ended in the divorce courts, a Las Vegas wedding is not synonymous with one that ends in tears. People tend to opt for the wedding capital of the world because here they are free of family pressures and can make all their own choices. Furthermore, thanks to the raft of amazing accommodation, romantic restaurants, shows and nightlife, the city is also becoming a honeymoon mecca.

Ceremonies

Like every other aspect of Las Vegas, the business of helping people to tie the knot is booming. Hotel ceremonies tend to be more ostentatious than those at ordinary chapels, but they have prices to match, too! One married couple were taken to their wedding site at the Venetian's St Mark's Square in an oversized white gondola, with a host of actors cavorting about as if it was a renaissance fair. After the gilt ceremony, the reception was held in the gardens area, where champagne and caviar celebrated the blessed union. All for a mere $12,000.

Little White Wedding Chapel

Jean Philippe's Patisserie at the Bellagio supplies superb cakes

Not quite as expensive, but definitely unusual, are the packages at the MGM Grand, in addition to the ceremonies at their two chapels, the Legacy and the Cherish. The first allows couples to take their vows at the top of the 250ft/76m Sky Screamer before descending into a 100ft/30m freefall dive at speeds of up to 70mph/113kph. The second is getting married in the trendy Studio 54 nightclub to the sounds of the 1970s.

Wedding queen of the West

Possibly the most famous wedding chapel in the world is the Little White Chapel owned by Charolette Richards, dubbed the 'wedding queen of the West'. In her time, she has married celebs including Joan Collins, Patty Duke and Bruce Willis. She is also a savvy business woman as well as a wedding planner and has an empire of wedding chapels and more exotic options. Contact details are in the A–Z of major wedding chapels on page 180.

- Little White Chapel
- Chapel l'Amour
- Chapel of Promises
- Crystal Chapel
- Gazebo Chapel
- Tunnel of Love: In 1991, Charolette noticed a disabled couple having difficulty getting out of their car to go into her chapel so she hit upon the idea of a drive-up window and opened it at A

You can even take your vows at Red Rock Canyon

Little White Chapel on the Strip. It became such a novelty that all kinds of couples began queuing up for the drive-through wedding. They come on motorcycles, roller-skates, in cars, limos, trucks, taxis and even boats! Now it includes a 'Tunnel of Love' in which couples are surrounded by floating cherubs, twinkling stars, birds on ribbons and signs everywhere saying 'I love you, I want you, I need you and I can't live without you'.

- A Little White Chapel in the Sky for balloon weddings
- We've Only Just Begun Wedding Chapel in the Imperial Palace Hotel on the Strip
- Speedway to Love Wedding Chapel for those wishing to get married at the Speedway.

Charolette also has a *Braveheart*-themed wedding ceremony in which costumed couples can tie the knot by moonlight in secluded woodland.

At A Little White Chapel you pay anything from $179 for the Economy package that includes a candlelight ceremony, music, four photographs and corsage and buttonhole to $579 for the Joan Collins Special, which includes the candlelight ceremony, music, photographs, bridal bouquets, corsages, buttonholes, garter, champagne glasses, lithograph marriage certificate, video recording, wedding cake and an etched marriage scroll. All the packages include a courtesy limousine service from your hotel to the Marriage License Bureau, on to A Little White Chapel and back to your hotel.

The chapel fee is $55, drive-up weddings cost $40, gazebo weddings $55, hot-air balloon weddings start at $1,000 and helicopter weddings start at $750. Some of the more exotic packages, including video taping, tuxedo rentals and the like, can go up to $1,500.

BRITTIP

If you do get married in Las Vegas you need copies of your marriage certificate, which you can now order via the internet. Go to co.clark.nv.us.

Happy day at the MGM Grand

A–Z of major wedding chapels

All Religions Wedding Chapel: 2855 Las Vegas Blvd S, 702 735 4179.

Bally's Celebration Wedding Chapel: 3645 Las Vegas Blvd S, 702 894 5222.

Candlelight Wedding Chapel: 2855 Las Vegas Blvd S, 702 735 4179, candlelightchapel.com.

Chapel by the Courthouse: 203 East Bridger Avenue, 702 384 9099, achapelbythecourthouse.com.

Chapel L'Amour: 1901 Las Vegas Blvd South, 702 369 5683, alittlewhitechapel.com, for weddings with up to 30 guests.

Chapel of Dreams: 316 Bridger Ave, Suite 103, 702 471 7729, lasvegasweddingchapelofdreams.com.

Chapel of Love: 1431 Las Vegas Blvd South, 702 387 0155.

Chapel of Promises: 1901 Las Vegas Blvd South, 702 369 5683, alittlewhitechapel.com, offers an elegant and traditional option.

Chapel of the Bells: 2233 Las Vegas Blvd S, 702 735 6803, chapelofthebellslasvegas.com.

Chaplain at Large: 1301 Las Vegas Blvd S, 702 382 5943.

China Town Wedding Temple: 4215 Spring Mountain Rd, 702 252 0400.

Crystal Chapel: 1901 Las Vegas Blvd South, 702 369 5683, alittlewhitechapel.com, for intimate weddings with up to 12 guests.

Cupid's Wedding Chapel: 827 Las Vegas Blvd S, 702 598 4444, cupidswedding.com.

Divine Madness Fantasy Wedding Chapel: 1111 Las Vegas Blvd S, Suite H, 702 384 5660 or toll-free on 1 800 717 4734.

Drive-up Wedding Window: 1301 Las Vegas Blvd South, 702 382 5943, alittlewhitechapel.com.

El Caribe: 2800 West Sahara 83656 Pecos-Mcleod, 702 382 5943, elcaribe.com.

Elvis Chapel: 727C South 9th Street, 702 383 5909, theelvisweddingchapel.com.

Emerald Gardens: 891 Las Vegas Blvd South, 702 242 5700, emeraldgarden.com.

Flamingo Hilton Garden Chapel: 3555 Las Vegas Blvd S, 702 733 3111, ceremonies here are $425–3,895, the latter including a mini-suite for one night, pianist at the ceremony, breakfast in bed, dinner and tickets for the cocktail performance of the Rockettes.

Gazebo Chapel: 1901 Las Vegas Blvd South, 702 369 5683, alittlewhitechapel.com.

Graceland Wedding Chapel: 6195 Las Vegas Blvd S, 702 474 6655, gracelandchapel.com.

Harrah's Las Vegas: 3475 Las Vegas Blvd South, 702 369 5000, harrahs.com.

Hartland Mansion and Café: 525 Park Paseo Drive, 702 387 6700.

Heavenly Bliss Wedding Chapel: 516 South 4th Street, 702 444 5444, heavenlyblisschapel.com.

Hitching Post Wedding Chapel: 1737 Las Vegas Blvd South, 1 800 572 5530, hitchingpostweddingchapel.com.

Jet Helicopter Weddings: 3712 Las Vegas Blvd South, 702 736 0013.

Las Vegas Garden of Love Wedding Chapel: 200 West Sahara Avenue, 702 385 5683, lvgardenoflove.com.

Las Vegas Helicopters Inc.: 3724 Las Vegas Blvd South, 702 736 0013, lvhelicopters.com.

Las Vegas Villa: 4982 Shirley Street, 702 795 8119, lasvegasvilla.com.

Las Vegas Wedding Chapel: 727 South 9th, 702 383 5909, lvchapel.com.

Las Vegas Wedding Reservations: 4036 Adelphi Avenue, 702 435 7922.

Little Chapel of Roses: 814 Las Vegas Blvd South, 702 382 9404.

Little Chapel of the Flowers: 301 Las Vegas Blvd South, 702 382 5943, alittlechapel.com.

Little Church of the West: 4617 Las Vegas Blvd South, 702 739 7971, littlechurchlv.com.

Little White Chapel at the Speedway: North Las Vegas, 702 382 5943, alittlewhitechapel.com.

Little White Chapel in the Sky: 1301 Las Vegas Blvd S, 702 382 5943, alittlewhitechapel.com; balloon wedding packages will set you back $1,500.

Little White Chapel: 1301 Las Vegas Blvd, 702 382 5943, alittlewhite chapel.com.

Long Fung Wedding Temple: 4215 Spring Mountain Rd, 702 252 0400.

Mount Charleston Hotel and Restaurant: 2 Kyle Canyon Road, Mount Charleston, 702 872 5500 or toll-free on 1800 794 3456, mtcharlestonhotel.com.

Rainbow Gardens: 4125 West Charleston, 702 878 4646, ilv.com/rainbowgardens.

Riviera Wedding Chapel: The Riviera Hotel on the Strip, 702 794 9494, theriviera.com.

San Francisco Sally's Victorian Chapel: 1304 Las Vegas Blvd South, 702 385 7777.

Scenic Wedding: PO Box 80601, 702 873 8316, vegasvows.com/ascenicwedding.

Sherwood Forest: 7768 West Sahara Avenue, 702 256 3202.

Silver Bell Wedding Chapel: 607 Las Vegas Blvd S, 702 382 3726.

Special Memory Wedding Chapel: 800 South 4th Street and Gass, 702 384 2211, aspecialmemory.com.

Speedway to Love Wedding Chapel: 4243 North Las Vegas Blvd, 702 644 3000.

Sunset Gardens: 3931 East Sunset Road, 702 456 9986.

The Wedding Room at the Cellar: 3601 West Sahara, 702 362 6712.

Tropical Gardens: 3808 East Tropicana Avenue, 702 434 4333.

Valley Outreach Synagogue: 1692 Long Horizon Lane, 702 436 4901, valleyoutreach.com.

Victoria's Wedding Chapel: 2800 West Sahara, 702 257 7303, avictorias.com.

We've Only Just Begun Wedding Chapel: Imperial Palace, 3535 Las Vegas Blvd South, 702 733 0011, imperialpalace.com.

Wedding on Wheels: 1301 Las Vegas Blvd S, 702 382 5943, alittlewhitechapel.com.

Wee Kirk o' the Heather: 231 Las Vegas Blvd S, 702 382 9830, weekirk.com.

Co-ordinators

In addition to the chapels there are several very good wedding specialists. Co-ordinators have no chapel themselves, but co-ordinate with a variety of vendors to make a memorable wedding for you, from themed to decadent.

A Viva Las Vegas Wedding

702 384 0771, vivalasvegasweddings.com
This company arranges an extraordinary number of differently themed weddings from *Star Trek* to Elvis and rock 'n' roll.

Bond: You can choose a Bond wedding ceremony for $1,100, which includes a limousine pick-up by Bond baddie Oddjob, two dancing Bond girls and a ceremony performed by a 007 impersonator who arrives by sports car.

Camelot: The Camelot theme includes Merlin or King Arthur as the minister, while you'll be treated like a king and queen. The basic package costs $700 and includes period music, knights, trumpeters and fair ladies. For an extra $100 you can have a soloist perform a medieval tune.

Getting married Elvis style

Elvis in Blue Hawaii: Here you have an Elvis impersonator and dancers from the Tropicana's *Folies Bergères* at your ceremony, which takes place in the Elvis Chapel. In addition to all the Elvis memorabilia, Hawaiian sets, showgirls and hula dancers, there will be theatrical lighting and fog, while 'Elvis' will sing 'Love Me Tender', 'Viva Las Vegas' and 'I Can't Help Falling In Love With You' ($700).

Gangster Chapel: Here you'll step back in time to a 1940s Mafioso shotgun wedding where the Godfather/minister opens the door to wedded bliss accompanied by two bodyguards and a waiter/soloist singing in Italian ($650).

Intergalactic: Your special day is presided over by Captain James T Quirk or Captain Schpock in the Starship Chapel, surrounded by life-size cut-outs of your favourite characters. The package comes with a Minister Transporter, an illusion entrance, theatrical lighting and lots of fog for $700.

Las Vegas: This package includes showgirls, keno runners, cocktail waitresses, card dealers and a Las Vegas-style singer/minister, plus theatrical lights and fog. It costs $650 and for another $250 you can even have Elvis or Marilyn Monroe at your wedding. Other packages include the Victorian ($600), the Disco ($650) and the Beach Party ($650).

Rock 'n' Roll Chapel: This is all about rock 'n' roll, complete with memorabilia and an electric guitar version of the Wedding March, while a rock star impersonator will sing during the ceremony for $650.

Graceland Wedding Chapel

Chapel of the Fountain at Circus Circus

Wedding Dreams of Las Vegas

1 888 2 WED N LV, weddingdreams.com
Another co-ordinator that provides a comprehensive series of packages.

Balloon trip: A beautifully romantic high-flying option is the sunrise balloon flight with champagne and hors d'oeuvres at $675. If you want a photographer to go up with you that will cost $1,275 and you can have guests at $150 per person.

Four lakes: Romantics may prefer to get married by the four lakes north of the Strip. The basic price of $549 includes minister, photos, bouquets and flowers, and optional extras include live music, a video and an Elvis impersonator.

Limo wedding: For an intimate affair, try the private limo wedding in which you'll also get champagne ($375) or get married in the privacy of a hotel room or suite for $499. For another $150 you can have a cake and non-alcoholic champagne reception for 15 people in your room.

New Beginnings: Skydivers will be in heaven with New Beginnings option at $1,200, which includes private use of a passenger jet liner, jump masters, minister, photos and a video.

Night flight: For $699 you can take a night flight over the lights of the Las Vegas Strip, have photographs and a video recording of the event as the minister conducts the service in mid-air. Or you can take a one-hour day flight over the Grand Canyon with a videographer. It'll cost you $1,846 plus tax!

Red Rock Canyon: You can get married in the great outdoors and even have an

Wedding chapel at the Imperial Palace

Elvis impersonator to provide the music. The price of $499 includes the minister, photos and flowers, while a limo service and 'Elvis' will cost extra.

Take the plunge: For daredevils, there is the bungee-jumping option at $499. You take your vows at the top of the 175ft/53m tower before taking the plunge.

Las Vegas Host

2680 Chandler Avenue, Suite 7B, 702 798 5246, lasvegashost.com
A full service for weddings at three different chapels in Las Vegas with five packages to choose from.

Candlelight Wedding Chapel: At this romantic location there are four packages at $179–499. Opened in 1967 (historic by Las Vegas standards!), this is the only free-standing chapel in the heart of the hotel district on the Strip and is where Whoopi Goldberg, Bette Midler and Michael Caine were wed.

Victorian Little Chapel of the Flowers: Prices at this pretty chapel are $195–3,150. Here you'll find a cosy atmosphere that includes polished brass chandeliers, etched glass and burnished cherry wood with Impressionist paintings.

Viva Las Vegas Wedding Chapel: Complete with fountain, silk trees and flowers and twinkling fairy lights, this provides the setting for the ultimate fantasy wedding. Packages start from $125, and include Elvis and other themed ceremonies.

Las Vegas Weddings and Room Co-ordinators

2770 South Maryland Parkway, Suite 416, 702 737 6800, lasvegasweddings.com
This company can book your rooms and organise every aspect of your wedding. Open 24/7, they arrange flowers, transport, clothes, reception and entertainments. They have 17 chapels and themes include Elvis and nature weddings. Or you can choose to take one of the packages arranged by tour operators from Britain (see page 248).

Candlelight Wedding Chapel

Wedding chapels at major resort hotels on the Strip

With all the resort-hotel websites, it's usually quickest to key in the main website address, then navigate via the menus. If you can't immediately see a weddings option, look under amenities.

Bellagio

702 693 7700, bellagio.com
East Chapel: The more intimate chapel holds a maximum of 30 guests, and is decorated in hues of cream, rose and peach, with antique green and bride's blue. The classy design allows you to say your vows at the altar with a beautiful full-length stained glass window as the backdrop.

South Chapel: Holds up to 130 guests in an elegant and refined classic European designed environment. Beautifully decorated in gold and muted colours with stained glass windows, it is also light and airy.

Caesars Palace

702 731 7110, caesarspalace.com
Caesars specialises in customising weddings to suit the most romantic tastes and a recent flurry of developments have led to the opening of some of the most attractive and varied chapel settings in any resort-hotel. For something even more special, you can also hire ancient characters – Caesar, Cleopatra, Roman guards, handmaidens and sirens are the favourites – to attend your ceremony at any of the chapels. Prices are $350–16,000.

Classico: Having opened in August 2005, this now offers the chance for 190 guests to enjoy a wedding ceremony in a classical environment. On a theme of beige, light blue and cream, it has chandeliers, stained glass windows and magnificent floral arrangements.

Intimate Garden: A stunning garden setting nestled in a private corner of the hotel's extensive grounds, this chapel can accommodate 125 guests. The resort's Roman-Greco theme is carried through with stone benches leading up to a grand arch flanked by aromatic herb and floral gardens.

Le Belle Luce Court: The new open-air Roman plaza chapel holds up to 230 guests. A dramatic waterfall forms the centrepiece of a lush, landscaped setting. It is at its best in the evening when the Strip lights add a romantic twinkling backdrop.

Romano: A more intimate affair for 35 guests, its décor is based around creams and blues.

Terrazza Garden: Small, beautiful and secluded, the Romanesque temple is surrounded by tropical palm trees, a blooming floral landscape, koi fish pond and fountains. Seats 114.

Tuscana: Based on the romance and charm of old world Tuscany, the colour scheme is creams and browns. Seats 85.

Circus Circus

702 734 0410, circuscircus.com
Chapel of the Fountain: Having recently undergone a major renovation, Circus Circus now also has an updated chapel. Once dark, it has been brightened up with a new white colour scheme. An Elvis wedding is an available option. Prices are $281–975.

East Chapel at the Bellagio

The Forever Grand Wedding Chapel

Excalibur

702 597 7777, excalibur.com
Canterbury Wedding Chapel: In keeping with the theme of the hotel, the chapel in a lovely gazebo has a medieval-gothic flavour with domed ceilings, stained glass windows and lots of dark wood. A large chandelier over the altar forms the perfect backdrop for photos and you can even look the part, too, by hiring period costumes. Now, where is that knight in shining armour...? Here a renewal wedding package costs $250 for the ceremony, music, one red rose, photo and bottle of champagne, while the wedding packages are $395–1,575; the latter includes room, dinner and breakfast.

Four Seasons

702 632 5000, fourseasons.com/lasvegas
Terrace and suites: The Four Seasons offers the serenity and prestige of the city's most acclaimed hotel in an exclusive, non-gambling environment. In addition to an outdoor venue, the Terrace, the Four Seasons also offers the chance to get married in some of the most amazing suites available in Las Vegas. Normally reserved for those who like to pay up to $10,000 a night for their hotel accommodation, this is a wonderful way to experience how the other half lives, at $3,000 a night! The Presidential and Panoramic suites, on the 35th to 39th floors of the hotel, come with stunning views of the mountains and desert. They are decorated in rich woods with floral and warm-hued upholstery and drapes. The Las Vegas Strip View suites feature floor-to-ceiling windows and – you guessed it – amazing views of the Strip.

Luxor

702 262 4444, luxor.com
Luxor chapels: Surprisingly, given the strong theming throughout this hotel, the two chapels of the Luxor are in keeping with the hotel, but not overtly Egyptian in feel. Elegantly decked out in creams and peaches, the larger chapel seats 100 guests, while the more intimate venue holds 60. Packages are priced at $479–1,425.

Mandalay Bay

702 632 7777, mandalaybay.com
Mandalay Bay chapels: There are two chapels within this resort, both set within an exotic island built on the shores of an 11acre/4.5ha tropical lagoon. The interiors are decorated in peaches and cream, while outside the chapel fountain provides a superb photo backdrop. Packages are $675–2,695.

MGM Grand

702 891 1111, mgmgrand.com
Forever Grand Wedding Chapel: A magnificent, cathedral-like archway announces your arrival at the lobby of this dual chapel. Lining the walls of the marble-floored area is a series of black and white photographs of movie stars in their wedding finery. Both chapels come in creams in blue with pretty domed ceilings. Packages are $699–3,999.

Cherish Chapel: Seats 25–30 guests.

Legacy Chapel: Seats 55–60 guests.

Wedding chapel at the Mandalay Bay

Mirage

702 791 7111, mirage.com
Customised ceremonies: The Mirage does not have a chapel, but can customise ceremonies to be performed in the banqueting space. You meet with their design team to discuss your requirements and tailor-make your own fairytale wedding.

Monte Carlo

702 730 7000, montecarlo.com
French-Victorian-styled chapel: The upmarket resort offers a refined chapel, which is decorated in soft, neutral colours with hand-painted murals. It seats 100 guests.

Paris Resort

702 946 7000, parislasvegas.com
In addition to two of the most romantic chapels in any resort hotel, you can also choose to get wed by the rooftop pool or on the observation deck at the top of the Eiffel Tower. Package prices are $800–10,000!

Chapelle du Jardin: An intimate chapel seating 30, it is decorated in pastel tones accented by charming garden murals.

Chapelle du Paradis: The cathedral-style setting of this beautiful chapel is enhanced by elegant columns, detailed gold-leaf designs, crystal chandeliers and angelic cherubs painted onto the blue-sky ceiling. Seats 90.

Treasure Island's Enchantment Wedding

Monte Carlo's beautiful chapel

Planet Hollywood

702 785 5555, planethollywoodresort.com/weddings.php
The chapel: The new Planet Hollywood is about cool lines and chic, designer flair. The old garish chapel from the Aladdin days is being made over, and at press time we had no idea what the new one will look like. Still, early word is that packages will be $499–749.

Stratosphere

702 380 7777, stratospherehotel.com
Holding the unique position of offering the highest chapels in all of America, they proudly sit 800ft/240m above the ground in the Stratosphere Tower; especially at night, they hold truly awesome views. Couples can also get wed on the indoor observation deck and then use the outdoor patio overlooking the Strip for their reception. Packages cost $155–2,975. An Elvis impersonator (of course!) is also available at an extra cost.

Garden Chapel: The smaller chapel seats 20.

Terrace Chapel: This seats 100 and is decorated in orange and grey.

Treasure Island

702 894 7444, treasureisland.com
Treasure Island Chapel: Enchantment, Destiny, Legacy and Elegance are the packages available here. White benches contrast with the terracotta hues of the décor to provide a romantic setting for your wedding. Packages cost $499–3,199.

The Venetian wedding experience

Venetian

702 414 4100, venetian.com

Chapels: This resort hotel is themed around the ageless beauty and romance of Venice and the storybook charm of old-world Italy. There are three chapels, each holding 40 to 50 guests and overlooking the pool deck and lush gardens. Cleverly, all three chapels can be opened out to provide space for a larger event.

Ponte al di Piazza: Alternatively, couples can choose to say their vows on the bridge over the square, which is said to serve as the stairway to longevity and prosperity as man and wife. Afterwards, you can start married life by floating down the Grand Canal in a beautiful gondola while being serenaded. Packages cost $750–4,500 and more.

Wynn Las Vegas

702 770 7100, wynnlasvegas.com

In keeping with the standards for privacy that pervade all aspects of Wynn's mega-resort, each of the wedding salons has its own private foyer where guests can gather before the ceremony, and a private bridal room for last-minute touch-ups! Delicate tones, deluxe upholstery and beautiful lighting are the other hallmarks of each chapel. Packages for these glamorous venues cost $790–19,350.

Lavender Salon: Designed to be intimate, yet can accommodate 120 guests. Despite its name, back-lit rose murals and rose petals strewn along the aisle are the main features of this chapel.

Lilac Salon: This chapel is perfect for smaller wedding parties and seats 65. White, creams and terracottas run throughout the salon and are reflected in the choice of flowers that line the aisle and altar.

Primrose Courtyard: Think luxurious fabrics in genteel Caribbean colours draped over an exterior altar and you get a good idea of what this chapel is about. A private courtyard under a canopy of trees that is surrounded by two fountains, it can seat up to 40 guests. It also available for pre-event cocktails or post-wedding cake and champagne.

Resort hotels off the Strip

Rio All-Suite Hotel

702 252 7777, riolasvegas.com

The Rio has three chapels, all located on the third floor masquerade village. Each has ivory brocade coverings and elegant bows.

Gardenia: This has gardenias and ivy floral arrangements and seats 50 guests.

Lily of the Valley: The largest chapel seats 130 guests.

Roses: With a rose trellis draped in muted pastel roses and ivy, this is suitable for 100 guests.

Poolside: The truly romantic may prefer the option of saying their vows at twilight on the soft, warm sand next to the pool. Located on the 50th floor terrace, it overlooks the twinkling lights of the Strip. Other alternatives include a range of breathtaking sites on the exclusive Rio Sesco Golf Course.

Imperial Palace

702 731 3311, imperialpalace.com

Chapel: The elegantly appointed chapel is on the fourth floor and is decorated in ivory and soft beiges with silk floral arrangements and crystal chandeliers.

Style and romance at the Venetian

Ritz-Carlton Lake Las Vegas

Tropicana

702 739 2222, tropicanalv.com
Gazebo: The outdoor island gazebo, an unusual and romantic chapel with a Polynesian theme, seats 30.

Island wedding chapel: This has been voted Best Wedding Chapel and Most Romantic Setting by the *Las Vegas Bride* magazine. Tucked away in the lush tropical foliage and tumbling waterfalls for which the hotel is famous, it seats 90. Packages start at $399 for the Aloha package and rise to $3,499 for the Blue Hawaii, which includes a five-night stay at the hotel.

Terrace of Dreams at the Bellagio

Resort hotels at Lake Las Vegas

Hyatt Regency Lake Las Vegas

702 567 1234, lakelasvegas.hyatt.com
Andalusian Gardens: A chapel with a gazebo.

Lotus Palmerai: The Lotus Court.

Chapel Fiorenza: Meaning Flowering Chapel, this new option is an Italian-themed chapel located on the Pontevecchio Bridge, which spans the resort's 320acre/129ha lake. A richly Italian décor theme features beamed ceilings, wrought-iron chandeliers, sconces, rustic stone floors, arched windows and wooden pews and it can accommodate 225 guests.

Ritz-Carlton Lake Las Vegas

702 567 4700, ritzcarlton.com
The Ritz offers three chapel locations, each designed to provide an unforgettable fairytale wedding.

Florentine Garden: Creating a Mediterranean ambiance with an enchanting courtyard with pastel stucco walls, the garden is surrounded by balconies that are used by trumpeters to herald the arrival of the bride and for launching rainbow streamers. Seats 150.

Pontevecchio Park: A serene location with breathtaking views of the lake, bridge and desert landscape. It can cater for 100–400 guests.

Tuscan Courtyard: An intimate private courtyard, with the pretty Italianate Monte Lago Village acting as a backdrop. Seats 20–50 guests.

9 GAY LAS VEGAS

A full guide to restaurants, bars and clubs

Surprisingly, for a city that claims to be so adult, there is relatively little available for the gay community. Nevadan anti-sodomy laws were only repealed in 1995 and a decade later, the city now has its first openly gay nightclub on the Strip – Krave.

There may not be the gay areas you'll find in many other cities, but there is an active scene and the annual Gay Pride Parade in April or May (call 702 733 9800 for details) is testimony to the presence of a gay community. For the most part, though, a lot of gay activity is immersed in the mainstream. Here is a guide to the specific amenities available to gay men and women.

Information

Gay and Lesbian Center

953 East Sahara Avenue between 6th Street and Maryland Parkway, 702 733 9800, gayvegas.com

A good place to start is the Gay and Lesbian Center. It is open Mon–Fri 10am–7.30pm – call ahead for schedules. It is a relatively new building and a new meeting point for gays. The Center's website is very helpful.

QVegas

qvegas. com

A leading gay newspaper, *QVegas*, maintains a great website full of information for the gay community.

The Gay Triangle

The Gay Triangle area around Paradise Road has several bars, Get Booked and the Mariposa coffee house. Pick up copies of the two free monthly gay papers – *QVegas* and *Out Las Vegas* – at any of those locations. This area is also lovingly referred to as the Fruit Loop by local gay and straight residents, for the business signs that show the rainbow colours of gay pride.

In this chapter

BRITTIP

As in New York, a lot of mainstream clubs, shows and restaurants have become popular hangouts for members of the gay community.

Pool fun is on offer at many hotels

Get Booked: At Paradise Plaza, 4640 Paradise at Naples Drive, 702 737 7780, this is a bookstore at the heart of the gay triangle at the corner of Naples Drive and Paradise Road, just south of Hard Rock Café, and a great source of information. It is open Mon–Thurs 10am–midnight, Fri 10am–2am, Sat noon–2am and Sun noon–midnight.

Another great gay area can be found along and between East Sahara and Karen Avenue, just to the west of Maryland Parkway. Here you will find Apollo Spa, Pride Factory, Spotlight Lounge, Badlands, Rainbow Lounge and the Las Vegas Lounge.

Accommodation

Alexis Park

375 East Harmon, 800 582 2228, alexispark.com

The closest hotel to the Fruit Loop area and host to a number of gay events. It has special discounted rates for people who call them on their 800 582 2228 number.

Blue Moon Resort

2651 Westwood Drive, just off the Strip, 702 361 9099, fax 702 361 9110, bluemoonlv.com

The $3.1m Blue Moon Resort opened in December 2002 providing a full-service gay resort for men only with 45 rooms and suites. Amenities include a Jacuzzi Grotto with 10ft/3m waterfalls to relax and enjoy the sun, a lagoon-style pool and sundeck with a clothing-optional area, plus a steam room.

Parlour suites provide 800sq ft/74sq m of space that are ideal for small meetings, entertaining guests or simply watching the TV and have large beds and armoires, large TVs, cable TV and electronic door locks.

Alexis Park

Lucky You

702 384 1129

An exclusively gay B&B just two blocks from the Strip within walking distance of gay bars. Well priced but no credit cards accepted.

The Ranch

1110 Ralston Drive, near Martin Luther King Boulevard, 702 631 7708

It's expensive and doesn't take credit cards, but is run by lesbians.

Riviera

2901 The Strip at Riviera Boulevard, 702 734 5110, theriviera.com

The most openly gay hotel on the Strip, it is the home of *La Cage*, a top drag show starring Frank Marino as Joan Rivers.

BRITTIP

Most nightlife starts quite late in Las Vegas and there is no last call as most of the venues are open 24 hours a day.

Blue Moon Resort

BRITTIP

Visit gaybar.com for up-to-date information and location maps for all the local gay bars.

Cafés

Garlic Café

Decatur Twain Shopping Center, 3650 South Decatur Boulevard, 702 221 0266
The only openly gay-owned café in town, you choose the strength of garlic. It's always busy and serves great food. Open daily 5pm–10pm.

Mariposa

Paradise Plaza, 4643 Paradise Road, at Naples Drive, 702 650 9009
Located in the heart of the Gay Triangle, this is a fun and friendly place with patio seating and great food. Open daily 3pm–3am.

Clubs and bars

Back Door Lounge

1415 East Charleston Boulevard, 702 385 2018
Has a happy hour every night from 5pm to 7pm. Monday night a free poker party starts at 7pm and there is a free barbecue on Saturday nights at 6pm. Very popular with Gay Latinos at the weekends.

Badlands Saloon

953 East Sahara Avenue, 702 792 9262
New home of the Gay Rodeo Association and probably the friendliest bar in town, the best times to visit are Sunday around 4pm and Tuesday and Thursdays around 7pm when the line-dancing classes get going.

Bar Code

5150 Spring Mountain Road, 702 221 5150
This is a trendy, alternative nightclub that puts on lots of sometimes kookie promotions most days of the week.

Charlie's Las Vegas

5012 South Arville Street, 702 876 1844, charlieslasvegas.com
Part of a popular chain of gay bars popular in Chicago, Phoenix and Denver. It sports a Country and Western theme with social events nightly.

Krave

Escape Lounge

4212 West Sahara Avenue, 702 364 1167, escapeloungelv.com
This is a new place designed for friends to have a quiet drink together and enjoy life.

Flex

4371 West Charleston Boulevard, 702 385 3539
A great mixed club with drink specials, dancing and live music.

Freezone Night Club

610 East Naples, 702 794 2300, freezonelv.com
All-round bar with restaurant. Tuesday is the Ladies 4 Ladies revue night, Thursday the all-male revue for Boys Night, and What a Drag! is held on Friday and Saturday. As its name implies: never a cover charge to enter.

Escape Lounge

BRITTIP

Some of the gay night spots are in quite out-of-the-way locations. For help finding them, look up addresses on mapquest.com.

Good Time Bar & Grill

1775 East Tropicana, 702 736 9494
Happy hours from 5–7am and 5–7pm. Monday is the most popular. No credit cards.

Krave

Miracle Mile, at the corner of Harmon Avenue and the Strip, 702 836 0830, kravelasvegas.com
The only gay nightclub on the Strip has been voted the best venue in town by many of the leading gay papers. There are events for men throughout the week – all starting at 11pm – with a GirlBar on Saturdays 9pm–3am.

Snick's Place

1402 South 4th Street, 702 385 9298, snicksplace.com
For the mature crowd. Sunday morning from 9am–noon is time for a Bloody Mary special.

Spotlight Lounge

957 E Sahara Avenue, 702 696 0202, spotlightlv.com
Over the last few years, the Spotlight has grown into a leader of the gay community, hosting a number of meetings and charity events to raise money for gay causes. It is also a great working class bar to relax.

Hanging out at the pool

Gay bath house

The Apollo Spa & Health Club

953E Sahara Avenue, Suite A-19, 702 650 9191, apollospa.com
Located in the north-west corner of Commercial Center, this is a bath house that caters for men.

BRITTIP

There are no exclusively female bars in Las Vegas, but two of the most popular with women are Freezone and Charlie's.

Good Time Bar & Grill

10 ATTRACTIONS

Thrill rides, children's attractions, museums and animal habitats

Yes, there really is more to Las Vegas than bright lights and gambling dens. There are a whole host of attractions that appeal to people of all ages, some amazing thrill rides and even a little – overpriced – culture in the form of art museums.

The high-tech wizardry that can be seen in so many nightclubs and production shows is also put to use in heart-thumping simulator rides and 3-D movies. And there is a raft of museums that celebrate aspects of the city's history and people – including Liberace and Elvis – and the Las Vegas Natural History Museum, while animals can be seen at several resort hotels and the local zoo.

In this chapter

As in other chapters, to save keying in a long website address, you can go to the home page for the resort-hotel, then follow the entertainment or attractions links.

Chaos at the Adventuredrome is not for the faint-hearted

Conventional rides

Many resorts around the Las Vegas area have added a number of thrill rides to get the blood pumping before you hit the gambling tables. Circus Circus draws top hand for the most rides, while the Stratosphere's skyreaching thrillers are some of the most wrenching. There are more too, including great rollercoasters at the Sahara and NYNY.

Adventuredome Theme Park

Circus Circus, 702 794 3939, adventuredome.com

The desert may be scorching hot outside, but here in this 5acre/2ha, fully enclosed elevated theme park – the largest space-frame dome in America – the temperature stays a comfortable 22°C/72°F all year round. Grand Slam Canyon is designed to look like a desert with a large rock canyon that gives way to caverns, pinnacles and steep cliffs, while a stream flows gently through the lush landscape. But this canyon is home to prehistoric creatures – well, life-sized replicas of them at least! – that make themselves known between two 140ft/43m peaks, a fossil wall, archaeological dig and a replica of an Indian cliff dwelling.

The **Canyon Blaster** is the only indoor, double-loop, double-corkscrew roller-coaster in America, and sends you careening between canyon walls at 55mph/88kph.

The two-minute long **Inverter** involves a 360-degree rotation in which you are held upside-down with only a harness and a T-bar separating you from the concrete floor 50ft/15m below.

Chaos twirls and whirls you anti-clockwise, backwards and upside-down on a circular platform amid the tracks of the Canyon Blaster. Lasting two minutes, it creates a 3-D effect as you rise, tilt and spin all at the same time, and due to the variation in speed and motion, no two rides are the same.

Slightly less scary is the Rim Runner

You know what to expect on the Inverter

In the **Sling Shot** you are shot up a tower at 4Gs of acceleration and then shot straight back down again.

The **Rim Runner** is a more relaxing ride, taking you on a scenic journey through botanical landscaping before plunging over a heart-stopping 60ft/18m waterfall.

BRITTIP

Save the Rim Runner thrill ride until the end of your Adventuredome visit as you will get soaked!

All in all there are 19 rides and attractions in the Adventuredome including **Laser Blast**, where sharpshooters take part in a high-tech war, bumper cars and a swinging ship, plus an IMAX simulator thrill ride (see page 196). Younger children are well catered for from plane and train rides to bumper-mobiles, plus strolling entertainers who juggle, mime and do magic tricks.

Open: Daily from 10am. It closes at 6pm Mon–Thurs, midnight Fri and Sat and 8pm Sun, though exact hours may vary according to the seasons, so do check.

Tickets: Entrance to the park is free, you just pay for the rides of your life! The main thrill rides cost $6 each, the large rides cost $4 each, the junior rides $4 each or you can buy an All Day Ride Pass at $14.95 for people 33–48in/84–122cm tall, and $22.95 for those above 4ft/122cm. Children under 33in/84cm ride free with an adult.

Desperado at Buffalo Bill's

Adventure Canyon at Buffalo Bill's

Buffalo Bill's Hotel, 31900 South Las Vegas Boulevard, Primm, 702 679 7433 or 1-800 FUN STOP, primmvalleyresorts.com
For amazing thrill rides on a Wild West theme, head to Buffalo Bill's in Primm, which is just 35mls/56km south of Las Vegas on Interstate 15.

America's tallest and fastest roller-coaster, **Desperado**, has a top speed of around 90mph/145kph and creates a G-force of nearly 4. A high-speed dive down a 55-degree hill into a tunnel starts the ride and is then followed by a 155ft/47m second hill, which leads to a zero-gravity sensation.

Turbo Drop creates a similar sensation to flying straight towards the ground in a jet fighter. Riders are nestled in padded saddles and shoulder harnesses, lifted 200ft/60m up in the air and plunged to earth at 45mph/72kph, creating positive G-forces close to 4.5.

The **Vault** is the first 3-D, digital projection motor ride in America. Each of the six motion pads drops, twists and turns as the screen takes you on one of 10 different rides ranging from the turbulent waters of Aquaride to the seriously rickety mine car on the Haunted Mine Ride.

Other rides: The Adventure Canyon Log Flume starts as a classic flume ride with a 35ft/11m drop, but once you splash down, you continue through an electronic shooting gallery that follows the park's Wild West theme. You take out a pistol as targets are lit up along the way, then if you shoot a bad guy you get points and if you shoot a good guy you lose points! There are plenty of other rides to make your visit worthwhile, plus the **Ghost Town Motion Theaters**.

Open: Mon–Thurs noon–6pm, Fri and Sat 10am–midnight and Sun 10am–7pm.

Tickets: The main rides are $5 or $30 for a full-day wristband, $22 for a half-day wristband. Little Wrangler passes for those under 4ft/1.8m are $12.

Manhattan Express

New York-New York, 702 740 6969, 1-800 NYFORME, nynyhotelcasino.com/entertainment
Based on the kind of rollercoaster that made Coney Island in the real New York so famous, the **Manhattan Express** ride twists, loops and dives around the perimeter and even through the New York-New York hotel, which can be a worry when you are sitting in 'Central Park' and hear a roar and rattling fling through the rafters. It has the world's first heart-line twist and dive that simulates the sensation felt by a pilot during a barrel roll in an aeroplane when the centre of rotation actually becomes the same as your centre of gravity! Incidentally, the Manhattan Express has been voted Best Thrill Ride in Nevada by *Nevada Magazine*'s reader survey.

Open: Sun–Thurs 11am–11pm and Fri and Sat 10.30am–midnight, weather permitting.

Tickets: $12.50 per person, second ride $6 or all-day pass $25.

Speed: The Ride and Cyber Speedway

Sahara Hotel, 702 737 2111, saharavegas.com/nascar
The Ride is the fastest roller-coaster in Las Vegas and literally slingshots riders at speeds of up to 70mph/112kph. You go through breathtaking loops as you zip your way around the Sahara before halting and repeating the experience in reverse!

The Manhattan Express

On **Cyber Speedway**, you really are in the driving seat. Driving an almost real-sized racing car, you speed around a track modelled on the Las Vegas Motor Speedway at speeds of up to 22mph/35kph doing seven laps in all against up to seven other drivers.

Open: Sun–Thurs 10am–midnight, Fri–Sat 10am–1am.

Tickets: $10 for one ride or $19.95 for both rides.

Stratosphere Tower

Stratosphere Hotel, 702 380 7777 or 1-800 99 TOWER, stratospherehotel.com/attractions.html

The **Big Shot** thrusts 16 passengers 160ft/50m into the air along the 228ft/70m spire at speeds of around 45mph/72kph, producing up to 4Gs with negative Gs on the way back down. What is so scary about the ride is not just the speed and force of it all, but the fact that you are so high up in the air in the first place!

Another great ride is the **High Roller** roller-coaster, one of the highest in the world.

Insanity – The Ride thrusts passengers 64ft/20m over the north edge of the tower at speeds that create forces of up to 3Gs, while at a 70-degree angle, providing a perfect view of nothingness beneath you – except a 900ft/277m drop to the Strip below (though no time for photos, folks!).

In **XScream** (i.e screaming to the extreme) passengers are propelled 27ft/8m over the edge of the tower at 30mph/48kph – again providing excellent views of the 900ft/277m drop.

Open: Sun–Thurs 10am–1am, Fri–Sat 10am–2pm. However, the rides are often not open on windy days.

Tickets: $15.95 for one ride including admission to Stratosphere Tower. Tickets to ride XScream, Insanity and the Big Shot are $25.95. An all-day pass $29.95.

XScream

The Big Shot

> **BRITTIP**
> For the best selection of thrill rides in town, the Stratosphere is the place to go. Thrill seekers with a car should head out of town to Buffalo Bill's Adventure Canyon in Primm.

Simulator rides and 3-D movies

SimEx Theater

Adventuredome Theme Park, Circus Circus, 702 794 3939, adventuredome.com

In **Escape from Dino Island** you are taken on a thrilling adventure to save T-Rex from extinction. For children over 42in/106cm only.

Fans of the Nickelodeon cartoon will love **SpongeBob SquarePants 4-D Ride**, where they get the chance to dive into Bikini Bottom and join SpongeBob and co on a 4D adventure.

Open: 10am–midnight.

Tickets: $6 per ride. All-day passes for the Adventuredome are also available (see page 194).

Merlin's Magic Motion Machines are at the fairytale Excalibur

Pharaoh's Pavilion

Luxor, 702 262 4555, luxor.com/entertainment

The Pavilion is home to a whole series of attractions including two IMAX movie theatres, one IMAX ride-film, The Tomb and Museum of King Tutankhamun and a virtual reality roller-coaster.

IMAX ride-film, **In Search of the Obelisk** tells the story of how a spectacular subterranean civilization was discovered during excavation works to build the Luxor hotel. As you arrive at an archaeological dig, it is apparent that evil forces are at work and before long you are taken on a high-speed chase twisting and turning through vast, cavernous areas.

In **Dracula's Haunted Castle**, the action starts on a dark and stormy night outside a foreboding castle. Two huge wooden doors creak open and an eerie-looking butler appears. You are then carried down dark hallways lit only by lanterns at break-neck speeds with horrifying skeletons jumping out and attacking you with swords and flying bats heading straight for your face!

In the **IMAX Theatre**, current 3-D films include: *Wild Safari 3-D, Mystery of the Nile, Magnificent Desolation: Walking on the Moon 3-D, Fighter Pilot* and *Sharks 3-D*.

Open: Daily 9am–11pm. Cinema hours vary but are normally 9am–midnight daily.

Tickets: $9.99 per ride or buy an attractions pass for $24.95. $11.99 per film.

Merlin's Magic Motion Machines

Excalibur, 702 597 7084, excalibur.com/entertainment

Here you'll find a series of hilarious rides produced by Iwerks Entertainment. In **Dino Island**, you get to explore a newly formed island upon which live dinosaurs now roam. In the heart-stopping **Comet Impact**, you are part of a team that must destroy a comet on a collision course with Earth.

Open: Daily 10am–11pm.

Tickets: $5 per ride.

BRITTIP

Merlin's Magic Motion Machines offer the best-value simulator rides on the Strip.

Pharaoh's Pavilion

Star Trek: The Experience™

Las Vegas Hilton, 3000 Paradise Road, 702 697 8700, lvhilton.com/entertainment
Be prepared to Klingon for dear life as you boldly explore the out-of-this-world experience of *Star Trek*. Home to two brilliant 'rides', there is now also a tour of *Star Trek the Experience: Secrets Unveiled*, while the theme restaurant, Quark's Bar and Restaurant, can be found in the Deep Space Nine Promenade of shops.

Those expecting a relatively tame encounter with the *Star Trek* crew, beware! In **BORG Invasion 4-D**, cybernetically enhanced beings known for absorbing other species into their ever-growing database of knowledge and technology are on the prowl. The first-ever cinema to use multiple-angle 3-D effects, it means the baddy can come at you from the front, right, left and overhead, so be warned. As for you, you are part of a group touring a research facility when it is attacked by the BORG and must try to reach the escape pod.

In **Klingon Encounter**, you are part of a group preparing to tour the USS *Enterprise* when everyone is beamed on to the ship through a gap in the time/space continuum and you find yourselves coming under attack from the Klingons (who are starboard bound, of course!).

Open: Sun–Thurs 11am–10pm, Fri–Sat 11am–11pm. Missions run from 11.30am–7.30pm Sun–Thurs and 11.30am–9.30pm Fri–Sat.

Tickets: Dual mission $36.99 adults, $33.99 under-12s and seniors. *Star Trek the Experience: Secrets Unveiled* is $39.99 or $29.99 when bought with a single tour ticket.

Fun rides

Eiffel Tower Experience

Paris, 702 946 7000, parislasvegas.com
You take a lift to about two-thirds of the way up the replica Eiffel Tower and then look out at the desert through an iron mesh. The hotel's tower is, in fact, only two-thirds of the height of the real Eiffel Tower, so your view is blocked by many of the tall buildings about. It is hard to get a decent view of the entire Strip and impossible to take any worthwhile pictures through the grille.

Open: Daily 10am–1am, weather permitting.

Tickets: Mon–Thurs adults $9, seniors and under-13s $7; Fri–Sun adults $12, seniors and under 13 $10.

BRITTIP

The Eiffel Tower Experience is probably the most expensive elevator (lift) ride in the world. Save your money and enjoy Strip views from any one of the fab restaurants with views (see page 105).

Gondola rides

Venetian, 702 414 4500, venetian.com/gondola.aspx
Supplying the full Venetian experience, the hotel puts on gondola rides around the Grand Canal Shoppes. They're pricey, but still cheaper than gondola rides in Venice! Tours start from St Mark's Square. Better yet

Star Trek: The Experience is a must for die-hard trekkies

are the newest gondola rides outside the main entrance of the Doge's Palace. These gondoliers are required to be Italian, or at least have travelled enough in Italy to be able to talk about it first hand. Plus, they must have great singing voices as they croon romantic melodies to their passengers. Many a wedding proposal has been made here. They even have a special wedding gondola, oversized and all in white, if you'd like to take your vows here.

Open: Sun–Thurs 10am–11pm, Fri–Sat 10am–11.45pm.

Tickets: Adults $15, under-13s $7.50, private gondola $60.

BRITTIP

The gondola rides are so popular that tickets sell out every day and the average wait for a ride is one hour.

Observation Deck Stratosphere Tower

Stratosphere, 702 380 7777, stratospherehotel.com

Take a ride up the Stratosphere's lifts to the top of the tallest free-standing observation tower in America, which has an indoor and outdoor observation deck where all the landmarks seen from different points of the circular deck are explained. The best time of day to see the Strip is just before sunset when you can make out all the landmarks before the town goes dark and everything lights up. Better still, start at the observation deck, then move up to the Top of the World Restaurant for a romantic dinner.

Open: Sun–Thurs 10am–1am, Fri–Sat 10am–2am.

Tickets: Adults $9.95, children 4–12 $6 (see page 196 for the details of the tower's thrill rides) free for Stratosphere guests.

Free shows

Bellagio Fountain Show

In the lake outside the Bellagio, bellagio.com

An incredibly stunning visual and audio experience as the now world-famous fountains perform carefully choreographed movements in time to operatic, classical and whimsical music.

Show times: Mon–Fri 3pm–midnight. Sat–Sun noon–midnight. Shows every half hour until 8pm, then every 15 minutes until midnight.

CBS Television City

MGM Grand, 702 891 5752, mgmgrand.com

A research centre that allows audiences to view TV shows in production and comment on them.

Show times: Free screenings begin daily at 10am until around 10pm and are conducted every 20 minutes.

Las Vegas Research Studios

Venetian, 702 732 2733, venetian.com

Here's your chance to have your say about up-and-coming products and shows. Screenings last between 15 and 20 minutes, after which you fill in an automated survey.

Open: Daily 11am–9pm.

Masquerade Show in the Sky

Rio All-Suite Hotel, 3700 West Flamingo, 702 252 7777, riolasvegas.com

A $25m Disney-esque spectacle in which dozens of Mardi Gras floats containing exotically costumed dancers literally 'float' about 20ft/6m above your head, accompanied to music.

Show times: Daily 3pm, 4pm, 5pm, 6.30pm, 7.30pm, 8.30pm and 9.30pm.

The Bellagio fountains show at night

BRITTIP

If you are travelling with children, be warned that the Masquerade Show in the Sky includes topless showgirls during the evening performances.

Sirens of TI

Treasure Island, 702 894 7111, treasureisland.com

A rowdy bunch of buccaneers do battle against alluring but treacherous Sirens in a spectacle full of singing, sword play, canon shots and, of course, at least one walking of the plank.

Show times: daily at 5.30pm, 7pm, 8.30pm and 10pm.

Animal magic

Lion Habitat

MGM Grand, 702 891 1111, mgmgrand.com/entertainment

A $9m multi-level lion habitat has been opened at the MGM Grand, in which visitors are encircled by lions via a see-through tunnel running through the habitat. Out of 24 lions, cared for by a veteran animal trainer, up to seven can be viewed in the habitat at any time. Three of the lions – Goldie, Metro and Baby Lion – are direct descendants of MGM Studio's marque lion, Metro.

Open: 11am–10pm.

Admission: Free, though an 'official' picture costs around $10.

A majestic lioness at the Lion Habitat

Two dolphins at the Dolphin Habitat

Secret Garden and Dolphin Habitat at the Mirage

Mirage Hotel, 702 791 7188, mirage.com/attractions

Here is your chance to get a closer look at the rare breeds of animal that Siegfried and Roy used in their magical illusion show. The $15m, 2.5acre/1ha natural **Secret Garden** habitat was specially built to house their Bengal tigers, panthers, snow leopards and Asian elephants.

BRITTIP

Make the most of the Mirage's free attractions by taking a look at the enormous tropical fish tank behind the resort's lobby during your visit to see the beautiful white tigers.

Next door is the massive **Dolphin Habitat**, which is home to a family of Atlantic bottlenose dolphins. Four connected pools, an artificial coral reef system and a sandy bottom replicate the dolphin's natural environment, which aims to provide a healthy and nurturing home for the marine mammals and educate the public about their role in the ecosystem.

Open: Mon–Fri 11am–5.30pm, Sat–Sun 10.30am–5.30pm.

Admission: $18 includes entrance to both habitats. On Wednesday and after the garden closes $6.

Walking through the Shark Reef tunnel

Shark Reef

Mandalay Bay, 702 632 7777, mandalaybay.com/entertainment

An aquarium you walk underneath so you are completely surrounded by water. It contains unusual and dangerous aquatic animals and fish from the world's tropical waters. More than 1,200 species are represented here from a 100ft/30m nurse shark to a tiny clown fish. Divers in the aquarium talk about the animals and answer questions via a high-tech underwater communications system.

The largest display of golden saltwater crocodiles outside Thailand can be seen here too. This is a seriously endangered species as there are only 12 left in the world. Other animals include moray eels, southern stingrays, angelfish, puffer fish, jellyfish and serpents and dragons featuring green tree pythons, known for their vivid green colour and razor-sharp teeth.

Be a dolphin trainer

One of the most exciting – if not expensive – new attractions to hit Las Vegas is the chance to become a dolphin trainer for the day at the Secret Garden and Dolphin Habitat at the Mirage. For a hefty fee of $720 per person (with two people per family as a maximum), it is possible to learn how to feed and play with dolphins as you accompany real trainers from 9.45am to 3.15pm. Throughout the day your activities and contact with the dolphins will be captured on camera and the photos put on a CD to take home. For further details or to make a reservation, phone 702 792 7889.

Open: Daily 10am–11pm; last admission at 10pm.

Admission: Adults $15.95, under-13s $9.95, under-5s free.

Southern Nevada Zoo

1755 North Rancho Drive, 702 647 4685, lasvegaszoo.org

A small zoo committed to conservation, education and recreation, it houses more than 50 species of reptiles and small animals of the great south-western desert. It is also home to other animals including an African lion, Bengal tiger, Barbary apes, monkeys, wallabies, flamingos, king vultures and North America's only tigrina, an endangered tropical cat.

Open: Daily 9am–5pm.

Admission: Over-12s $7, 2–12s $5 and under-2s free.

Superb royal white tigers

The Tank

Golden Nugget, 702 385 7111, goldennugget.com

While primarily for guests staying at the Golden Nugget in downtown Las Vegas, sometimes staff will let you slide in. The Tank is the new $30m swimming pool complex, including a three-storey water slide. But the coolest part is the shark tank – yes, sharks! The Tank is designed in such a way that while going down the water slide you go through a tube through the middle of the sharks! It is the closest you can come to these cold-blooded killers without donning a mask and fins!

Tiger Habitat

Mirage, 702 791 7111, mirage.com/attractions

A showcase for the famous white tigers that once took part in Siegfried & Roy's magic show, with a pool, waterfalls and all-white background to make the tigers feel secure.

Open: 9am–2.30am.
Admission: Free.

Wildlife Habitat at the Flamingo

Flamingo Hotel, 702 733 3111, flamingohotel.com

Surrounded by lush pines, palms and magnolia, this is the only place in town where you can see the flamingos up close.

Lions at the Southern Nevada Zoo

Impeyn and silver pheasants can also be seen here, along with Gambel's quails, a crown crane, two ibis, ducks, turtles, parrots and penguins. The penguins are fed daily at 8.30am and 3pm – a sight not to be missed!

Open: 24/7.
Admission: Free.

Wildlife Habitat at the Flamingo

The Las Vegas Guggenheim

Art galleries

Being but 100 years old, Las Vegas has a limited run of culture to draw on. What there is happens to be imported at a tidy cost. Thus her museums have some fine pieces but they are few and pricey to see. Most of the galleries at the Bellagio, Wynn and Venetian often charge a wad of cash for just a peek at a bit.

One lovely counterpoint, though, is that several of the high-end shopping areas, including places like Grand Canal Shoppes and Forum Shops, have some dazzling art galleries. And away from the resorts, there are some fascinating places to check out.

Bellagio Gallery of Fine Art

Bellagio, 702 693 7871, bgfa.com
This originally opened to show off the previous owner Steve Wynn's masterpieces, which included Rembrandts, Monets and Picassos, but he took the paintings with him when he sold the hotel to the MGM Grand. Now it showcases travelling art exhibitions and is theoretically non-profit-making. The exhibitions are on a small scale, rarely more than 12–20 pieces or so, but cost is steep, so you should only come by if the current exhibition is particularly of interest to you.

Open: Daily 9am–10pm.

Admission: Adults $15, students $12.

Guggenheim Hermitage Museum

Venetian, 702 414 2440, guggenheimlasvegas.org
Russia's famous Hermitage Museum, which is based in St Petersburg, has joined forces with the Solomon R Guggenheim Foundation in New York to create this museum at the Venetian. The gallery houses some remarkable Russian artefacts and masterpieces that are part of travelling art exhibitions, again, very good quality but on a fairly small scale.

Open: Daily 9.30am–8.30pm.

Admission: Adults $19.50, students $14.50, under-13s $9.50, under-6s free.

Las Vegas Art Museum

9600 West Sahara Avenue, 702 360 8000, lasvegasartmuseum.org
Fine art exhibits in three galleries that are changed on a monthly basis. The museum also runs art classes for adults and children and art competitions.

Open: Tues–Sat 10am–5pm, Sun 1–5pm.

Admission: Adults $6, seniors $5, students $3, under-12s free.

The Wynn Collection

Wynn Las Vegas, 702 770 3590, wynnlasvegas.com
Casino mogul Steve Wynn's private collection includes Picasso's *Le Rêve*, (the painting that originally inspired him for Wynn Las Vegas), Matisse's *The Persian Robe* and *Pineapples and Anemones* and Manet's *Portrait of Mademoiselle Suzette Lemaire in Profile*. Oh, and there's also a portrait of Steve Wynn himself by Andy Warhol! Named one of the top 10 private collectors by US magazine *ARTnews*, Wynn has been collecting art for years and now has a collection that spans 400 years of art history. The one drawback? There are only 13 to 15 pictures on display at any one time.

Open: Sun–Thurs 10am–11pm, Fri–Sat 10am–midnight.

Admission: Adults $6, under-12s free.

The Wynn has a considerable art collection

Attractions

Bellagio Conservatory and Botanical Gardens

Bellagio, 702 693 7111, bellagio.com
This glorious display of exotic plants and flowers provides row upon row of blooms that create a unique tapestry to reflect each season and holiday. The combination of the fragrances, textures and colours are heavenly, while the inspirational conservatory with its glass-topped atrium and sweeping staircase is simply divine. This is a wonderful place to come and release the tension of otherwise intense Las Vegas.

Open: 24/7.

BRITTIP

Feel a photo opportunity coming on? Then the perfect spot to capture yourself in Vegas is at the gorgeous Botanical Gardens in the Bellagio.

The Cloud

Fashion Show Mall, 702 369 0704, thefashionshow.com
One of the most eye-catching attractions on the Strip hovers 128ft/39m above a pedestrian plaza right outside the Fashion Show Mall. Nearly 500ft/152m long, the steel canopy is called The Cloud and is a wonderful source of shade during the day. At night, giant images are projected on to its surface to highlight promotions and events happening at the mall, while a further four massive LED screens are used to broadcast videos and other live broadcasts from the city.

The Conservatory at Chinese New Year

Ethel M Chocolate Factory and Cactus Gardens

2 Cactus Garden Drive, Henderson, 702 433 2500, ethelm.com
This large American sweet-making factory, just 5mls/8km from the Strip, gives an insight into the entire process. The tour ends with a free sample, but as you'll also find yourself in the factory shop, you won't be alone in deciding to buy a box of chocolates. Afterwards step outside to see the 2.5acres/1ha of cactus gardens and the Living Machine, a revolutionary new waste water recycling plant – the first of its kind designed for treating industrial waste water.

Open: Daily 8.30am–7pm.
Admission: Free.

Ethel M Chocolate Factory

Imperial Palace Auto Collection

Guinness World of Records

2780 Las Vegas Boulevard South, 702 792 3766
Affiliated to the book, record-breakers are brought to 3-D life with the help of life-sized replicas, colour videos and computerised databanks. Included are the tallest man, the fattest man and fastest-talking man, plus the musical records of Michael Jackson and videos of world records being set.

Open: Daily 9am–8pm.

Admission: Adults $6.50, students and seniors over 62 $5.50 and 5–12s $4.50.

BRITTIP

Re-creating some of the world's most bizarre facts is either a trainspotter's dream come true or the most boring subject in the world. Your position will inform your enjoyment of the Guinness World of Records attraction.

Imperial Palace Auto Collection

Imperial Palace Hotel, 702 731 3311, autocollections.com
More than 600 cars make up this collection but only 250 are ever on show at one time. Some of the vintage, classic and special-interest cars include the Chaser, the world's fastest petrol-powered police car, a 1986 Ford Mustang, which was specially built for the Nevada Highway Patrol, President Woodrow Wilson's 1917 Pierce Arrow car and a 1961 Lincoln Continental that was once owned by Jacqueline Kennedy Onassis.

Open: Daily 9.30am–9.30pm.

Admission: Adults $6.95, seniors and under-13s $3.

Laser Quest

7361 West Lake Mead Boulevard, 702 243 8881
This is serious boys' rough-and-tumble stuff that will appeal to all ages of the male species. Simply don a vest with a laser sensor and shoot at other players as you find your way through a multi-level maze with enough twists and turns to keep you guessing for several hours.

Open: Tues–Thurs 6–9pm, Fri 4–11pm, Sat noon–11pm, Sun noon–6pm.

Admission: $7.50 per person for 20 minutes of play.

Guinness World of Records

BRITTIP

Going to fight it out at Laser Quest? Remember that lasers are just like light beams and can ricochet off reflective spots throughout the Quest – a pretty neat way to do away with your opponents (or be done away with)!

Las Vegas Mini Gran Prix

1401 North Rainbow Boulevard, 702 259 7000, lvmgp.com

In the unlikely event that you do turn up in Sin City with children in tow, then this is the place to come to stop them feeling they have to spend their entire sojourn being kept out of all the adult activities. There are a few fun slides, but the real draw here is the fun mini-car races, which take place in Grand Prix-style cars of various shapes and sizes. To ride a Kiddie car you must be four years old or at least 54in/1.37m tall. To ride a Grand Prix car you must be 16.

Open: Sun–Thurs 10am–10pm, Fri–Sat 10am–11pm.

Admission: $5.50 per ticket or $25 for five tickets.

Madame Tussaud's

Venetian, 702 414 4100, mtvegas.com

This is the Las Vegas version of the popular wax museum franchise. Five theme areas include the Big Night, a special VIP party with Whoopi Goldberg and Brad Pitt among others; the Sports Arena with Mohammed Ali, Babe Ruth and Evander Holyfield (who is missing part of his right ear!); Rock and Pop with Elton John and Tina Turner; Las Vegas Legends with Frank Sinatra and Marilyn Monroe; and the Finale, a state-of-the-art tribute to modern Las Vegas legends including Wayne Newton and Siegfried and Roy. The entrance is just off the Doge's Palace at the south end of the square.

Tiger Woods at Madame Tussaud's

Old Las Vegas Mormon Fort

Take the moving walkway until you see two wax figures standing guard at the entrance. These figures change regularly, rotating between basketball's Michael Jordan, Johnny Depp as *Pirates of the Caribbean*'s Jack Sparrow, Muhammad Ali and Don King (the wild-haired boxing promoter). It is a great photo opportunity!

Open: Times vary but generally daily 10am–10pm.

Admission: Adults $22.95, seniors and students $17.95, children $12.95, family $62.80.

Old Las Vegas Mormon Fort

State Historic Park, 908 Las Vegas Boulevard North, 702 486 3511, parks.nv.gov/olvmf.htm

This is the oldest surviving non-native-American structure in Las Vegas and dates back to 14 June 1855 when the Mormon missionaries arrived in New Mexico Territory. Their aim was to convert the indigenous inhabitants and provide a safe way-station between Mormon communities in Great Salt Lake City to the north and San Bernardino to the east. The 150sq ft/14sq m adobe-walled fort was still being built when the fort was abandoned in 1858 and subsequently was used by lead miners before becoming a ranch. To think, Sin City could have been a conservative Morman haunt like Salt Lake City!

Open: Daily 8.30am–4.30pm.

Admission: Adults $2, under-13s $1, under-6s free.

The Tomb and Museum of King Tutankhamun

Planetarium and Observatory

Community College of Southern Nevada, 3200 East Cheyenne Avenue, 702 651 4759

Southern Nevada's only public planetarium and observatory has multimedia shows on astronomy plus hemispheric motion pictures. Public observing sessions are held after the last showings.

Open: Shows are on Fri 6pm and 7.30pm, Sat 3.30pm and 7.30pm. Public observing sessions are held at about 8.30pm, weather permitting. The shop is open Fri 5pm–8pm and Sat 3pm–8pm.

Admission: Adults $5, under-12s and over-55s $3.

Ron Lee's World of Clowns

330 Carousel Parkway, Henderson, 702 434 1700, ronlee.com

Ron Lee is a well-respected artist and sculptor, and his work has been used by all manner of film companies. He is also responsible for the M&M candy sculptures so popular around the world. Here you can see how clown and animation characters are made in an impressive 35-minute self-guided tour. A Warner Bros production facility, you will see famous cartoon characters including Popeye, Betty Boop, ET and Rocky. It includes a museum of clown memorabilia, Jitters Café and gift shop and a beautiful, jewel-encrusted musical carousel, which you can ride for $1.

Open: Mon–Fri 9am–4pm, Sat 10am–4pm.

Admission: Free.

The Tomb and Museum of King Tutankhamun

Luxor, 702 262 4555, luxor.com/attractions

This is touted as an exact re-creation of King Tut's tomb as it was discovered by Howard Carter in 1922. Hidden for centuries, the tomb and its artefacts had been untouched by grave robbers. The replica includes stone chambers housing statues of the gods, wooden boats intended to carry King Tut on his final voyage to the afterlife and vessels for food and drink. Most impressive of all the replicas is the gold-plated sarcophagus and the shabtis – figurines made of semi-precious stones symbolising workers to help Tut with his duties.

Open: Daily 9am–11pm.

Admission: $9.99 or attraction pass $34.95 (see Pharoah's Pavilion, page 197).

A figurine from Ron Lee's World of Clowns

Museums

Atomic Testing Museum

Desert Research Institute, 755 East Flamingo Road, 702 794 5161, ntshf.org
Once classified as top secret, the most chilling episodes in Nevada's history have been re-created at this museum. Tracing the history of the Nevada test site, which from 1951 until 1992 saw more than 900 nuclear weapons being tested for the US government, you enter an interactive bunker to witness bomb blasts. As the seats vibrate and gusts of air blow through the theatre, it is easy to get a feel for the power of the bombs. Exhibits include replicas of bomb shelters, offices and guards station from the Nevada test site and nearly 400,000 declassified documents. They include letters from Albert Einstein and the captain of a Japanese fishing boat caught in the fall-out tests carried out in the Pacific.

Open: Mon–Sat 9am–5pm, Sun 1–5pm.
Admission: Adults $10, students, seniors and military $7, children 6 and under free.

Clark County Heritage Museum

1830 South Boulder Highway, Henderson, 702 455 7955, heritagecenter.us
This museum covers a time span of 12,000 years of southern Nevada history and includes Heritage Street, a living history area, and a Nevada ghost town. There are old railroad cars, a fully restored 1920s bungalow built by a pioneer Las Vegas merchant, a replica of a 19th-century frontier print shop, plus ranching displays and a nature walk.

Open: 9am–4.30pm.
Admission: Adults $1.50, under-16s and seniors $1.

Elvis-A-Rama

Elvis-A-Rama Museum

3401 Industrial Road (one block west of the Strip), 702 309 7200, elvisarama.com
You can't miss the great neon gold record and guitar bursting out of the roof! With more than $3m-worth of memorabilia, you can see hundreds of items belonging to the king of rock 'n' roll. In addition to the displays of his jumpsuits, army uniform and film costumes, there are video displays of Elvis in action throughout the museum. Plus, twice a day Elvis impersonators, Justin Kurtis or Donny Edwards, perform a fast-paced tribute to the King.

Open: Daily 10am–7pm. Shows at 2pm and 4pm daily.
Admission: Museum $12.95, show only $17.95, show and museum $27.

Atomic Testing Museum

Las Vegas Gambling Museum includes gaming memorabilia

BRITTIP

The Elvis-A-Rama Museum has a free shuttle service between the museum and any hotel on the Strip between the Stratosphere and Mandalay Bay. Call the museum to arrange a pick-up time.

Las Vegas Gambling Museum

450 Fremont Street, 702 385 1883

It's a subject close to the heart of the city, so it was only a matter of time before a clever entrepreneur opened a historical showcase. Covering everything from the building of the Hoover Dam to the history of Fremont Street, Howard Hughes, Liberace, Elvis and the Rat Pack, memorabilia include gaming chips from casinos past and present.

Open: Daily 10am–8pm.

Admission: Adults $2.50, seniors $1.25.

Las Vegas Historic Museum

Tropicana, 3801 South Las Vegas Boulevard, 702 739 2222

This is a small but fascinating look at the tumultuous history of Sin City. From mobsters to corporations, the museum charts the history of Las Vegas in an intimate and easy-to-follow environment. Top of the must-sees is the section on mobsters, including Bugsy Siegel's death certificate, the Rat Pack and Elvis exhibits in the headliner section, and an area dedicated to unearthing the history of prostitution and brothels in rural Nevada. There are even a series of TV screens upon which videos of famous casino implosions and fires are shown.

Open: Daily 9am–9pm.

Admission: Adults $6.95, seniors $5.95. You must be over 18 or accompanied by an adult to enter the museum.

Notorious mobster Bugsy Siegel

Las Vegas Natural History Museum

Las Vegas Natural History Museum

900 North Las Vegas Boulevard, 702 384 3466, lvnhm.org
Wildlife existed in the Las Vegas valley long before humans arrived and created casinos! Here you can take a walk on the wild side and discover the scenic and wild natural beauty of southern Nevada. It includes exhibits representing the many different habitats in the Las Vegas area with a diverse variety of plants and wildlife. The historical side is represented by animated dinosaurs, while there is an international wildlife room, small live sharks in the aquarium, and a hands-on exploration room for children. There is also an extensive wildlife art gallery with award-winning wood sculptures.

Open: Daily 9am–4pm.

Admission: Adults $7, seniors, military and students $6, 3–11s $3, children 2 and under and members free.

Singer Lynn Ross at the Liberace Museum

Liberace Museum

Liberace Plaza, 1775 East Tropicana Avenue, 702 798 5595, liberace.org
The man known as Mr Showmanship lives on in one of the most popular attractions in Nevada. One building houses 18 rare and antique pianos, including Liberace's favourite Baldwin grand piano, and others owned by Chopin and George Gershwin, plus Liberace's cars. Another building is devoted to his famous stage wardrobe of multi-sequinned, bejewelled and rhinestone-studded costumes and famous rings that used to dazzle audiences around the world. The third contains an extensive collection of Liberace's memorabilia including hundreds of rare Moser crystals from the Czech Republic, a monogrammed set of dinner plates that once belonged to President John F Kennedy, and Liberace's violin, made by the famous violin-maker George Winterling.

A portion of the proceeds from the museum, gift shop and café go to the Liberace Foundation for the Performing and Creative Arts, which has donated thousands of dollars to schools, universities and other organisations for music, dance, drama, film and visual arts.

Open: Tues–Sat 10am–5pm, Sun noon–4pm.

Admission: Adults $12.50, and seniors and students $8.50.

The Neon Museum

Lied Discovery Children's Museum

833 North Las Vegas Boulevard, 702 382 3445, ldcm.org
Here children can touch, see, explore and experience more than 100 hands-on exhibits in one of America's largest – and most exciting – children's museums. Children crawl and slide through the Toddler Towers, become a star on the Performing Arts stage, pilot the Space Shuttle or Gyrochair, create colour computer prints and toe-tap a tune on the Musical Pathway. They can also stand in a giant bubble, play at being a disc jockey at the KKID radio station or use their bodies to generate electricity.

Open: Tues–Sun 10am–5pm.

Admission: Adults $7, children 1–17 $6, seniors and under-1s free. Children under the age of 11 must be accompanied by an adult.

Marjorie Barrick Museum of Natural History

4505 South Maryland Parkway, 702 895 3381, http://hrcweb.nevada.edu/museum
Another genuinely fascinating offering at the University of Las Vegas campus, the real interest in this museum is its emphasis on the lives and traditions of the Paiute and Hopi Indians. A museum dedicated to the natural history of the region, one of the other main exhibits shows the reptiles that live in Nevada's deserts, including the venomous Gila Monster lizard, plus an open-air habitat for desert tortoises.

Open: Mon–Fri 8am–4.45pm, Sat 10am–2pm.

Admission: Free.

Neon Museum

East end of the Fremont Street Experience, 702 387 NEON, neonmuseum.org
Once the City of Neon, now all that remains of many of Vegas' most famous older hotels are their neon signs. Here you'll find the Hacienda Hotel sign before the building was imploded to make way for the Mandalay Bay, plus the original Aladdin's genie lamp and many other historical neon signs with their spectacular

Duelling armadillo puppets at the Lied Discovery Children's Museum

colours, intricate animation and sheer size. A small museum with big appeal!

While there are lots of exhibits inside, the best part is out the back at 'The Boneyard' where the massive signs are kept. This area is constantly being used by movies and TV shows for location work. Many of the best signs have been refurbished and mounted in the areas of the Fremont Street Experience and the East Fremont Street Entertainment District. You can download a free walking tour from the website.

Open: 24/7.

Admission: Free. Guided tour $5 adults, $3 students, under-5s free.

Nevada State Museum

700 Twin Lakes Drive, 702 486 5205, springspreserve.org

The history of southern Nevada from mammoths to gambling is presented in three galleries – Biology, Earth Science and History/Anthropology. There is also a display explaining how neon has been used in the city.

Open: Daily 9am–5pm except major holidays.

Admission: Adults $4, seniors $3, under-18s free.

Ravine Walk at the Nevada State Museum

11 OUTDOOR ADVENTURE

Every kind of fun from cowboy cook-outs to horseback riding

Las Vegas is a wonderful city, and practically everything you'd like to do in the great outdoors in America is right on its doorstep in a plethora of stunning environments. Nearby are Red Rock Canyon, where ponderosa pines and Joshua trees grow out of towering cliffs of Aztec sandstone, the Valley of Fire, a Martian landscape of vivid red, pastel and white sandstone, and Mount Charleston, which looms 12,000ft/3,658m above sea level.

The biggest jewel in Las Vegas's crown of outdoor splendours, though, is the Grand Canyon. A whole raft of companies organise plane and helicopter flights to – and even down to the bottom of – the 10ml/16km wide and 1ml/1.6km deep natural wonder. Many of those companies also offer trips a little further north to the stunning Bryce Canyon and Zion National Park, famous for cascading waterfalls.

On top of that, there are a whole host of brilliant ways to experience this great region, from white-water rafting and rock climbing, to horse riding and following the cowboy trail. At certain times of the year, it is possible to go skiing in the morning at Lee Canyon on Mount Charleston, then head off to Lake Mead for a spot of water-skiing in the afternoon. Where else could you find such a dramatic mix of marvels? Arrive in Las Vegas and you are just moments away from a world of beauty and adventure.

In this chapter

Hoover Dam from the South

Places to see

Hoover Dam

South on Highway 93 just past Boulder City, 30mls/50km south-east of Las Vegas, 702 494 2517, hooverdam.com
Visitor Center: Open daily, except Thanksgiving and Christmas Day, 8am–6pm.
Admission: Adults $10, 7–16s $5, under-7s free.
This amazing construction – it's 726ft/221m high and 1,244ft/379m long – is filled with enough concrete to build a two-lane highway from San Francisco to New York, and it literally changed the face of America's West. Blocking the Colorado River at the Black Canyon, which spans Nevada and Arizona, the dam put an end to centuries of droughts and floods caused by the mighty Colorado. Work began on the dam in 1931 and the $165m project was completed by 1935. Its offspring, Lake Mead, now produces drinking and irrigation water for the entire Las Vegas Valley, while the electric power plant creates enough energy to sell to Nevada, Arizona and California.

The dam will be more difficult to reach through to the end of 2008. The government is building a new road through the rugged terrain to go from Nevada to Arizona. They are also placing in more robust security checkpoints along the way, so while this process is going on expect some extremely slow going.

BRITTIP

If you're touring in an RV (recreational vehicle, or camper van) you will have to park on the Arizona side of the dam as they have been banned from the parking garage at Hoover Dam for security reasons.

Hoover Dam near Boulder City

Spectacular view of the dam

Discovery Tour: This gives you access to the 165m Visitor Center, a three-level, 110ft/33m diameter circular building, which stands 700ft/213m above the base of the dam. From the indoor and outdoor observation decks are stunning views of the dam, Lake Mead and the waters of the Colorado River re-entering the Black Canyon after passing through the dam's giant turbines.

BRITTIP

As you leave Boulder City and head for Hoover Dam, watch out for stupendous views of Lake Mead at the junction with Highway 93.

A gallery houses an environmental exhibit, technology exhibit and the story of the settlement of the lower Colorado River area. The rotating theatre is divided into three segments and you move between the three areas to see different films about the making and history of the dam.
Boulder City/Hoover Dam Museum: At Boulder Dam Hotel, Boulder City, museum 702 294 1988, hotel 702 293 3510, bcmha.org, Mon–Sat 10am–5pm, Sun 12–5pm, admission $2. Here you'll see a free movie about the building of the dam plus historical memorabilia from the workers. While you're there, take a peek at the renovated home in the museum, which in its time has accommodated movie star James Cagney and reclusive billionaire Howard Hughes.
Other activities: While you're in the area you can also take a river raft trip (see page

The awe-inspiring Lake Mead

223), try a tandem jump (see page 238). An excellent stop-off point during your day trip is **Harry's Café** (702 294 2653, open 7am–8pm). Boulder's oldest diner, its 1950s-style environment makes for a fun pit stop.

Lake Mead

Visitor Center is 4mls/6km north-east of Boulder City, 702 293 8990, nps.gov/lame or lakemead.areaparks.com
Visitor Center: Open daily 8.30am–4.30pm.
Admission: Free.
Other useful numbers: Lake Mead Marina 702 293 3484; Alan Bible Visitor Center 702 293 8906 (Mon–Fri) park info
The dazzling-blue Lake Mead, created by the construction of the Hoover Dam, is about 25mls/40km south of Las Vegas. It is 110mls/177km long and has 550mls/885km of freshwater shoreline. It is the Las Vegas outdoor retreat of choice and many permanent residents have boats here. Here you can try out anything from boating to swimming, scuba-diving, water-skiing, camping and fishing, while six marinas provide docking space for boats, plus restaurants and other services. Every December, a Parade of Lights is held at Lake Mead marina, with a flotilla of powerboats, houseboats and sailing boats covered in lights. A newer, annual event is the hydroplane race held in September.

The Visitors Center contains a botanical garden and exhibits on natural history. Here you will find details of a self-guided tour, with tape recording, of the lake's Northshore and Lakeshore roads, plus information about facilities and services.

Marinas: Two not-so-scenic roads – Lakeside Scenic Drive (Highway 146) and Northshore Scenic Drive (Highway 167) provide access to the marinas around the Nevada shoreline of Lake Mead, which include **Las Vegas Bay Marina** (702 565 9111), **Calville Bay Resort** (702 565 8958), **Echo Bay** (702 394 4000) and **Overton Beach Resort** (702 394 4040). These are all full-service marinas offering houseboat and daily deck cruiser rentals, restaurants and gift shops. At night, Callville Bay provides a barbecue on the patio overlooking the lake.

If you'd like to explore a little further afield, head off south to **Lake Mohave** and **Cottonwood Cove Resort and Marina** (1000 Cottonwood Cove Road, Cottonwood, 702 297 1464). It's a full-service marina offering luxury houseboats, small boats and personal watercraft rentals about one and a half hours south of Las Vegas.
Hiking: During the cooler winter and early spring months, you can take a hike in the Lake Mead National Recreation Area on Saturday mornings to learn about the history of the people of the area, from the mining era onwards. Each hike is limited to 25 people and you can make reservations by phoning 702 293 8990.

Valley of Fire State Park

6mls/10km from Lake Mead and 55mls/88km north-east of Las Vegas using Interstate 15 and Highway 169, 702 397 2088, desertusa.com/nvvalparks.nv.gov/vf
Visitor Center: Open daily 8.30am–4.30pm.
Admission: $6 per vehicle.
The park – the oldest in Nevada – gets its name from the red sandstone formations that were formed from great, shifting desert sand dunes during the age of the dinosaurs 150 million years ago. Complex geological movements and extensive

Stunning scenery in the Valley of Fire

erosion have created the spectacular wind carvings in the colourful rock formations. There are shaded areas with restrooms at Atlatl Rock, Seven Sisters, the Cabins, near Mouse's Tank trail head and White Domes. At the Visitor Center, there are exhibits on the geology, ecology and history of the park, plus the nearby region.

This whole area was extensively used by basket-making peoples and later by the Anasazi Pueblo farmers from the nearby Moapa Valley from 300BCE to 1150CE. It was probably visited for hunting, food gathering and religious ceremonies, though the lack of water limited their stays. Wonderful reminders of the time these ancient tribes spent here can be seen in the extraordinarily detailed Indian petroglyphs that tell the stories of their lives. The fantastic scenery and fascinating history make it well worth a day's visit.

Nature's way: The whole area is dominated by creosote, burro and brittle bushes, plus several different types of cactus. Spring is a wonderful time to visit as this is the time to see desert marigold, indigo bushes and desert mallow in bloom. The park is visited by many species of bird, but those in residence include raven, house finch, sage sparrow and, of course, the famous road runner – beep beep!

The animals tend to be nocturnal, coming out to forage for food when the desert heat has begun to fade, and include many different types of lizard, as well as snakes, coyote, kit fox, spotted skunk, black-tailed jack rabbit and ground squirrel. The desert tortoise is now so rare it is protected by Nevada State law. Early mornings or late afternoons are the best time to see the wildlife, but keep your distance.

One of the best ways to explore the park is by hiking through it and maps of trails are provided at the Visitor Center.

Arch Rock: A 2ml/3km scenic loop road provides views of some of the valley's most interesting rock formations, for example Arch Rock and Piano Rock. You'll get a true wilderness experience at the secluded Arch Rock Campground with its primitive facilities!

Atlatl Rock: Here you will find outstanding examples of ancient Indian rock art or petroglyphs, including a depiction of the atlatl (at'-lat-l), a notched stick used to throw primitive spears and the forerunner of the bow and arrow.

BRITTIP

Atlatl Rock is a great location for campers and the campsite is well-equipped with modern WC and shower facilities.

Beehives: Unusual sandstone formations weathered by the eroding forces of wind and water, there are three group camping areas nearby, available by reservation only.

Cabins: Now a picnic area, these historic stone cabins were built with native sandstone by the Civilian Conservation Corps in the 1930s as a shelter for passing travellers.

Mouse's Tank: Named after a renegade Indian who used the area as a hideout in the 1890s, this is a natural basin in the rock where water collects after rainfall, sometimes remaining for months. A half-mile round trip trail leads to Mouse's Tank from the trail head parking area, passing numerous examples of prehistoric Indian petroglyphs.

Amazing rock formations in the Valley of Fire

Rock climbing at Red Rock

Petrified logs: Logs and stumps washed into the area from an ancient forest about 225 million years ago are exposed in two locations.
Rainbow vista: A favourite photo point with a panoramic view of multicoloured sandstone.
Seven Sisters: Fascinating red rock formations, which are easily accessible from the road. Picnic areas provide a relaxing stop.
White Domes: Sandstone formations with brilliant contrasting colours, picnic area and trail head. White Domes is an 11ml/17.7km round trip drive from the Visitor Center. Duck Rock is a short hike.
Other sights: Clark Memorial, Elephant Rock, the deep red sandstone of Fire Canyon and the amazing Silica Dome.

Red Rock Canyon

17mls/27km west of the Las Vegas Strip on Charleston Boulevard (Highway 159), 702 515 5350, redrockcanyonlv.org or sunsetcities.com/redrock.html

Red Rock Canyon is part of the Red Rock Canyon Conservancy Area, an area to the west of Las Vegas that includes the Spring Mountain Range, home of the Spring Mountain Ranch, Mount Charleston and Bonnie Springs Old Nevada.

Once the home of ancient Native American tribes, this magnificent canyon was formed by a thrust fault – a fracture in the earth's crust where one plate is pushed horizontally over another – 65 million years ago. It is home to feral horses and burros (donkeys), as well as native wildlife such as desert bighorn sheep and coyotes, which you can see on the 13ml/21km Scenic Loop Drive (see opposite).

The Calico Vista points are good stopping points, offering great views of the crossed-bedded Aztec sandstone. For easy access to the sandstone, stop at the Sandstone Quarry car park where you can see large blocks of stone and other historic evidence of quarry activity that took place during the turn of the last century. You can have a picnic at Red Spring and Willow Spring, while there are also great views of wooded canyons and desert washes at Icebox Canyon, Pine Creek Canyon and Red Rock Wash. The Bureau of Land Management runs the Conservancy Area and there is a new free Visitors Center at the entrance to the Scenic Loop Drive for touring information, open 8am–4.30pm November to March, and 8am–5.30pm April to October.

BRITTIP

It is advisable to stop at the visitors' centre before going into the park's Scenic Drive Loop to acquaint yourself with the park regulations, including where you can drive and park.

Scenic Loop Drive: Open daily Nov–Feb 6am–5pm, Apr–Sep 6am–8pm and Mar–Oct 6am–7pm. Entrance to the loop costs $5 for motorists and $2 for motorcyclists; free for hikers and cyclists.

The 13ml/21km scenic drive is a one-way road. Cyclists are permitted to ride on the scenic drive, but must obey traffic laws. Sightseeing, photography and hiking trails are accessible from the designated pullouts and parking areas. If you would like to go hiking or rock climbing in Red Rock or Mount Charleston, see page 222.

Cycling at Red Rock

Pahrump Valley Winery: 3810 Winery Road, Pahrump, *775 751 7800*, pahrumpwinery.com. Just north of Red Rock is Nevada's only vineyard and it regularly produces award-winning Chardonnay, Cabernet and Burgundy. Open 11am–4pm; call for schedule of free tours.

Bonnie Springs Old Nevada

16mls/26km west of Las Vegas, 702 875 4191, bonniesprings.com
Open: 8am–5pm.
Admission: $20 per car (up to six people and includes a $10 restaurant coupon) or $3 per person on a bus. Price includes access to the zoo.
Originally built in 1843 as a stopover for the wagon trains going to California down the Old Spanish Trail, Bonnie Springs has been used as a tourist attraction since 1952. Now this replicated old American West mining town includes gunfights in the street, hangings, an 1880 melodrama, miniature train, US Post Office, blacksmith display, wax museum and Boot Hill Cemetery.

You can go horse riding from here – a one-hour guided horseback ride costs $40 – while there is a petting zoo, duck pond and aviary. Breakfast, lunch, dinner and cocktails are also available. A shuttle service to the village and ranch from Las Vegas is provided through Star Land Tours (702 296 4381).

Spring Mountain Ranch State Park

15mls/24km west of Las Vegas, via Charleston Boulevard (Highway 159), in the Red Rock Canyon National Conservation Area, 702 875 4141, http://parks.nv.gov/smr.htm
Open: Daily 8am–4.30pm. The main ranch house is open daily 10am–4pm.
Admission: $6 per vehicle.
The many springs in these mountains once provided water for Paiute Indians and later

Spring Valley

Sailing on Lake Mead

brought mountain men and early settlers to the area. This 520acre/210ha oasis was developed into a combination working ranch and luxurious retreat by a string of owners who have given the area a long and colourful history. Chester Lauck of the comedy team Lum & Abner, and millionaire Howard Hughes are past owners of the ranch.

In the mid-1830s a campsite was established along the wash that runs through the ranch. The spring-fed creek and grassy meadows formed a welcome oasis for travellers using this as an alternative route to the Spanish Trail through Cottonwood Valley. The use of the site by pack and wagon trains continued until their replacement by the railroad in 1905.

At the ranch house, you can find information about the ranch and surrounding areas and take a self-guided tour. Guided tours throughout the historic area are available weekdays at noon, 1 and 2pm, weekends at noon, 1, 2 and 3pm.

BRITTIP

There are often fire restrictions in this area, so check the website for the latest information.

The remote trail was also perfect for outlaws and was used extensively by those involved in slave trading, horse stealing and raids on passing caravans. One of the most famous was mountain man Bill Williams, after whom the ranch was first named.

Riding at Mount Charleston

In 1876 it was taken over by two men and named Sand Stone Ranch. The name stuck until it was leased in 1944 to Chet Lauck, the Lum part of comedy duo Lum & Abner and renamed Bar Nothing Ranch. A ranch house was built as a family retreat and Lum created a boys' camp. In 1955, German actress Vera Krupp bought the property, expanded the ranching business side and renaming it Spring Mountain Ranch.

At 3,800ft/1,158m, it is usually up to 10°C/15°F cooler than Las Vegas with cold winters and thunderstorms and flash floods in summer. Visitors can see wonderful plants including the Joshua tree, Mohave yucca, indigo bush, desert marigold and globe mallow. Animals are harder to spot as many are nocturnal, but include lizards, snakes, antelope ground squirrels, kit fox, jackrabbits, coyote, rock squirrel, badger, mule deer and bighorn sheep.

What's on: A Living History programme re-creates the ranch's past in the spring and autumn, including demonstrations of pioneer skills. The Super Summer Theater puts on outdoor performances every June, July and August, while the Theatre under the Stars features musicals and plays for the whole family. Gates open at 6pm, shows start at 8pm. There is also a picnic area.

Mount Charleston

35mls/72km north-west of Las Vegas on Highways 95 and 157, 702 514 5400, sunsetcities.com/mt-charleston.html

Camping: 1-800 280 CAMP (2267). Camping allowed from May to September. Cost depending on campsite, picnic area and trail.

Set in the lush Toiyabe National Forest, Mount Charleston looms nearly 12,000ft/ 3,657m above sea level. One of the most beautiful areas in the Las Vegas Valley, Lee Canyon Road, the Kyle Canyon section of Charleston Park Road and Deer Creek Road have all been designated Scenic Byways because of their extraordinary scenery and panoramic views. The area is about 17°C/30°F cooler than Las Vegas, making it a perfect escape from the city heat for a day.

Charleston Peak was the birthplace of the Paiute people, so for the Native Americans it is sacred land. To respect this, the scale and extent of the road system remains fairly limited.

Camping is popular here, along with horse riding, and in the winter you can ski at Lee Canyon (see Activities, page 222).

BRITTIP

Day trips to the Grand Canyon, Bryce Canyon and Zion Canyon from Las Vegas are available via helicopter, small plane or coach (see page 222).

There are plenty of watersports on Lake Mead

Further afield

Full details of the Grand Canyon, Zion, Bryce and Death Valley are given in Chapter 15 on pages 261–278 and details of air and bus tours are in this chapter on page 221.

Grand Canyon: nps.gov/grca. If you're planning to go on a bit of a tour, then you're bound to want to see the Grand Canyon close up and for real. But it is also possible to take plane and helicopter rides to this, the most spectacular canyon on earth – even landing on the canyon floor and having a spot of lunch on the banks of the Colorado. With Heli USA you can combine a flight to the Grand Canyon with a river rafting trip.

Zion National Park: 435 772 3256, zion.national-park.com. North of Las Vegas and the Grand Canyon in southern Utah is the majestic Zion National Park with its beautiful waterfalls cascading down red rocks, and its hanging gardens. Once a home to the ancient Anasazi, its history and majesty are presented in an adventure film on a giant screen at the Zion Canyon Cinemax Theater (435 772 2400, zioncanyontheater.com).

Bryce Canyon: bryce.canyon.national-park.com. Nearby in Utah is the equally beautiful Bryce Canyon, once home to both Native Americans and cowboys of the Old West. Both Zion and Bryce offer hiking, biking, horse riding, rock climbing and bird watching.

Death Valley: 760 786 3200. West of Las Vegas in eastern California, this is the hottest place on earth, with average summer temperatures of 45°C/131°F. Here you will see miles of sand that has been hardened into a sea-like landscape by the heat of the sun, extinct volcanos and wind-carved rock formations.

Many companies offer day trips to Death Valley and to break up the monotonous terrain on the way, you'll be taken through the beautiful Titus Canyon, some ghost towns and be shown Native American Indian petroglyphs. Once there, you'll be shown all the Death Valley highlights including Furnace Creek, Zabriskie Point, Bad Water and Scotty's Castle.when it became final.

Spooky sights

ET Highway

About 140mls/237km north of Las Vegas, 1 800 NEVADA 8

A 98ml/158km stretch of road on Route 375, a few miles north of the notorious Area 51 and the super-secret Groom Lake Air Force Base, this is where the American Air Force is believed to have tested the Stealth and U-2 aircraft and where numerous American TV shows have claimed aliens from outer space have undergone examinations at the top-secret Department of Defense site. UFO buffs often gather on ridges above Area 51 and use high-powered telescopes and binoculars to spy on the secret location. Their favourite meeting points are at the bars in nearby Rachel, where they exchange tales about extra-terrestrials.

Now the road has been officially dubbed the ET Highway by the Nevada Commission on Tourism, which has even created a new programme called the ET Experience.

Extraterrestrial Highway

Pioneer Saloon

Goodsprings, south of Las Vegas, 702 874 9362

Founded in the old mining town, this has much historical memorabilia and is worth dropping into to soak up some old-Americana atmosphere. Sitting on top of the US Army Cannon Stove, once used to warm people up on cold winter nights, is a piece of melted aluminium from the aeroplane in which film star Carole Lombard died. The plane crashed into Double Deal Mountain in January 1942 and her husband Clark Gable sat in the bar for days after, hoping for a miracle. Open daily from 10am.

Bonnie and Clyde's 'Death Car'

Primm Valley Hotel, 702 386 7867
The original car driven by Bonnie Parker and Clyde Barrow in their final shoot-out with the FBI on 23 May 1934 is on display at Whiskey Pete's Hotel. The infamous duo who held up gas stations, restaurants and small banks in Texas, New Mexico, Oklahoma and Missouri were shopped by a friend. At a cost of $75,000, Clyde's bullet-ridden and bloodstained shirt is now on display too! Worth visiting if you're going to Buffalo Bill's Turbo Drop and Desperado (see page 195).

Ghost towns

The old gold and silver mining towns are the stuff of many a Western movie and it is possible to visit some of these abandoned sites.

Goldfield Ghost Town (on Interstate 95 north of Scotty's Castle) was once Nevada's largest city after gold was discovered in 1902. Known for its opulence, it was called the Queen of Camps and had 20,000 residents at its peak, with mines producing $10,000 a day in 1907. A flood in 1913 and a fire in 1923 destroyed much of the town, but still standing are the Courthouse and Santa Fe Saloon among others. For details contact the Goldfield Chamber of Commerce (702 485 6365) or 775485 9957 for visitor information.

In 1904 gold was discovered in the Amargosa Valley and the town of Rhyolite (just outside Beatty on Interstate 95, then 374) was born. At its peak, it housed 10,000 people and had more than 50 saloons, 18 grocery stores and half a dozen barbers. But it became a ghost town in 1911 after losing its financial backing. You can still see the Cook Bank Building, school and jail, plus a house built in 1905 entirely of bottles.

Tours

Air tours

You can fly to all the major sights mentioned in this chapter either in a small plane or by helicopter. Flight packages or helicopter flights are offered by many of the tour companies listed. Scenic Airlines is the largest. These tours may be pricey – anything up to $650 – but they offer a marvellous opportunity to see amazing scenery in a very short space of time.

Generally, a short flight will include the Las Vegas Strip, Western Grand Canyon, Hoover Dam and Lake Mead and will cost around $59. The next step up will be the above plus a complete aerial tour of the Grand Canyon for around $209. The more expensive prices will include extras such as a champagne lunch on the Grand Canyon rim or, in the case of a helicopter flight, on the Canyon floor next to the Colorado. Combination tours may include lunch with Native Americans, river rafting, hiking and canyon sunset/sunrise. Some companies offer an overnight stay at the Grand Canyon, Bryce Canyon or Monument Valley. Tour companies are listed on pages 225–228.

Bus tours

The prices are cheaper, but the days are longer as you get to see all the sights covered by the air tours – only on the ground, of course! Tour companies are listed on pages 225–228.

Ghost town at Belmont

Flying to the Grand Canyon

The Maverick Helicopters' pilot looked the spitting image of Tom Cruise and the theme from *Mission: Impossible* was blasting down our earphones as we took off from McCarran Airport. Suddenly the helicopter banked steeply and we five passengers had an altogether too-close-for-comfort view of the ground. Then, just as suddenly as we'd banked to the right, the helicopter straightened up and we found ourselves inching over the 'matchbox' houses at what seemed to be a snail's pace. In reality, we were speeding out of the Las Vegas Valley at 130mph/210kph, heading east to the West Rim of the Grand Canyon.

Within minutes, we were flying over the $1m homes in the exclusive community of Lake Las Vegas and its two golf courses. Next came the 110ml/177km long Lake Mead, the largest man-made lake in America providing a beautiful blue contrast to the pale brown rocks, and then the Hoover Dam. My thoughts that the scenery had a volcanic look to it were confirmed when our pilot pointed out an extinct volcano.

It took half an hour to reach the Grand Canyon and after a brief flyover, we landed on its rocky floor. Our pilot immediately jumped out and started preparing our champagne drinks with light snacks. It seemed a perfect way to spend 40 minutes – quaffing champagne and looking around at this millions-of-years-old natural wonder.

All too soon, it seemed, we were taking off again, but before we started our return journey we were taken on a small flight through the canyon. The half-hour ride back to Las Vegas passed all too quickly as we headed for our final treat – a flight down the entire length of the famous Strip for a bird's-eye view of all those amazing buildings. (For information on helicopter flights to the Grand Canyon see page 265.)

Activities

All the contact details for the various companies are in the A–Z on pages 225–228.

Bike tours

Red Rock Downhill Bike & Hike Tours: Cyclists will love these half- or whole-day tours through the Red Rock Canyon and Valley of Fire.

Single Track Tours Las Vegas: Professionally guided mountain bike tours for both the beginner and professional at $115 per person.

Hiking

Grand Canyon Tour Company: They do half-day and full-day hikes with guides who tell you all about the geology and human and natural history of the Grand Canyon. You will be given drinking water, high-energy drink mixers and snacks.

There's stunning scenery for hiking

HikeThis!: Guided hikes starting at $95 per person for one to four people, plus rock scrambling deep in the canyons, over creek bed stones and massive sandstone boulders.

Rocky Trails: You can hike just about anywhere with Rocky Trails, one of the largest dedicated hiking organisations, which specialises in providing geological tours of everywhere from Red Rock to Valley of Fire, Mount Charleston and even Death Valley. Tours cost $119–195 including lunch. Or you can hike down the Grand Canyon – still the best way of seeing one of the most beautiful places on earth.

Horse riding

Available at Red Rock Canyon, Bonnie Springs Old Nevada, Mount Charleston and Valley of Fire.

Cowboy Trail Rides Inc.: You can go on horseback rides, custom and group trail rides and pack trips in southern Nevada, Utah and Northern Arizona. Trips are tailor-made and can last an hour or seven days.

Mount Charleston Riding Stables: A three-hour ride to the Fletcher Canyon filled with beautiful aspen trees and huge evergreens. Overnight wilderness rides are also available. A 90-minute ride through Cedar Ridge will provide panoramic views of the high desert valley below and the surrounding Spring Mountains. Allow four

Canoeing at Pyramid

hours to include travel to and from your hotel. Costs $79 per person. An incredible three-hour ride along the legendary trails of Robbers Roost is also available.

You will see where the outlaws rode to escape their crimes, follow a trail hidden by dense foliage, see the cave, secret passageway and streams that supplied water – all tucked away in the forest. Allow five hours to include travelling time. Cost $99 per person.

Off-road adventures

ATV Action Tours: ATV has the sole licensing permits for many desert regions, mountains and other points of interest in south-west Nevada. They combine the off-road experience in Land Rovers, Jeep Cherokees and Wranglers with short hiking excursions, climbing large rock formations and searching for petroglyphs. Definitely the most fun way to get back to nature without breaking into a sweat! Tours cost $89–245.

LookTours: This company is now also offering ATV tours alongside a Hoover Dam and Lake Mead, 4x4 Off-road Hummer Adventure for $169 (or $159 if booked over the internet). It includes around 2½ hours of four-wheel, off-road adventure through the Mojave Desert, including Lava Butte, Rainbow Gardens and Lizard Eye Ridge, plus Hoover Dam and Lake Mead. Total time around six hours including lunch. You can even combine the tour with a rafting trip down the Colorado.

Other companies: Since ATV set the ball rolling, many other tour companies are now offering Hummer Tours – the term used to describe off-road adventures in 4x4 Hummers. Those companies include Grand Canyon Tour Company and Rebel Adventure Tours. The Hummer tours can be combined with other activities such as jet-skiing and rafting.

Rafting

Two basic types of rafting are easily available from Las Vegas.

Black Canyon River Raft Tours: You can take a gentle ride in a motorised raft down an 11ml/18km stretch of the Colorado, starting at the base of the mighty Hoover Dam and stopping for lunch (and a cooling swim). Along the way you will see hot water springs bubbling out of cliffs, flora and fauna and the amazing desert bighorn sheep, who think nothing of living on the perilous slopes of the Grand Canyon. These rides usually last around seven hours and cost $79–125. Plenty of other tour companies offer similar tours.

Grand Canyon Tour Company: The other kind of rafting is a lot more expensive, but more authentic and involves rapids. One- or two-day trips on rapids with strengths of between four and seven (on a scale of one

Amargosa is great for quad biking

to 10) are available with Native Americans from the Grand Canyon area. The Grand Canyon Tour Company offers trips from Lees Ferry in Arizona (about 21/2 hours' drive from the South Rim of the Grand Canyon) that can also be combined with a hike down the Grand Canyon. Otherwise most of their trips start at three days and go up to two weeks between April and September, costing around $250 per day.

Skiing and snowboarding

Just 35 minutes away from Las Vegas in Mount Charleston's Lee Canyon, you can ski or snowboard from Thanksgiving to Easter. Beginner packages for skiing cost $70 for ski rental equipment, lift ticket and a one-hour group lesson. For snowboarding it costs $70 for the rental equipment, lift ticket and a one-hour group lesson. Lift prices for those with experience are $38 for adults and $25 for under 12s. In summer (mid-June to October) ski-lift chair rides to the top of the ski runs are only $5 for adults and $3 for under 12s.

Water activities

Cruising, boating, fishing and jet-skiing are all available on Lake Mead.

Lake Mead Cruises: The largest provider of cruises and jet-skiing runs breakfast, midday, dinner and dinner-dance (Friday and Saturday only) cruises on the glassy waters of Lake Mead on board the *Desert Princess*, an authentic 300-passenger paddle-wheeler, which is climate-controlled inside. Breakfast cruises cost $36.50 (under-12s $18), midday cruises $22 (under-2s $10), early dinner cruises $46 (under-12s $25) and dinner-dance cruises $58. Apart from the dinner-dance cruise on which no children are allowed, all under-2s go free. All prices include tax. You can either board at Hoover Dam or at Lake Mead Marina.

Jetski at Laughlin

Lake Mead Jetski Tours: Package ($209) includes a two-day orientation class and 90 minutes on the water. Each tour is accompanied by a guide who will narrate the trip via a hands-free, waterproof, two-way radio on each personal jet-ski. Lunch is provided.

Overton Beach Watercraft: Further north at Overton Beach Marina you can hire everything from personal watercraft to patio and fishing boats. Overnight packages are even available. Personal watercraft can seat two or three people and have storage compartments with a built-in cooler for your packed lunch. Patio boats for up to 10 people are perfect for fishing or cruising and come with a motor, radio/cassette, cooler, cushioned bench seating and an awning. Costs are $125 for four hours, $195 for eight hours. Fishing boats hold four people and come with a Fish Finder and Pole Holder to increase your odds! Costs are $65 for four hours, $100 for eight.

Snowboarding at Mount Charleston

Petroglyphs at the Valley of Fire

A–Z of tour companies

As you can see, the outdoor options are numerous, so to make life a little simpler I have tried to list most of the major tour companies in this simple A–Z format. In many cases the companies have their own websites through which it is possible to book excursions and trips in advance. This is probably most useful for those planning to do something quite specialist, such as rock climbing or trying to go off the beaten track, as times and dates may be specific.

Adventure Photo Tours: 702 889 8687, adventurephototours.com. Private or semi-private photo safaris with professional and well-informed guides to Red Rock, Valley of Fire, Lake Mead and ghost towns in seven-seater Ford Expeditions, with pick-up from your hotel.

Adventure West Tours: 702 735 4188. Tours of the western rim of the Grand Canyon from $89 and the Heart of the Canyon tour from $199, which includes a helicopter ride to the floor of the canyon plus a boat ride on the Colorado River.

Annie Bananie's Wild West Tours: 702 805 9755, anniebananie.com. Experienced 'cowboy' guides take you on a trip through ancient and western history.

ATV Action Tours: 888 288 5200, atvactiontours.com. Get to the other side of Las Vegas Valley in a Jeep Cherokee or Wrangler off-roader and then take a short hike. Also offers custom tours – including overnight stays at a dude ranch (see page 262), in a mountain cabin or even camping under the stars.

Black Canyon River Raft Tours: 702 293 3776, blackcanyonadventures.com.

Cactus Jack's Wild West Tour Company: 702 731 2425.

Cadillac Reservations and Tours: 1 800 556 3566, lvhelicopters.com. Offers a selection of helicopter flights to the Grand Canyon, but they do not land in the canyon.

Cowboy Trail Rides: 702 387 2457, cowboytrailrides.com. Fun horse rides through Mount Charleston ranging cost $45–329 a person. Their five-hour WOW ride, that takes you through untouched wilderness, will make you think you are in 1800s Old West.

Creative Adventures: 702 361 5565. Specialists in the Spirits and Ghosts Tour, which takes you to the wild country along the Colorado to Native American country before touring Searchlight, once a bustling mining town at the turn of the last century.

Drive Yourself Tours®: 702 565 8761, grandcanyonwest.com. Pop a tape in the cassette machine and take yourself off to Red Rock, Valley of Fire, Mount Charleston, Hoover Dam, Lake Mead or the Grand Canyon, listening to information about points of interest. The tapes come with maps.

Grand Canyon Tour Company: 1 800 2 CANYON, grandcanyontourcompany.com. All kinds of tours by most methods of transport.

Gray Line Sightseeing Tours: 702 384 1234, grayline.com. The big bus trip specialist, covering everywhere from Hoover Dam to Bryce Canyon and Death Valley. If you pay for your tour in advance, you'll get a free round trip transfer from the airport to your hotel or a free Laughlin Day Tour.

BRITTIP

Watch out! Some tour companies offer two-for-one or other big discounts, making their prices appear very competitive, but they don't include taxes and other extras, which can bump up the cost considerably.

Fishing on the Walker River

Cowboys ...

You can't get away from them in Nevada – even the casinos are packed with Stetsons bobbing around among the slot machines. One of the most exciting festivals the city has to offer is the annual National Finals Rodeo held in the second week of December. Great contests include saddle bronc riding, bareback riding, bull riding, calf roping, steer wrestling, team roping, steer roping and barrel racing.

Annie Bananie's Wild West Tour: Here you can get the best of the Wild West in comfort and style for $99 per person. Experienced 'cowboy' guides take you to Lake Mead for lunch at the historical Calville Bay Marina, before your air-conditioned coach whisks you off to the Black Mountains, Rogers' Springs, the Valley of Fire and the Moapa Indian Reservation.

Bonnie Springs Old Nevada: A visit here (see page 218) will give you a real taste of the Wild West.

Cactus Jack's Wild West Tour Company: Offers horseback trail rides.

Grand Canyon West Ranch: You can get a taste for real-life ranch action at any of the many ranches dotted throughout Nevada, Arizona and California that allow non-cowboys on board for a bit of fun (see page 266 for a full description of the different types and how to get in). One of the nearest – just 45 minutes by helicopter from the Las Vegas Strip – is the new Grand Canyon West Ranch, which nestles in the mountainous area between the west end of the Grand Canyon and the 6,000ft/1,828m Music Mountains of Arizona. Heli USA (see below) offers overnight packages, including helicopter flight, at this working cattle and guest ranch for $354 adults, $254 children.

Accommodation consists of rustic two or four-person cabins with authentic roll-top bathtubs and log fires. A herd of long-horn Corriente cattle roam the ranch along with the wild animals such as deer, mountain lion, bob cats, rattlesnakes and lizards. Self-drive packages with cabin stay start at $99 per person mid week.

Oatman: About 20mls/32km east of Laughlin is Oatman in Arizona. Once a thriving mining town during the gold rush, wild burros now wander the streets of this popular TV and Western movie backdrop. At weekends you can take a trip back to the Old West with free cowboy gunfights and showdowns on Main Street. For details phone the Chamber of Commerce (928 768 6222 or 928 768 3839).

Wild Wild West Horseback Trail Rides: If time doesn't permit a stay, try these trail rides available through Look Tours, including a free pick-up from your hotel to the Sage Brush Range on the Moapa Indian Reservation. Choose from an Old West Breakfast Ride, Dalton Gang Lunch Ride ($99 and six hours each) or the John Wayne Sunset Dinner Ride ($119). Including a hearty feast prepared by cowboys and cowgirls, the trails are designed to be user-friendly for both novice and experienced riders.

Moapa Reservation

Heli USA Airways: 01438 749049 (UK) or 702 736 8787 (Las Vegas), heliusa.com. Offers a comprehensive selection of flights to the Grand Canyon with overnight stays, plus exclusive stays at the Grand Canyon West Ranch (see Cowboys panel, above).
Hike This!: 702 393 4453, hikethislasvegas.com. Offers guided hiking and rock scrambling tours around some of the most spectacular scenery in southern Nevada.
Keith Prowse: 0871 232425, keith prowse.com. For helicopter, aircraft and land tours.
King Airelines: 702 433 7770, kingairelines.com. Discounted aeroplane and helicopter tours to the Grand Canyon, 365 days of the year, ranging in length from three to seven hours.

... and Indians

Three tribes have dominated Nevada's Native American history – the Northern Paiute, Southern Paiute and the Shoshone. Between them they have etched their stories in the rock petroglyphs of the Valley of Fire and other sacred places including Mount Charleston. The modern-day Native Americans still remain an important force in Nevada, with major Indian reservations at Moapa plus Fort Mojave Reservation in the southernmost tip of the state. They still live by their ancient codes and, even though they now run their own casinos and restaurants, maintain their heritage through traditional pow wows.

Originally, the pow wow was designed to bring various tribes together in a friendly way. It was a festive gathering where they exchanged gifts, heard the latest news and sold foods and crafts. Rodeos were an attraction, but the highlight was always the tribal dance competition for which they would dress in tribal regalia.

Bruno's Indian Museum: 1306 Nevada Highway, Boulder City, 702 293 4865. This promotes and gives information about the Native American artists of the south-west, of which 2,000 are represented by the museum. Open 10am– 5pm.

Grand Canyon Tour Company: Another way to get the 'Indian' experience is to go on a one or two-day rafting trip with a Native American river guide on the Colorado River. This company (see page 225) offers rafting from Diamond Creek to Pierce Ferry.

Hualapai Indians: Most of the major tour companies offer Grand Canyon flights or helicopter tours to the West Rim combined with a barbecue lunch with the Hualapai Indians, who will tell you about their legends and culture. The trips have been so successful that the Hualapai have even built a tiny village overlooking the Grand Canyon where you can shop for souvenirs or check out the small museum.

Lost City Museum of Archaeology: 721 South Moapa Valley Boulevard, Overton, 702 397 2193. Another great place to go, this is just north of Red Rock Canyon. For $5 adults (under-18s free) you will find artefacts from the Anasazis who lived in the Moapa Valley from the 1st to the 12th centuries CE. Displays include a reconstruction of the basket-maker pithouse and pueblo dwellings. The museum is located 66mls/106km north-east of Las Vegas on Highway 15 and Highway 169 near Overton. Open daily 8.30am–4.30pm.

Moapa River Indian Reservation: Pow wows still take place today and are a wonderful way to experience the Indian culture. Of course, it cannot be guaranteed that a pow wow will be organised for your trip, but you can still get a taste of the Native American way of life by coming here, just east of the Valley of Fire off Interstate 15. The store at the entrance is famous for its duty-free tobacco, alcohol and fireworks. But be warned: fireworks are not allowed outside the reservation and police do stop and search cars periodically.

Lake Mead Cruises: 702 293 6180, lakemeadcruises.com. Cruises and jet-skiing on Lake Mead.
Lake Mead Jetski Tours: 702 558 7547, worldwidejetskis.com. Jet-ski tours on Lake Mead.
Las Vegas Tour Desk: 702 310 1320, lasvegastourdesk.com. Specialises in air tours to the Grand Canyon.
Las Vegas Tours: 702 895 9976, lasvegastours.com. Champagne picnics at the bottom of the Grand Canyon.
Look Tours: 702 233 1627, looktours.com. Winner of the 2005 Best Sightseeing Tour Company by the Nevada Commission on Tourism, the company offers every conceivable tour option and combination you could wish for – by aeroplane, bus, helicopter, raft and ATV or

Houseboat on Lake Mead

Hummer. It's worth checking out the website and booking directly to take advantage of the internet deals.

Maverick Helicopter Tours: 888-261 4414, maverickhelicopter.com. Custom charters and tours to Grand Canyon, Bryce, Zion, Monument Valley and Death Valley. Also offers personalised videos to take home.

Mount Charleston Riding Stables: 702 387 2457, mountcharlestonridingstables.com. Cowboy-trail rides to a variety of destinations.

Overton Beach Watercraft: 702 394 4400. Hire of anything from personal watercraft to patio and fishing boats.

Rebel Adventure Tours: 702 380 6969, rebeladventuretours.com. Off-road Hummer tours to Lake Mead and Hoover Dam and Grand Canyon, also combined with jet-skiing, lunch with Native Americans and white water rafting.

Red Rock Downhill Bike & Hike Tours: 702 617 8965. Half- or whole-day cycling tours through the Red Rock Canyon and Valley of Fire.

Rocky Trails: 702 869 9991, rockytrails.com. Run by a geologist, this company specialises in hiking tours that give you a real insight into the wonders of Red Rock, Valley of Fire, Mount Charleston and Death Valley.

Scenic Airlines: 01992 463465, scenic.com. Since Eagle Airlines bought out Scenic, this is now the largest air tour company in Las Vegas. It offers every single destination you could think of – and every combination. In addition to the Grand Canyon, Zion Canyon, Bryce Canyon, Monument Valley and Lake Powell, you can also do overnight stops and get the Native American experience. Plus, of course, the night flight over the Strip.

Heli USA tours

BRITTIP

Some tour companies offer free day-long trips to Laughlin, but these are just a classic way to get you to spend money at the casinos there.

Single Track Tours: 702 813 5730, singletracktours.com. Professionally guided mountain bike tours of the Las Vegas area.

Sky's the Limit: 702 363 4533. Hiking and rock climbing.

Sundance Helicopter Tours: 702 736 0606, helicoptour.com. Mostly helicopter trips to the Grand Canyon – landing on the canyon floor – but also do combinations with rafting, the Harley Davidson Café and Pahrump Valley Vineyard.

Single Track Tours take you through stunning scenery

12 GOLF AND OTHER SPORTS

Getting some golf action, plus spectator and extreme sports

Las Vegas is most famous for staging big-name fights between boxers, but its climate – especially in the spring, autumn and winter months – makes it perfect for golf and there has been a huge increase in the number of courses built over the last decade.

The irony is that the time when most Brits visit Las Vegas – the summer – is actually low season, so you should get some pretty good deals at golf courses then. The peak season is October to May, as the Americans consider the summer months far too hot to be playing golf! Fortunately, in the summer golf courses are open early in the morning and later in the afternoon.

BRITTIP

If you want to arrange a round of golf, go for an afternoon slot as the early mornings tend to get very busy. It's also a lot cheaper at many places – ask about 'twilight' rates, which means any time after 1pm.

In this chapter

The number of golf courses is stunning. Many hotels are affiliated to different golf courses, which offer resort guests reduced-price tee fees. All the same, fees for those courses and others in central Las Vegas will be two to three times more expensive than those out of the city, so I have given details of golf courses in Boulder City, North Las Vegas, Laughlin and Pahrump. A few Henderson courses are still well priced, but

There are plenty of golf courses

most of those in the sought-after Lake Las Vegas area are now very expensive. Generally, the prices given include a cart.

A full listing of golf courses open to visitors follows below, but two very useful numbers are:

Stand-by Golf: 702 597 2665 (7am–9pm), stand-bygolf.com. For same-day and next-day play at reduced prices at many golf courses in the Las Vegas area.

Golf Reservations of Nevada: 702 732 3119, worldgolf.com/courses/unitedstates/nevada.html . For advance tee-time reservations for individuals and groups at major courses in the area.

Golf courses in Las Vegas

Angel Park Golf Club

100 South Rampart Boulevard, 888-629 3929, angelpark.com
Two 18-hole resort courses. Rounds cost $65–160 depending on the season. Twilight and reduced summer rates available. Reservations up to four months in advance.

Badlands Golf Club

9119 Alta Drive, 702 566 7618, badlandsgc.com
27-hole resort course. Rounds cost $95–205 depending on season. Twilight rates available. Reservations up to 60 days in advance.

BRITTIP
The Badlands is considered the golfing equivalent of an ultimate thrill ride. Carved through canyons, each of the 27 holes is known for dramatic shot values.

Bali Hai Golf Club

5160 Las Vegas Boulevard, 888-427 6678, bali-hai-golf-club.com
Stunning tropical-themed course just south of the Mandalay Bay with a fabulous clubhouse. Rounds cost $250 and up depending on the season. Reservations up to six months in advance.

BRITTIP
The Bali Hai Golf Club is not only fantastically located just by the Four Seasons and Mandalay Bay hotels, but also has a divine restaurant, Cili, run by celebrity chef Wolfgang Puck.

Bear's Best Golf Club

11111 West Flamingo Avenue, 702 804 8500, bearsbest.com
A collection of Jack Nicklaus's favourite 18 holes in a dramatic setting with a desert-style clubhouse. Rounds cost $195–245.

Callaway Golf Center/ Divine Nine

6730 Las Vegas Boulevard South at the corner with Sunset Road, 702 896 4100
Nine par-3 holes. Rounds cost $25–45. Driving range hits on to 12 greens with various hazards.

BRITTIP
The Callaway Golf Center is also home to the Danny Gans Junior Golf Academy that offers free golf instruction to children aged 11–16.

Bali Hai Golf Club

Desert Pines

Desert Pines Golf Club

3415 East Bonanza Road, 866-447 4653, waltersgolf.com
Named after the hundreds of mature pines that line the 18-hole public course, it also has covered hitting areas and an automatic ball delivery system. Rounds cost $35–160. Reservations up to six months in advance.

Desert Rose Golf Club

5483 Club House Drive, 702 431 4653, http://desertrose.americangolf.com
Palm trees, water and bunkers highlight the 18-hole county course, which has a wash between the holes. Rounds cost $65–95. Twilight rates available. Tee times seven days in advance.

Las Vegas Golf Club

4300 West Washington, 702 646 3003, americangolf.com
18-hole city course. Rounds cost $75–105. Reservations 60 days in advance.

BRITTIP
Don't forget your sun protection factor 30 and a hat when playing in summer. In autumn, take a sweater with you for late-afternoon games as it can get quite chilly when the sun goes down.

Las Vegas National Golf Club

1911 East Desert Inn Road, 702 734 1796, americangolf.com
18-hole public course. Rounds cost $75–185. Twilight rates available. Floodlit driving range. Reservations 60 days in advance.

Las Vegas Paiute Golf Resort

10325 Nu-Wav Kaiv Boulevard, 20mls/32km north of city on the Snow Mountain exit near Mount Charleston, 866-284 2833, lvpaiutegolf.com
Three 18-hole public courses on the Las Vegas Paiute Tribe Indian Reservation. Green fees start at $150 and go up depending on the season. Reservations up to 60 days in advance.

Badlands

BRITTIP

The Snow Mountain course at Las Vegas Paiute Golf Resort is considered the best public access course in Las Vegas by *Golf Digest* magazine.

Painted Desert Golf Club

5555 Painted Mirage Drive, 702 645 2880, americangolf.com
18-hole public course. Rates vary according to the season. Reservations up to 60 days in advance.

Rhodes Ranch Golf Club

20 Rhodes Ranch Parkway, 702 740 4114, rhodesranch.com
Rates vary according to the season. Reservations up to 60 days in advance.

Shadow Creek

888 778 3387, shadowcreek.com
18-hole resort course specifically for the MGM Mirage group, which includes the MGM Grand, the New York-New York, Bellagio, Treasure Island and the Mirage. One of the highest ranking courses in America – accessible to MGM Mirage guests from a mere $500!

Painted Desert

BRITTIP

When reserving your tee time, also check the cancellation policy and how much notice you need to give before forfeiting any money!

Golf at Lake Tahoe

Boulder City

Tournament Players Club at the Canyons

9851 Canyon Run Drive, 702 256 2500, tpc.com
18-hole resort course. Rounds cost $125–265 depending on the season. Reservations up to a year in advance.

Golf courses north of Las Vegas

Aliante Golf Club

3100 East Elkhorn, North Las Vegas, 866 447 4653, aliantegolf.com
A tournament quality course of 18 holes, with green fees running at $30–130 depending on the season.

Craig Ranch Golf Course

628 West Craig Road, 702 642 9700, http://thegolfcourses.net/golfcourses/NV/4123.htm
18-hole public course. Rates vary according to season. Reservations seven days in advance.

North Las Vegas Golf Course

324 East Brooks, 702 633 1833
Nine-hole city course (the ninth hole is on a hill and has a great view of Las Vegas). Rates vary according to season. Reservations seven days in advance.

Golf course in Boulder City

Boulder City Golf Course

1 Clubhouse Drive, Boulder City, 702 293 9236, bouldercitygolf.com
18-hole city course. Rates from $40 for Clark County residents and $50 for non-residents. Reservations one week in advance.

Golf courses in Henderson and Green Valley

Black Mountain Golf and Country Club

500 Greenway Road, Henderson, 702 565 7933, golfblackmountain.com
18-hole semi-private course. Rates from $70. Tee times up to four days in advance.

DragonRidge Golf and Country Club

552 South Stephanie Street, Henderson, 702 614 4444, dragonridgegolfclub.com
With great views of the Las Vegas Valley and bent-grass greens, this will test even the best golfers. Cost $130–225. Reservations up to 30 days in advance.

Legacy Golf Club

130 Par Excellence Drive, Henderson, 888-629 3929, thelegacygc.com
18-hole resort course. Cost $65–170 depending on the season. Tee times up to 120 days in advance.

Reflection Bay Golf Club

75 MonteLage Boulevard, Henderson, 702 740 4653, reservations 877 698 4653, lakelasvegas.com/golf_reflection.asp
Jack Nicklaus's prestigious course includes five holes played alongside 1.5mls/2.4km

Reflection Bay

BRITTIP

Jack Nicklaus's nationally ranked Reflection Bay Golf Club is part of the exclusive MonteLago Lake Las Vegas Resort, which includes shops, restaurants, a casino and two waterfront hotels. For more details of the whole area, visit lakelasvegas.com.

of Lake Las Vegas shoreline, while other holes are decorated with water features. Green fees vary daily. Tee times up to 30 days in advance.

Rio Secco Golf and Country Club

2851 Grand Hills Drive, Henderson, 702 252 7777
18-hole resort course owned by the Rio All-Suite Hotel. Mostly for Rio's and Harrah's hotel guests. Reservations 90 days in advance.

Wildhorse Golf Club

2100 Warm Springs Road, 702 434 9000, americangolf.com
18-hole public course. Rates vary seasonally. Reservations up to 60 days in advance.

BRITTIP

The Wildhorse Golf Club's 18th hole is one of the most difficult in the Las Vegas Valley, thanks to the surrounding bunkers and four lakes!

Balloons over Laughlin

The Community Center at Sun City Summerlin

Golf courses in Laughlin

Emerald River Country Club

1155 West Casino Drive, Laughlin, 702 298 0061
Demanding 18-hole resort course next to the Colorado including five holes along the river, 54 bunkers and plenty of changes in elevation. Rates vary $45–125 depending on the season. Reservations up to 30 days in advance.

BRITTIP

The Emerald River Country Club has received a three-star rating – the highest – from *Golf Digest*.

Mojave Resort Golf Club

9905 Aha Macav Parkway, Laughlin, 702 535 4653, mojaveresortgolfclub.com
An 18-hole course that hosts the Southern Nevada Golf Association Championships. Rates vary depending on the season, $50–900. Reservations one week in advance or 30 days with a credit card.

Golf courses in Summerlin and Pahrump

Sun City Summerlin Golf Club

Palm Valley: 9201-B Del Webb Boulevard, 702 363 4373. 18-hole semi-private (preference is given to residents).
Highland Falls: 10201 Sun City Boulevard, 702 254 7010. 18-hole course.
Eagle Crest: 2203 Thomas Ryan Boulevard, 702 240 1320. 18-hole course. Rates vary $45–110. Call for reservations.

Sam Boyd Stadium

Willow Creek Golf Club

1500 Red Butte, Pahrump, 775-727 4653, wcgolf.com
An 18-hole championship course surrounded by the Nopah and Spring Mountain ranges. Rates $20–60 depending on the season. Reservations seven days in advance.

BRITTIP
The Willow Creek Golf Club – a pleasant 45-minute journey from Las Vegas – has a beautiful course famous for having the best rates in southern Nevada.

Spectator sports

Las Vegas has it all still to do in the sporting arena. It doesn't have a professional football or basketball team – both are university (or college, as they are called in America) teams, but sometimes NBA (basketball) friendlies are held during October, which are worth going to see.

The city is most famous for hosting major championship boxing events two or three times a year – and has done so since 1960, largely as a result of the fact that this was the only city in America where you could legally gamble on a winner. Most of the middle and heavyweight fights take place at Caesars Palace, the MGM Grand or the Mandalay Bay. Tickets start at $100 and rise to a steep $3,500 or more for ringside seats. Best place to do your homework is on the Ticketmaster website ticketmaster.com.

American Football

Sam Boyd Stadium, Boulder Highway, 702 895 3900
The UNLV team's season runs between September and December. Tickets cost between $15 and $25.

Baseball

Cashman Field, 850 Las Vegas Boulevard North at Washington Avenue, 702 386 7100
Home of the Las Vegas 51s, who play from April to September as part of the Pacific Coast League.

Basketball

Thomas & Mack Center, 4505 Maryland Parkway on the UNLV campus, 702 895 3725, thomasandmack.com
The city's team is the UNLV Runnin' Rebels, who play all their games here between November and May. During October, NBA teams sometimes play exhibition games here, and in 2007 the NBA's All-star Game was hosted here. There is also a strong movement to move an NBA franchise to Sin City.

Las Vegas Speedway Park

7000 Las Vegas Boulevard North, 1-800 644 4444, lvms.com
Lying 17mls/27km north of the Strip, the 1,500acre/607ha speedway opened in 1996 at a cost of $200m and seats 107,000. Facilities include a 1.5ml/2.4km superspeedway, a 2.5ml/4km road course, a 0.5ml/0.8km dirt oval, drag strip, go-kart tracks and racing school. Check out Midnight Madness on Fridays and Saturdays for drag racing that starts at 10pm as part of the test and tune sessions that begin at 5pm. Phone ahead for schedules of upcoming events and tickets.

Ryan Schnitz at the Speedway Park

Ice hockey

702 84 7777, lasvegaswranglers.com
Ice hockey is a big deal in America and desert-bound Las Vegas doesn't disappoint. For some fierce action try the local Wranglers' matches. Visit the website or phone for a schedule.

For general sports events try UNLV Sports on 702 739 3267.

BRITTIP

Try Nevada Ticket Services on 702 597 1588 or lsvegas ticket.com to book anything from basketball to football, hockey, baseball, National Finals Rodeo, pro bull rides, Superbowl and Final Four.

Wrestling

wwe.com
The city doesn't hold its own events, but does play host to several World Wrestling Federation and World Championship Wrestling events. Either check out the local paper when in town or look at the website in advance.

Bungee jumping is only for the brave!

Extreme sports

There are many different ways to have fun in Las Vegas and if extreme thrills are your thing, then you can do anything from a terrifying bungee jump to taking part in a race at the Speedway. For details visit vegas4visitors.com/recreate/recreate-extreme.htm.

AJ Hackett Bungee

aj-hackett.com/world/cdlasvegas.htm
If it's sheer exhilaration you want, jump off the 180ft/55m tower, then cool off in the pool! Hours are seasonal. Various packages are available with T-shirts and videos. AJ Hackett is planning a move so it's worth checking out its website to confirm location in advance.

BRITTIP

You must be a minimum of 13 years old to do a bungee jump and weigh at least 90lb/40kg. Under-18s must also be accompanied by a parent or legal guardian.

Open: Mon–Fri 11am–8.30pm, Sat and Sun 11am–10.30pm, weather permitting. Last lift goes up half an hour before closing and hours change in autumn and winter.
Cost: For first-time jumpers $54 for one jump. Subsequent jumps $25 each with fourth jump free. Groups of five or more get $5 off per person. T-shirts and jump videos also available.

Flyaway Indoor Skydiving

200 Convention Center Drive, 702 731 4768, flyawayindoorskydiving.com
Learn how to fly in America's only indoor skydiving simulator, where the vertical wind tunnel allows you to beat gravity and fly! First-time flyers are given a 20-minute class in safety and body-control techniques. Experienced skydivers can also get valuable 'air' time to improve their skills without having to pack a rig and wait for the right weather. Video coaching programmes are also available in which your air tunnel flight is recorded to help you improve your style.
Open: Mon–Sat 10am–7pm, Sun 10am–5pm. Classes every half hour from 11am to an hour before closing.
Cost: $60 for first flight, $95 for two flights, $175 for five flights and $250 for learn-to-fly coaching package including five flights, video services and personalised coaching.

Major annual sporting events

April: Big League Weekends (baseball) – Cashman Field Center, 702 386 7100.

April: Spring Pro-Am Golf Tournament – Sunrise Golf Club, 1-800 332 8776; and Las Vegas Senior Classic – Senior PGA Golf Tournament, 702 382 6616.

September: Pro-Am Golf Tournament – Sahara Country Club, 1-800 332 8776.

October: Ice hockey season. A schedule is available in August for the Thomas and Mack Center, 702 895 3725, thomasandmack.com; and for the Las Vegas Invitational PGA Golf Tournament.

December: National Finals Rodeo Christmas Gift Show at Cashman Field Center, 702 386 7100. National Finals Rodeo at the Thomas and Mack Center, 702 895 3900. For a schedule call 702 656 1401. Las Vegas Bowl Collegiate Football Game – Big West Conference v Mid-American Conference at Sam Boyd Silver Bowl, 702 731 2115.

BRITTIP

Dress the part for your indoor skydive – make sure you're in comfy clothes with socks and trainers.

Sky diving is an awesome experience

Laser Quest

7361 West Lake Mead Boulevard, 702 243 8881

You wear a laser-sensing vest and shoot it out with other laser-wielding players in a maze of corners, turns, walkways and mirrored walls. Lasers are, of course, lightbeams, so you can even hit someone from around a corner if you get it to ricochet off the right point. Great for children up to the age of 80!

Open: Tues–Thurs 2–9pm, Fri 2–11pm, Sat noon–11pm, Sun noon–6pm.

Cost: Flat rate of $7.50 per person for 20 minutes of play.

Las Vegas Mini Grand Prix

1401 North Rainbow Boulevard, 702 259 7000, lvmgp.com

Take Exit 82a off US 95 for the ride of a lifetime on children's Grand Prix, Nascars, go-karts and kiddie karts. There is also a games arcade and snack bar.

Open: Sun–Thurs 10am–10pm, Fri–Sat 10am–11pm except Christmas Day and depending on the weather.

Cost: $5.50 per ticket or $25 for five. Cars available for from four to over 16-year-olds.

Las Vegas Parachute Center

Just behind the Goldstrike Hotel at Jean airport, 702 877 1010 (south-west of Las Vegas)

Take a tandem skydive after a 30-minute lesson for $169 ($199 including transport from your hotel). Open daily 8am–11am, jumps are by appointment only.

You can even get married in the air!

Race Car Tours

Las Vegas Motor Speedway, 7000 Las Vegas Boulevard North, 866-807 4697, lvms.com

This is home to the city's NASCAR events and drag races, where you can also get a piece of the action yourself. After minimal instruction you're allowed behind the wheel of a full-sized, 600HP racing car for six laps at speeds of up to 145mph/233kph at a cost of $399. For a mere $75 you can be a passenger in a two-seater racing car as a professional instructor does six laps around the Speedway. For $129 you can even experience a real race as a passenger in a qualifying run as a professional reaches speeds of up to 180mph/290kph!

Rocks and Ropes

3065 East Patrick Lane, Suite 4, 702 434 3388, rocksandropes.com

This indoor climbing facility has more than 7,000sq ft/651sq m of sculpted and textured walls for climbing, 30ft/9m ceilings, top rope and lead climbing and a mega-cave with a leadable 40ft/12m roof so people can learn everything they need to know to go rock climbing for real! Cost: $10 one day, $6 equipment rental, includes 45 minutes' instruction.

Skydive Las Vegas

Boulder City Airport, 1401 Airport Road, Boulder City (near Hoover Dam), 702 759 3483, skydivelasvegas.com

You freefall for 45 seconds before enjoying a seven-minute parachute ride in a tandem jump. By appointment only.

Las Vegas Motor Speedway

Xtreme Zone

Adventuredome Theme Park, 702 794 3939, adventuredome.com

A combination of rock climbing and aerial bungee jumping creates an interactive experience with multiple difficulty levels. The Zone's rock-climbing attraction combines traditional harnesses and handholds with cutting-edge belay technology to make it as safe as possible. The aerial trampoline combines a standard trampoline with a hydraulic system and bungee cords so you can climb up to 20ft/6m and then flip and spin yourself back and forth. You must weigh 40–265lb/18–120kg to climb the wall and 30–220lb/13.5–99kg to experience the bungee.

Xtreme Zone is part of the Adventuredome complex

13 GETTING THERE

The tour operators, doing it your own way and specialist planners

Of course, with Las Vegas your dream destination you still have to get there. You have a lot of choices. After all, if you are going to fly across an entire ocean and most of a continent to get there, you might as well make it worth the trip! Do you use the city as a fantastically cheap base for visiting all the natural wonders on its doorstep? Maybe you head off on a fly-drive tour; or even start in Los Angeles and San Francisco and take in all the wonderful places that you can reasonably visit in the amount of time available to you?

Then there are the other factors, like how many of you are travelling, or whether you will be visiting friends in, say, San Diego or Phoenix. In that case you could take advantage of the incredibly cheap offers to Las Vegas that are advertised in the local papers and travel from there. If you have children and teenagers in your party, you'll probably be best with an airline/tour operator that caters well for the family market. You may even want to do a part fly-drive and add on a ranch or golfing holiday or an adventure trek.

In this chapter

The visitor figures show that Brits tend either to go on a long-weekend package to Las Vegas or do a combination of any of the above. It is for this reason that if you have ever picked up a brochure on visiting Las Vegas and California there seems to be so much information and so many options to wade through from multi-centre

Highway 50

packages, fly-drives, coach tours, open-jaw flights (see page 243) and so on. It'll take some time to make sense of one brochure, let alone compare a few to see what suits you best. Then there is the other option – to organise your trip totally independently.

To try to make life easier, I've tried to outline the options available, what to look for and what to ask for.

BRITTIP

When shopping around for flight prices, make sure the figure you are given includes all taxes and airport fees to make a proper comparison.

Specialist tour operators

Not your local travel agents, but those who specialise in organising holidays to Nevada and California and produce a brochure to display their products. I say this because Las Vegas in particular has quirks all of its own and someone with little local knowledge is unlikely to provide you with the best deals or choice of options.

What's good about the specialist North American tour operators is that the big outfits have massive buying power and so can offer some of the best prices available for both hotels and car-hire services. In many cases you can go for a 'land-only' deal for a nominal charge, which gives you the option to arrange your own flights through some of the cheap flight brokers who advertise in the weekend national newspapers (more about that in the independent travel section, page 251). Most do not advertise this, though, so you will have to ask.

All the main specialist North American operators provide tailor-made packages, which mean that you can take advantage of any special deals and arrangements they may have with, for instance, hotels,

McCarran International airport

The bright lights of Las Vegas

theme parks and local airline companies offering scenic flights around the Grand Canyon area and San Francisco.

The bigger guys – such as American Connections, Virgin, Kuoni, Jetlife, Premier and Getaway Vacations – can pack in a lot of added-value extras. You can get room upgrades for honeymoon and anniversary holiday-makers, free transfers to the hotel (rarely part of a North American package), free accommodation and/or free meals for children, extra nights free, free flights to London from regional airports and so on. You may also like to know that out of the large tour companies operating in North America, Virgin Holidays, Kuoni, Travelsphere, Jetsave and Page & Moy did particularly well in the 'would you recommend this tour operator to a friend?' stakes as part of a *Which?* tour operator survey.

Local knowledge

Big is not always best in this market, as good knowledge of the location is very important, along with the operator's determination to provide you with what is best for you (which may involve making alternative suggestions to your own best-laid plans) and offer a generally good level of service. Smaller outfits such as Just America (justamerica.co.uk) do not claim to be the cheapest, but with a high level of return custom and recommendation-to-friends business, they know their emphasis on getting things right for a slightly higher cost means all the difference between an okay holiday and a fantastic one. Their policy is based on not packing too much

Arches National Park

into one trip so that you travel to see destinations, not see destinations as you travel. Overall, it makes them very good value for money.

Another smaller UK operator, Funway Holidays, (funwayholidays.co.uk) works alongside United Vacations, which sends more than one million people a year to Las Vegas, so they have tremendously good buying power and very good access to hotels in Las Vegas. More than 30 hotels are featured in the brochure (the average tends to be about five or six), including all the recently opened resorts such as The Palms.

In addition, Funway's relationship with Las Vegas means they are likely to be able to get you into top resort-hotels when other tour operators may not. They also provide a whole raft of extras, including vouchers for free admissions to parks and shows and 25% discounts on helicopter tours to the Grand Canyon. Overall, it makes them one of the best operators to Las Vegas. They also have some great arrangements for self-drive tours.

What to look for

Using a tour operator is great if you want to get everything sewn up before you go, but remember they're in business to make money and, while their brochures may be in one sense accurate, not all of them will point out any negatives. Also, it is useful to bear in mind that even if something is not included in the brochure, such as open-jaw tickets (see page 243) or air passes (see page 244), you should always ask your preferred operator if they can arrange those for you.

The following sections will show you how to take the good, watch out for the bad and reject the downright ugly that tour operators have to offer.

Scheduled flights

Charter services to Las Vegas come and go – and are seasonal at best, so it really is down to scheduled flights. In the case of America generally, and Las Vegas in particular, this is a good thing as most of the airlines fly every day to a whole range of locations in North America – many at easy-to-catch times of the day – and from a range of regional airports in the UK.

Given the way most Brits tend to move around Nevada, Arizona and California during a holiday to the region, this provides the essential flexibility required when organising a trip. What tends to follow on from scheduled services is the ability to make a stop on the way to your final destination (stopover); fly into one city and out from another (open-jaw) and even fly between cities (using multi-centre packages or air-pass vouchers). And if you tend to do a lot of long-haul travelling, you can even arrange it so that you get frequent-flyer points. Most of the operators offer a minimum of three airline prices, some up to six, except for airline-run operators, such as American Holiday (American Airlines); NorthWest Airlines; United Vacations (United Airlines) and Virgin.

The Sphinx at the Luxor

Frequent-flyer points

Did you know that every time you fly you could be clocking up frequent-flyer mileage points that will eventually give you free air travel or other perks such as last-minute availability, lounge access and free upgrades or discounts off attractions and excursions in the USA? Very often your holiday booking does give you free air miles, but you may not know about it. Even if you do not claim the benefits, your travel agent still has the right to do so and some like to keep this nice little perk under their hats! So, before you go on holiday, register with the airline for their loyalty scheme and keep your booking passes to prove that the flights were taken. Discounted flights may not qualify, but it's always worth checking.

Many of the North American specialists will automatically offer frequent-flyer points on American Airlines flights, though you may have to pay an additional £49 for the privilege of collecting them. Having said that, AA give you one Advantage mile for every mile you fly, which is over 10,000 if you're flying from London to Los Angeles – enough to earn you one free ticket to certain European destinations.

If you have a family, it is a good idea to register the whole family in the scheme so each person can build up their points. Some schemes, such as Virgin's Flying Club Frequent Flyer (0870 161 6059), expect their economy-class passengers to complete three return economy flights before qualifying, though upper class or premium economy passengers qualify immediately. British Airways offer both air miles and travel points, the latter granting lounge facilities and even free travel insurance with enough credits.

When arranging to join a frequent-flyer programme, ask if there is a bonus for joining at that particular time as different airlines offer bonuses. For instance, not so long ago Virgin was offering a bonus of 2,000 points on joining and Continental a special activation bonus of a whopping 5,000 miles when you take your first Continental Airlines holiday. The scheme offers free upgrades and free tickets.

Also, for those who have an American Express card, they have an excellent travel site (americanexpress.com/membershiprewards) where you can book everything you need, get frequent travel points for Amex and double up frequent flyer points for the airlines and hotels you use. These transcontinental trips can add up quickly when you are dipping twice.

Finally, following the lead of a partnership between MGM Mirage and American, most major resorts have teamed up with one airline's frequent-flyer programme or other to get points bonuses. So any time you spend money at the hotel you can earn even more points, or use your points for free shows, tours, or what have you.

Assessing flight choices

Flights to Las Vegas from Britain have multiplied at a happy rate. Direct service is still primarily via Virgin via London or Manchester, so for convenience they have the best options. Competition for passengers, though, has made going indirect through hubs much cheaper and you can save hundreds of pounds by waiting for change-overs in airports.

Harrah's Hotel and Casino

Indirect service is available through a host of airlines, including a partnership of British Airways/USAir, plus Continental, BMI, Virgin, American and United, although recently KLM Royal Dutch has consistently been having the lowest fairs, with their London-Amsterdam-Minneapolis-Las Vegas route generally much cheaper than others, although you will spend at least seven extra hours travelling.

So when comparing prices for flights, the first thing you need to look for is whether you are getting a direct flight with Virgin or whether you are going via a hub city – which you will do with any of the other carriers – and how much longer that will add on to your travel time. When weighing up cost differences, bear in mind that flying into a hub city tends to involve changing planes to a less comfortable domestic plane, where you will also be charged for your drinks.

Combine relaxing with the high life

If you do opt to use a non-direct service, also remember that some tickets may provide better stopovers than others, which will make arranging a decent multi-centre deal easier.

The next thing is to take into consideration any differences between flying at the weekend or midweek – there is normally a surcharge for Friday and Saturday flights.

Finally, always ensure the price you are quoted includes all airport taxes and non-negotiable fees – they can amount to a fair bit and you don't want those kinds of surprises!

BRITTIP

Always check around for best flight prices before booking, as there may be good deals on offer.

Open-jaw flights

Fly into one city and out from another. It's usually very simple to work out the cost – in most cases, you add the cost of flying to one destination to the cost of flying to the other, divide by two and add a £1. This means you don't have to backtrack and it can save you quite a lot of money on a touring trip. Very few operators advertise open-jaw so you will have to ask whether it can be arranged or shop around.

Multi-centre packages

Fly into one city, look around, fly on to another, look around, fly on to another, look around and then fly home. This kind of package tends to be one of the most popular in the Las Vegas/California holiday market with the trio of Las Vegas, Los Angeles and San Francisco as the leading lights. It's a good idea if you don't want, or don't have, enough time to drive between all the main places you want to see, but it is a more expensive option, generally, than using your full quota of stopovers, or the open-jaw system.

Stopovers

The alternative to the above is to use the stopover system whereby you break your journey at various points. Most of the airlines offer this service, with the first stopover usually free and subsequent stopovers (up to a maximum of three) being charged at around £60 a stop. Some airlines now offer two free stopovers.

BRITTIP

Do bear in mind that if you opt for the direct Virgin flight there will be no stopovers to take advantage of.

If you want to use this system, you have to ensure that the route you are booking is the correct one for you as the first, free, stopover is usually limited to the 'gateway' city – the first place where the plane lands in the United States and where you'll go through American immigration. Watch this, as many of the American airlines use 'hub' cities as their gateway cities, such as Detroit or Minneapolis in the case of NorthWest Airlines, and you may not consider Delta's hub cities of Atlanta or Cincinatti to be as exciting a stopover point as New York or Los Angeles, for instance. With other airlines, including NorthWest, it may pay to route your trip via Amsterdam so that you get a more interesting 'gateway' city.

Las Vegas from the air

BRITTIP

To make best use of your free stopover, check your 'gateway' city is a reasonable destination, such as New York or Chicago, rather than Cincinatti or Atlanta!

Extra stops

These are similar to stopovers, except you'll pay an extra fee, usually £60. If you want to fly to more than one place not covered by your free stopover allowance, or if the place you want to go to isn't on the route, go for an air pass (see below).

BRITTIP

When booking flights, be sure to claim your free air miles or find out about the airline's loyalty scheme before you go, to be on track for free air travel or other benefits such as priority booking, lounge facilities and upgrades.

Child and youth discounts

Most airlines give child discounts (ages 2–11), usually at 50% off the published price during mid and low seasons and at 40% during peak season. The peak season does vary a little but a rough guide is July–August and the Christmas period around 15–27 December. Very few airlines offer youth discounts for 12 to 16-year-olds (a paltry 10%, which could be matched by shopping around the flight shops) but your best bets are tour operators who use United Airlines and Virgin.

Infant fares

The old days of tour operators publishing very cheap infant fares, but then adding on up to £60 of taxes are, thankfully, mostly gone, though some still continue this practice. A good fully inclusive price these days is around £70, but do check that the price you have been quoted includes all taxes.

Travelling with children

One point to stress is that many airline crews are being quite strict with child passengers. There have been numerous instances in recent years of children not being allowed to travel because of bad behaviour. It is quite a long trip, so make sure you bring enough things to keep your children merrily occupied.

Regional departures

More and more airlines are running routes directly from regional airports in the UK to Las Vegas and California. But in most cases you will have to pay a supplement to fly to London (though Kuoni offers free flights in connection with transatlantic BA and United Airlines flights). In almost all cases, if you want to fly from Glasgow, you will have to pay a supplement of around £45–50. However, United Vacations and US Airtours offer free connections from many regional UK airports.

Air passes

If you plan to visit more than the one city covered by your free stopover or, for whatever reason, are likely to make quite a few flights between certain destinations, an

Circus Circus is popular with families

The Stratocoaster

air pass is the way to go. But you must buy before you go as North American residents are not permitted to buy air passes, so they won't be available once you get to the US.

The airlines and smoking

Virgin and most of the American airlines have a total non-smoking policy on their transatlantic flights. In fact, smoking is banned by law on all flights in US airspace, so even if you do get a transatlantic flight that allows smoking, if you switch to a domestic plane for the final leg of your journey you will not be allowed to smoke on that plane.

Code share

Many airlines enter into alliances with each other to share routes, which can offer you more choice of routes and fares. It means that your flight is marketed by one airline, with the airline's flight number, but when you board you find the service is operated by a different airline. Some tour operators will inform you in advance, but they may not always know as these alliances are constantly changing. Be careful of this if you have a particular dislike for one airline or know that you definitely want to fly with a certain company. A *Which?* survey of airlines found that Virgin was among the most highly rated, yet it currently has a code-share alliance with Continental, who came pretty near the bottom of the same report.

Kids stay free

Many operators offer this as an extra, but it is standard policy at many hotels to allow children to stay free in the same room as an adult. If you're NOT being offered this as an option, go elsewhere!

Las Vegas showgirls

Length and type of visit

Fly-drive and tailor-made tours

These have to go hand-in-hand in the North American market as there are so many options it would be daft for any tour company to force people into taking one particular tour (that's what coach trips are for!). Chapter 15 The Grand Canyon and Surroundings gives a good insight into great places to visit within easy striking distance of Las Vegas.

Coach and Tauck tours

If you don't want to worry about car hire, driving and all the other arrangements you will need to make, and you don't mind a coach-load of people crowding into an attraction at the same time as you, then this could be the way to go. Coach tours are not necessarily all-inclusive, though, and may not include meals so that you have the option of choosing where to eat.

Tauck tours are the posher version and usually include everything. Run by an American company, you will be greeted and treated as an individual, while the tours themselves tend to be shorter so you have more time to relax and explore sights by yourself. In addition, you are put up in first-class hotels with character.

Extras

Grand Canyon flights

One of the added bonuses of visiting Las Vegas is that you can experience the amazing scenery of Arizona's Canyonlands, plus other natural wonders Bryce Canyon and Zion Park, without the long drive. A whole host of scenic flight operators work out of Las Vegas (details in

Dirty South tour bus

A Grand Canyon flight is a must

Chapter 11 Outdoor Adventure), but if you want to make sure of your seat or tie up all loose ends before you go, many of the tour operators are offering these flights. Again, ask even if they're not advertised as they may be able to arrange a scenic flight for you.

BRITTIP

Don't try to see too much in too short a space of time – you don't want to spend your whole holiday driving and you may even want to leave time for an adventure tour or ranch holiday.

Show tickets

You can buy these in advance to ensure you get a seat, but don't overdo it as you may miss out on cheap deals locally.

BRITTIP

If you are flexible and don't mind waiting until the last minute, you can save lots of money on show tickets. There are many half-price ticket stands along the Strip and Fremont Street and shows that aren't overbooked will sell tickets through these dealers at cut rates to put bums on seats. You can often get tickets for shows at 50% off by buying a ticket on the day of performance from one of these shops. But sorry, this won't do for hard to find tickets, so Cirque extravaganzas are rarely available this way.

The tropical Mandalay Bay

Hotel vouchers

The three basic kinds of hotel vouchers are the Liberty and TourAmerica Hotel Passes and the North American Guestcheque. In all cases you buy vouchers at a certain price in advance that are valid for one night at a participating hotel – usually a chain hotel. You can book the hotel in advance and the room will accommodate up to four people. It can be a very good way of planning your holiday budget and pre-paying as far as possible. But one major drawback is that if you buy more than you need, there is usually a charge for redeeming any unused vouchers. Often it amounts to the value of one voucher and in some cases it can be one voucher plus an administrative charge of £25.

Another drawback is that you do not benefit from any promotions that participating hotels and motels may run locally. And do bear in mind that these chain hotels don't have much character and some may even seem a little soulless.

- Purchasing the vouchers does not automatically give you the right of accommodation, so it is always best to book as far in advance as possible, especially if you intend to travel in the peak seasons.
- If you intend to arrive after 4pm, you will need a credit card to guarantee your reservation. If it is a hotel/motel in a particularly busy area, such as one of the major sights that is not near a big town or city, I'd recommend you ask them to send or fax the confirmation of your reservation.
- There are often many hotels of the same chain in the same town, so it is best to make a note of the full address so you go to the right one!

BRITTIP

If you're in Los Angeles check the local papers for good deals on the Amtrak rail service between LA and Las Vegas.

The American way

Motorbike hire

Okay, so you fancy yourself as a modern-day cowboy enjoying the ultimate touring experience of travelling along those wide-open roads on anything from a Harley Davidson Electra Glide to a Fat Boy or Road King. You can do that from LA and Las Vegas, but it'll be a lot more expensive than a car. The few operators that offer this include American Holidays and Jetlife.

Amtrak and Greyhound

Greyhound's International Ameripass allows you to go where you want, when you want, travelling by coach day or night. High season May–Sep $278 for 10 days, $384 for 21 days. Low season Jan–May, Oct–May $254 for 10 days, $344 for 21 days. Amtrak rail passes for Western states start from $210 for 5–30 days; 15 days adults $325, kids 2–15 $210; 30 days adults $405, kids 2–15 $270. National and other regions are also available. Amtrak covers all the major destinations and sights in California and there is the new non-stop daily service between Los Angeles and Las Vegas for $38 return. The trip takes 5½ hours. Few tour operators advertise Amtrak travel, but others may arrange it for you if you ask. Take a look at amtrak.com.

Motorbikes in Laughlin

Other things you need to know

The seasons

There are four: low or off-peak, low shoulder, high shoulder and peak. Basically, the most expensive times to travel are Christmas, July, August, Easter and during the American bank holidays: President's Day (George Washington's birthday) – the third Monday in February; Memorial Day – the last Monday in May and the official start of the summer season; Independence Day – 4 July (in the middle of the high season); Labor Day – the first Monday in September and last holiday of summer; and Thanksgiving – always the fourth Thursday in November.

BRITTIP

Hotel prices in America are for accommodation only and do not include breakfast.

Low or off-peak season tends to be November, then January to the end of March excluding the bank holidays and Easter. May, June and October are low shoulder and all other times are high shoulder.

Best times to travel

Without a doubt, Monday to Thursday. Flights are cheaper, airports less crowded for departure and arrival, and hotels in Las Vegas, in particular, are far less busy. The very best days to arrive in Las Vegas are Tuesday to Thursday morning.

A–Z of specialist tour operators

visitlasvegas.co.uk

American Holidays

02890 310000, americanholidays.com
They have some excellent fly-drive packages.

Archers Direct

0871 423 8425, archersdirect.co.uk
Packages to California and Las Vegas that are busy indeed.

Bon Voyage

0800 316 3012
One of the bigger operators, but surprisingly, offers very few extras.

Funway

0870 220 0626, funwayholidays.co.uk
Funway offers bonus offers available at certain hotels: free meals and breakfasts for children, free children's clubs, free nights, free shuttle bus service. Plus with every booking: fun books, packed with money-saving deals on sightseeing trips, attractions, shows, shopping and dining; free reduced rate phone card; free Rand McNally Travel Planner and VIP shopping discount card in conjunction with the Shop America Alliance. Funway's sister company in America is very big in Las Vegas. It has its own car rental and sightseeing options that can be reserved via its website.

You'll need formal clothes for restaurants such as Joël Robuchon

Jetlife

0870 787 7877, jetlife.co.uk
If you fly with Continental Airlines to the western states, you will get a free car upgrade.

Jetset

0870 700 4000, jetsetholidays.co.uk
Jetsave offers free accommodation for children at certain hotels, Greyhound Ameripass and Air Passes. However, does not give clear details of the 'fully inclusive' insurance and car hire prices, so check that the package DOES include everything you want.

Just America

01730 266588, justamerica.co.uk
Has the best value, easiest-to-use arrangements for car hire. Also specialises in a highly personalised, tailor-made service.

Kuoni

01306 742888 (reservations), 07000 458664 (brochures), kuoni.co.uk
One of the UK's best long-haul tour operators, Kuoni offers extra nights free, room upgrades, free sports, meals and drinks and food discounts. There are also special deals for honeymooners and those celebrating silver or golden wedding anniversaries (though you'll have to take a copy of your marriage certificate with you!).

North America Travel Service

0845 122 8899, northamericatravelservice.co.uk
Specialises in fly-drives but offers very little information about flights and availability of open-jaw and stopovers. Also offers some free night deals at certain hotels, and has separate brochures for coach, Tauck and adventure tours.

NorthWest Airlines

08705 074074, nwa.com
Offers flight discounts for teenagers. Tickets come with a complete travel planner and online reservations, plus it has its own frequent-flyer centre.

Premier Holidays

0870 889 0850, premierholidays.co.uk
Premier Plus offers include extra nights free at certain hotels, free transport to attractions, breakfasts, upgrades for honeymooners, tea and coffee and use of health clubs.

Trailfinders

0845 058 5858, trailfinders.co.uk
The UK's largest independent travel agent, this is renowned for tailor-made itineraries and a good selection of discounted flights. One of the few tour operators still offering Amtrak passes and the only company that still offers the Greyhound Ameripass in its brochure.

Unijet

0870 533 6336, firstchoice.co.uk
The only company offering chartered flights direct to Las Vegas, it is famous for its amazingly cheap long-weekend and week-long deals.

United Vacations

0870 242 2901, unitedvacations.co.uk
No regional departures, unless you fly via

The Doge's Palace at the Venetian

Amsterdam, but free connecting flights from regional airports during off-peak times. Books of vouchers for cheaper dining and attraction entrance fees.

USAirtours

0871 210 6750, usairtours.co.uk
Offers free drinks, breakfasts, shuttle to the Strip in Las Vegas, and free extra nights at certain hotels.

Virgin Holidays

0870 220 2707, virginholidays.co.uk
Virgin offer free kids' funpacks on flights, free breakfasts, free meals for children and extras for honeymoons and anniversaries at certain hotels. Don't forget to join the frequent-flyer programme if you qualify. Plus $50 discount at Virgin Megastores and better deals for single parents.

Escorted tour companies

APT International Tours

020 8879 7444, aptouring.com
APT give discounts if you have travelled with APT before, plus a travel bag.

Jetsave

0870 162 3503, jetsave.co.uk
Jetsave give generous discounts for groups of 15 or more, plus free places depending on the number travelling. No supplements for single travellers if prepared to share a room.

Page & Moy

0870 833 4012, pageandmoy.com
Consistently rated highly by repeat-visit travellers.

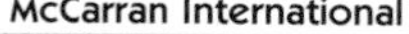

McCarran International

Flying over LA International

Travelsphere

0870 240 2460, travelsphere.co.uk
National Express pick-ups to point of departure for £5; savings on hotel airports and regional departures.

Airports

McCarran International airport

Just 1ml/1.6km from the Strip and 5mls/8km from downtown, McCarran International airport is one of the slickest, most modern and easy-to-use airports in America. In a passenger survey of 36 major airports – which looked at speed of baggage delivery, ease of reaching gates, ground transport, cleanliness, quality of restaurants, attractiveness, ease of parking and following signs – McCarran came sixth.

The airport is among the 10 busiest airports in the world and deals with 800 flights a day and around 30.5 million passengers a year. The latest runway – opened recently at a cost of $80.5m – has given the airport the capacity to handle 60 million passengers a year. It has direct flights to 62 US airports and nine international destinations and more than 5,000 cars a day use the parking facilities.

Like many other aspects of life in Las Vegas, the airport has the very latest technology. There is no need for departing passengers with tickets to go to ticket counters inside the terminals – they can check in their luggage at the ticketing/departure kerb. It is the first airport in America to use Common Use

Terminal Equipment (CUTE). This allows airlines to use any gate as needed, which creates more efficient scheduling of gates and faster boarding for passengers. In addition, all facilities are accessible to the disabled and amplified phone sets are dotted throughout the terminal.

Los Angeles International airport

If you are planning a touring holiday or perhaps an open-jaw flight, you may want to come into or out of Los Angeles airport, a major international airport with all the best facilities.

Independent booking

There may be many different reasons why you want to organise all or part of your trip independently. Some people (jammy dodgers, I call them!) fly to San Francisco or Los Angeles to visit friends and then decide to go off to Las Vegas and other parts of California or Arizona on trips. But by nature we Brits are an independent lot and one of the most appealing ideas for us is just to fly to the west coast of America and hit the open road. Whatever the reason, the following tips will help you to save money in all the right places so you have more to spend on enjoying the sights and buying those essential pairs of trainers etc!

Flights

Competition in the transatlantic flight market is fierce, which is good news for us the customers. It also means that it makes sense to shop around for the best deal you can get. I recommend that you read the tour operators section (see pages 248–250) first, so you can acquaint yourself with all the terms and deals available.

Wonder websites

Check out the following for up-to-date prices, the best deals and to book.

hotelanywhere.co.uk: A British-owned website providing discounts on hotels anywhere in the world.

quikbook.com: A service providing discounts on hotels from coast to coast in America. It promises there are no hidden cancellation or change penalties, and pre-payment is not required.

hotels.com: A great internet discount reservation service.

hotelconxions.com: Another good website for checking out availability at well-booked Las Vegas hotels and reserving a room.

Once you have worked out what your priorities are, then you have a pretty good chance of beating the prices quoted in the brochures by phoning round the transatlantic flight bookers that advertise in the weekend newspapers. *The Sunday Times* is particularly good. Remember, too, that the tour operators specialising in the North American market also have access to deals being offered by the airlines, so can often beat their own published prices! Low and low-shoulder seasons (see page 248) are particularly good for brilliant deals, such as flights to Las Vegas or Los Angeles for £300 or even less.

You can even go for a totally no-frills, mega-cheap flight with 'consolidated' fares. These are the old-style bucket-shop fares which have now been legalised. The travel agent negotiates deals on your part, so you get very cheap fares and they're happy, too, as they earn better commission rates. The main restriction with these fares

McCarran is a first-class airport

is that you can only use one airline and sometimes it may involve flying via that airline's 'home' country, for instance, somewhere in Europe. Also you won't get free or extra stopovers, but you can get around this by buying air passes for internal flights (see page 244). These air passes are not available in the States so you need to buy them before you go.

Hotels

If you're happy touring around Nevada, Arizona and California staying in the rather soulless chains such as Days Inn, Ramada and so on, you could take advantage of many of the special deals that are advertised in local papers and find a room on an ad hoc basis. Generally this is no problem at all in cities and towns, but it may be worth booking a few days in advance for rooms at major sightseeing destinations, such as the Grand Canyon or Furnace Creek in Death Valley. Even if you'd prefer accommodation with a little more character, you can still find cheap deals through agents once you are in America (see opposite).

Las Vegas is one of the weirdest cities on earth for hotel prices. In most cities around the world, hotels tend to be busy during the week and offer incentives to fill their rooms at weekends. With Las Vegas, the reverse is true. So many Americans from Salt Lake City to Phoenix and Los Angeles use Las Vegas as a weekend destination that occupancy rates are a staggering 96% on Friday and Saturday nights (even with 135,313 rooms to fill).

On top of that, the city hosts huge conventions and special events such as rodeos and prize fights that tie up hotels, restaurants, transportation, showrooms and traffic for a week at a time. For these reasons, although Las Vegas hotels have their rack (standard) room rates, prices vary wildly above or below that rate according to how busy it is and how much they think they can get away with! Having said that, the price of accommodation is probably cheaper than anywhere else in North America and given the class and quality of facilities on offer, you can live like a king or queen very cheaply at top resorts in Las Vegas.

BRITTIP

Some of the best internet sources for booking Las Vegas Hotel rooms are lasvegasadvisor.com and hotels.com.

Cheap deals: If you happen to be in southern California in December or January and pick up a local paper, you may see promotional offers direct from Las Vegas hotels in which the rooms are practically being given away. On the basis that an empty room is a liability, they will be happy to do this just to get your foot in the door – and their casino! The deals often include not only incredibly cheap rooms, but also free shows and meals.

In addition, the travel sections of the Sunday papers just about anywhere in the States – and at just about any time of year – are good for picking up fantastic deals to Las Vegas.

By far the best places to buy good Las Vegas deals from are southern California (Los Angeles and San Diego), Phoenix, Denver or Chicago. The package usually includes room, transport and possibly rental car and shows. Even if you've already got your transportation sorted, you can still take advantage of the special deals by asking for the 'land only' part of the deal.

In almost all cases, you will get a better deal on Las Vegas hotels once you are in the States (with the possible exception of Funway, which has access to so many hotels at great prices), especially if you are travelling at low or shoulder seasons.

BRITTIP

A smart way to find the cheapest hotel rate? First, check online or with booking companies for hotels at a good rate. Then check the hotel's website – they often have internet deals that are lower than anything else available.

In the unlikely event that you can't find deals for Las Vegas in the *LA Times* or other local papers, contact airline tour

Airport check-in at the MGM Grand

A room at Skyrise Tower at the Circus Circus

companies such as American Airlines Fly-Away and Delta Dream Vacations and ask if they have special deals at particular hotels.

National Reservation Bureau: Good American agents to use include the National Reservation Bureau on toll-free number: 1 800 638 5553 (but don't phone from a hotel room as you'll be charged the hotel phone rates). Prices will vary according to the time of year but when I looked they had rooms at Circus Circus from $46 (approx £23 at $2.01 to the £ or £11.50 a head for two adults) at the Excalibur from $55 (£13.50 a head for two) and at the Luxor from $65 (£16 a head for two) among many others.

Other Las Vegas agents that will help not just with the price of a room, but actually get you in at the inn, so to speak, include Las Vegas Travel, toll free on 1 800 286 9195 and Gold Reservations, toll free on 1 800 627 4465.

BRITTIP

Most hotels in America work on a per-room price basis, though there may be a maximum number of adults allowed. In addition, the room usually consists of a double or two double beds – the latter can't be guaranteed, but can be requested. In some cases there may be a small extra charge if there are more than two adults, but this won't be much.

No room at the inn: It is also worth using one of the agents mentioned above if you're having trouble booking yourself into one of the top resort-hotels as they are more likely to have rooms. Once agents are given blocks of rooms to sell, as far as the reservations manager is concerned, those rooms are not available.

One word of warning: If booking a hotel yourself, always guarantee your first night with a credit card (even if you do not plan to arrive late). If you do, then sending a deposit is not needed. If you are booking by phone, make sure you are given a reservation or confirmation number so you can verify the reservation. With a confirmation number, no written confirmation is needed. I have had times when my reservation was cancelled by a mistake from the hotel. With the confirmation number, the hotel cannot turn you away. They must find you a room of at least the same standard or better than the one you reserved and at the same rate.

BRITTIP

Most hotels will allow children under a certain age to sleep for free if sharing a room paid for by one or more adults.

The internet

Take care when making bookings via the internet. As with all independent travel arrangements, you do not have a tour operator to complain to (and, possibly, get money back from) if things go wrong. Stick to bigger hotels and car-hire firms if you are booking some time in advance as you are not covered if the company goes bust before you arrive for your holiday.

Probably the biggest drawback to internet bookings, though, is that there have been concerns about the security of sending credit card details over the internet. Larger sites will use a secure server to process credit cards, and they are generally safe. If they do not, or for any reason you feel uncomfortable about giving

The Monte Carlo

the site your information, you can take details from the internet and make arrangements via the phone, fax or by letter. However, you would not likely get any special internet promotional rates by doing it this way.

The specialists

So you've seen the bright lights of the big cities, taken in the amazing natural wonders of the West and had a flutter in Las Vegas – what more could you want? Well, the truth is that we Brits not only have an independent spirit, we also have romantic notions of the rugged outdoors and cowboy lifestyle. The chances are that if you've gone all the way to the West, you'll want to add on a ranch holiday or 'soft' adventure tour such as rafting, cycling, climbing and motorbiking or perhaps go horse riding, bird watching, play a little golf, do the jazz thing or get a real taste of California wines. The following companies offer those services.

Adventure

Hemmingways: 0870 742 2673, hemmingways.co.uk
Outlaw Trails: 01892 515612, outlawtrails.com
Ranch America: 0845 277 3306, ranchamerica.co.uk
Trailfinders: 0845 058 5858, trailfinders.com
Trek America: 0870 444 8735, trekamerica.com

Bird watching

Ornitholidays: 01794 519445, ornitholidays.co.uk

Golf

Destination Golf USA: 020 8891 5151
The American Golf Holiday: 023 8046 5885, americangolfholiday.com

Jazz

Ashley Tours: 01886 888335, ashleyjazztours.co.uk

Ranching

American Round-Up: 01404 881777, americanroundup.com
NAR: 0870 777 8877
Ranch America: 0845 277 3306, ranchamerica.co.uk
Jetlife: 0870 787 7877, jetlife.co.uk
Kuoni: 07000 458664, kuoni.co.uk
United Vacations: 0870 242 2901, unitedvacations.co.uk
Virgin: 0870 220 2707, virginholidays.co.uk

Wine

Arblaster and Clarke: 01730 263111, winetours.co.uk
Winetrails: 01306 712111, winetrails.co.uk

Shadow Creek Golf Club

14 DRIVING AND CAR RENTAL

How to get out and about on the open road

It's the grand dream, isn't it – driving along the American highway, the only car on a stretch of road that goes on for so long you only lose it on the horizon, music blasting, shades on and not a care in the world? Believe me, it truly is an experience not to be missed. You cannot help but get a sense of being so much closer to nature when all around you is space, space, space on an unbelievable scale.

And while (thanks to the sheer size of America) you might on occasion feel as if you are driving through great swathes of nothingness, at least the skies are likely to provide some spectacular sights of their own, from multi-coloured sunsets to heavenly blue vistas and massive rainfalls that you can see from miles away. I once spent a whole day driving on a straight open road surrounded by Arizona desert landscape, with blue skies each side and a monumentally large downpour straight ahead – and not a drop fell on me until the night (when my tent almost got washed away!), which just gives you a feel of how vast the country is.

I tell you all this to help convey the scale of what you will encounter on a touring trip around the west of America, so be warned: unless you want to spend your entire time driving during your two weeks, don't try to tackle too much all in one hit.

The other point is that while you may have some reservations about your ability to drive on the wrong side of the road in a foreign country, it really is not a problem in America. The reality is that driving in America is both easier than driving in Britain and a great deal more fun, too. The whole system of getting on and off freeways and turning left and right is so much easier when driving on the right-hand side of the road.

In this chapter

Car rental

Now you must decide what type of car to hire and who to hire it from. Most of the tour operators have special deals going with Alamo, though one or two use Avis, Budget or Dollar. The prices have become pretty standardised since 2000, but the best deal can be found through the tour operator Just America (see page 249), which offers many extras included in the price – and at a lower rate than any other operator.

The Strip, looking north

Costs

Many of the tour operators give the price of hiring the car separately from what it will actually cost you to walk away from the rental desk with your car keys, though others do now show all-inclusive prices. This makes sense as there are charges you must pay in addition to the car hire fees: extended protection, collision damage waiver (CDW), airport user fee, state local surcharges and taxes, under-age driver fees and child seat (if you need one). In any case, when checking the price of hiring a car, make sure you look at the right area and right dates, as prices vary from place to place. Florida and California are cheaper than Western USA prices, which makes a big difference. Some rental companies consider Arizona and Nevada to be part of a region including California, while others consider them separate, and thus a higher rate.

BRITTIP

Pre-renting can help you avoid hard-sell tactics by car hire staff wanting you to take out personal insurance. If you have extended protection and travel insurance (see Chapter 16) you'll be well covered.

Additional driver fees: This is rarely required by most car hire chains, but when it is, it reaches $7 per driver per day.
Airport user fee: This will cost you up to 14% of the total charge.
Cash deposit: Very few places will even accept a cash deposit, much preferring a credit card to act as deposit. For places that do take cash deposits, be ready for delays as the counterperson has to go

The pool at the MGM Grand

through rarely used forms. The deposit tends to be around $100 per week. In addition, you will often be asked to provide an additional credit card in the driver's name to cover any incidentals such as the deposit or under-age driver charges. If you want to leave a cash deposit, you'll be asked to show two forms of identification, for instance passport, driving licence or other government-issued photo card.
Child seat and deposit: Children up to the age of five must, by law, travel in a child seat in America, and you should book these in advance. The cost will be $5–8 per day plus $50 deposit (on a credit card).

Alamo car park, Las Vegas International airport

Grand Canal shops

Collision damage waiver (CDW): At $20.99 per day, this covers you for $10,000–50,000 worth of damage to your hire car regardless of the cause, plus theft or loss.
Environmental tax: A further $2 per day if car rental is arranged in the UK.
Extended protection: Many Americans do not have any or enough insurance and if they caused the accident, you would have no one to sue for damage to your property or for personal injury (the car is covered by CDW, see above). This type of insurance covers all liabilities and costs about $8–14 per day.
One-way drop-off fees: Most companies charge if you want to pick up your car in one location and drop it off in another, which can easily add $100–300 on to your rental costs. The exceptions tend to be if you pick up and drop off in the same city, though always check.
Rental surcharges: During peak periods, you will be charged around a further £23 per week or £5 per day for your car rental. The peak seasons tend to be from 15 July to 31 August and from 20 to 27 December.
State/local surcharges and taxes: 5–15% of the total cost depending on exact location of rental.
Under-age driver fees: All the UK deals are for drivers with a minimum age of 25 and drivers under 25 will have to pay a further $20 per day.
Comprehensive Alamo rentals: The all-inclusive packages and comprehensive insurance cover schemes you take out in advance in the UK tend to cost £23–46 a day in Las Vegas/Nevada. They include extended protection, CDW, airport user fee and state/local surcharges and taxes, and generally work out cheaper than paying for all the above on arrival (and saves a lot of time when you go to collect your car).

Documents and systems

Documents: You will need a UK driving licence or a driving licence from your country of residence. An international driving licence is not acceptable.
Limits: You will not be allowed to drive your hire car in Mexico or off-road in America. Many Las Vegas car hire providers will further restrict your driving to Nevada, Arizona and California only.
Hiring cars locally: You may only wish to hire a car for a few days while you are on holiday, and this can easily be arranged when you arrive. You'll find phone numbers for all the major car-hire firms in a local phone directory, but remember that the prices they quote you will not include all the extras outlined above, so be sure to include those when you do your calculations. (For names and contact numbers of car-hire companies see page 17.)
Pre-rental: Some tour operators are now offering you the chance to fill out all the necessary paperwork before you leave home so when you arrive you can just pick up your car keys and go. Not only does this save you time, but it also means you can bypass efforts by the counter staff at American car-hire firms to give you the upgrade hard sell! In any case, you will generally get a better deal for bigger cars if you arrange this in advance. The possible exception is in Las Vegas where they practically give away upgrades on a quiet week. But be warned, if you arrive in Las Vegas when the city is packed, it may be difficult to find a car of your choice.

Native American dancer

Choosing the right car

Sorry, but size *is* an issue! Where your flight includes car rental, it will normally be for a small, economy-size car, which probably won't be much good for a tour even if there are only two of you. The biggest problem is the boot size – the boots of all American cars are much smaller than their European equivalents and you do have to take into account that you will need to accommodate your luggage.

This is what the different price brands will provide:

- **Economy:** Usually a Chevrolet Aveo or similar, equivalent to the UK's Vauxhall Corsa. Considered big enough for two adults.
- **Compact:** Usually a Chevrolet Cavalier or similar, equivalent to a UK Vauxhall Astra. Considered big enough for three adults.
- **Intermediate:** Usually an Oldsmobile Alero, equivalent to the UK's Vauxhall Vectra. Considered big enough for four adults.
- **Full size:** Usually a Chevrolet Impala or similar, equivalent to the UK's Vauxhall Omega. Again, large enough for four adults.
- **Convertible:** Usually a Chrysler Sebring or similar, equivalent to the UK's Vauxhall Astra Convertible. Large enough for three adults.
- **Luxury van:** Usually a Chevrolet Venture or similar, equivalent to the UK's VW Sharan. Large enough for seven people.
- **4-wheel drive:** Usually a Chevy Blazer or similar, no UK equivalent. Large enough for five people.

You might want to choose something unusual

Automatics: All American hire cars will be automatics, unless you specifically get a high-performance car like a Maseratti at a speciality care hire. Some things may confuse you at first if you are not familiar with automatics, for example you won't be able to drive until you put the car into D for drive and you probably won't be able to take the keys out of the ignition until you have put the car into P for park. D1 and D2 are extra gears, which you only need to use when going up or down very steep hills.

BRITTIP

Most accidents that Brits are involved in tend to take place on left turns, so take extra care here. Remember, too, there is no amber light from red to green, but there is one from green to red.

Traffic calming in Death Valley

Accidents and emergencies

If you have even a minor accident, the police must be contacted before the cars can be moved. The car-hire firm will also expect a full police report for the insurance paperwork. In the case of a breakdown, there should be an emergency number for the hire company among the paperwork they gave you. Always have your driving licence with you (remember an international driving licence is not valid) and your car-hire agreement forms in case you are stopped by the police at any time. If you are pulled over, keep your hands on the wheel and always be polite. If they find out you're British you could just get away with a ticking off for a minor offence (but not for speeding at 95mph/153kph!).

Most American cars have cruise control, which lets you set the speed at which you want to travel and then take your foot off the gas pedal (the accelerator). There are usually two buttons, either on the face of the steering wheel or on the switch that controls the car lights, for cruise control, one to switch it on and the other to set your speed. You take off cruise control by pressing the on button again or by simply accelerating or braking.

BRITTIP

During the summer in the desert, don't immediately enter your car. The temperature can be as high as 82°C/180°F. First open it and let the hot air escape. Better yet, reach in to turn on the motor and the fan or air conditioner (easy enough to do in an automatic, no clutch to bother with and no need to be seated). Let the hot air blow out of the car before seating.

Air conditioning: In the California/Nevada/Arizona area it would be rare for a car not to have air conditioning but you must keep the windows closed to make it work.

BRITTIP

The temperature inside a car exposed to the fierce, desert sun of summer Las Vegas can reach 82°C/180°F! Never leave any children, pets or anything that can possibly melt inside a car for any length of time. And never touch metal with a bare hand!

Fuel/gas: You've hit the highway and need to fill up, but just bear in mind that for the most part interstates (the main roads) do not have gas stations – you will have to get off, though they are not usually too far away. Practically all gas stations are self service.

On the road

Rules and regulations

Here are a few things you should know.

Alcohol limits: The legal limit for blood alcohol in America is lower than in Britain and the police are very hot on drink-drivers (drunk-drivers in American parlance). Generally a single drink can put you at or over the limit if you are a smaller person! It is also illegal to carry open containers of alcohol in the car itself.

Parking: It is illegal to park within 10ft/3m of a fire hydrant or a lowered kerb and you should never stop in front of a yellow-painted kerb – they are for emergency vehicles and you will get towed away! Never park on a kerb either.

Seat belts: These are compulsory for all passengers. Babies and small children are required to be secured in child safety seats (available through most car-hire agencies).

Speed: No speeding, please! The speed limits on the main Interstates are well signposted and tend to be 55–70mph/88–112kph – 75mph/120kph on some lonely stretches in Nevada and Arizona – while the MINIMUM allowed is 40mph/64kph.

Bighorn sheep

Be warned, the Americans take their speed limits very seriously. Most traffic police won't bother you if you are only 5–8mph8–12kph over the posted limit, but 10mph/16kph or more and you are in danger of a fairly pricey fine. Go 20mph/32kph or more over the limit and you risk astronomical fines ($300 or more), 30mph/48kph and you might possibly enjoy a short term in gaol.

School zone: Flashing orange lights suspended over the road indicate a school zone ahead, so go slowly.

School buses: These cannot be overtaken in either direction while they are unloading and have their hazard lights flashing.

Signposts and junctions: One of the most confusing aspects of driving around towns in America is the way they hang up road names underneath the traffic lights at every junction. The road name given is not for the road you are actually on, but the one you are crossing. Another thing to be wary of is that there is very little advance notice of junctions, and road names can be hard to read as you approach them, especially at night. So keep your speed down if you think you are close to your turn-off so you can get into the right lane. If you do miss your turning, don't panic, as nearly all roads in American towns are arranged in a simple grid system so it will be relatively easy to work your way back.

Sometimes you will meet a crossroads where there is no obvious right of way. This is a 'four-way stop' and the way it works is that priority goes in order of arrival. When it is your turn, pull out slowly. If two come together at the same time, the one on the farthest 'right' has priority. If two cars stop facing each other, the one going straight has priority over any car turning.

At red lights, it is possible to turn right providing there is no traffic coming from the left and no pedestrian is crossing, unless specified by a sign saying 'No turn on red'. A green arrow gives you the right of way when turning left, but when it is a solid green light, you must give way to traffic coming from the other direction.

U-turns: These are forbidden in built-up areas and where a solid line runs down the middle of the road.

Las Vegas Convention Center

15 THE GRAND CANYON AND SURROUNDINGS

Must-see sights within easy reach of Sin City

Arizona and the Canyonlands

In California it's quite often the people and urban developments that make the state a truly remarkable experience. In Arizona it is the history and natural wonders that make it one of the most beautiful and thrilling of all of America's 50 states. This is the land of cowboys and Native Americans, of gold-mining and ghost towns, of movie-making and centuries-old history and of one of the seven great natural wonders of the world: the Grand Canyon.

Without a shadow of a doubt it has some of the most spectacular landscapes ever crowded into such a compact area. On top of the Grand Canyon, there is the Petrified Forest, Walnut Canyon, Sunset Crater and Montezuma's Castle.

Arizona is a massive state, encompassing the cities of Phoenix (its capital) and Tucson. Travelling to these destinations would require a big investment in time. Getting to the Grand Canyon and the Canyonlands, however, is feasible within a matter of hours from Las Vegas.

Going native

Arizona has the largest Native American population and more land devoted to reservations than any other state. In addition, the prehistoric Native American tribes, such as the Hohokam of southern Arizona, the Sinagua of the central, and the cliff-dwelling Anasazi (ancient ones) of northern Arizona provide some extremely old historical ruins (rare in America). These are a monument to their high degree of sophistication in dry farming, water management, plus their far-flung trade routes and jewellery, pottery and textile-making.

In this chapter

And let us not forget, of course, that Arizona was the birthplace of possibly the best known Native American of them all, Geronimo. The Apache warrior engaged nearly three-quarters of America's military ground troops in his pursuit after the Civil War and up to 1886 when he surrendered – having never been captured – at Skeleton Canyon in Southern Arizona!

Native American artefacts

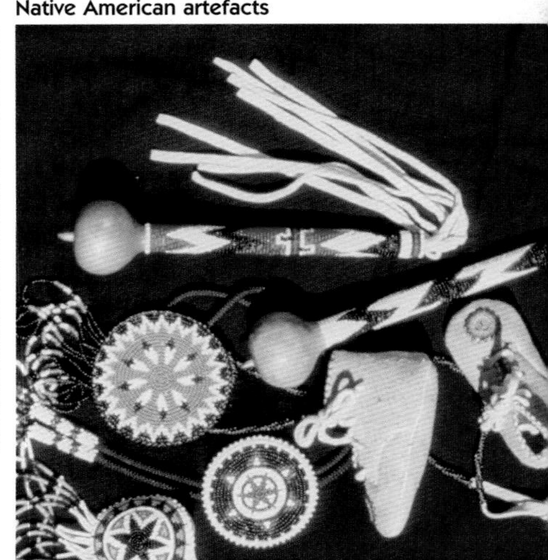

Ranching

Peeples Valley and Yarnell: On the cowboy front, even today mining and ranching are the most important industries of the small communities of Peeples Valley and Yarnell on Route 89 north of Wickenburg. The lush grasslands are home to a thriving cattle industry that has cowboys still riding the plains. The whole area down to Wickenburg is known as the Dude Ranch Capital of the World because of all the ranches that allow you to visit and participate in the activities.

Prescott: The old capital of Arizona, surrounded by Prescott National Forest, the pine-covered Bradshaw Mountains and the Yavapai Indian Reservation, is known for its boulder-strewn granite dells and grasslands. Stately Victorian homes are a reminder of its heyday years, while the rowdier side of frontier life is remembered on Whiskey Row, where 26 saloons once attracted cowboys from far and wide. The annual Frontier Days celebration is held here at the beginning of July, complete with fireworks, dancing, rodeo performances, a parade and cowboy golf tournament.

The cowboy life

The Ruby Mountains near Elko

Jerome: Further north on State Route 89A is Jerome, which sprang up during the gold-mining boom on Cleopatra Hill overlooking the Verde Valley. Once the ore diminished, it became known as America's largest ghost city and is now home to a colony of artists and visitors who walk the steep, winding streets to see the historic buildings and browse through shops and boutiques.

The best historic sites are the town's 'travelling jail', which has slid downhill 225ft/69m since a dynamite explosion dislodged it from its foundations during the 1920s, and Jerome State Historic Park, once the mansion of mining developer 'Rawhide' Jimmy Douglas.

Campe Verde: This is to the south-east (along Route 260), established in 1864 as a cavalry outpost to protect Verde River settlers from Indian raids. The old fort still stands in the middle of the town.

Montezuma Castle National Monument: Just north, along Interstate 17, are these well-preserved cliff dwellings, a five-storey, 20-room dwelling built in and under a cliff overlooking Beaver Creek. It was misnamed by early settlers who thought it had been inhabited by Aztecs, but it was actually built by Sinagua Indians in the 12th and 13th centuries.

Clarkdale: Further north is Clarkdale, where you can see the 100-room pueblo that housed 250 people from the 13th century until they mysteriously disappeared some time in the 15th century. Clarkdale is home to the scenic Verde Canyon Railroad, a renovated New York Metro Line train that transports passengers along a 40ml/64km

The river threads across the canyon floor

route through cottonwood forests and the base of a desert mesa (table). En route you'll see bald eagles, great blue herons, deer and javelina.
Flagstaff: This is just a little further north and considered to be the gateway to the Grand Canyon.

The Grand Canyon

Grand Canyon National Park, PO Box 129, Grand Canyon, AZ 86023, 928-638 7888, nps.gov/grca
Open: The park is open 24 hours a day. Visitor Center in Canyon View Information Plaza open 8am–5pm.
Admission: $25 per vehicle, $12 per person arriving by other means. Admission is for seven days but does not cover fees for use of overnight campsites, which are extra. Under-15s free. Free planning guides are available in advance from the National Park Service. Write in for a Trip Planner, Backcountry Trip Planner or Accessibility Guide.

BRITTIP
To avoid the crowds (five million people visit each year) and searing heat, go in March, April, September or October either before 10am or after 2pm.

Two billion years in the making, the majestic spectacle stands from between 4,500ft/1,370m to 5,700ft/1,740m high for an amazing 277mls/446km with an average width of 10mls/16km. To geologists, it is like an open book, as they can immediately see that the bottom layer is two billion years old while the top is a mere 200 million years old, with the geological ages in between represented in its colourful stony strata.

Viewing it from one of the many vantage points on the South Rim, you will see the myriad rock formations change colour according to the sun's position throughout the day. The best times to see it (and the quietest) are at sunrise or sunset. You can also walk out over the Canyon on the Skywalk – a glass bridge suspended over the West Rim. But in some ways you can only get a feel for its awesome, breathtaking hugeness by descending into its depths by mule. If you don't have the one or two days to spare needed for the trip, you can stop at the new IMAX theatre at Tusayan and watch the *Grand Canyon – The Hidden Secrets* film.

Seeing the Grand Canyon

More than five million people a year flock to the South Rim to view the Grand Canyon. Closer to the Colorado River than the North Rim, it also provides better views of the canyon.

You can either drive straight to the Grand Canyon Village or head for the Canyon View Information Plaza and the Visitors Center and bookstore, where you can pick up a copy of the park's newspaper for up-to-the-minute information on facilities, activities and transportation options, and a map.

From here you can walk to Mather Point, which gives wonderful views of the Canyon, before making use of the free shuttle service to the Grand Canyon Village for further views.
The film: The IMAX theatre, 928 638 2468, at the south entrance in Tusayan has shows at half past the hour 1 Mar–31 Oct 8.30am–8.30pm, 1 Nov–28 Feb 10.30am–6.30pm, daily, on a 70ft/21m screen with six-track stereo sound. Adults $12, 6–12 $8, under-6s free.

Sunset over the Canyon

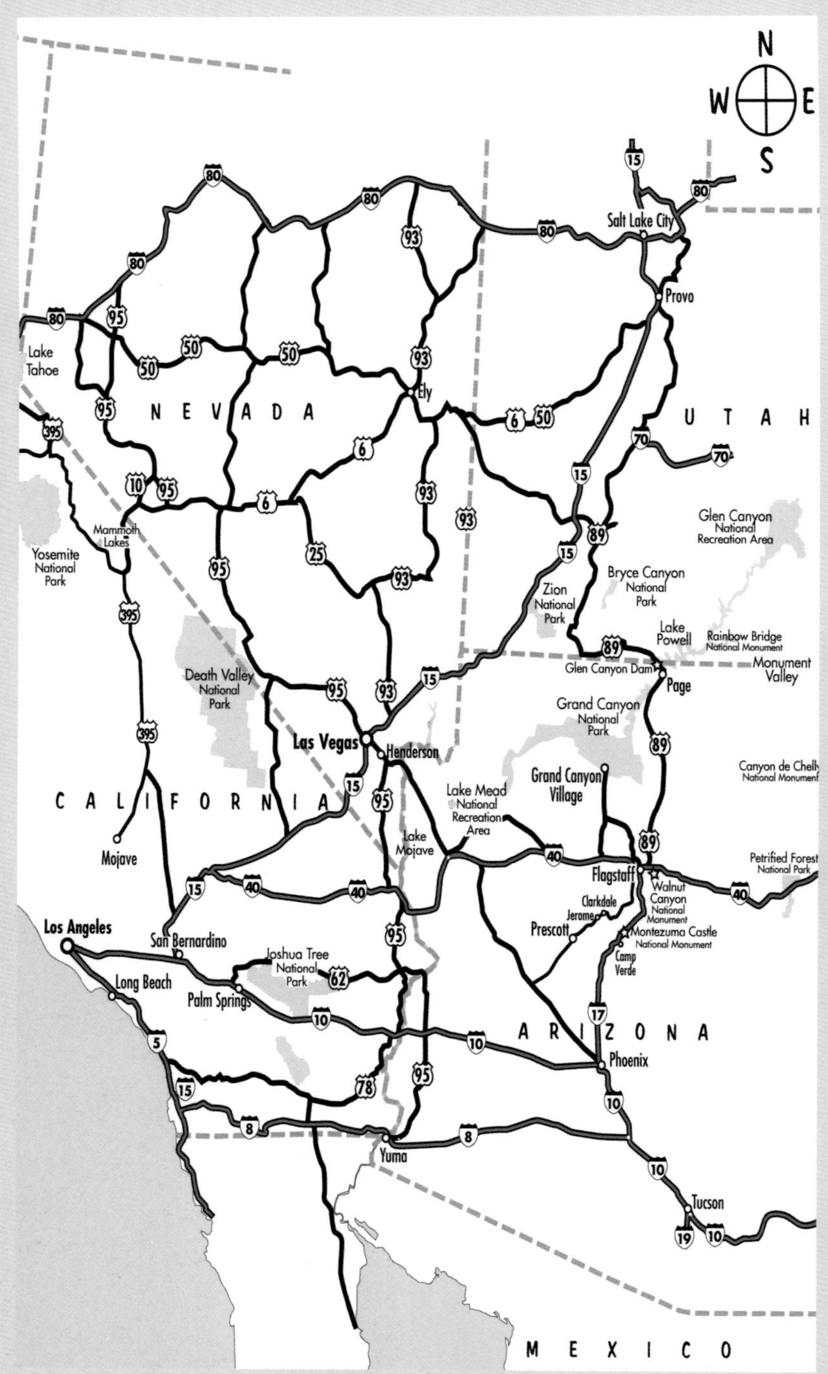
N
W
E
S
NEVADA
UTAH
CALIFORNIA
ARIZONA
MEXICO
Salt Lake City
Provo
Lake Tahoe
Ely
Mammoth Lakes
Yosemite National Park
Death Valley National Park
Las Vegas
Henderson
Glen Canyon National Recreation Area
Bryce Canyon National Park
Zion National Park
Lake Powell
Rainbow Bridge National Monument
Glen Canyon Dam
Page
Monument Valley
Grand Canyon National Park
Grand Canyon Village
Canyon de Chelly National Monument
Lake Mead National Recreation Area
Lake Mojave
Mojave
Flagstaff
Walnut Canyon National Monument
Petrified Forest National Park
Clarkdale
Jerome
Prescott
Montezuma Castle National Monument
Camp Verde
Los Angeles
San Bernardino
Joshua Tree National Park
Long Beach
Palm Springs
Phoenix
Yuma
Tucson

Helicopter view

By train: The Grand Canyon Railway, 1 800 843 8724, runs a 1920s Harriman coach steam train from Williams to the South Rim, travelling through 65mls/105km of beautiful countryside.

By bus: Guided tours to the South Rim from Flagstaff are run by Nava-Hopi Bus Lines. Call 928 774 5003 for times and prices.

Staying on the floor of the Canyon: Phantom Ranch offers 10-bunk dorms with toilet and shower, plus private cabins. For reservations, contact AMFAC Parks and Resorts, 14001 East Iliff Avenue, Ste 600, Aurora, CO 80014 or call 303 297 2757.

Horseback rides: With the Apache Stables in Tusayan, adjacent to the park. Write to PO Box 158, Grand Canyon, AZ 86023, apachestables.com or call 928 638 2891.

Rafting the Colorado: Trips include half-day floating excursions, motor boat trips and 18-day expeditions on rowing boats. You need to book at least six months in advance and companies include:

- **Arizona Raft Adventures:** 4050 East Huntington Drive, Flagstaff, AZ 86004, 1 800 786 7238, azraftcom.
- **Arizona River Runners:** PO Box 47788, Phoenix, AZ 85068, 1 800 477 7238, arizona riverrunners.com.
- **Canyon Explorations Inc.:** PO Box 310, Flagstaff, AZ 86002, 928 774 4559.
- **Canyoneers Inc.:** PO Box 2997, Flagstaff, AZ 86003, 1-800 525 0924, canyoneers.com).
- **Diamond River Adventures:** PO Box 1300, Page, AZ 86040 (928 645 8866, diamondriver.com).
- **Hualapai Tribal River Runners:** 887 Route 66, Peach Springs, AZ 86434, 928 769 2419, grandcanyonresort.com.
- **Outdoors Unlimited:** 6900 Townsen Winona Road, Flagstaff, AZ 86004, 928 526 4511, outdoorsunlimited.com.
- **Wilderness River Adventures:** PO Box 717, Page, AZ 86040, 928 645 3296, riveradventures.com.

Flightseeing: Flights by small aircraft or helicopter. Companies include:

- **Air Grand Canyon:** 6000 Janine Drive, Prescott, Arizona, 928 638 2686.
- **AirStar Helicopters:** PO Box 3379, Grand Canyon, AZ 86023, 702 262 6199, airstar.com.
- **Kenai Helicopters:** PO Box 1429, Grand Canyon, AZ 86023, 928 638 2764.
- **Papillon Grand Canyon Helicopters:** PO Box 455, Grand Canyon, AZ 86023, 928 638 2419.

Skywalk over the Canyon rim

Lodging: For full and up-to-date details of lodges near the rim, write to AMFAC Parks and Resorts (see page 234).

North Rim

Through Jacob Lake on Highway 67, this is a lot quieter than the South Rim and home to Canyon Trail Rides (435 679 8665, canyonrides.com), which runs one-hour forest rides, half-day trips into the Canyon and full-day trips to Roaring Springs where you can frolic in the natural pools. Here you can stay at the Grand Canyon Lodge from late May to mid October. For reservations, write to AMFAC Parks and Resorts (see page 265). The Kaibab Lodge, five miles north of the park, is also open from mid-May to early November. For reservations 928 638 2389, kaibablodge.com.

Howdy pardner!

Arizona is real cowboy country and if there is one way to see the stunning scenery, wide-open expanses and narrow gorges, it is on the back of a horse – as a cowboy. Nowadays, it is very easy to be a real 'city slicker' as a whole host of ranching options are available, depending on your riding abilities and needs for luxury items, such as a bed. The types of ranches are:

Guest ranch: This is where you live as a 'guest' of the ranch owners in an environment that is designed to entertain you while providing plenty of horse riding opportunities and Western activities. It's the soft option that will give you a feel for the way of life but no hands-on experience.

The north rim

Dude ranch: Vacation-based rather than the seriously business-like working ranches, you'll do a lot of riding, while Western activities from Wild West shows to rodeo visits, square dances, barbecues and sports provide plenty of fun.

Resort ranch: These offer the Western experience but also have golf, tennis and ballooning, and the whole environment is much more luxurious than dude or working ranches.

Working ranch: Still in business to raise livestock and grow crops, these are home to the real cowboys. Depending on the time of year and the work that is necessary on the ranch, you'll be able to learn to drive cattle, brand and rope steers, eat

A helicopter view over the Grand Canyon

Spring Ranch near Las Vegas

around a camp fire and sleep under the stars. Round-ups take place in spring and autumn when the ranchers prepare their cattle to be moved to summer and winter ranges. It's a high-activity time at the ranches so the hours are long and the work is physically demanding. On the cattle drives you are likely to travel 6–12mls/9–19km a day, but ride at least three times as far as you bring in strays from the flanks. Evenings spent around the campfire hark back to bygone days in what is a truly wonderful, friendship-forming experience. Horse drives are a much faster version as the horses like to travel at speed. Only for very seasoned riders with lots of cross-country experience, but the long-distance gallops are a real thrill.

- **American Round-Up:** 0870 747 2624. Offers the full range.
- **Ranch America:** 01923 671831. Also offers a range of holidays.
- **Equitour:** 01865 511642. Part of Peregrine Holidays Ltd, these are excellent for working ranches all over America's West and even provide riding clinics to bring you up to speed!

Trail rides with Outlaw Trails: 01892 515612, outlawtrails.com. For horse-riding vacations with a difference try Outlaw Trails, which runs specially tailored, fully researched trips to the old trails used by outlaws determined to avoid the long arm of the law. Closest to Arizona is the Robbers Roost trail in Utah in which you'll see the way stations and trail used by the Wild Bunch of Butch Cassidy and the Sundance Kid, the Hole in the Wall Gang and Robbers Roost Gang. Robbers Roost land is sprawled across 320sq mls/830sq km of high desert and you'll ride through pinion, sage and cedar flats, a maze of rock gorges and canyons, plus long mesas, arches, pinnacles and high-shouldered buttes. If you attempt any of the 'climbs' used by the outlaws, you'll get a pretty good idea of what brilliant horsemen they were! The seasons and numbers are limited because of the weather and nature of the trips, but the trails are perfect for lovers of the historical West who want a great big chunk of adventure.

Joshua tree, southern Nevada

Watch the birdies!

You've seen them in cartoons, now you can see the birds of the Arizona deserts and mountains in real life. The south-eastern corner of the state is the most popular bird-watching area of North America and more than 400 species can be found here from migratory water fowl to native birds, nesting birds, grassland birds and mountain birds.

You can watch greater roadrunners chase lizards across the desert floors, black-chinned hummingbirds buzz around like bees, acorn woodpeckers drill holes in roadside telegraph poles and painted redstarts flit in the dappled light of oak woods with **Ornitholidays** (01794 519445). The company organises a three-week trip at the end of April/beginning of May when the desert is comfortably cool and many birds are nesting while others are starting to migrate to their breeding grounds in the north. All this along with spectacular views of the Grand Canyon.

Another favoured time of the year is in August when the city of Sierra Vista has a birding festival complete with bat stalks and owl prowls.

Other Arizona marvels

Once you've been there, done that at the Grand Canyon, don't miss out on many other natural and historical wonders Arizona has to offer.

Sunset Crater: 928 526 0502, nps.gov/sucr. Leave the South Rim on Highway 64 and take the 89 south to Sunset Crater Volcano National Monument. An active volcano more than 900 years ago, it now rises to 1,000ft/305m and rangers here offer geology, seismology and other tours while the Visitors Center can provide you with maps for self-guided trails.

Walnut Canyon: 928 526 3367, nps.gov/waca. Further south, join the Interstate 40 going east and take in Walnut Canyon National Monument for an awe-inspiring view of how Sinagua Indians lived in homes built out of the limestone cliffs. The Visitors Center Museum displays artefacts that make it possible to imagine how they existed.

Meteor Crater: 1 800 289 5898. Nearby, this dates back 22,000 years when an enormous meteor travelling at 33,000mph/53,100kph plunged to Earth. Because of its resemblance to the lunar landscape, the 570ft/174m deep crater was used as a training site for Apollo astronauts and the museum displays a 1,406lb/638kg meteorite, the largest found in the area.

Sunset Crater

Petrified Forest: 928-524 6228, nps.gov/pefo. Further east is the Petrified Forest National Park and Painted Desert Visitors' Center and Museum. There are more fossilised trees to be found here than anywhere else in the world with million-year-old agate logs lying in profusion on the ground.

Canyon de Chelly: 928 ,674 5500, nps.gov/cach. Further north on Route 191, you can view the Indian cliff-dwelling ruins at Canyon de Chelly National Monument. At the base of sheer red cliffs and in canyon walls, the ruins date back to the 12th century and you can get to them on scenic rim drives, four-wheel-drive vehicles, horseback or on foot. Phone the visitors centre for details. Rich with history, the Anasazi Indians lived here until 1300 and the Navajo arrived in 1700, using it as a base to raid nearby Indian and Spanish settlements.

Monument Valley: 928 871 6647, navajonationparks.org/monumentvalley.htm. Take Highways 59 and 163 to see one of the best-used locations for filming Westerns such as John Wayne's *Stagecoach*. To the left of this area is the Navajo Nation, the largest of all the Indian reservations – extending across 25,000sq mls/64,750sq km, it is bigger than the state of West Virginia – which is home to just 175,000 Native Americans, who welcome visitors for sightseeing and shopping – buy silver and turquoise jewellery, exquisitely woven rugs, intricate kachinas and other crafts.

The land encompasses mile upon mile of desert and forest land, interrupted only by spectacular mesas, buttes and rock

Lake Powell

formations. The Navajos provide hiking, horseback or four-wheel-drive tours through some of the most popular sites such as Canyon de Chelly and Monument Valley.

BRITTIP

Did you know that more people have died of drowning in the desert than of thirst? It's all due to flash floods, and the reason why they've got such a high mortality rate is that they are so violent and so quick you literally have no time at all to react.

Lake Powell: From this area, take Route 98 up to the shores of Lake Powell, a 25m acre/10m ha lake with more shoreline – 1,960mls/3,154km – than California, which was formed by the completion of the Glen Canyon Dam in 1963. Today it's a home for houseboats and pleasure craft that explore the 96 canyons discovered and mapped by intrepid, one-armed explorer John Wesley Powell in the 19th century.

Rainbow Bridge Natural Monument: 1 866 875 8456, nps.gov/rabr. A natural stone arch carved by the relentless forces of wind and water, only became easily accessible after the lake came into being. It is an amazing 290ft/88m high and 275ft/83m wide. Now boat rentals, tours and accommodation are all available at the Wahweap Lodge and Marina on the lake's southern-most shore. Phone for reservations.

Glen Canyon Dam: 928 608 6404, nps.gov/glca. Offers self-guided tours and day-long and half-day float trips along the Colorado river from the base of the dam, from March to October. Phone for details. The town of Page, founded as a construction camp for crews building the dam, has plenty of restaurants and accommodation.

Cochise County: This southeast corner of Arizona is an 1800s Old West museum all by itself. This area is just a one or two-hour drive from Tucson and includes such historical areas as Texas Canyon and Skeleton Canyon, where Geronimo waged war against the American Army with no more than 42 men. There is the old mining town of Tombstone, infamous for the gun battle between the Earps and the Clantons in the OK Corral. Finally, in Fort Huachuca lies the old museum and remains of Camp Huachuca, home to the famous Buffalo Soldiers, two regiments of freed African Americaln slaves who battled Puma and Apache native tribes for decades.

Glen Canyon Dam

Utah and the Wild West

Often overlooked thanks to the fame of the neighbouring Grand Canyon and Arizona, the south-western corner of Utah is home to an area known as the Grand Circle. Stunning national parks include Zion National Park, Kolob Canyons and Bryce Canyon. The Grand Circle also takes in Lake Powell and the Glen Canyon National Recreation Area, which straddles Utah and Arizona, and Nevada's Lake Mead National Recreational Area (see page 215).

The beauty of Utah's natural wonders is matched by its sense of wilderness. Despite an increase in visitors, it is still an untamed environment with often only primitive facilities available, while the rich cowboy and outlaw history touches many sights and locations throughout the region.

Zion National Park

Within remarkably easy striking distance of Las Vegas, it takes just two hours to drive to the south-western end of the Grand Circle along Interstate 15 in the direction of St George. The entrance is on the south side just beyond the town of Springdale, where you will find the visitor centre and two camping sites.

BRITTIP

Within Zion National Park is the Kolob Canyons area, which has its own Visitor Center.

Visitor Centre: 435 772 3256, zion.national-park.com. Open year-round 8am–5pm except Christmas Day, and provides everything from books, to information, maps, an introductory video and backcountry permits and even has a small museum. 7-day pass $25 per car or $12 per person.

Zion Canyon

Zion National Park

The natural rock sculptures and vividly coloured cliffs that tower above the floor of Zion Canyon pull in nearly 2.5 million visitors a year, making it one of the most popular sights in the region. To the Mormon pioneers who discovered it after the Paiute Indians had left, the beautiful rock structures so resembled natural temples they called it Little Zion. An early Methodist minister was so awe-struck that he gave many of the towers and cliffs that rise up 3,000ft/914m into the sky biblical names such as Three Patriarchs, Angels Landing and the Great White Throne.

Seeing the sights

Zion Canyon Scenic Drive: One of the easiest ways to appreciate its beauty is to take this 7ml/11km trek along the canyon floor – a narrow, deep gorge that is the centrepiece of the park, surrounded by wondrous monoliths that stand between 2,000ft/610m)and 3,000ft/914m high. Along the bottom of the canyon flows the Virgin River. It may look small, yet it has the power of the once-mighty Colorado and is almost single-handedly responsible for carving the gorge – admittedly over a 13 million-year period!

The Zion-Mount Carmel Highway: A 13ml/21km drive up steep switchbacks and through tunnels to Checkerboard Mesa. The road was considered an engineering marvel when it was completed in 1930 and cuts a swathe through rough up-and-down terrain to connect lower Zion Canyon with the high plateaux to the east.

Two narrow tunnels, including one over 1ml/1.6km long, were blasted through the

View across Zion Canyon

cliffs to complete the job. As you travel from one side of the tunnel to the other, the landscape changes dramatically. On one side are the massive cliff walls of Zion Canyon, on the other is an area known as Slickrock Country. Here rocks coloured in white and pastels of orange and red have been eroded into hundreds of fantastic shapes and etched through time with odd patterns of cracks and grooves. It is followed by the mountains of sandstone known as Checkerboard Mesa – one of the best examples of naturally sculptured rock art.

Seasons in the sun

Each season provides a spectacular array of colours in Zion. Spring sees the waterfalls cascading into the Virgin River. Summer – easily the busiest time of year – is the time to enjoy the striking sight of the deep red cliffs peeking out above the lush green foliage. Come autumn those leaves turn brilliant red and gold, while in winter a layer of snow adds a pristine cleanliness to the rugged landscape.

BRITTIP

The best times to visit Zion National Park are May and September, when the weather is at its finest and the crowds are at their smallest.

Things to do

You can cycle, take a tram ride or go on a horse ride through the park, yet most people agree that the best way to experience the full majesty is to hike.
Guided walks: These are offered along fairly easy trails – some of which are accessible by wheelchair. True adventurers, though, will want to do the 16ml/26km hike through The Narrows, which involves wading through the Virgin river. Be aware, though, that advance preparation and a permit are necessary to do this.

Guided horse rides are available from the end of March to early November. Call 435 648 2555 or 435 648 2700 for information.

BRITTIP

It is not advisable to drink untreated water from streams or springs. Water can be bought at the visitor centre, campgrounds, Zion Lodge, Grotto Picnic Area and the Temple of Sinawa.

Bicycles: These are only permitted on established roads and the Pa'rus Trail, which leads from the campgrounds to the Scenic Drive junction.
Camping: This is allowed only in the campgrounds or in designated back country sites with a permit.
Climbing: Information is available at the visitor centre. But many of Zion's cliffs are sandstone with much loose or 'rotten' rock and climbing tools and techniques used for granite are often less effective here.

Mountain biking in Austin

Kolob Canyons

In the north-western reaches of Zion National Park, just off Interstate 15 at Exit 40 about 45mls/72km from the entrance to Zion. Visitor Center: 435 586 9548.

Kolob Canyons Road is one of two scenic routes, which provides stunning views of the spectacular finger canyons, carved out by springs along the edge of Kolob Terrace. It will take you 5mls/8km into the red rock, running perpendicular to the walled Finger Canyons and providing a high viewpoint at the end.

The Kolob Terrace Road overlooks the white and salmon-coloured cliffs at the left and right forks of North Creek. Both routes climb into forests of pinyon and juniper, ponderosa pine and fir, while aspen trees are found at Lava Point. In early spring the Kolob is still buried under thick snow, and in summer there is still a feel of mountain coolness to the air.

Lodging in Zion National Park

Zion Lodge, 303-297 2757, zionlodge.com Open year-round and provides a choice of motel rooms, cabins and suites. It is the only lodge in the park and the only restaurant. There is also a gift shop and post office.

Lodging in Springdale: The Zion Park City

Bumbleberry Inn: 97 Bumbleberry Lane, 435 772 3224, bumbleberry.com. Large, spacious rooms with private balconies or patios overlooking wonderful scenery in a quiet, off-road location. Facilities include a heated pool, indoor Jacuzzi, indoor racquetball, games room, restaurant and gift shop.

Canyon Ranch Motel: 668 Zion Park Boulevard, 435 772 3357, canyonranchmotel.com. New and remodelled cottages, some with kitchens, around a quiet, shady lawn with panoramic views of Zion. Amenities include new pool and Jacuzzi.

Cliffrose Lodge & Gardens: 281 Zion Park Boulevard, 1-800 243 8824, cliffroselodge.com. At the entrance to Zion National Park along the Virgin River. All rooms have excellent views, while there is also a large pool and 5acres/2ha of lawns, trees and flower gardens.

El Rio Lodge: 995 Zion Park Boulevard, 435 772 3205, elriolodge.com. Clean, quiet and friendly 10-roomed lodge with a green shady lawn, sundeck and fantastic views of Zion Park.

Lodging in Rockwell

Hummingbird Inn B&B: 37 West Main, Rockville, 435 772 3632, on Highway 9, just outside Zion National Park. All four guest rooms have private baths and a large country breakfast is included. The inn has a Jacuzzi plus an upstairs deck and a library/games room loft. Outside activities include croquet, horseshoes and badminton.

Lodging in Hurricane

Half-way between Zion National Park and St George. Visitor info 435 635 3402.

Pah Tempe Hot Springs: 825 North 800 East, 35-4 Hurricane, 435 635 2879. A tiny retreat where no smoking or alcohol is allowed, but where massage and therapy programmes are available, plus a relaxing hot mineral pool along the Virgin river.

Kolob Canyon

View across Bryce Canyon

Park Villa Motel 6: 650 West State Street, 435 635 4010. Luxury units with fridge and microwave, just 1ml/1.6km from mineral hot springs. Facilities include heated pool and spa, laundry, kitchen and cable TV.

Bryce Canyon

1 888 467 2757, nps.gov/brca and nationalparks.org
72mls (116km) from Zion National Park. Follow Highway 89 towards Hatch, then turn into Highway 12 to Bryce village and the Visitor Center is just inside the entrance on Highway 63.
Visitor centre: 435 834 5322. Open 8am–8pm May–Sept, 8am–6pm Oct–Nov, 8am–4.30pm Dec–Mar, 8am–6pm April except Thanksgiving, Christmas and New Year's Day. Provides information, books and back country permits. The park is open daily 8am–8pm daily except as above.

A short introductory video on the park is shown on the half hour and on the hour and short geology talks are given in the visitor centre museum. bryce.canyon.national-park.com
Admission: Seven-day pass $10 per person, $20 per car. You can buy a National Parks Pass by phone or from the website.

Hoodoos and other formations

Bryce Canyon National Park consists of 37,277acres/15,097ha of scenic, colourful rock formations and wonderful desert and has been home to Indian tribes for about 12,000 years – including the Anasazi and Fremont. The most recent tribe to inhabit the region was the Paiute, who were still here when explorers John Wesley Powell and Captain Clarence E Dutton 'discovered' the area in the 1870s.

In 1875, Ebenezer Bryce settled in the Paria Valley to harvest timber from the plateau and neighbours called the nearby canyon Bryce's Canyon – a name that stuck!

The canyon is a geological wonder – home to a series of horseshoe-shaped amphitheatres carved from the eastern edge of the Paunsugunt Plateau. Erosion has shaped colourful Calron limestones, sandstones and mudstones into thousands of spires, pinnacles and fins that together provide unique formations known as hoodoos.

The Paiutes called the hoodoos Legend People who had been turned to stone by coyote because of their evil ways. In fact, they are fantastically shaped and incredibly tall pillars of rock that have been created by a series of massive land movements and river erosions.

BRITTIP

The best times to see large mammals in Bryce Canyon are summer mornings and evenings in roadside meadows.

The result is a geological paradise filled as it is with wonderful examples of the effects of sedimentation from both fresh and sea waters, erosion through wind, water and ice and earthquake and volcanic action over a period of millions and millions of years. The plateaux , staggering vertical columns, gullies and canyons are a joy to behold, while the high elevations – between 6,000ft/1,830m and 9,000ft/2,740m – provide panoramic views of three states and a perfect spot for stargazers.
Sights to look out for: The monoliths of Thor's Hammer, Deformation, Uplift and the Grand Staircase.

Bryce Canyon

Nature's way

The differing and diverse soil and moisture conditions throughout Bryce Canyon have allowed more than 400 species of wild flower to grow including rare gentian, bellflower, yarrow, gilia, sego lily and manzanita.

The meadows and forests are also home to many animals from foxes to deer, coyote, mountain lions and black bears. Elk and pronghorn antelope, reintroduced nearby, can also sometimes be spotted in the park.

On top of that there are more than 160 bird species who visit the park every year. Most migrate to warmer climates in the winter, but those that stay include jays, nuthatches, ravens, eagles and owls.

Scenic drives

A scenic drive along the 18mls/30km of the main park road affords outstanding views of the park and southern Utah scenery. From many overlooks you can see further than 100mls/160km on clear days.

Rainbow or Yovimpa Points: On crisp winter days, views from Rainbow or Yovimpa Points are restricted only by the curvature of the Earth. Driving south from the Visitor Center to Rainbow Point, you gradually climb 1,100ft/335m. En route you will notice how the pines change to spruce, fir and aspen. Both points provide magnificent views of a large chunk of southern Utah. On most days you can see Navajo Mountain and the Kaibab Plateau, which is 90mls/145km away in Arizona. On the clearest day you can even see as far as New Mexico. In the foreground are the colours of the long-eroded slopes and remnant hoodoos. While you are here, search out The Poodle to the north west of Rainbow Point, and the Pink Cliffs behind it.

The park road ends at Rainbow Point with a road loop that turns you back towards the park entrance.

Rainbow Point

Fairyland Canyon

Agua Canyon: This displays some of the best contrasts of light and colour in the park. Look for small trees atop a hoodoo known as the Hunter, while in the distance you will also be able to see the rims of southern plateaux and canyons.

Fairyland Canyon/Point: This offers stunning views of the Fairyland Amphitheater and its fanciful shapes, the Sinking Ship, Aquarius Plateau and Navajo Mountain in the distance. Because Fairyland Canyon lies between the entrance station and the park boundary, and 1ml/1.6km off the main road, many visitors miss this viewpoint, yet it has some of the most spectacular views in the park.

Farview Point: This provides a panoramic view of the neighbouring plateaux and mountains and far to the south-east even the Kaibab Plateau of the Grand Canyon's North Rim. The Natural Bridge is actually an arch that was formed by the combined forces of rain and frost erosion rather than the work of a stream.

Paria View: This looks out across hoodoos in an amphitheatre carved by Yellow Creek. The Paria River valley and Table Cliffs Plateau form the backdrop. To the south, the White Cliffs, weathered out of Navajo sandstone, can also be seen.

BRITTIP

Picnic tables, water and WCs are available at Sunset Point, Yovimpa Point and the south end of the north campsites. There are also picnic tables along the road to Rainbow Point, but no amenities.

Thor's Hammer at Bryce Canyon

Ponderosa Canyon: This area reveals a series of multi-coloured hoodoos that are framed by pine-covered foothills and the Table Cliffs Plateau to the north.

Bryce Amphitheatre: The Sunrise, Sunset, Inspiration and Bryce Points ring Bryce Amphitheatre, the largest natural amphitheatre in the park. The Queen's Garden Trail begins at Sunrise Point. From Sunset Point, you can hike to Thor's Hammer and Wall Street. Inspiration Point offers the best view of the Silent City. The Under-the-Rim Trail begins at Bryce Point. From each point you can see as far as the Black Mountains in the north-east and Navajo Mountain in the south.

Things to do

You can avoid driving round the park by using the shuttle bus system, which has three different shuttle lines and leaves every 10 to 15 minutes. The Visitor Center provides details of birding, camping, hiking, photography, star gazing, wildlife watching and trail rides. At the Visitor Center, you can also get a schedule to join a National Park Service ranger to explore the Canyon's natural and cultural history and learn about the forces that shaped the landscape.

Cycling is only allowed on paved roads and there are no mountain biking trails.

Guided horse rides are available in the morning and afternoon from April to October. For details contact Bryce Canyon Lodge (435 834 5361).

Lodging in Bryce Canyon and Bryce

Bryce Canyon Lodge: 435 834 5361, brycecanyonlodge.com. Provides 70 rooms including three suites, one studio, motel rooms and cabins. The lodge also has a restaurant, gift shop and post office, and provides the only hotel accommodation inside the canyon. There are also two campsites in the canyon itself, while back country camping is possible for a fee of $5.

Best Western Ruby's Inn: Highway 63, 435 834 5341, rubysinn.com. Provides 369 rooms including suites, handicapped rooms and non-smoking room. Facilities include in-room spa, cable TV, indoor swimming pool, spa, hot tub, restaurants, general store, gallery and gift shops. Also offers trail rides, air tours, chuckwagon cookouts, rodeo, ATV rides and cross-country skiing.

Bryce Canyon Lodge

Bryce Canyon Pines Motel: Highway 12, 435 834 5441, brycecanyonmotel.com/lodging. Has 51 rooms including two with kitchenettes and a room for the disabled. Facilities include a restaurant, swimming pool, gift shop, campsite and horse riding.
Pink Cliffs Bryce Village Inn: At the junction of highways 12 and 63, 435 834 5300. The 53 rooms include 14 bunkhouses that are open seasonally. Amenities include a restaurant, café, swimming pool, trading post and barbecue dinners.

Death Valley National Park

From Las Vegas you can reach the park's southern end via Highway 95, which takes you to Amargosa Valley and Death Valley Junction. You can also get there by heading to Pahrump and then following the State Line Road to Death Valley Junction.

BRITTIP

At around $179, Death Valley tours are not cheap but Rocky Trails (see page 222) do offer a great experience if you want to see it close up!

Furnace Creek Information Center

760 786 3200, nps.gov/deva, open daily 8am–5pm
This is the largest of all America's national parks outside of Alaska and covers more than 5,156sq mls/13,354sq km. At the bottom of the 300ml/483km long Sierra Nevada mountain range that stretches to Lake Tahoe in the north, it is the hottest place on earth. In summer the average temperature is 45°C/131°F and the rocks almost reach water-boiling point. The lowest point – 282ft/86m below sea level – in all of America is in the heart of the Valley.

Death Valley

Scotty's Castle

Wimps can visit in March and April when it is just 18°C/61°F and admire the desert spring blooms that shoot out of the sculpted rocks. But let's face it, the whole point of going to Death Valley is to drive through it at the hottest time of year! I would, however, advise giving yourself – and your car – an even chance of making it across in one piece by setting off early in the morning and making sure both your car radiator – and you – have plenty of water.

The National Parks of California warn you not to stop your car in the heat of the day (it'll probably not restart until night-time) and don't drive too quickly, again to prevent overheating. Always ensure you have enough petrol as stations are thin on the ground, but can be found at Furnace Creek, Stovepipe Wells, Scotty's Castle and Panamint Springs.

Just bear in mind that if you do break down you'll be on your own for some time as there is no public transport in the Valley and not many Americans are daft enough (mad dogs and Englishmen and all that) to go through in the summer. However, if you're sensible you will survive and will be amazed by the breathtaking beauty of the miles and miles of sand and rocks that have been hardened into a sea-like landscape by the melting sun.

BRITTIP

Death Valley may be the extreme when it comes to heat, but summer in all the regions surrounding Las Vegas is very hot, so always ensure you have plenty of water with you – dehydration is no fun.

Artists Palette, Death Valley

The main sights include Furnace Creek, the ruins of Harmony Borax Works, Zabriskie Point with its gorgeously golden hills that are best seen at sunrise or sunset, Badwater and the amazing heights of Dante's View where you get precisely that – a spectacular vista of the white salt lakes that stretch to the Panamint Mountains.

Other sights include Scotty's Castle, an incongruous mansion retreat built for American millionaire Albert Johnson in the 1920s, Ubehebe Crater, a 500ft/152m deep hole, which is all that remains of a volcano, the 700ft/213m high Eureka sand dunes and Racetrack Valley, so named because it is a dry mud flat covered in wind-blown boulders.

If you're mad enough to go hiking, try the 14ml/22.5km round trip to the top of Telescope Peak, which does at least get cooler as you get higher!

Some people opt to stay at Furnace Creek, though I can't see the point of being boiled alive for quite so long! However, if you do wish to stay, head for the rustic **Furnace Creek Ranch** (760 786 2345, furnacecreekresort.com) which has a pool, stables, restaurant, bar, shop, tennis courts and even an 18-hole golf course – the lowest anywhere on Earth!

Mammoth Lakes

Mammoth Lakes Visitors Bureau: toll free in the US 888-466 2666, from elsewhere 760 934 2712, visitmammoth.com

A short one-and-a-half-hours' drive north of Big Pine in Death Valley National Park on Highways 190 and 136 is the majestic world of Mammoth Lakes. At the gateway to Yosemite, it is one of the best places in the Sierra Nevada for outdoor activities and is second only to Tahoe as a ski resort in winter. The magical setting and 50ml/80km trail make it popular with mountain bikers, while expert guides offer climbing, kayaking and hang-gliding.

The whole area is also good for golf, canoeing, swimming and searching out wildlife, gold mines and ghost towns. Recent investment in Mammoth Mountain mean there is now a new 18-hole championship golf course and a pedestrian resort, Gondola Village, with shops, restaurants, a skating pond and gondola, which connects the centre of town to the heart of the mountain for unmissable views. **Lodgings include:** Holiday Inn (3236 Main Street, 760 924 1234); Mammoth

Ponderosa Pines

Mountain Inn (1 Minaret Road, 760 934 2581) and Sierra Nevada Inn (164 Old Mammoth Road, 760 934 2515). Or you can write to the Mammoth Lakes Visitor Bureau at PO Box 48, Mammoth Lakes 93546 (760 934 2712, visitmammoth.com) for a free vacation planner.
Good for breakfast and lunch: Blondies (3599 Main Street, 760 934 4048). Good for dinner is Alpenrose (343 Old Mammoth Road, 760 934 3077).
Good for getting around in town: Mammoth Shuttle on 760 934 6588.
Other useful contacts: Devil's Postpile National Monument (760 934 2289, nps.gov/depo); Mammoth Museum (5489 Sherwin Creek Road, 760 934 6918); Mammoth Mountain Bike Park and Adventure Challenge Course (1-800 626 6684); Mammoth Mountain Ski Resort (760 934 0745) and Tamarack Cross-Country Ski Area at Mammoth Lakes (760 934 2442).

Yosemite National Park

This has to be one of the most stunning natural sights in America. Mile-high cliffs gouged out by glaciers thousands of years ago are topped with pinnacles and domes from which waterfalls cascade. Coyotes and black bears roam the valley floor, which is never more than a mile wide. In winter, roads in the park get blocked by snow and in summer by the thousands of visitors who flock to the area.

Yosemite National Park

Visitors' Bureau: 209 372 0200, nps.gov/yose.
Yosemite Sierra Visitors Bureau: 41969 Highway 41, Oakhurst 93644, 559 683 4636, yosemitethisyear.com.Guided tours, including trips around the valley and into the mountains, are bookable through most of the hotels in the area. Full details of mountain biking, fishing, boating at Bass Lake, steam train, the historic park and Native American museums are available here. Write to them for a visitors' guide.

BRITTIP

Fill up with petrol on your way into Yosemite as there are no petrol stations in the park.

Yosemite Area Traveller Information Centre: 209 372 0200/0265, yosemite.com. This is another useful office which can give you all the latest information on park and surrounding road conditions (essential at all times except summer), transport, recreation, lodging, camping and dining options.
Yosemite View Lodge: Yosemite Motels, PO Box 1989, Mariposa, CA 95338, 209 742 7106. Adjacent to the wild and scenic Merced River, Camp Grizzly opened early in 1999. Based on a theme of a 1950s summer camp, it provides educational nature trails, barbecue-style dining, country line dancing and other special events. Contact them to book and get more information on motels in the area.

BRITTIP

Some roads close from late autumn to early summer – check in advance and have tyre chains at the ready for sudden falls of snow if driving in winter.

Other useful numbers: Yosemite Mountain Sugar Pine Railroad (559 683 7273, ymsprr.com) which runs steam trains through the Sierra National Forest near Yosemite Park; Yosemite Sightseeing Tours (559 658 8687, yosemitetours.com); All-Outdoors Whitewater Trips (1 800 247 2387) for half, one, two and three-day rafting trips from April to November; and Whitewater Voyages (1 800 488 7238) for wonderful runs down the Merced with guides, food and equipment.

16 SAFETY FIRST

Safety, insurance, hints and tips on makng the best of your holiday

No one wants to think about anything going wrong with their dream holiday, but it is worth thinking about a few commonsense aspects of safety and security so that you can avoid any preventable problems.

General hints and tips

Don't allow your dream trip to Las Vegas and beyond to be spoilt by not taking the right kind of precautions, be they for personal safety or of a medical nature.

In the sun

Let's face it, most Brits tend to travel to America at the hottest time of the year – the summer – and most are unprepared for the sheer intensity of the sun. Before you even think about going out for the day, apply a high-factor sunblock, as it is very easy to get sunburnt when you are walking around, sightseeing or shopping. Reapply regularly throughout the day. It is also a good idea to wear a hat or scarf to protect your head from the sun, especially at the hottest time of the day from 11am to 3pm, so you do not get sunstroke. If it is windy, you may be lulled into thinking that it is not as hot, but this is a dangerous illusion – especially in the desert valley of Las Vegas! If you are spending the day by the pool, it is advisable to use a sunshade at the hottest time of the day, and apply waterproof sunblock regularly, even when you are in the pool, as the UV rays travel through water. Always make sure you have plenty of fluids with you when travelling. Water is best. Try to avoid alcohol during the day, as this will have an additional dehydrating effect.

At your hotel

In America, your hotel room number is your main source of security. It is often your passport to eating and collecting messages, so keep the number safe and secure. When checking in, make sure none of the hotel staff mentions your room

Be safety conscious in your hotel

BRITTIP

Use a business address rather than your home address on all your luggage.

number out loud. If they do, give them back the key and ask them to give you a new room and to write down the new room number instead of announcing it (most hotels follow this practice in any case). When you need to give someone your room number – for instance when charging a dinner or any other bill to your room – write it down or show them your room card rather than calling it out.

When in your hotel room, always use the deadlocks and security chains and use the door peephole before opening the door to strangers. If someone knocks on the door and cannot give any identification, phone down to the hotel reception desk.

When you go out, make sure you lock the windows and door properly. Even if you leave your room just for a few seconds, lock the door.

Cash and documents

Most hotels in tourist areas have safety deposit boxes, so use these to store important documents such as airline tickets and passports. When you go out, do not take all your cash and credit cards with you – always have at least one credit card in the safe as an emergency back-up and only take enough cash with you for the day. Using a money belt is also a good idea. Keep a separate record of your travellers' cheque numbers. If your room does not have its own safe, leave your valuables in the main hotel safe.

Emergencies

For the police, fire department or ambulance, dial 911 (9-911 from your hotel room).

If you need medical help in Las Vegas, there are three main options, all of which are open 24 hours a day, seven days a week: **Harmon Medical Center**, 150 East Harmon Avenue (702-796 116); **Fremont Medical Center**, 4880 South Wynn Road (on the corner of Tropicana and Wynn, 702-871 5005); and **UMC Hospital**, 1800 W Charleston Boulevard (702-383 2000).

Cars

Most of the advice is obvious, but when we go on holiday we sometimes relax to the point of not following our basic common sense. Never leave your car unlocked and never leave any valuable items on the car seats or anywhere else where they can be seen.

Travel insurance

The one thing you should not forget is travel insurance when travelling anywhere around America. Medical cover is very expensive and if you are involved in any kind of an accident you could be sued, which is very costly indeed in America.

If you do want to make savings in this area, don't avoid getting insurance cover, but do avoid buying it from tour operators, as they are notoriously expensive.

The alternative, particularly if you plan to make more than one trip in any given year, is to go for an annual worldwide policy directly from insurers. The worldwide annual policies can make even more sense if you're travelling as a family.

In all cases, you need to ensure that the policy gives you the following cover:

- **Actual coverage of the United States** – not all plans include America;
- **Medical** cover of at least £2 million in America;
- **Personal liability** cover of at least £2 million in America;
- **Cancellation and curtailment** cover of around £3,000 in case you are forced to call off your holiday;

Keep your winnings safe!

Check insurance for sports cover

- **Lost baggage and belongings** cover at around £1,500 – most premiums only offer cover for individual items up to around £250, so you will need additional cover for expensive cameras or camcorders;
- **Cash cover** (usually around £200) and documents including your air tickets, passport and currency;
- **24-hour helpline** to make it easy for you to get advice and instructions on what to do;
- **Membership of the Financial Ombudsman Service** in case you are unhappy with the outcome of a claim.

Check and check again

Shop around: You do not have to buy your policy from your tour operator, so don't let them include it as a matter of course. You will almost certainly be able to get a better deal elsewhere.

Read the policy: Always ask for a copy of the policy document before you go and if you are not happy with the cover offered, cancel and demand your premium back – in some cases you will only have seven days in which to do this.

Don't double up on cover: If you have an 'all risks' policy on your home contents, this will cover your property outside the home and may even cover lost money and credit cards. Check if this covers you abroad – and covers your property when in transit – before buying personal possessions cover.

Look at gold card cover: Some bank gold cards provide you with insurance cover if you buy your air ticket with the gold card, so it is worth checking, although there will be terms and conditions.

BRITTIP

Put away maps and brochures in the glove compartment, as these will be obvious signs that yours is a tourist's car.

Check dangerous sports cover: In almost all cases mountaineering, racing and hazardous pursuits such as bungee jumping, skydiving, horse riding, windsurfing, trekking and even cycling are not included in normal policies. There are so many opportunities to do all of these activities that you really should ensure you are covered before you go. Backpackers and dangerous sports enthusiasts can try Insure & Go (0870 901 3674, www.insureandgo.com). The Travel Insurance Club (01702 423398, www.ticltd.co.uk) is also an excellent place to look for travel insurance. It specialises in insurance for backpackers aged 18–35 and the cover includes walking holidays, sports and activities, skiing and scuba diving, bungee jumping and abseiling; as does Leading Edge (0870 112 8099, www.leadingedge.co.uk).

Make sure you qualify: For instance, if you have been treated in hospital in the six months prior to travelling or are waiting for hospital treatment, you may need medical evidence that you are fit to travel. Ask your doctor for a report giving you the all-clear (you will have to pay for this) and if the

Get full coverage on car insurance

insurance company still says your condition is not covered, shop around.

Insurance policies

This is a competitive market, so it pays to shop around to find the best policy for you. Some companies offer discounts if you already have another policy with them. These companies are worth checking out for annual-cover or single-trip travel insurance.

To compare deals, visit www.moneysupermarket.com or phone 0845 345 5708. It has cheap deals from more than 450 policies to compare from online, with links directly through for purchasing. You can also compare leading providers of the most comprehensive deals at www.top4deals.com/travel-insurance.

Atlas Direct (0870 811 1700, atlasdirect.net)
Citybond Travel (0870 444 6431, citybond.co.uk)
CostOut (0191 497 3202, costout.co.uk)
Direct Travel (0845 605 2700, direct-travel.co.uk)
Eagle Star (0800 587 5048, eaglestar.co.uk)
Egg (08451 233 233, egg.com)
Flexicover Direct (0870 990 9292, flexicover.com)
James Hampden (020 7398 8080, jameshampden.co.uk)
Leading Edge (01892 836622, leadedge.co.uk)
Marks & Spencer Financial Services (0800 068 3918, marksandspencer.com)
More Than (0800 300 866, morethan.com)
MRL Insurance Direct (0870 876 7677, mrlinsurance.co.uk)
National Australia Group: Clydesdale Bank (0845 601 8336, cbonline.co.uk) Nationwide BS (0500 302012, nationwide.co.uk)
TravelPlan Direct (0870 7744 177, travelplan-direct.com)
Worldwide Travel (0870 112 8100, worldwideinsure.com)

Other useful contacts

The Association of British Insurers (ABI) (020 7600 3333, abi.org.uk)
Financial Ombudsman Service (0845 080 1800, financial-ombudsman.org.uk)

Now how do you say that?

17 INDEX

Major page references are in **bold**, illustrations are in *italics*. A=Attraction H=Hotel S=Show.

Acknowledgements

With thanks to everyone who supplied photographs for this book, in particular MGM Mirage.

America's Shopping Places 84, 85; Bebe Sport 93 top; Benetton 93 bottom; Blue Man Group 65; Blue Moon Resort 190; Cesars Palace 29; Candlelight Wedding Chapel 183 bottom; Cirque du Soleil 60, 61, 62, 63; Comedystop.com 70 bottom; Ethel M Chocolate Factory 204 bottom; Fleur de Lys 110; Four Seasons24, 26, 32; General Growth Properties Inc. 80, 82; Golfamerica.biz 231, 233; Hard Rock Café123; Hard Rock Hotel 144 bottom; Harrah's 74, 86, 143, 146 top, 160 bottom, 242; Heli USA 228 top; Ian Parker 263 top; Imperial Palace 53 bottom, 69, 168, 183 top, 205 top; Las Vegas News Bureau 6, 7, 9, 11, 21 top, 59, 90, 94 top, 115, 147 bottom, 167 bottom, 195, 215 bottom, 230; Lasvegas.com 15; Leonardo.com 14, 16, 41 top, 49, 73, 137 bottom, 155 top, 176; Lied Discovery Children's Museum 211 bottom; Little White Wedding Chapel 178; Lvcasinoinfo.com 57, 83, 196, 280; Lynn Ross 210; MGM Mirage 8, 10 bottom, 18, 23, 27, 28, 30, 31, 33, 34–38, 44, 51 tp, 66 bottom, 71, 74 bottom, 77, 97–103, 105–108, 111, 114, 117, 118, 120, 121, 126–136, 137 top, 138, 139 top, 140, 141, 144 top, 146 bottom, 148 bottom, 152, 153 bottom, 154 bottom, 161 bottom, 162, 163, 167 top, 168, 170–175, 177, 178 top, 179 bottom, 182 top, 184–186, 188 bottom, 193, 194, 197, 199–201, 204 top, 207 top, 238 bottom, 241 bottom, 244, 248, 252, 253, 256, 279; Nevada Commission on Tourism 11, 12 bottom, 213, 214, 215 top, 216–227, 229, 232 bottom, 234, 239, 240, 241 top, 245–247, 257 bottom, 258, 259, 261, 262, 269–277; Nevada State Museum 212; N9ne Group 147 top; Painted Desert Golf Club 232 top; Palace Station 57; Paris Las Vegas 40; Planet Hollywood 41 bottom, 42, 139 bottom, 160 top; Planet99.com 145, 191, 205 bottom; Rainforest Café 124; Rio All-Suite Hotel 52, 53 top, 112, 142; Ritz-Carlton 55, 188 top; Rob Bender 78; Ron Lee's World of Clowns 207; Ryan Schnitz 235 bottom; Sahara 67, 119; Scott Hooper 158; Shadow Creek Golf Club 254; Singletrack Tours 228 bottom; Skydive Las Vegas 237; State Historic Park 206 top, Stratosphere 21 bottom, 43; The Palms 50, 51, 109; Tillerman 122; Tim Martin 268; Tommy Rocker's 152 top; Tropicana 54, 164; View Images 64 top.